Boys Abducted

A series edited by
Lee Edelman, Benjamin Kahan,
and Christina Sharpe

Boys Abducted

The Homoerotics of Empire and Race in Early Modernity

ABDULHAMIT ARVAS

Duke University Press *Durham and London* 2025

© 2025 DUKE UNIVERSITY PRESS. All rights reserved

Typeset in Garamond Premier Pro by Westchester Publishing Services

Library of Congress Cataloging-in-Publication Data
Names: Arvas, Abdulhamit, [date] author.
Title: Boys abducted : the homoerotics of empire and race in early modernity / Abdulhamit Arvas.
Other titles: Theory Q.
Description: Durham : Duke University Press, 2025. | Series: Theory Q | Includes bibliographical references and index.
Identifiers: LCCN 2024029757 (print)
LCCN 2024029758 (ebook)
ISBN 9781478031581 (paperback)
ISBN 9781478028413 (hardcover)
ISBN 9781478060635 (ebook)
Subjects: LCSH: English literature—Early modern, 1500–1700—History and criticism. | Turkish literature—Early modern, 1500–1700—History and criticism. | Boys in literature. | Homosexuality in literature. | Gay erotic literature. | Exoticism in literature. | Abduction in literature. | Imperialism in literature.
Classification: LCC PR408.H65 A78 2025 (print) | LCC PR408.H65 (ebook) | DDC 823/.3093538—dc23/eng/20250101
LC record available at https://lccn.loc.gov/2024029757
LC ebook record available at https://lccn.loc.gov/2024029758

Cover art: Ali Yaycıoğlu, *Finality 23: When life is in red then blue*, 2022. Pastel. Courtesy of the artist.

Contents

A Note on Transcriptions and Translations
vii

Acknowledgments
ix

Introduction
1

PART I
Boys Encountered

———

1
Traveling Boys in the Mediterranean
45

2
Mapping Boys on the Horizon
81

3
(In)Visible Boys in English Abductions
109

PART II
Boys Transformed

4
Refashioning Boys
141

5
Regendering Boys
169

PART III
Boys in Modernity, East and West

6
Staging Boys, 1690–1990
199

7
The Orientalization of Boy Love
A Conclusion
221

Notes	Bibliography	Index
233	277	309

A Note on Transcriptions and Translations

Transcriptions of Ottoman Turkish (in the Arabic script) into the Latin alphabet in this book follow Modern Turkish orthography, omitting diacritical marks including the hamza, the letter ʿayin, and indication of long vowels. Popular words in English are spelled in their English usages (i.e., pasha, qadi, the Qur'an).

All translations, unless otherwise noted, are mine, and originals are included in notes throughout the book. I used translations that have previously been done when possible. Translations by others and any alterations or corrections made to them are clearly marked in the endnotes.

Acknowledgments

Acknowledgments are where the scholarly voice usually gets more personal. This is probably why I always start a book by reading that section first—if you are reading this, we are obviously of the same mind, dear reader. The personal is political, we are told. The personal is pedagogical, too. I start with my brief personal journey in developing this project that spanned over almost a decade, during which I accumulated immense debts of gratitude. The list of generous, supportive, brilliant minds reflects the politics and pedagogy of vital friendships, alliances, coalitions, collaborations, and camaraderie in building bridges for survival and growth.

The seeds of this book go back to my graduate school years with exciting and energetic moments of flourishing studies and conversations around sexuality, race, gender, and globality. As I was trying to find ways to engage with all these critical schools as a graduate student, I quickly realized how compartmentalized our early modern subfields were. I spent year after year running from the queer room to the race room to the global room in order to hear debates in each field. It was exhausting! It was not merely that sexuality/race/empire were fundamental to my critical inquiries, but it was also that my early modern sources were forcing me to gain mastery in all of them, since none of these critical issues were isolated from the others. This process pushed me to consider early modernity beyond a single national literature paradigm. I was ready to take the challenge. My first step was to put together the reading list for my comprehensive exam. While my doctoral program required a list of 125 books on average, I ended up with more than 400 books on race, sex, and globality on my exam list. Again, it was an exhausting yet a most rewarding experience. I was at the Department of English at Michigan State University, a state school with limited funding, so I had to teach a class every semester. As an international student, I had the pressure of mastering languages, perfecting writing in a second language, and finishing on time while at the same time facing resistance to studying early modern literature. In the meantime, I was told by some respectable scholars that as an international student I had little to no chance of becoming a successful early modernist in the United States.

While I was developing the project surrounded by such difficulties and burdens, a most generous network of advisors, mentors, and friends welcomed, encouraged, and supported me at every stage. They made me feel that I belong and should move on with confidence. On the top of the list are Jyotsna Singh and Valerie Traub, who, as the best advisors one can have, enthusiastically mentored and guided me. Jyotsna, in her inspiring Sufi attitude, gently pushed me to consider early modern sexuality more globally by thinking with the Ottomans. Valerie, in her always brilliant, critical, and rigorous mode, attended to every sentence I wrote and made me think and write better. She has continued her unmatched mentorship; she generously read and commented on the whole book manuscript, which made a huge difference. Other members of my committee—Ellen McCallum, Stephen Deng, and Tamar Boyadjian, as well as my former mentors Serpil Oppermann and Craig Dionne—have never stopped supporting me. Cajetan Iheka has been my most dear fellow traveler since graduate school years; I am grateful for our genuine friendship and intellectual camaraderie.

During and beyond graduate school, the encouragement, curiosity, and openness of many motivated me to pursue the project and kept me in the intellectual circles I call home. These include David Halperin, Gayle Rubin, Kim F. Hall, Will Fisher, Jeffrey Masten, Ian Smith, Urvashi Chakravarty, Emily Weissbourd, Mario DiGangi, Arthur Little Jr., Daniel Vitkus, Jonathan Burton, Jane Degenhardt, Marjorie Rubright, Stephen Spiess, Ari Friedlander, Joey Gamble, Vin Nardizzi, Anjali Arondekar, Dennis Britton, Drew Daniel, Kadji Amin, Eng-Beng Lim, Joseph Boone, Amrita Dhar, Patricia Akhimie, Zarena Aslami, Iqbal Khan, Victor Lenthe, Susanne Wofford, Miles P. Grier, Simone Chess, Colby Gordon, William West, Wendy Wall, Sawyer Kemp, Nandini Das, Misha Teramura, Alan Stewart, Stephen Guy-Bray, Timothy Francisco, Laureen Eriks Cline, John Garrison, Kirk Queensland, Christopher Shirley, Amrita Sen, Janet Bartholomew, Lisa Barksdale-Shaw, Will Tosh, Karen Newman, Don Rodrigues, Harry McCarthy, Jordan Windholz, Margo Hendricks, Ambereen Dadabhoy, Robert Stagg, Noémie Ndiaye, Jeremy Chow, Anita Raychawdhuri, Martine van Elk, Qais Munhazim, Debanuj Dasgupta, and Max Fox. Our conversations and discussions made it possible for me to revisit tensions, differences, alignments, and fault lines among various fields and provided strategies for developing this book with confidence. For such enriching exchanges, I am also grateful to Ottoman and Turkish studies scholars whose insights have been illuminating. Emine Evered generously spent time with me each week for a year at MSU, reading Ottoman manuscripts together. The inspiring and encouraging conversations with Selim Kuru and the late Walter Andrews were invaluable; so too were those with Baki Tezcan, Ali Yaycıoglu, Ramazan Hakkı Öztan, Ezgi Sarıtaş, Mostafa Minawi, Gülay Yılmaz, Evren Savcı, and Aslı Niyazioğlu.

This book was written as my career was moving me across the country from Michigan to New York, Santa Barbara, and Philadelphia. At Vassar College, my colleagues were most welcoming and nurturing. I particularly thank Judith Dollenmayer, Barbara Page, Zoltan Markus, Hiram Pérez, Chris Grabowski, Paulina Bren, Gabrielle Cody, Paul Russell, Mita Choudhury, Amitava Kumar, Andrew Davison, Katherine Hite, Leslie Dunn, Ben Morin, Zachary Cofran, Louis Römer, Johanna Römer, Pınar Batur, and Beth Darlington. I have immense gratitude for my Vassar besties Katie Gemmill, Tara Mulder, Christina Owens, Pauline Goul, and Marius Drager for their friendship and for enthusiastically joining my dance parties and bringing fun and companionship to my days in Poughkeepsie.

At the University of California, Santa Barbara, I worked with great colleagues and friends who contributed to the growth of the book. Weekly gatherings with my companions and intellectual comrades Terrance Wooten and Utathya Chattopadhyaya and our passionate discussions of many parts of this book at Elsie's as well as at various hiking sites and on the beach at nights during the pandemic shaped my thinking tremendously. Terrance's brilliantly capacious Black Studies lens and Utathya's forceful and wide-ranging intellect calibrated my thinking. Bernadette Andrea was, and still is, a most supportive colleague, mentor, and collaborator. Other members of my Santa Barbara family kept me going: Bishnu Ghosh, Bashkar Sarkar, Paul Amar, Christina Vagt, Julie Carlson, Eileen Joy, Aranye Fradenburg Joy, Mireille Miller-Young, Charmaine Chua, Sherene Seikaly, Jennifer Tyburczy, Leila Shereen Sakr, Dwight Reynolds, Lisa Hajjar, and Ben Olguin. My conversations with amazing thinkers and artists Jessica Nakamura, Leo Cabranes-Grant, Ninotchka Bennahum, Christopher Pilafian, Risa Brainin, Irwin Appel, and Brandon Whited helped me further think about the project creatively with theater, dance, and performance studies.

At USCB, I was awarded the Junior Faculty Manuscript Workshop Grant by the University of California Humanities Research Institute, thanks to which I was able to bring together fabulous readers to workshop the first full draft of the manuscript. I am forever grateful to Bernadette Andrea, Arthur Little Jr., Kaya Şahin, William Germano, and Carla Fraccero for accepting my invitation to join the workshop, for reading the manuscript with great care and scrutiny, and for improving and enriching it on so many levels.

My colleagues at the University of Pennsylvania have been enthusiastically supportive from the first day I joined the department. I thank every single member of Penn English for welcoming me so warmly. In particular, I owe an immense debt to my most generous and brilliant colleagues who made time to closely read the whole manuscript for a day-long workshop: Ania Loomba, Melissa Sanchez, Zachary Lesser, Heather Love, David Eng, Suvir Kaul, and Chi-ming Yang. Their feedback contributed tremendously to the growth and betterment of the project. The fabulous Seçil Yılmaz also generously read the whole manuscript and provided feedback, for which I am thankful. For their collegiality, friendship, and unfailing support at Penn, I am grateful to Dagmawi Woubshet, Whitney Trettien, Pearl Brilmyer, Margo Crawford, Caroline Batten, Rita Copeland, Rahul Mukherjee, Paul Saint-Amour, Emily Steiner, David Wallace, David Kazanjian, Al Filreis, Simcha Gross, Eve Trout-Powell, Harun Küçük, Oscar Aguirre-Mandujano, Ian Fleishman, Heather Hughes, Meta Mezaj, Kevin Platt, David Kim, Brian Rose, and the late Robert Ousterhout.

In addition to the abovementioned friends who read the whole manuscript, I want to pay my special gratitude to those who read parts of the book and provided insightful suggestions: Terrance Wooten, Utathya Chattopadhyaya, Cajetan Iheka, Stephen Hutt, Margo Hendricks, Leo Cabranes-Grant, Paul Amar, Jeff Masten, as well as all the brilliant students in my graduate seminars "Comparative Histories of Sexuality" and "Histories of Race and Sexuality" at Penn. Their feedback made a huge difference. I thank all members of and participants in the research initiatives I have been a part of or organized in the process of developing this book. Some of my ideas were shaped while I was a research affiliate in the Early Modern Conversions Project; special thanks to Paul Yachnin and Steven Wittek, both of whom always included me in the interdisciplinary Conversions events and gave me space to share my work. Other members Bronwen Wilson, Patricia Badir, and Benjamin Schmidt were always supportive. During my summer research fellowship on "Conversions" at the University of Cambridge, Rob Clines, Ivana Horacek, Anuradha Gobin, and Bill Acres were a great source of joy and companionship. Research groups I collaborated with, including New Sexualities, Mediterranean Studies, and Early Modern Center at UCSB, Med/Ren at Penn, and the Theater Without Borders, generated impactful engagements and exchanges. The amazing seminarians at the panel "Queer | Race | Global: Early Modern Crossings" (which I co-organized with Bernadette Andrea) at Shakespeare Association of America meeting broadened my horizon.

I wrote this acknowledgment in Oxford where I was a Visiting Fellow; I thank Exeter College for hosting me so generously and providing me with the time and space I needed for the final stages of the book. My thanks also go to the Folger Shakespeare Library for supporting this project with a research fellowship and to the Office of the Vice Provost for Research and the School of Arts and Sciences at Penn for a generous grant from the University Research Fund. I deeply appreciate Margo Crawford, chair of Penn English, for her support in providing book subvention funding. I thank *English Literary Renaissance*, especially Adam Zucker, for publishing an article version of chapter 1. A part of chapter 5 appeared in the first special issue on Early Modern Trans Studies in the *Journal for Early Modern Cultural Studies*, for which I thank the editors of the issue, Colby Gordon, Simone Chess, and Will Fisher, as well as the *JEMCS* editor Daniel Vitkus.

Working with Duke University Press has been a wonderful experience. I thank the series editors, Lee Edelman, Benjamin Kahan, and Christina Sharpe, for inviting me to publish under Theory Q and for reading the manuscript with enthusiasm before I submitted it to the press. I am particularly grateful to Benjy for working so closely and willingly with me and for cheering me on, motivating me, and encouraging me at every stage of the publication process. Ken Wissoker was always there whenever I needed him and was a most phenomenal editor to work with. Assistant editor Ryan Kendall was highly communicative and helpful at every stage. I am highly appreciative of the editorial team for finding the most generous and helpful peer-reviewers; the two anonymous readers, to whom I am forever thankful and indebted, moved the project up to the next level with their invaluable, brilliant suggestions and insights.

Throughout my grad school years, I always dreamed of going back to Turkey and teaching there. By the time I finished my PhD, however, my beautiful country was nearly in ruins in the hands of inept people. I was not able to go back. In the meantime, while I was fighting against an immigration issue to be able to stay in the United States during the Trump era, my friends and colleagues, many of whom are listed above, did not hesitate a second to write letters in my support. I thank every single one of you! Your letters contributed a lot to making it possible for me to be able stay and work in the United States and write this book.

My loving family and caring friends always make me feel special, respected, protected, and empowered to pursue difficult questions, no matter where. My biggest gratitude goes to every single member of my family—my resilient mother, my loving sisters and brothers and their partners, and my beautiful nephews and nieces—for being so patient with me living abroad. My friends from Turkey have never stopped trusting and supporting me and showing me love from afar: İlyas Kudaş, Nevin Öner, Zeynep Elibol, İbrahim Coşkun, Osman Coşkun, Niyazi Oral, Ömur Duruerk, Mücahit Arvas, and Fatih Kurt. I thank most affectionately my Philadelphia friends, who quickly made this beautiful city of love home for me, especially my admirable Potato Boys who were exposed to many moments of my crises and stood by my side in love, support, and patience: Andy Thierauf, Chris Sanjuanelo, Bryan Myer, Stephen Hutt, Tyler Fenstermaker, Benja Newman, and Erhan Seyhan Gezen. Thank you, Sarah Wasserman, for our long walks and talks. And a huge thank you to my NYC friends, Miguel Andonaegui and Jerico Bleu, and Katie Gemmill and Kareem Amin, for always caring for me and hosting me at your lovely homes so beautifully whenever I needed to. A special thank you to the special Joe Cofler, who was truly a most affectionate champion of support during the final stages of completing this manuscript.

Finally, my affectionate gratitude goes to all my lovers across cities, countries, continents, whose intimacies have kept me sane.

Introduction

This book pursues beautiful boys. It traces the literary and historical figurations of beautiful boys who were violently abducted in the sixteenth and early seventeenth centuries. These boys, both fictional and real, were made exotic, different, other—be it in Mediterranean waters or on trading ships, in the margins of maps, on the horizon of poetic imaginations, on the edges of celebrated paintings, in English households as servants and in Ottoman courts as slaves, or as objects of desire in the streets of London and Istanbul or even in the deep forests of ancient Greece as imagined on the English stage. Using the abducted beautiful boy as a salient point of contact, I explore two distinct textual and visual traditions—English and Ottoman—contrapuntally to reassess the relationships among homoeroticism, race, and empire. In a period of geopolitical crossings, religious conversions, global trade, new imperial visions, and changing socioeconomic structures, the beautiful abducted boy, I argue, is a site for exploring the complex homoerotic subtexts of racial and religious difference and imperial violence in both the emergent empire of England and the far more vast and powerful Ottoman Empire.

In both of those societies, the early modern boy was a distinct yet incoherent and mobile social, sexual, and gender category. Factors such as age, class, status, geography, race, kinship relations, employment, service, and sexual availability constituted, commenced, and terminated the stage of boyhood.[1] Historically, when moving from childhood to boyhood and entering an ambiguous gender phase, usually around ages seven to ten, boys were, like all other genders, defined within a spectrum in opposition to and subordinated to the adult man in a nonbinary gender system.[2] In this transitional stage, boys were inferior and subservient to men in multiple hierarchical registers: as apprentices in various occupations; as students at school; as pages in households; as minions in courts; as varlets in streets, brothels, taverns, or bathhouses; and as actors or love objects in theaters and literary imaginations. Actual boys were prominent in England's world of the theater, while figural boys were central to the Ottoman poetic tradition, appearing as the most common subject of male desire (sometimes instead of women, sometimes alongside them). In fact, often their juvenile bodies, androgynous appearance, and youth marked them as the more appealing, if not the ideal, form of human beauty and object of desire.[3] At the same time, they were often unremarked upon in historical archives.

The emergence of the boy linguistically—"boy" or "lad" in English and "*oğlan*" or "*gulam*" in Turkish—relates the term to service in a gendered power hierarchy. The earliest definitions of "boy" in English from the 1300s connect the term to status: "a male servant, slave, or assistant"; "non-white slaves, non-white servants, labourers"; "a male person of low birth or status."[4] It was only in the mid-fifteenth century that the boy appears in reference to "a male child or youth."[5] Any reference to boys—youth, lad, child, son, page, groom, servant, wag, apprentice, imp, ganymede, ingle, catamite, varlet, toy, crack, ward, orphan—suggests a hierarchical pattern.[6] Likewise, in Ottoman Turkish, "*gulam*" refers to both servant and boy; and other terms used for boys such as "*mürahik*," "*mümeyyiz*," "*emred*," "*şabb-ı emred*," "*emred*," "*oğlan*," "*uşak*," and "*mücerred*" denote hierarchical orderings in relation to the adult man. While the age of the boys sometimes functioned crucially in their transition to legal majority and manhood (usually between ages fourteen and twenty-one), it was mainly their status and class, financial independence, household mastery (i.e., marriage), and physical, sexual, and mental maturity (i.e., body hair, the ability to discern right from wrong) that morphed the boy into an adult man.[7] The term's temporal flexibility can be observed in early modern sodomy trials involving boys "aged 29 years or thereabouts."[8] The term "boy" was also used in an affective sense, sometimes to disparage, other times to praise.[9] From a gender category to a term of endearment or insult, the term "boy" marked some men as boys due to their social status and race.[10] While boyhood was an ephemeral status for most, for others, it lingered permanently. This book mainly follows boys in the latter category.

Boys Abducted: The Homoerotics of Empire and Race in Early Modernity concerns racially, religiously, and culturally exoticized boys; boys who were forcibly taken from their lands and made objects of servitude and desire; boys who, in many instances, would always remain boys. Traffic in (and the fate of) these boys has long been rendered invisible in scholarship compared to that of domestic, local boys or women as objects of the male gaze, exchange, possession, and captivity.[11] While boys have been objects of desire for women, this study follows the Sedgwickian formulation of the homosocial competition between men. It therefore focuses on the boy as an object of abduction and conversion in contestations between men as a means to challenge a historiography that has presumed ahistorical, normalized heteronormativity in patriarchal regimes. The abducted boy stands next to, but ultimately apart from, such better-known figures in early modernity as the boy student, the boy actor, the apprentice boy, the favorite boy, the royal boy, the print boy, the lovely boy, and the masterless boy. The abducted boy is a literary figure whose prototype is the beautiful, abducted Ganymede of Greek myth and who was imbricated in early modern imperial and colonial politics as a result of the revival of Greco-Roman models and of increasing cross-cultural interactions and exchanges. The abducted boy, therefore, is as much a historical figure as a classical prototype.

I use abduction to refer to various acts of displacement. Stemming from the classical Latin term "*abdūcere*," "abduct" began to be commonly used in the early seventeenth century with significations of "to lead away, carry off, remove, to withdraw, to entice away, to captivate, charm, to appropriate, take away, to pull away or aside, to turn aside, divert."[12] Throughout the book, the category "abducted boy" therefore capaciously refers to boys who were forcibly dislocated from their native lands through enslavement, captivity, recruitment, or kidnapping and who were often eroticized as sexually available beautiful boys or Ganymedes, be it figuratively or literally. My use of the aesthetic category of "beautiful" in reference to the abducted boy, on the other hand, aims to highlight the mimetic deployments of this embodied figure who mediates the manifold tensions between homoerotic desire, literary eroticism, and the violent history of abductions and enslavements that were often motivated by religious and racial difference. The term "beautiful," of course, signifies differently in different historical and cultural contexts. The boys in this project certainly appear as the epitome of beauty with their androgynous, vulnerable bodies and their promising and energizing youth. However, it is not within the scope of this project to detail what constitutes beauty in the period I study. My examples thus offer ambiguous, often veiled descriptors for beauty. While paradisical idealizations of the boy as beautiful sometimes expand into the realm of platonic aestheticization, at other times, the celebration of his body (hairless, youthful, slender, white, fair), language (accent, simple, innocent), and habits (naked, Christian clothing, [un]circumcised) signals erotic excitement about (and attraction to) the boy. More than his appearance, however, the orderly hierarchy in which the boy is framed and idealized renders him beautiful and desirable. Beauty in this sense appears as an effect of the boy's orderly disposition and as a situated function that does cultural work. Beauty also appears in some sources as enabling a certain level of agency and benefit, empowering boys to get what they want. When possible, I point to physical descriptions and definable characteristics to show how beauty is gendered and racialized, but overall, I leave beauty as ambiguous as it is to maintain the lack of an existing consensus on what constitutes the beautiful.[13]

Tracing the abducted beautiful boy in a cross-cultural framework, this book makes visible the fraught relations between sexuality and race and between erotic desire and violence, as well as the homoerotics of imperialism in both the English and Ottoman contexts. What distinct yet inextricably intertwined (his)stories of sexuality and race do abducted boys narrate as they cross boundaries between nations and empires both as captives and eroticized beloveds? The abducted boy offers a history of sexuality and race, where the racial and the queer converge and conflict through the figure of the boy as he circulates in aesthetic, erotic, commercial, and imperial economies. Abducted and forced to cross borders, the beautiful boy reveals both desirable and undesirable cross-cultural inflections in the shared yet contested space of the Mediterranean. Subject to violent forms of conversion and assimilation, the boy enables us to apprehend the homoerotics of empire, particularly how sexuality and race, as well as religion, combine in producing the hierarchization of human difference.

Boys in Counterpoint

In my transnational and contrapuntal examination, I investigate the abducted boy who traverses borders beyond national and linguistic boundaries. As will be evident in this introduction and throughout the book, I move across representational and historical archives, in various sites between Istanbul and London, and across scholarly fields, resisting overspecialization and fidelity to a single critical school in search of larger structures of eroticism and empire. In doing so, I am inspired by queer historiography's frame of "cruising" in the archives for discursive formations rather than outing individuals by thinking with modern terms and identities. As Jeffrey Masten notes in his foundational work of early modern queer literary historiography, "the desire to sleep with the dead" is an "impossibility, even as it figures as an intractable curiosity or desire, of searching the annals of the past for erotic subjects motivated by our desires and living our practices, with the cultural and political meanings we associate with these desires and practices." Hence, rather than outing the Renaissance, it is vital to "account for the abiding differences in the ways this period represented sexuality."[14] Additionally, following José Esteban Muñoz's projection of "cruising" not for sex but for varied, creative potentialities, for imagining and mapping a queer "utopia," my queer historicist method enables me to look back to the past and unpack the complex assemblages and fusions of cultural, gender, racial, and religious differences that operate to produce sexuality in the labyrinth called history.[15]

This book therefore cruises the English Channel as well as the Mediterranean, crosses back and forth between England and Ottoman Turkey to map out imperial structures in which the abducted boy is located. In etymological relation to the concept of crossing, "cruise" appears in the English language in the seventeenth century, corresponding to the Dutch "*kruisen*" (to cross), which means "to sail crossing to and fro, to traverse and cross the seas."[16] The emergence of "cruise" coincides with the usage of "cross"—stemming from medieval "croise" or "croyse" (from the Old French "*cruiser*" and the Latin "*crusiare*")—which began to mean "to pass over a line, boundary, river, channel, etc.; to pass from one side to the other of any space," as can be exemplified in the words of Valentine in *The Two Gentlemen of Verona*: "How young Leander crossed the Hellespont."[17] (I examine Leander's crossing in chapter 1.) With the rise of England's engagement in a maritime economy, cruising and crossing became a part of the English language. The original early modern connotation ("to sail to and fro over some part of the sea without making for a particular port or landing-place, on the look out for ships, for the protection of commerce in time of war, for plunder") did not gain a queer signification ("to walk or drive about [the streets] in search of a casual sexual [esp. homosexual] partner" for pleasure) until the twentieth century.[18] Nonetheless, the term's relation to crossing makes it possible for my project to queer its early modern signification. As Ian Smith reminds us, early modern "queer," which derived from the German "*quer*," which meant "to pass or extend across from side to side of, to traverse, cross; also to cross direction of, to run at an angle to," is related to crossing, traveling, and turning.[19] And Daniel Vitkus's study of "turning Turk" has shown that "to turn" signifies not only religious conversion but also crossings, changes, transformations, and perversions that connect religious conversion to sexual transgression.[20] Interestingly, in Turkish, "*dönme*" (convert/turned) also signifies change not only in religion but also in gender and sex.

With its complex links with crossing, traveling, and turning, cruising in conceptual terms orients me throughout the book to intentionally search for representations of boys in multiple, often-neglected archives and repertoires, while it also requires me to heed the complexity of multiple intersections, including the different registers in which they appear. Methodologically, then, cruising enables crossings from one context to another, and within them, the discovery of unexpected affinities as well as deliberate connections in the pursuit of the subject. It offers the potential to better explore startling historical interrelations that ultimately provide a critique of the present. Cruising involves being volitionally open to risks and vulnerabilities, being led or oriented by different sites and persons without knowing what awaits at the end. It requires missing out on something, since every road taken is a turn not taken. It is the excitement of the process rather than the final product that orients the cruiser.

At the same time that cruising describes the sense of floating and crossing that constitutes both the method and the object of my study, it also necessitates addressing the unequal power dynamics in which the abducted boy exists as both subject and figure. My analysis follows boys not merely as objects of pleasure but also as objects of plunder, taking cruising done for "plunder," as in its early modern sense, rather than cruising done just for "pleasure," as in its modern usage. As Muñoz would be the first to admit, cruising is implicated in hierarchies of race, class, and (even in male homoerotic spaces) gender. Cruising in historical archives in search of queer affinities may result in what might be troublesome in our contemporary codes of sexual desire and ethics, as Carolyn Dinshaw writes: "The community across time formed of such vibrations, such touches, is not necessarily a feel-good collectivity of happy homos."[21] In particular, a queer-historical pursuit of boys unearths what Kadji Amin terms "disturbing attachments" in a "deidealized" queer historiography.[22] In the representations of abducted boys in the following pages, boys are situated in eroticized hierarchical structures that encompass coercive facets of the cultural and social world of homoeroticism before modernity.

Such accounts, which might be difficult to face and follow for contemporary readers in the context of modern discussions of sexual abuse and child trafficking, show what Rachel Hope Cleves calls "the historical ordinariness of pederasty."[23] Throughout the book I deliberately distinguish this historically ordinary pederasty from modern pedophilia, which are often conflated.[24] Pederasty as a conventional erotic mode includes various asymmetries regarding not only age but also social status, gender, and generational and racial difference, while pedophilia, a modern Western category of crime, refers to adult desire for prepubescent boys in particular (a topic I explore further in chapter 6). In contrast to today's almost-normative age-egalitarian ideals for same-sex relations in the West, in the premodern world, most erotic relations between men and boys, as well as between men and women, were structured in asymmetries and inequalities. Lines between sex and abuse and between pleasure and violence were quite blurry and different from our contemporary demarcations of them. Early modern erotics often demanded hierarchy, not mutuality. Hence, sex was, as David Halperin aptly puts it, "something done to someone by someone else, not a common search for shared pleasure or a purely personal, private experience in which larger social identities based on age or social status are submerged or lost."[25] Pederasty, then, was "a relation of structured inequality between males" not only in terms of different ages ("men" and "boys") but also in terms of different social statuses (freeborn men and slaves, citizens and noncitizens) that determined nonreciprocal sexual patterns, positions, desire, and pleasure—older man chases and enjoys the younger boy, who is not expected to enjoy sex.[26]

Indeed, rather than the negative and visceral feelings attributed to pederasty under the spectacle of pedophilia today, early moderns often framed pederasty and socioeconomic dependencies in positive terms for generating social ties and healthy maturation for boys through homosocial friendship, pedagogy, companionship, social acculturation, and promotion. Such celebrations of unequal and sometimes exploitative relations in strict patriarchal structures ultimately served to privilege adult men at the expense of boys, women, and socially and racially marginalized others. In Western modernity, however, as Amin has uncovered, pederasty was made a racialized sexuality of imperialism in the long durée and was "made retrograde" in the West and associated with Arab-Islamic cultures in the twentieth century.[27] Amin's observation complements other postcolonial queer explorations of the brown boy/white man dyad in colonial and racial contexts that reveal the projection of pederasty onto non-European spaces and cultures in which white men must save brown or black boys. While pederastic modernity locates a white man/brown boy dyad outside Europe, the following chapters show instances not only where pederastic desire was the historical ordinary in the West but also where brown men saved white boys from white men.

To what extent was the traditional and normative pederastic erotic dynamic, intricately and intimately blended with violence and exploitation, utilized in imperial and colonial projections in early modernity? Throughout the book I investigate the man/boy dyad by focusing not mainly on the age of boys (the boys I analyze are not prepubescents but are often what we would call adolescents aged around fourteen or above who were considered to be capable of consent) but on their social status in order to show how race, religion, and class mark the boy as the subject of adult male desire in a pederastic matrix. It is worth noting that in early modernity, puberty was the threshold for consent to sex or marriage and that rather than a strictly chronological age, factors including gender, physical development, class, geography, and race functioned crucially in determining sexual maturity. By particularly tracing boys placed in a multilayered pederastic matrix in Ottoman and English cultural productions from the early modern period, this study unveils the entanglements of asymmetrical power relations in the eroticization of boys in imperial imaginings. Beautiful boys were often put in celebrated homoerotic imaginaries and relations, yet religious and racial difference, coercion, and violence framed their eroticization and ultimately their abduction. They were objects of plunder taken for pleasure.

Accordingly, a historical queer exploration of sexuality must contend with violence, and such violence was often racially inflected, inasmuch as many boys were enslaved due to their racial and religious difference. *Boys Abducted* explores boys in a particular scenario in which they share object status with other boys in aesthetic and erotic deployments yet differ from them as historically vulnerable youths—as traveling boys crossing borders—in an imperial economy of abduction, enslavement, captivity, conversion, and racialization.[28] The abducted, converted, assimilated boys evoke the transformation of boys from one identity into another. They are the objects of desire, service, and slavery. Religiously and ethnically different, they appear as cupbearers, racialized servants, and eroticized beloveds. Hence, their representations reveal homoerotic undercurrents of empire and race.

My use of "homoerotics of empire" or "homoerotics of race" throughout the book draws from Joseph Boone's *The Homoerotics of Orientalism*, which maps out in a transregional and transhistorical framework how male homoeroticism operates inside and outside the dominant structures of Orientalism in contradictory ways that challenge a binary separation of East and West, Islam and Christianity. Tracing a large archive of Western representations of the East, Boone mainly considers Anglo-European and American fantasies and perception (both homoerotic fascination and homophobic aspersion) of homoerotic heritage in the Middle East. Instead of a standpoint located in the Anglo-European and American context, I pursue a synchronic approach with a specific focus on both early modern English and Ottoman contexts, not simply showing similarities between the two but offering the Ottomans' own epistemological basis for producing sexuality in order to open up new ways to approach English texts and discourses. In doing so, my particular attention to early modernity unearths templates that complement the genealogies of homoerotic subtexts of Orientalist imaginations that would fully emerge in the following centuries that Boone has mainly focused on. This also reveals the homoerotics of Orientalism as a changing phenomenon. That is, the pervasive homoeroticism attributed to the Ottomans in an age when traveling English boys and men were under the threat of captivity shifted in Orientalist modernity of the nineteenth century, which attributed not only sodomy but an aggressive and uncontrollable heterosexuality to "lustful Turks" in their harems. With a focus on early modern texts and contexts, the following chapters highlight imperial and racial desires and anxieties that were projected in and through homoerotic dynamics before modernity.

My mapping of abducted boys in English and Ottoman cultural and literary archives enacts a mode of contrapuntal reading instead of staying in one national context. My approach and analytics stem from my training in English literary studies as well as from my critical lens on the cultural history of a society I grew up in as a nomadic queer Muslim subject, moving as a boy from an eastern, Kurdish-majority town to a western, Turkish-majority city in Turkey, then moving to the United States for graduate studies in English. Cognizant of this background and training, I attend to Ottoman and English texts and contexts in their own cultural, philological, and geotemporal specificities while paying attention to interconnections. In my multidirectional exploration, I follow Walter Andrews and Mehmet Kalpaklı's comparative study of love in Ottoman, Italian, and English contexts, as well as Sahar Amer's intercultural examination of medieval French and Arab lesbianism. I analyze texts and contexts in an intercultural and interrelational mode rather than in an explicitly comparative way. As Ania Loomba has cautioned, "comparison has historically served to shore up Eurocentric and discriminatory ideologies," and "the irreversibility of comparative terms is itself shaped by a Eurocentric view of history, and of what we regard as universal and what as particular. To push the comparison ... is to challenge such a view and make available more complete intersections than have hitherto been visible."[29]

In order to unveil such intersections without creating hierarchical genealogies and patterns between the Ottoman and English contexts, I deploy and expand the contrapuntal method as developed by Fernando Ortiz and Edward Said. Ortiz explores the intertwined histories of sugar and tobacco in Cuba, suggesting that these are "counterpoints" that illuminate what he calls "transculturation," or the complex transformation of different cultures that have been brought together by colonialism.[30] In *Culture and Imperialism*, Edward Said uses a related but different term, "contrapuntal," to trace transculturation by reading together cultural and literary texts from both colonizing and colonized contexts. Said suggests that we need to "reread" the cultural archive "not univocally but contrapuntally, with a simultaneous awareness both of the metropolitan history that is narrated and of those other histories against which (and together with which) the dominating discourse acts."[31] In other words, literary texts encompass the cultures of the colonizer and the colonized, both of which are necessary to fully understand the dynamics of the colonial encounter. A contrapuntal method sees these two cultures not as binary opposites but as intersecting. Thus, Said offers "a global analysis, in which texts and worldly institutions are seen working together, by avoiding a partial analysis offered by the various national or systematically theoretical schools."[32] Building on Raymond Williams's concept of a "structure of feeling," Said's contrapuntal approach seeks to reveal "structures of attitude and reference" in which "structures of location and geographical reference appear in the cultural languages of literature, history, ethnography, sometimes allusively and sometimes carefully plotted, across several individual works that are not otherwise connected to one another or to an official ideology of 'empire.'"[33]

While both Ortiz and Said use contrapuntal analysis in the frame of imperial and colonial encounters (and Boone uses it in the frame of Orientalism), I extend the method to put into counterpoint not the colonizer and the colonized but two empires on different levels of colonialism in the sixteenth and early seventeenth centuries: English and Ottoman, and hence Christian and Islamicate, texts and contexts in a time frame when the two had intensifying mercantile and diplomatic encounters and exchanges. At the same time that the Ottoman Empire was an already established power whose territorial domination included almost one-third of Europe in the period I cover, England was emerging as an international player with imperial aspirations and began trafficking in the Ottoman Mediterranean shortly after its exclusion from the European Catholic League. Putting into contact these two contexts that have so far been considered unrelated reveals recurring structures of feelings, attitudes, and references in the context of the construction of sexual and racial imageries.

Rather than centering a diachronic argument regarding historical change or direct lines of borrowing and influence, I deploy the contrapuntal method as a way of connecting texts from both contexts by situating them in the same geohistorical plane in order to uncover the imaginaries of homoeroticism as related to imperial ideas and practices in early modernity. My focus inevitably reveals the shared aesthetic and moral repertoires and common ideological ground of these two realms. Hence, when possible, I point to both similarities and differences as well as transmissions between these two cultures. In certain cases, when such infiltrations are evident, I will argue that we can discern the co-construction, rather than a simple national construction, of sexuality, race, and the homoerotics of empire.

In my contrapuntal framing, each chapter explores the abducted boy in various discursive formations by means of cross-readings of multiple texts beside and against one another, wherein the historical, literary, and aesthetic slide into one another across artificially created borders. I am aided in this by the fact that early modern literatures are predominantly literatures of comparison, reworking, intertextual allusion, adaptation, translation, and misreading—not only in the Ottoman context of harmonizing Arabic, Persian, Turkic, Italian, and Byzantine cultures (as is evident in the Ottoman language itself) but also in the English context, where we can see the influences of Greek, Latin, Italian, French, Spanish, Arabic, and Persian languages and contexts and borrowings from those languages. At their very formation, then, early modern literatures typically resist an insular, national-literary boundary, and thus they are open to tracings of queer affinities contrapuntally among multiple contexts.

Starting with perhaps the most famous, certainly iconic, abducted boy, Ganymede, this book investigates many such affinities. Ganymede has long been a favorite subject in the history of sexuality as the homoerotic companion, the seductive lover, the corrupter, the beautiful youth, the sex toy, the friend, the student, or the servant. I emphasize, instead, the violence of his abduction. The myth itself originates from a violent encounter, the war between the Greeks and the Trojans, the eastern and western sides of the Mediterranean. As a result of this encounter, Ganymede is seized as plunder by Jove and put in an interspecies and intergenerational pederastic relation. In order to foreground Ganymede's effect and function in historical and literary abductions and to lay out the larger historical and critical frameworks of this project, in the following three sections and in a cruisy mode with fluctuations and sudden turns in various archives, I first discuss how a focus on Ganymede's abduction makes visible not only the erotic titillation embedded in his forceful ravishment as the object of adult male desire but also his instrumentalization in the service of the imperial male fantasy of owning youthful servants from other lands in early modernity. Subsequently, I discuss why the Ottomans matter for exploring the history of sexuality in a transcultural context. My framing of the Ottoman Empire in the same geotemporal coordinates as England serves not to idealize the Ottomans in the global Renaissance but to offer a critical global approach to investigate thorny relationships between sexuality and race, pleasure and violence, and homoerotic and imperial desire.

The Ganymede Effect

Whenever a boy appears in an early modern abduction plot, the alluring Ganymede is in the air. Take, for example, Robert Greene's romance narrative *Menaphon*, in which the Thessalian pirate Eurilochus, "driving before him a large booty of beasts to his ships," sees the beautiful boy Pleusidippus on the shore of the Mediterranean Arcadia and gazes on his face "as wanton Jove gazed on Phrygian Ganymede in the fields of Ida." And "hee exhaled into his eyes such deepe impression of his perfection, as that his thought never thirsted so much after any prey, as this pretty Pleusidippus' possession."[34] The boy's beauty delights the pirate's eyes and enchants his heart, and he kidnaps the boy as a form of booty, later presenting him as a gift to the king of Thessaly. Ganymede, in the story, is evoked to instigate the abduction of the beautiful boy who becomes an object of admiration, and henceforth, abduction and circulation between men. But why does Ganymede appear in such plots that are often set in the Mediterranean, and what work does his appearance do?

Ganymede was a Phrygian boy abducted by Jove (Zeus) who, lured by the boy's beauty, took the form of an eagle and carried him away to Olympus, where Ganymede was transformed into an immortal cupbearer to the Gods. Beginning with ancient Greek and Roman narratives by Homer, Plato, Virgil, and Ovid, the story of Ganymede has generated two overarching yet conflicting interpretations: a platonic view that neglects the carnal elements of the myth, taking it as signifying a spiritual union with God (*amor spiritualis*), and an erotic view that relates the myth to homosexual love and pederasty (*amor carnalis*).[35] While Homer's *Iliad* stresses the beauty of Ganymede as the "comeliest of mortal men,"[36] Socrates of Xenophon's alternative *Symposium* downplays the boy's comeliness and the pederastic associations of the myth by declaring that it is Ganymede's "spiritual character that influenced Zeus," as signified by his name, which means "to rejoice in wise councils."[37] Plato's *Laws* claims that the Cretans were "the inventor of the tale" because the practice of pederasty (which Plato defined as sexual mentorship between an adult male and a young boy) was institutionalized there; however, his *Symposium* idealizes Ganymede as a companion and lover who, in misogynist fashion, is superior to women.[38] These two competing interpretations, fluctuating between Ganymede as a figure of ideal love and an object of pederasty, shaped medieval and early modern explications of the myth.[39]

While the story underwent many mutations, visual and literary representations from the late fourteenth century onward coalesced around Ganymede as an icon of homoerotic male desire.[40] In Europe, Ganymede's popularity reached its apogee in the sixteenth century when he was associated with homoerotic love, pleasure, desire, favoritism, and beauty. Even when his abduction was evoked in the form of rapture, ravishment, rape, transport, theft, plundering, and conversion, such violent acts were presented in erotic terms.[41] The most famous version of the myth circulating in the early modern period was derived from Ovid's Latin *Metamorphoses*. In Arthur Golding's 1567 translation, Ganymede's story as narrated by Orpheus (a character also associated with homoeroticism) in a "milder" style to "tell of prettie boyes / That were the derlings of the Gods: and of unlawfull ioyes" makes most visible the homoerotic aspect of the abduction for English readers.[42] In Ovid's depiction, Jove, who "did burne erewhyle in loue of *Ganymed*," "thrusts up" the Trojan boy in the form of an eagle and makes the boy his eternal cupbearer.[43] This passionate flaming homoeroticism, presented in "milder" terms in Ovid, is made visually explicit in early modern paintings such as Michelangelo's *Ganymede*, which, as is evident from its copies, depicts in a highly eroticized mode the moment of Ganymede's abduction (fig. I.1).[44] Jupiter, in the shape of an eagle, aggressively holds the boy's body, grasps Ganymede's legs with his talons, and surrounds his body with his wings while Ganymede's legs are parted, suggesting, in Leonard Barkan's words, "an image of anal penetration."[45] So too does Peter Paul Rubens's *The Rape of Ganymede* aggressively eroticize the abduction by emphasizing the grasping talons of the eagle and phallic quiver thrusting into the boy's buttocks (fig. I.2). The god indeed thrusts up "burn[ing] erewhyle in loue."

This association of the mythic boy with homoerotic desire became such a preeminent trope in the Renaissance that the term Ganymede came to refer to any beautiful boy, including popular mythical youths such as Orpheus, Cupid, Hercules, Adonis, and Hermaphroditus.[46] Moreover, by 1591 the name Ganymede itself became a common noun, "ganymede," in English.[47] Thomas Blount's 1656 dictionary *Glossographia* defines Ganymede as "the name of a Trojan boy, whom Jupiter so loved (say the Poets) as he took him up to Heaven, and made him his Cup-bearer. Hence any boy that is loved for carnal abuse, or is hired to be used contrary to nature, to commit the detestable sin of Sodomy is called a Ganymede; an ingle." As a corrupt form of the name Ganymede, "catamite" started to be used in English to signify, in Blount's definition, "a boy hired to be abused contrary to nature, a Ganymede."[48] Ganymede, a classical signifier now in reference to real-life boys, as is evident in Blount's use of "any boy," has a literary erotic history: "say the Poets."

Indeed, Ganymede as the boy-object of male desire appears ubiquitously in literature and on stage, including in Christopher Marlowe's plays, William Shakespeare's comedies, and Richard Barnfield's sonnets.[49] In Shakespeare's *As You Like It*, for instance, Rosalind cross-dresses as the seductive, saucy Ganymede who

FIGURE 1.1. *Ganymede*, copy after Michelangelo, sixteenth century. Harvard Art Museums/Fogg Museum.

instructs Orlando how to love. Ganymede also shows up as a threat to sexual order in anti-sodomy satires such as Henry Peacham's *Minerva Brittana*, which links the boy to buggery, incest, murder, counterfeiting, and witchcraft. Peacham pictures the boy as an active agent not on the back of an eagle but on a cock, where he viciously holds not a wine cup but poison. Following the

FIGURE 1.2. *The Rape of Ganymede*, Peter Paul Rubens, 1536–1538. Museo Del Prado.

premodern discourses that often mark boys as seducers rather than as victims of older male desire, this Ganymede boy is presented not the passive victim of abduction but a seductive youthful threat.[50] Similarly, in John Marston's *Certaine Satyres*, he is "One who for two daies space / Is closely hired ... an Open Ass."[51] Ganymede also appears in or shapes initial letters in print, and he functions as an inviting emblem, as on the sign for Thomas Walkley's bookstore in London called The Eagle and Child; it is possible that the sign was designed to attract certain types of book buyers.[52]

The early modern revival of Ganymede imagery has been attributed to the prominence of Ovid in the humanist curriculum.[53] Retellings of classical myths were a means for humanist writers to reflect on prevailing styles of eroticism in humanist pedagogy and to explore contemporary social issues. My focus on figurations of Ganymede in abduction plots produced in the historical context of cross-cultural interactions further brings to the fore the real-life traffic in boys, highlighting and attempting to negotiate the complex geopolitical tensions between erotics and violence in literary representations and social practices. That is, when put in the historical context of cross-cultural encounters, forms of homoeroticism ubiquitously enabled with Ganymede also reveal how local homoeroticism is often in dialogue with, if not attached to, pederastic homoeroticism imagined to be elsewhere, especially in the so-called East, where hierarchical relations between masters and servants, kings and minions were eroticized. It is therefore not accidental that multiple figurations of Ganymede appear in accounts of cross-cultural relations, especially in literary and dramatic English representations of Turks. Thomas Goffe's *The Couragious Turke* stages Ganymede as a character in a masque in the Turkish court who lectures the sultan on the superiority of love between men. In John Mason's play *The Turke*, Ganymede stands for a loving companion in a pastoral setting in which Bordello renounces the love of women, inviting his servant Pantofle to be his Ganymede.[54] The Venetian merchant Vitelli of Philip Massinger's *The Renegado* sells in an Ottoman marketplace in Tunis "crystal glasses, such as *Ganymede* / Did fill with Nectar to the Thunderer."[55] Travelers such as Michel Baudier invoke the mythic boy in describing real-life servant boys in the Ottoman lands, where men "speak not but of the perfections of their *Ganimedes*."[56] Servant boys in the Persian court are called "Ganymede boys" in the traveler Thomas Herbert's account.[57] Such depictions, which associate Ganymede with abducted and converted boys in eastern courts, seem to have set the terms for the formation of the later Orientalist and colonial deployments of Ganymede.[58]

How did early modern travel writings that represent abducted European boys as Ganymede influence literary imaginations? How were such travel writings influenced by literary depictions? What effect did such images of Ganymede have on the real-life abductions of boys? To what extent were actual boys who were abducted as booty expected to perform as Ganymedes to make their masters feel like powerful gods? Is it simply coincidental that "ganymede" emerged as a common noun in English when England commenced its overseas trade relations in the Mediterranean? In order to answer such questions in this book, I locate beautiful abducted boys like Ganymede in the Mediterranean space of the early modern period, from the 1550s to 1620s.

This was a period of rising global encounters: Western Europe was trading and expanding in the Mediterranean and the colonial Americas, while the Ottomans were broadening their empire into the Balkans and North Africa. Both the English and the Ottomans were participating in the economy of captivity—being captured or capturing other boys. As a power in the Mediterranean market, the Ottomans practiced an institutionalized policy of abducting boys as *ganimet* (spoils of war, booty), which recalls the iconic Ganymede, as I analyze in the first chapter. In Aşıkpaşazade's Ottoman history, one of the earliest accounts of this practice, the writer proposes "let's give these boys to Turkish households so that they can learn Turkish; after they learn the Turkish language, we can bring them up as the janissaries."[59] From the fifteenth to the mid-seventeenth centuries, the Ottomans brought thousands of Euro-Christian boys into Istanbul every year and converted them so they could assimilate into Ottoman culture and society and help rule the empire.[60] These *ganimet* boys were eroticized not only in European travelogues that called them Ganymede but also in Ottoman literary and visual imaginaries as beloveds, beautiful servants, or obedient cupbearers. In England, it was a common practice to seize English boys from their homes or schools and turn them into actors and singers for royal performances. In the sixteenth century, like Ottoman abductions, such abduction methods were expanded to take up "other" boys from other lands. In alignment with Aşıkpaşazade's account of Ottoman abductions, Robert Johnson's *New Life of Virginea* instructs the Englishmen that "for the poore Indians . . . Take their children and traine them up with gentleness, teach them our English tongue, and the principles of religion."[61] Englishmen trafficked in not only Native American but also African and Indian boys at the dawn of the African slave trade and with the rise of the East India Company. The abducted boy then became a rising figure in literary imaginations in the form of beloved servants, companions, or objects of admiration. As the following chapters reveal, representations of these boys in Ottoman and English cultural representations locate the abduction of boys—institutionalized or not—within a homoerotic matrix of imperial power relations by creating an erotic bond between a hierarchically superior man and a boy abducted from "other" lands.

Drawing on this historical context, *Boys Abducted* terms such deployments and evocations of Ganymede in abduction plots "Ganymede effects." The Ganymede effect refers to allusions to and refigurations and reminiscences of the iconic Ganymede in accounts about abducted boys—imaginary and real—and to an affective mode that emerges through the boy in these abductions and their representations. The myth of Ganymede sometimes effected real-life abductions; other times, abductions inspired reconfigurations of Ganymede in representations. Wherever Ganymede appears in these texts, he carries with him and performs a dual affective function: pleasure and violence, simultaneously. That is, Ganymede's function is not just as a signifier; he calls into play the mixed, hybrid, or concurrent affect that surrounds the materials at the center of this book's investigation.[62] This effect, function, and affective mode is troublingly homoerotic. It travels along with Ganymede-like boys, marking both pleasure and violence at work in their coerced abductions. These boys' lives—and representations of them—hold violence and pleasure (their own, that of others) in constant and oscillating tension.

Part of the project of this book is to maintain a balance between a queer affirmation of cross-generational encounters—resisting, by following queer studies on pederasty, an ahistorical, knee-jerk dismissal of pederasty as universally, morally wrong and recognizing that for some men and some boys, erotic encounters might be mutually desired—with simultaneous recognition of the more widespread experience of sexual coercion and violence visited upon abducted boys. While some scholars have analyzed pederasty as a corrupting force in premodern Europe, others have stressed its potential for social benefits.[63] Alan Sinfield has noted that pederasty can take reversible forms and offer power to the younger party. Following this potentiality and deploying pederasty as a part of queer historiography and analytics, Amin proposes to take pederasty as "less a matter of parsing properly queer from uninterestingly normative or starkly oppressive forms of pederasty than of patiently charting the intertwined perils and potentials of pederasty's marginalized erotics of social power."[64]

Drawing on such insights and examining various figurations of the abducted boy in early modern Ottoman and English historical contexts, this book offers the adult man/abducted adolescent boy dyad as an inevitable component of early modern erotics steeped in violence in the normatively non-egalitarian erotic structures of the past. I argue that native boys who were abducted, exchanged, and circulated were made a part of larger cultural, economic, and political practices that contributed to and sustained the homoerotics of imperialism. The exotic, foreign, racialized boy, both as a literary trope and as a historical subject, is not simply a curiosity or an esoteric figure of desire, but is rather a site of ideological negotiations of imperial, racial, religious, and colonial trajectories in the gendered power hierarchies of early modernity.

Analyzing the Ganymede effect thereby reveals queer affinities and overlapping structures of feelings, attitudes, and references in cultural imperial imaginings in seemingly unconnected languages, literatures, and histories. The term emphasizes the complex connection between the figurative and historical accounts of abducted boys wherein Ganymede, both as a signifier and a generatively performative figure, exposes underlying myths, archetypes, and discursive crossings as he emerges in the historical boys who were abducted as booty while also eroticized as beloveds, and sometimes as seductive and corrupting lovers, in literary and visual representations.

Queering the Renaissance with the Ottomans

Ganymede-like abducted boys in palimpsestic Mediterranean settings—a multilayered space of both the classical past and contemporary encounters—provide a prolific point of entry for considering sexuality in global contacts. This book views cross-cultural encounters as playing a prominent role in producing sexuality because they mediate and complicate sociopolitical and cultural concerns and their attendant negotiations. As Ann Laura Stoler persuasively argues, the history of sexuality simply cannot be charted in Europe alone.[65] In early modern England and in Europe in general, religious and cultural differences were often mapped onto sexual differences, as Alan Bray observes in Edward Coke's seventeenth-century formulation of the "infernal trio of sorcerers, sodomites, and heretics."[66] Sodomy was often elsewhere, foreign. (Likewise, "buggery," from "bugger," signified not only anal sex but Bulgarians and heretics, etymologically related to the Latin *"bulgarus"* and the French *"bougre."*[67]) Sodomy was used as a means of generating and marking religious and racial difference, and as an unnatural, alien, heretical transgression, it was ubiquitously attributed to the Ottoman lands and persons. The compendium of the travels of the Shirley brothers, for instance, claimed that "for their vices, they [Turks] are all *Pagans*, and *Infidels*, *Sodomites*, and Liars."[68] William Lithgow noted Turks were "extreamely inclined to all sorts of lascivious luxury; and generally adicted, besides all their sensuall and incestuous lusts, unto *Sodomy*."[69] Women too, as George Sandys reported on Constantinople, engaged in "unnatural" same-sex activities in Ottoman lands: "Much unnaturall and filthie lust is said to be committed daily in the remote closets of these darkesome *Bannias* [bathhouses]: yea women with women; a thing uncredible, if former times had not given thereunto both detection, and punishment."[70] Sodomy became a predominant trope in English representations of the Turks; and such sodomitical attributions have often been analyzed as stereotypical othering tools.[71]

The projection of stigmatized deviance upon the Ottomans, however, is only one side of the story in exploring sexuality in the Anglo-Ottoman context. Vilified forms of sexuality—sodomy, and its ofttimes corollary, same-sex male eroticism—were commonplace tropes in Ottoman literature. One of the aims of this book is to explore how Ottoman sexual discourses expand our understanding of the expression of sexuality in early modern England and thus alter our general picturing of them. Is the "global Renaissance" that includes the Ottomans *queerer* than what we have thought so far in the project of queering the Renaissance, and if so, given the framework of violence I have been discussing, what do we make of its queerness?[72]

But first, a brief note on the Ottomans *in* and *of* Europe is necessary to foreground cultural crossings that will appear in following chapters. This book reframes some of major early modern English literary texts in the much-ignored Ottoman context. My transnational approach to early modern literature and the history of sexuality and race challenges the distorted image of the early modern past as governed by fixed geopolitical, ethnic, and religious boundaries by paying attention to discursive and material contacts and exchanges between nations and religions, especially in the historical Mediterranean context.[73] Comparative charts of similarities, intricate networks, processes of circulations, and possible connections present an early modern world that was far more complex and dynamic than that offered by nationalistic ethnographic perspectives that emphasize differences in the framework of strictly divided cultural borders of the modern nation-states.

There are striking parallels and crossings between the cultural imaginaries of early modern societies, or what Sanjay Subrahmanyam calls "connected histories." Besides the flow of things, people, and technologies in the early modern world, "ideas and mental constructs, too, flowed across political boundaries in that world, and—even if they found specific local expression—enable us to see what we are dealing with are not separate and comparable, but connected histories."[74] In pursuit of such connected histories, and challenging the New World–centric new historicist scholarship that has framed Europe simplistically against its colonial others, the global turn in early modern English literary studies has focused on cross-cultural encounters, which, as Jyotsna Singh asserts, "generated not only material exchanges within varying and uneven power relations, but also a rich and complex cross-pollination of art, culture, belief systems, and technologies between England and its 'others,' both within and outside Europe."[75] This global turn has historicized England's engagements and investments in the so-called East with a particular focus on extensive exchanges and interactions in the Mediterranean following the Ottoman capitulations (certain rights and privileges accorded to foreign nationals by the Ottoman sultan) that were granted first to the Turkey Company (1581), which in 1592 became the Levant Company, for trade privileges in the eastern Mediterranean (the Levant) and along the Barbary coast of North Africa. The purpose of England's engagement in this space was that, as noted in the letter of Queen Elizabeth I to the Ottoman sultan, through "mutuall trafique, the East may be joyned and knit to the West."[76]

Indeed, from religious conversions to communal cohabitations and personal interactions, extensive political, social, military, commercial, cultural, and personal crossings between the English and the Ottomans knit the two together. Rich and complex cross-pollinations became evident in the cultural appropriation of Ottoman goods, styles, and images in England. These included royal and aristocratic interest in Turkish fashion and products, the personal exchanges of letters and gifts between Elizabeth I and Safiye Sultan, and the circulation of the portraits of the Ottoman sultans and other Ottoman objects in the marketplace, to name a few.[77] Numerous English writers chronicled Ottoman history and society in detail, and English travelers and ambassadors to the Ottoman court left varied accounts of their encounters—Richard Knolles's *The Generalle Historie of the Turkes*, Richard Hakluyt's *Principal Navigations*, George Sandys's *A Relation of a Journey*, Samuel Purchas's *Purchas His Pilgrimage*, Paul Rycaut's *The Present State of Ottoman Empire*, and William Harborne's and Thomas Roe's records of their ambassadorships, among others. These accounts assembled a rich archive that engendered popular images of the Ottomans in Elizabethan and Jacobean literature and theater. In the forty-year period from 1580 to 1620, more than sixty English plays appeared with Islamic themes, characters, or settings, whose Turkish costumes, acting styles, and gestures on the English stage were often drawn from more than 3,000 printed texts about Islam, Turks, Moors, and the Ottomans.[78]

In this period of increasing cross-cultural exchanges and encounters, reading English and Ottoman cultures together challenges the presumption of the two as incommensurable.[79] The traditional Eurocentric literary view of a fixed universal Europe has long imprisoned early modern cultural imaginations and their artistic products in the spheres of strictly divided, ostensibly unconnected Eastern and Western literatures. These demarcations, as I discuss elsewhere, have a recent history going back to the nineteenth-century Orientalist project of creating the West in opposition to the Orient.[80] The great Orientalist E. J. W. Gibb's first and influential English collection of Ottoman poetry in six volumes, *A History of Ottoman Poetry* (1900–1909), for example, renders impossible a comparison of cultural productions from the Ottoman and English contexts—temporal, intellectual, and moral—in the Renaissance even though he recognizes correspondences between them in the Middle Ages: "The genius of the Middle Ages and the genius of the Renaissance are so opposite that mutual comprehension seems impossible. In the West the latter killed the former; but into the East it could not pass."[81] Gibb recasts the fiction of a secular Renaissance as a new, morally and intellectually higher code. His use of "the genius" of the age alongside of "the guidance of the new-found Hellenism" refers to the nineteenth-century signification of "the Renaissance" not only as a descriptive historical phrase but also as a spirit of Western civilization and modernity, going back to the Eurocentric conceptualization articulated by Jules Michelet's *La Renaissance* (1855), Jacob Burckhardt's *The Civilisation of the Renaissance in Italy* (1860), and Walter Pater's *The Renaissance* (1873), among others.[82] While "West" and "East" once shared cultural similarities, even identical imaginings in spite of linguistic and religious differences in the Middle Ages, an ideologically constructed imperialist notion of the Renaissance and Europe began to separate the two cultures in hierarchal terms: namely, a modern, advanced civilization versus a premodern stasis. Gibb's *History* is symptomatic in revealing a shift in marking Ottoman literature as incompatible with European cultural productions.

Instead of portraying the Ottomans as the solely Islamic, distinctively non-Western other, and thus as peripheral to European culture and history, my effort to chart, when possible, convergences and divergences between the two realms presents an early modern world that confutes Islam/Christian, East/West, Europe/Rest divisions and situates the Ottomans as central to European culture, geography, and politics. European and Christian cultures were intricately adopted and blended in the Ottomans' empire-building politics and in its social and cultural productions as much as traditional Islamic cultures were—whether through cross-cultural encounters, conversions, neighborhood interactions, imperial multiculturalism, or abduction and enslavement of Euro-Christians. Challenging the orientalizing and therefore racialized discourse by Gibb and his followers, Walter Andrews points to an "Ottoman Renaissance" as a period of intense and creative cultural and artistic activity in the Ottoman Empire from approximately 1453 to 1625 "paralleling the broader burgeoning of culture(s) in Europe commonly called 'the Renaissance.'"[83] While the Ottomans figure prominently in the cultural, political, economic, and social life of Europe, Western cultural re-formations and social developments, in turn, traveled to the Ottoman Empire from the mid-fifteenth century onward. This bilateral transmission, to quote Andrews, "breaks down artificial barriers that separate East from West, Ottomans from Europeans, barriers that are constituted more by the structure of our present scholarly institutions than by actual conditions during the Renaissance."[84] Like Western Europe, Ottoman society witnessed the emergence of new cultural and aesthetic forms that included architectural achievements, monumental historiographies, reworkings of classics, translations, the emergence of a distinctive Ottoman literature that broke away from Persian imitations, the elite patronage of arts and literature, artistic productions of Italian artists and artisans in Istanbul, and the secularization of cultural imaginings. Further interconnections in universalist imperial claims, new economic modes and commerce, cartographic developments, changing gender and sexual dynamics in a shared period and space of ideas, persons, and objects challenge a situating of the Ottomans and Europeans in wholly antithetical and oppositional terms.[85]

In fact, Europe as a continentally and culturally unified formation also stems from the nineteenth-century reimaginings of power dynamics—the West versus the rest—in conceptualizing a more definitive geographical continental divide. The Ottomans were no less European than England was in the early modern period. As Michael Wintle shows, Britain itself was historically sometimes included in and other times excluded from the cartographic theater of Europe. In addition to the Ottomans' self-conscious claim of Roman heritage in their empire-building process, the geographical coordinates of the empire (their capital city and almost one-third of their territory was located in Europe) impede an imagination of the Ottomans outside Europe and solely under Persian and Arabic influences. The Ottoman sultans declared themselves as Caesars (*kaysers*), emperors, or universal monarchs, claiming their imperial dominion over both Asia and Europe and therefore over both Islamic and Christian worlds. Some humanists recognized the Ottoman sultan as the universal emperor in the Roman sense. On the Habsburgs' rivalry with the Ottomans in claiming the universal imperium, for instance, Jean Bodin marked the Ottomans as the victor: "If there is anywhere in the world any majesty of empire and of true monarchy, it must radiate from the sultan. He owns the richest parts of Asia, Africa and Europe, and he rules far and wide over the entire Mediterranean and all but a few of its islands."[86] Other humanists and chroniclers linked the Ottomans with Trojans.[87]

Likewise, some Ottoman intellectuals did not see religion as a demarcating feature between the Ottomans and Western Christendom but located the Ottomans in European geography as a European power.[88] Hajji Ahmed's 1559 map, the earliest known Turkish-language map designed for public sale, for instance, divides the world into four continents (Asia, Europe, Africa, and the

New World), on the top of which is Europe under the hegemony of the Ottomans, carrying the legacy of the Romans and of Alexander the Great:

> Europe: This continent is special in that it is small compared to the others but at the same time more densely populated and intensively cultivated. The arts and sciences flourish there, and the fighting spirit of its people has served as a constant source of illumination, such that it is more beautiful and secure than other renowned and famous provinces. And furthermore it should be known that the greatest rulers of all ages have compared this land to the Sun, and most of them have ruled from here. These include the mighty Alexander the Great . . . and today in the year 967 of the Muslim calendar it is ruled by His Majesty Suleyman of the House of Osman, Sultan of Sultans and Refuge of the Rulers of the World, who is an even greater source for the illumination of humanity.[89]

Noting France, Spain, Italy, Portugal, and Germany as other parts of Europe, the Ottoman intellectual and cartographer confirms the Ottoman sultans, in Giancarlo Casale's terms, "as the physical embodiment of Europe."[90] Furthermore, Ahmed connects the Ottomans' imperial domination over lands they conquered to European colonialism in the Americas as he describes Spanish colonial activities, especially regarding the native people of Peru: "These people once upon a time were all pagans, but now most of them have become Catholics . . . [They have] learned the Spanish language and customs, just as the people of Anatolia and Karaman have learned the language and customs of the Turks."[91] Alongside a perspective that connected the Ottomans to an Islamic world and lineage, a view often shared by educated, freeborn Muslims of the empire, as Casale observes, a strong intellectual discourse emerged that envisioned the Ottoman Empire as a European state.

Such complex imperial self-projections call for a reconsideration of early modern literary imaginings beyond the narrow confines of single-language national literature within the nation-state paradigm. The Ottoman literary elite amalgamated Arabic, Persian, and Byzantine traditions as the poets of Rum (Roman lands) and identified themselves not as Turk but as Rumi, or Roman.[92] Rumi, or Rumice (in the Roman manner), became a signifier for Ottoman cultural productions that alluded to and combined Persian, Arabic, Hellenistic, Roman, and late antique traditions and figures. Early modern European writers were cognizant of such blending of languages, traditions, and ethnicities in the Ottoman social fabric. The English writer John Foxe claimed that "there are few now remaining, which are Turks indeed by birth and blood."[93] Rycaut observed that, in structuring their empire, the Ottomans followed the Romans, "who well knew the benefit of receiving strangers into their bosom," and as a result, "no people in the world have ever been more open to receive all sorts of Nations to them, then they, nor have used more arts to increase the number of those that are called *Turks*."[94] Jakab Harsány Nagy, a seventeenth-century Transylvanian humanist, likewise, warned his European readers against assuming an essential Turkish identity: Turkish character, he wrote, "is not one nation [*millet* in the Turkish text; *una gens* in the Latin] but consists of all sorts of people of the world: Germans, Poles, French, English, Dutch, Hungarians, Muscovites, Czechs, Rus, Cossacks, Serbs, Bulgarians, Albanians, Abkhazians, Georgians, Kurds, Persians, Arabs, Greeks, Armenians, Tatars, Wallachians, Moldavians, Circassians, Croatians, Italians, Jews, Indians, and many others. Whoever wishes to speak of the Ottoman character [*Osmanlinin tabiati*], he must know the character of all [these] people [nations]."[95] Instead of a religiously unified Europe in opposition to the Islamic Ottomans, these examples, as well as those in following chapters, present a continental belonging and cultural legacy that went beyond religious difference and went back to the Romans as foregrounding Europe that included the Ottomans as its primary imperial player.

In this transnational imperial context, Anglo-Ottoman encounters and interactions proved to be critical in shaping certain English imaginaries at home. Building on Amer's intercultural approach to medieval lesbianism in the Arab Islamicate and in Christian European contexts, I also recognize the difficulty, if not impossibility, of a sole focus on literary sources and influences and direct lines of transmission in premodern forms of transcultural crossings in cultural materials and texts. Instead, I consider what Amer suggests, "not only linguistic and textual context (the intertextual), but also the sociohistorical and cultural codes inscribed within each text (the intercultural)."[96] I too propose that although Ottoman and English writers probably did not read one another, English bodies entered the Ottoman lands, where they interacted with the Ottomans; drank at their taverns and coffeehouses; observed their lives and customs; heard their stories, songs, and poems; saw their performances; attended their festivals; and most likely experienced some Ottoman bodies more intimately. Such overseas interactions and encounters generated the genre of tales or news from Turkey in England.[97] Besides the figurations of the Ottomans in influential European texts that circulated in England, including Niccolò Machiavelli's *The Prince*, Baldassare Castiglione's *The Book of the Courtier*, and many humanist writings, English chronicles and travelogues captured not only Ottoman history and imperial structure but also its contemporaneous society, culture, and language. In taverns, Ottoman stories and tales circulated as they were narrated by seaman, merchants, travelers, and writers, including

Richard Hakluyt, the great compiler of *The Principal Navigations, Voyages, and Discoveries of the English Nation*.[98] As a result, not only Ottoman goods but also Ottoman voices and ideas infiltrated into England and contributed to English imaginaries via travelogues, poems, and plays on public stages.[99] The accounts of abducted boys (as the following chapters will show), for instance, created mythologies of the janissaries in relation to Ganymede in England, and descriptions of Ottoman eunuchs in travelogues echoed on the English stage.

In locating sexuality in cross-cultural connections and trajectories, this book includes Ottoman sources not simply to expand the geographic reach of Western historiography but to challenge, reconsider, and "provincialize" Eurocentric sexual histories by bringing to the forefront Ottomans' own sexual epistemologies as models in order to reconfigure our approach to English representations.[100] In spite of differences and putative otherness, cultural productions from the two contexts demonstrate complex and curious parallels and connections in representations of sexuality. It is indeed not surprising if we also take into account the shared foundational authorities, discourses, and conceptualizations—theological (similarities between the Bible and the Qur'an), classical (especially the influence of Plato and Aristotle and the popularity of Alexander the Great), and medical (Galen and Avicenna). In both English and Ottoman cultures, there was a Roman influence. Galenic theories of the humoral body and Avicenna's (Abu Ali al-Ḥusayn bin Abdullah ibn al-Ḥasan bin Ali bin Sina) medical propositions on sex and gender difference in his *Al-Qanun fi't-Tibb* (Canon of medicine) were not only essential parts of the medical curriculum but were also operative in natural philosophy, moral philosophy, and physiognomy to the mid-seventeenth century.[101] On such shared grounds, in particular, I shift the angle of vision to ask: What do we see in early modern England when we look at sexuality from a standpoint located in the Ottoman lands, specifically in its capital Istanbul?

One thing in particular stands out: in the Ottoman Empire, domestic and public relations and political power were organized and managed around highly institutionalized orderly homosocial and homoerotic male bonds, especially between adult men and boys. Further, despite theological denunciations of sexual relations outside marriage, same-sex male homoeroticism was central to Ottoman literature in various genres from the fifteenth through the eighteenth centuries.[102] These included the ghazal (lyric poetry) the *mesnevi* (narrative poem), shadow theater, the *şehrengiz* (catalogue of beautiful men), the *tezkire* (biography), the *dellakname* (catalogue of bathhouse boys), and the *bahname* (book of libido).[103] In exploring this literature, I particularly draw on and am in dialogue with Andrews and Kalpaklı's *The Age of Beloveds*, which introduces and mediates early modern Ottoman sexuality alongside European literary and critical sources mainly for a Euro-American audience and reveals multiple symmetrical discourses on love and the beloved across cultures.[104] Recognizing how poetic genres make possible the expression of homoerotic love, they persuasively show that beautiful boys, whether they appeared in miniatures, poetry, or historical narratives, were not merely a rhetorical device or, as hitherto suggested, an abstract, disembodied metaphor mediating the passage to the divine, but derived from and represented a distinct social class of boys who were objects of desire and devotion in the homosocially structured empire.[105]

Whereas Andrews and Kalpaklı catalogue and conflate all such boys under the term "beloved" in their portrayal of widespread homoeroticism in Ottoman cultural productions and society, I suggest that these boys often differed from one another based on their class, age, ethnicity, race, or religion. They were *şehir oğlanları* (city boys), *levends* (adventurous youths), *emreds* (beardless youths), libertines, *suhtes* (theology students), *evbaş* (lower-type boys), prostituting boys, *hamam* boys (bathhouse boys), Galata boys, Frank boys (European boys), and janissaries. Although cognizant of these categories, Andrews and Kalpaklı's project mainly traces the nature of love in Ottoman culture wherein the boy stands as a beloved erotic object of male desire. Even their suggestive discussion of the parallels between the cupbearer boy in this poetic tradition and the iconic Ganymede serves to display erotic symmetries regarding the prevalence of boy love in both the Ottoman and European contexts, although they do not explore what the boy's religious and cultural difference conveys in such figurations.[106] In contrast, I argue in this book that not all boys accrue the same meaning. What necessitates the deployment of not a Muslim boy but a Christian boy in this literary culture? And, to extend this line of thought into the English context, what does Shakespeare's racially othered Indian boy in *A Midsummer Night's Dream* signify that the white youth of his sonnets do not or cannot? Can Ottoman accounts of various categories of boys guide us to highlight differences among boys in English representations?

The Darker Side of the Global Renaissance

As I have begun to intimate, if the sexual arrangements and representations in the early modern Ottoman world appear queer to us moderns, this queerness was not always something we might want to idealize. In pursuing representations of boys at thorny intersections, my study crucially presents sexuality not as an isolated category of analysis but as one that is inseparably intertwined with race and empire because it is marked by the asymmetries and violence generated by racial and imperial histories on the darker side of the "global renaissance."[107] I use "the darker side," evoking Walter Mignolo's *The Darker Side of the Renaissance* about Spanish colonialism, in reference to the exchanges of imperial, colonial, and racial technologies, violent practices, and discourses on a global level. Specifically, in this section, I call for a critical approach to the Ottoman past and imperial ideology as it appears in comparative or global early modern studies. I map out some aspects of Ottoman slavery and racialization, empire building, and race making in order to provide an essential background for understanding the hierarchization and eroticization of abducted, enslaved boys in the following chapters.

Remarkably, foundational studies of the "global renaissance" that emphasize cross-cultural encounters and exchanges have often ignored the exchanges of not-such-fun things, or the darker side of the global Renaissance. In its important task of questioning and historically probing what constitutes the West and its Eastern other by stressing the Ottomans' relevance to and power in Europe, such work initiated a global turn as they marked the Renaissance as an era "before Orientalism."[108] In part intent on challenging Said's initial conceptualization of Orientalism as knowledge-production about the East, critics have stressed an early modern Europe that had not colonized Turkey but had equal or pragmatic relationships of exchange with the Ottomans. They suggest that all of Said's understanding of East-West relationships applies only to the nineteenth century and after, when Europe became a global imperial power.

However, by suggesting that early modern Europe was not in a position to engender Orientalist discourses and attitudes, such critiques engage in two fallacies: they simplify and thereby misread Said and they orientalize the Ottomans in a way that Said did not. Said does not present an ahistorical, universal Orientalism but instead makes an explicit distinction between a modern Orientalism in post-Enlightenment discourse and its other "latent" forms.[109] His examples from antiquity and the premodern period reflect his Foucauldian genealogical investigation that offers not a point of origin but a messy genealogy of orientalisms (in plural) in multiple sites and their transhistorical operations, in which texts offer palimpsestic tropes that then circulated and contributed to form nineteenth-century Orientalism.[110] Critiques of (and deliberate distancing from) Said on the part of early modern critics have served to mark, if not cement, the Ottomans as essentially different from Europeans and render them almost invisible in discussions of imperialism, colonialism, and race-making processes in early modern English studies.[111] Nowhere in his *Orientalism* does Said present the Ottoman Empire as orientalized; rather, his analysis centers on places in North Africa and what is now called the Middle East that were once *conquered* by the Ottomans. In fact, one can even claim, by noting Said's probably deliberate neglect of the Ottomans in his book, that the Ottoman Empire might be one of those imperial powers that actively contributed to the formation of modern Orientalist thought and imagination. By taking into account Ottoman culture and imperialism in relation to Western empires—thus following Said's *Orientalism* and his even more complex investigation of *Culture and Imperialism*—this book will unearth complex genealogies of orientalisms in early modern cross-cultural encounters and exchanges.

Formations of sexuality, race, and empire in England existed not simply in opposition to but alongside and in dialogue with the Ottomans. By considering the darker side of cross-cultural contacts between the English and the Ottomans while also contrapuntally lingering in their queer sites and imaginaries, I do not suggest an equal dialogic partnership; rather, as I will show, there were asymmetric transferences, crossovers, and cultural negotiations between England and the Ottoman Empire. Western powers were not essentially and innately powerful, nor were they culturally isolated from non-Western imperial practices and discourses. Ania Loomba has recently cautioned that "we cannot challenge a crude narrative of an endless clash of cultures by simplifying past histories of contact into a narrative of mutuality and equity. If we do so, we cannot explain why and how modern Western empires were born and shaped during the Renaissance, or indeed understand why so many of the cultural achievements of the Renaissance are overtly marked by imperial ambition (or question such ambition)."[112] Countering the model of connected histories for its inadequacy in fully excavating cultural differences and ideologies among different imperial models, Loomba offers a model of imperial histories in order to better investigate the genesis and dynamics of Western empires. I connect this imperial history model with the connected history model discussed earlier based on the premise that no single imperial culture was immune from the influences of another. In doing so and in relying on studies that have shown how certain practices of enslavement moved from Islamicate societies to Christian ones, I ultimately query the darker side of connected histories with a focus on sexuality at the intersection of race as they were co-produced and made into the grammar of imperial rule.

The Ottoman Empire was hardly disconnected from Western empires, considering their cultural and geographical commonalities and exchanges. In this respect, it is important to dispel the idea of viewing the Ottomans as somehow exceptional in their egalitarianism. There is an unfortunate tendency in comparative histories to single out (and often celebrate) the Ottoman Empire by emphasizing its difference from European imperialism. Jonathan Burton, for example, sets "the multi-ethnic cosmopolitanism and tolerance of the Ottomans against the racial practices that developed in contemporaneous Portuguese, Spanish, English, and Dutch empires."[113] He suggests that the Ottomans took up the legacy of the Roman empire, and in doing so, "extended the benefits of citizenship to the diverse peoples they conquered.... [They] allowed confessional diversity, intermarried at the highest echelon, and most importantly recruited a core of metropolitan elites through the *devşirme*, or child tribute."[114] It is true that Ottoman imperial practices were different in many ways from European colonial practices in the Americas and later in the rest of the world. Nevertheless, in the mid-sixteenth century, the Ottoman intellectual Hajji Ahmed likened Spain's colonization in the Americas to the Ottomans' conquest of Anatolia. Uncritical deployments of the Ottoman Empire as an egalitarian imperial structure characterized by the happy cohabitation of various communities for centuries bury the brutal aspects of Ottoman slavery while risking the erasure of the relationships between religious and racial difference and political subjecthood and sovereignty in this period. Such celebratory assessments of Ottoman slavery and imperialism are usually built on a conventional Turkish nationalist glorification of Pax Ottomanica, a view that idealizes the early modern Ottoman Empire as the cradle of tolerance where the peaceful coexistence of various religions and ethnic groups was uninterrupted.[115] This kind of simple opposition between East and West simply reverses the ideological bias of Orientalism but keeps alive its binary structure. We need to be careful not to romanticize, orientalize, or infantilize the Eastern and Islamicate empires of the past by stoking a nostalgia that might bring unintended political consequences and serve to feed into a nativism that is uncritically obsessed with a presumably glorious past. Empires, after all, are built on various forms of control, hierarchization, oppression, exploitation, violence, and subjugation in order to maintain their global power.

While being an Ottoman subject was beneficial to some Christians and Jews, and while some European Christians willingly converted to obtain some of the benefits that specifically accrued to Muslims, the Ottoman Empire was by no means an egalitarian society. Being conquered meant being subjected to a variety of restrictions and control that included higher taxation and wearing obligatory belts (*zünnar*) that marked religious difference for subject Christian and Jewish populations, even if they were not forced to convert. To become an elite through *devşirme*, the systematic practice of capturing, converting, assimilating Christian boys (the subject of my first chapter), was not something that every non-Muslim willingly agreed to. In fact, this coercive practice was traumatic for families and their children, as is evidenced in native sources from the lands under Ottoman control.[116] While some families, especially Bosnians, might have regarded the system as beneficial for their sons, others resisted and resented *devşirme*, which transformed the abducted Christian boys into permanent slaves, or *kul*, a term used for "slave" but that can also be translated as "servant to God," signifying that the power dynamics of Ottoman absolutism were similar to those between God and human and between creator and the created.[117] Hence, my focus on abducted boys shall reveal that the Ottomans effectively turned boys not into equal subjects in an egalitarian structure but into objects and, in particular, into vehicles for enacting, maintaining, and representing the legitimacy of the empire itself.

Certainly Ottoman slavery was different from Western slavery, in which a slave was mostly a chattel deprived of civic rights and in which children inherited slave status. Ottoman slavery, in general, was more similar to European servitude and bondage. *Devşirme* boys, for example, were *kuls*, slaves of the sultan, but at the same time, they had privileges that other subjects of the empire did not. They were considered part of the sultan's household and were paid salaries. They were exempt from taxation, and they themselves owned properties and slaves. Others, such as purchased slaves, had the legal right to negotiate their contracts or change their master if they wished. Slavery was not invariably inherited; the sons and daughters of the slaves were sometimes free. Also, slaves could be liberated at their master's will, usually upon their religious conversion. Slaves, therefore, had opportunities and means to rise to positions of power and influence.[118] Despite these differences, the lack of individual consent and will relegated many of these boys to the condition of slavery for the rest of their lives. Within the viciously combative and competitive structure of the Ottoman palace, *devşirme* slaves were always under the threat of a death order from the sultan.[119] Importantly, religious difference was an essential marker of hierarchization that legitimized their enslavement even if they converted to Islam upon their recruitment. Furthermore, they were exposed to consistent attacks as unreliable converts or because of their non-Muslim lineage. As one sixteenth-century intellectual put it: "Either on their father's or their mother's side, the[ir] genealogy is traced to a filthy infidel."[120] In this book, I explore such moments when religious difference was racialized.

The suppositions that Islamic law was supreme in the rule of the empire and that Islamic "tolerance" was universal should also be critically examined in light of the state policies of maintaining control by the demarcation and hierarchization of peoples. Otherwise, such assumptions risk ignoring the historical changes that took place in ideologies, thus imprisoning Islamicate society in a fabricated fable of a unified, never-changing matrix of a singular Islam. As I further discuss in chapter 1, the Ottomans distorted Islamic laws to enslave Christian boys from their own imperial population, boys who were supposed to be under the authority and protection of laws, in order to maintain their imperial power via the *devşirme* system. Islamic law therefore was not the only source of imperial rule and it was not interpreted in a single way. As Chouki El Hamel rightly remarks, "Relying solely on Islamic ideology as a crucial key to explain social relations, particularly the history of black slavery in the Muslim world, yields an inaccurate historical record of the people, institutions, and social practices of slavery in the Arab world."[121] This assessment is particularly significant for understanding the Ottomans, considering that they embraced Roman heritage and accepted common law (in addition to Islamic Shari'a law) in forming and governing the empire. Although that empire housed multiple different religious groups, they were often strictly segregated into zones that had restricted access to outsiders. Therefore, rather than assuming that religion alone can serve as an accurate lens for analyzing Ottoman imperial politics and social and cultural practices, we need to acknowledge imperial politics, cultural-historical specificities, and contextualized, plural Islams.

In pursuing racially and religiously marked abducted boys, this book assesses emergent racial ideologies and distinctions as critical components of the empire, since racial and religious differences were crucial factors in the abduction of boys. While race has started to be carefully investigated in early modern English studies in the past few decades, only recently have Ottomanists began to pay attention to emerging racial discourses in early modernity. They nevertheless tend to avoid using the term "race" in describing the human difference produced in the period.[122] Yet not to use the term "race" in premodern studies, Geraldine Heng reminds us, "would be to sustain the reproduction of a certain kind of past, while keeping the door shut to tools, analyses, and resources that can name the past differently."[123] Terms of larger generality such as "otherness" or "difference," Heng establishes, do not serve strategic, epistemological, and political commitments to understanding human culture and society. Also, such attempts to distance race/racisms of the past from the present risks blurring the ways that discourses, ideologies, and practices in the past penetrate into the present. My use of "race" and "racism" in both English and Ottoman early modern contexts throughout the book aims to denaturalize human hierarchizations and to highlight a genealogy of race as inextricably interlinked with and articulated through the infrastructures of slavery, colonial and imperial practices, religious difference, and eroticized and gendered power hierarchies. This does not mean neglecting local sociopolitical and cultural specificities; rather, it means attending to "transregional conversations about race [that were] centuries in the making."[124]

On race as an analytic tool for exploring human difference transhistorically and transregionally, Heng's definition is particularly illuminating: "*Race is a structural relationship for the articulation and management of human differences, rather than a substantive content.*"[125] In this book, I consider that early modern race and racisms were ways to make fundamental differentiations and hierarchizations among humans not only in Europe but also in the Ottoman realms. By the seventeenth century, in addition to prior racial discourses of climate theories, physiognomy, humoral theory, and theological renderings of the Hamitic curse, a racialism based on skin color had appeared in Arab-Islamicate regions.[126] El Hamel remarks that "the expansion and racialization of black slavery in Morocco and in the adjacent Atlantic world was taking place at the same time... from common roots in a Mediterranean concept of slavery and Abrahamic traditions."[127] Documenting the rise of the new slavery practices that ignored the Islamic prohibition on enslaving Muslims, El Hamel convincingly demonstrates how black Muslim Africans began to be enslaved, indeed, began to be seen as "natural slaves." Influenced by such Arab-Islamicate racial discourses, Ottoman intellectuals generated racialized ideas in parallel with the Ottomans' imperial investments in Africa and with the simultaneous rise of a black population in Istanbul from the second half of the sixteenth century onward.

Antiblackness appears to have functioned as a structural tool for denying legitimacy to black African bodies in the rule of the empire, even though a few had honor and status at court. While white European boys were abducted as slaves to serve in higher status in courtly and military affairs, black African boys were castrated to serve as eunuchs in domestic spaces. Black and white eunuchs were strictly separated; black bodies were seen as inferior in the natural order of things and were thus put closer to women in the harem in the patriarchal structure of the empire. It is worth asking, as I do in chapter 5, why not a single black boy became a grand vizier while some white boys who were made eunuchs, such as the Bosnian Hadım Ali Pasha, the Bulgarian Hadım Mesih Pasha, and the Albanian Hadım Hasan Pasha, did. In fact, biographies of black Ottomans, rare as they are, show that they had particular difficulty advancing their careers compared to their white counterparts.[128] Whether they were black or white, only a very few of these slaves among countless others rose to power. Likewise, none of the black female slaves became the favorite (*haseki*) or mother queen (*valide sultan*) in the harem. The Ottomans very successfully sold a dream of exceptional access to power for a few enslaved men, women, and boys, a dream whose basis in racialized abduction and coercion we are still in the process of uncovering.

In this context, this book treats the homoerotics of abductions, which put enslaved boys in beautified gendered and eroticized power hierarchies, as inseparable from racial formations and dynamics. In doing so, it shows that homoeroticism was a potent force in the creation, maintenance, and imagination of racial hierarchies and empire across both East and West. As the following chapters will discuss, abducted boys were selected on the basis of their physical appearance and were often depicted in erotic terms. It was the whiteness of the boys that determined their value, their promotions, and their appraisal in literature. Some Ottoman writers celebrated white European beauty and encouraged reproductive unions with the Ottomans of European descent so as to create an ideal population. Intellectual discourses by elite writers not only signaled and established a racial vocabulary infused with sexual desire but also revealed how the white beauty routinely idealized in Ottoman literature functioned to construct somatic hierarchies. Conventional readings of this aesthetic celebration of whiteness and of white and black as merely metaphors ignore the racial dynamics of imperial and sexual power hierarchies. Protesting the privileging of whiteness as the ideal norm by these intellectuals, one rare black Ottoman elite, to whom I return in chapter 5, wrote: "[God] said 'the noblest one among you in the eyes of God is the most pious'; He did not say 'the most good-looking, the most handsome, and the whitest.'"[129] It is important to discern how skin color here is perceived as interlinked with beauty. In contemporary Ottoman accounts and in literary examples, as the following chapters illuminate, the imperial gaze is consistently fused with an erotic gaze on good-looking white boys, a gaze that sometimes idealized whiteness and other times condemned blackness. As Carmen Nocentelli observes for the European context, "Love and empire accompanied each other from the beginning of Europe's expansion overseas."[130] So, too, for the Ottomans.

Asymmetrical Intersections: Queer/Race

Throughout the book, my queer-race hermeneutics carefully attends to the often-contradictory and problematic infusion of homoeroticism into the imperial and racial gaze by bridging sexuality and queer studies of the early modern period with studies in early modern race and globality.[131] Cultural and literary works with queer imaginaries present social hierarchies of race and sexuality as vulnerable, contradictory, and ambiguous. The literary and cultural history this book offers presents homoeroticism as troubled by hierarchy, race, slavery, and coercion and thus sometimes used as an imperial tool to take control of, dominate, and exploit populations and lands during this time period. My queer analytics considers sexuality to be inseparable from race in its focus on gaps, contradictions, pleasure, and playfulness. Hence, this book aims not only to unearth homoerotic dynamics of the past that seem to us today to be part of queer historiography but also to queer the past in terms of deconstructing the rhetorical historical, literary, and visual strategies that contributed to producing the structures of the hierarchization, articulation, and management of human difference that are in fact artificial, unstable, mobile, and malleable.

Exploring race and sexuality with the early moderns requires a capacious focus on conjunctions, crossroads, and overlapping discourses. Sexuality is constituted vis-à-vis the projected other via the attribution of transgressive acts onto foreign sites and people. Likewise, race is always construed in terms of othered populations in complex interrelations with various overlapping discourses and forms of knowledge production and is therefore permeable and adaptable, or, as Peter Erickson and Kim F. Hall characterize it, "always protean and sticky, attaching to a range of ideologies, narratives, and vocabularies in ways both familiar and strange."[132] As Ian Smith signals, "Race is constitutionally queer insofar as it is never a unified, fixed category but posits a social identity produced from a number of intersecting, overlapping conceptual conjunctions—including color, religion, geography, and sexuality."[133] In an age of intensifying global traffic, it is thereby vital to investigate, as the following chapters do, the porous and mobile categories of sexuality and race interrelationally in a comparative context in order to denaturalize, unsettle, upset, and subvert hierarchies of human desire and human difference, both of which are categorized in relation to "the other" in order to create the natural order of things in the past (and in the present).

A historical exploration of the homoerotics of asymmetrical differences faces the difficulty of demarcating objectification from attraction, violence from pleasure, identification from disidentification, and coercion from desired hierarchical attachments. A queer analytics that scrutinizes sexuality and race together, as black feminism and the queer of color turn in queer studies have persuasively shown, can offer productive vectors for questions around sexuality and various asymmetrical differences, including those related to race, nationality, religion, age, class, or gender.[134] As Jennifer C. Nash aptly put it, "The persistence of race as a social, cultural, and economic project is fundamentally related to its hold on all of our erotic imaginations.... Race is an erotic project, not simply because it pleasures majoritarian subjects, but because it shapes minoritarian desires and pleasures as well, constituting how minoritarian subjects imagine their bodies, longings, and desires."[135] In the early modern context, Valerie Traub likewise probes the self/other relationality in sexual desire and acts: "Subject to both incitement and prohibition, sexuality is often a site of simultaneous allure and danger, inviting identifications with and disavowals of 'others' in complex and ambivalent ways. Sex can involve genuine appreciation, curiosity, and vulnerability, the acceptance of someone who appears different from the self. It can also involve individual and structural forms of coercion, exploitation, and domination, including projecting onto others one's own disavowed desires."[136] Traub builds on the "survivance strategies" first articulated by Gerald Vizenor that Bernadette Andrea centrally deploys in her examination of Muslim women in British literature ("the union of active survival and resistance to cultural dominance"), and her observations on sexuality call for a careful examination of varying dynamics in interracial relations.[137] As Traub writes, "All cross-race liaisons, within and without slavery, took place within a broad framework of asymmetrical power. While most were the result of sexual assault and exploitation, others were born of mutual desire, opportunism, accommodation, and/or creative 'survivance.'"[138]

Indeed, the boy in both English and Ottoman contexts often seems to be a passive subordinate party in same-sex male couplings due to his age, status, race, religious difference, or putative sexual role—be it as a ganymede, a minion, a servant, a favorite, a catamite, or an ingle. A focus on these boys with an awareness of the potential slipperiness of sexual roles and positionalities, however, unveils the boy's sometimes-active subjectivity in empowering himself for survivance in a male homosocial structure that normally places him at the bottom of the hierarchy. The literary examples I analyze reflect a glimpse not only of the historical realities that create a context for the burgeoning trope of the abducted boy but also of moments of creative subversions of normative hierarchies in interracial, intergenerational same-sex relations. The abducted boy in survivance sometimes finds alternate routes with his alluring beauty and desiring self. Some boys in the cultural texts I analyze are represented as active agents who orient, direct, participate, plot, seduce, or facilitate, defying the ahistorical perception of boys as universally sexless and innocent.[139] The abducted boy in representation, I suggest, had the potential to upset gender, sexual, and racial categories with his desirable body, youth, sexual activity, and religious, racial, and cultural difference. Although in real life many such boys remained enslaved throughout their lives, some others made a transition from servitude to a position in the ruling elite, from being solely an object of another's erotic gaze to the subject who converts the gazing adult, and, in some cases, from being the eroticized abducted boy to a poet who eroticized boys who were abducted.

Of course, cultural texts and literature both reflect and shape fantasies and histories and sometimes cover, legitimize, and aestheticize certain forms of violence as displaying some elements of pleasure. Genres such as the romance, the ghazal, and the epyllion might blur the line between coercion and consent in ways that can illuminate the historical complexities of these categories, which are different from our modern understanding.[140] Literary representations attribute a certain level of erotic subjectivity and power of resistance to boys, who are repeatedly positioned as not merely passive but also as active agents.[141] The early modern period, as Masten puts it, regularly returns to the question of "boy-desire," which is a question of not only the almost universal desire for boys but also "the desires of such young men *themselves* (toward a variety of objects)."[142] Exploring historically this literature that eroticizes boys while complicating the status of the boy merely as victim, the following chapters ask: Why did Marlowe not allow a coercive homosexual intercourse in the Mediterranean world of *Hero and Leander*, which emerges in stark contrast with travelogues that depict this space as a zone of exploitative boy-lovers (chapter 1)? What does the apparent sign language that abducted boys developed among themselves for arranging their erotic pursuits tell us about their sexual agency in developing same-sex sexual relations (chapter 1)? Why does the conqueror of Constantinople, Ottoman sultan Mehmed II, praise a beautiful Christian boy in his poetry, wherein the boy's beauty eventually engenders the conversion of the Muslim sultan (chapter 2)? How do beautiful boys in early modern cartographic representations actively shape, direct, and orient the viewer's perspective and body (chapter 2)? Why does Shakespeare deploy classical pederastic homoeroticism in Oberon's abduction of the Indian boy in Mediterranean Athens, an act that generates the happy ending of *A Midsummer Night's Dream* (chapter 3)? What are we to make of the stories about English boys who escaped their English party to become a part of Turkish households with boy-lovers (chapter 4)? How should we understand the boy who castrates himself in order to be in closer proximity to the sultan's body in the sultan's private chambers (chapter 5)? To what extent can sex and pleasure become forms of resistance for abducted boys (chapter 6)?

Disclosing the subjectivity and resistance that the abducted boys sometimes register makes explicit the performative and subversive elements of the racial, gender, and erotic categories produced by and within power relations. A recognition of such boys as both desiring and resistant to desire does not reflect exactly the experiences and actions of all historical boys, nor should it prevent us from recognizing historical real-life abuses. Nonetheless, these representations defy the simplistic and ahistorical picturing of adolescent boys as invariably lacking in sexual desire, power, or agency to fight and overcome oppression—assumptions that are mostly rooted in modern policing or pathologizing of nonconforming desires in terms of various modes of present egalitarianisms.[143] As mentioned above, premodern ideals and norms of sexual desire were different from ours; in pederastic relations, boys were often seen as seductive, corrupting, desiring agents rather than as corrupted innocent victims of assault.[144] Literary scenarios and imaginative possibilities often provide transformative imaginaries and alternatives that go against the historical context by offering discrepancies, gaps, ambiguities, and contradictions. Boys in each chapter will offer moments when the racially or religiously othered and hierarchically less powerful boy is not always a silent or powerless subject but one who uses various means and queer possibilities to survive, resist, or fulfill his desire in the hegemonic imperial structure.

Crossings with Boys

In addition to moving between English and Ottoman contexts and beyond single national-language paradigms, my contrapuntal readings in the chapters that follow inscribe a cross-genre pattern that addresses a wide array of texts: on the one hand, Ottoman poems, historical chronicles, prose works, festival accounts, and miniatures; on the other hand, English plays, poems, travelogues, chronicles, and maps and paintings produced in Western Europe. Often, generic conventions and tropes—be it the beloved boy in the ghazal tradition, Ovidian homoeroticism in the epyllion, or erotic Mediterranean encounters in the romance—make it possible for writers to express homoerotic scenarios. Yet as I will show, they are inseparable from historical conditions and geopolitics and contribute to discourses around homoeroticism, race, and empire. The wide range of genres and texts in this study thus aims to uncover discursive formations and cultural imaginings in which the figure of the beautiful abducted boy traverses literal geographic boundaries by means of his abduction as an object and sometimes as the subject of same-sex male desire. Identifying boy abductions as an important component of imperial imaginings in both cultures, my study unearths the homoerotic cultural landscape of the so-called West and East by evincing a shared visual and textual repertoire.

The three chapters in Part I, "Boys Encountered," analyze the abduction and conversion of beautiful boys in the sites of cross-cultural encounters. The early modern sexual and gender economy Ottoman and English domains shared surpasses a binary matrix of male versus female. Instead, it operates across a wider spectrum, one that includes the boy. The figure of the abducted beautiful boy in poetic, cartographic, and dramatic representations in Part I demonstrates not only the gendering but also the eroticization of spaces and imperial visions. Chapter 1 revisits Marlowe's invention of Leander's homoerotic abduction in the Hellespont in his retelling of the otherwise classical heteroerotic story in his much-celebrated poem *Hero and Leander*. Marlowe's poem belongs to the short-lived genre of epyllion, which has often been analyzed as a literary reflection of the humanist training English male poets underwent in their youth. This chapter, however, situates the poem and its Mediterranean setting in the geohistorical context of the sixteenth century and connects the Ganymede imagery Marlowe creates in this geographic space to beautiful Christian boys abducted by the Ottomans as *ganimet* (booty). I analyze the representation of Leander through the icon of Ganymede together with the Ottoman elite's cataloguing of beautiful servant boys, including Mustafa Ali's *Kava'idu'l-mecalis* (The rules of social gatherings), which racially hierarchizes boy slaves from various ethnic and religious backgrounds based on their youthful beauty, which functions to regulate racial and imperial hierarchies. By putting the servant boy as an object of desire in Ottoman accounts into dialogue with Leander, I highlight how the Mediterranean space makes possible Marlowe's imagining of exciting homoerotic alternatives in which the boy can also resist sexual coercion. This contrasts with contemporary travelers' sodomitical, anti-sex narratives in which boys are often permanently imprisoned in a coercive master/slave matrix in the Mediterranean.

Chapter 2 begins with the Ottoman poet Aşık Çelebi's imperial desire to save beautiful white boys from white Christian Europeans. This chapter merges the poetic and cartographic gaze on boys by zooming in on the cross-cultural encounter zones to show how those boys' bodies signify the spaces from which they were abducted. I bring into conversation the spatial representations of boys such as Aşık Çelebi's "Ode to the Danube" and the Ottoman poet Avni's (Mehmed II) verses on the town of Galata (the Christian neighborhood of Istanbul), in which the beautiful Christian boy embodies Western Christendom, with representations of Ganymede-like boys on the margins of Western European maps of the Danube River (the fluid border space of contact between the Ottomans and Europeans, especially the Habsburgs). This chapter proposes that early modern representations of territory conceptualized such cross-cultural spaces as embodied by the beautiful boy who evokes a competition for land between men that is loaded with cross-religious desire. In doing so, it also calls into question the traditional trope of the land as female in colonial discourse. Attentive to the various work that different genders do, this chapter argues that figurations of the boy as a gendered and eroticized embodiment of territory in relation to liminal borders points not only to imperial and military contestations between men but also to masculine tensions between homoerotic, cross-religious pleasure and sodomitical anxiety. Further questioning what the boy's body does and how his beauty functions in spatial imaginings, this chapter unveils the boy's potential for engendering religious conversion, probing simplistic dichotomies of subject/object and active/passive.

While English accounts were highly critical of the Ottoman practice of abducting European Christian boys, chapter 3 turns its focus exclusively to English abductions in the Mediterranean context, tracing the fate of boys the English abducted from foreign lands. The early modern English practice of abducting and converting boys extends the argument from the previous chapters to blur an English/Ottoman, West/East binary about coercive abductions and conversions. Often the boys the English abducted and converted from Africa, India, and the Americas were relegated to lifelong servitude and were vulnerable as domestic servants to their masters' sexual advances. In this hierarchical paradigm, I turn to Shakespeare's *A Midsummer Night's Dream* as a Mediterranean play to closely analyze the abductions of the Indian boy of exceptional beauty. Focusing on Oberon's abduction of the boy in the Mediterranean zone around Athens, I scrutinize the homoerotic dynamics of territorial domination created via the racialized boy. I further put the Indian boy into dialogue with black African boys of English portraiture in the ensuing decades, wherein the trope of white master/black servant emerges simultaneously with the rise of "other" boys in England who were abducted and transported from their native lands. The repertoire of exotic boys in visual imagery and in the streets of London shows that as England was establishing itself as an imperial state, abducted boys became a medium for colonial agents to display their imperial claims. Preceding these boys, the Indian boy of Shakespeare's imagining anticipates and queers the appearance of exotic boys in an established racial hierarchy.

Part II, "Boys Transformed," examines material transformations, especially bodily conversions of the abducted boy via circumcision and castration. Tracing white English boys who were circumcised and black African boys who were castrated upon their abduction in the Mediterranean economy of captivity and slavery, the two chapters in this part show how abducted boys were embodied fusions of racial and gender ideologies in producing subjects. Chapter 4 analyzes the traveler Thomas Sanders's account of two English boys who were captured and forcefully circumcised in the Mediterranean, which was imagined as a dangerously sodomitical space for English youths. Circumcision was a hotly debated and frequently referenced practice in English writing. Mapping circumcision discourses in a broad spectrum of texts including chronicles, travelogues, medical tracts, ethnographic treatises, and plays such as Robert Daborne's *A Christian Turned Turk* and Shakespeare's *Othello*, the chapter asks: If circumcision narratives reveal religious, economic, and sexual anxieties, to what extent do these anxieties intersect with trepidation about traveling boys who were abducted, enslaved, and converted in the Mediterranean? Ottoman bodies and their everyday practices were perceived as a great threat to male bodies in Europe, and Christian boys who were imagined as abducted, castrated, and sodomized by Turks evoked a nightmare that manifested itself particularly in circumcision narratives. In contrast, circumcision was celebrated in entirely positive terms in Ottoman accounts, as is demonstrated in Ottoman festivity books such as *Surname-i Humayun* (The book of the imperial festival). Such grand festivities, I show, functioned constitutively in the formation of European discourses not only about circumcision but also about Ottoman magnificence. Exploring circumcision as performing political as well as gender and sexual work, this chapter emphasizes that the religious conversion of boys upon their abduction necessitated conversions of their bodies, which became sites of cultural, religious, political, and erotic negotiations.

Chapter 5 transitions from circumcised boys to castrated boys in the Ottoman court and their travels to the English world. While previous chapters trace white European boys who were abducted and transformed by the Ottomans, this chapter turns to black youths in the Ottoman capital. With the Ottoman expansion into Africa in the second half of the sixteenth century, there emerged a rising number of once-boy-now-eunuch black slaves in Ottoman lands. The bodies of these black boys were refigured, reinscribed, resignified, and re-formed and were put in a more explicit racial hierarchy when the Ottomans began to strictly separate black and white eunuchs. Focusing on this racial separation, this chapter examines an emerging antiblack racial discourse in treatises produced by Ottoman elites. As a reaction to racist attacks, and in parallel to the strict separation of black eunuchs from white eunuchs at court, some black writers praised blackness in their writings. This chapter concludes by suggesting that the figurations of such racially marked boys, eunuchs, and men traveled throughout Europe via chronicles, travelogues, stories, and other narratives. They eventually appeared on the English stage in Shakespeare's Mediterranean plays *Anthony and Cleopatra* and *Twelfth Night* and in Ben Jonson's *Volpone*, among others.

These two parts of my argument are synchronic and contrapuntal, not a diachronic narrative of historical change. In Part III, "Boys in Modernity, East and West," however, I bring forward the temporal dimension of the literary history I have narrated so far by tracing the eroticized boy via a transhistorical exploration, gesturing toward a historical shift in both England and the Ottoman Empire. Chapter 6 reconsiders *A Midsummer Night's Dream* only to take a transhistorical turn to modernity with an eye on the Anglo-American staging history of the Indian boy in the historical context of (in)visible abducted boys that were made legible in previous chapters. While the Indian boy has mostly been rendered invisible since his first probable appearance on stage in 1692, he has at other times appeared on stage as a little boy, a girl, an adult man, an orientalized teen, an African American youth, and even a puppet. What story does the absent presence of the Indian boy on the Shakespearean stage narrate? What shifts in sexual and racial histories does the Indian boy's (in)visibility perform? How can an early modern text illuminate our modern-day sexual concerns? This chapter explores these questions through the 1991 Shakespeare Santa Cruz production of *A Midsummer Night's Dream* by putting into dialogue postcolonial, critical race, and queer analytics to exemplify a transhistorical intersectional lens. This approach demonstrates that the (in)visibility of the Indian boy on stage speaks of a sexual and racial history, of interracial and intergenerational desire, while marking erotic continuities and ruptures from the early modern period.

The book's concluding chapter moves from the early modern period to the nineteenth century to finish the project with a dialogue with contemporary queer explorations of the boy in our (post)modern global context. While in the early modern period, the boy is prominent in Ottoman and English cultural representations, the orientalizing modernity of the nineteenth century rendered perverse the expression of boy love in both cultures. Hence, we witness the fading of beautiful boys and boy-lovers in both contexts. Instead, in the context of a pederastic modernity, boy love began to be attributed to an imagined orient by the Western colonial ideology; the brown boy became an object to be saved by the white master from the oriental pederast. Predating this, the abducted boy of the early modern period offers a history wherein boys are violently made amorous and glamorous components of the grammar of empire.

PART I

Boys Encountered

I
———

Traveling Boys
in the Mediterranean

In the Hellespont, the beautiful boy of Christopher Marlowe's *Hero and Leander* (1598), "amorous Leander, beautiful and young," cries out to his captor: "You are deceav'd, I am no woman, I," not understanding that he has been abducted precisely because he is a boy (51, 676).[1] When Leander swims naked to see his beloved Hero on the western side of the Hellespont, his alluring body charms "kingly" Neptune, who mistakes him for Jove's beautiful cupbearer Ganymede and takes him away (650). Leander's abduction as Ganymede, which Marlowe inserts in his retelling of the story by the Greek poet Musaeus, seems to follow the classical trope of the abducted boy that appears frequently in early modern literature.[2] Marlowe's deployment of the trope as Leander swims across the Hellespont, however, calls for an exploration of the geopolitical significations of such erotic scenarios and landscapes. Why does the poem include a homoerotic abduction plot in an otherwise heteronormative classical love story? How does the Hellespont, a geographical locale of the greater Mediterranean notorious for piracy throughout the early modern period, contribute to the literary rendering of abductions of boys? And to what extent does the beautiful traveling boy embody the tensions between literary eroticism and the history of abductions, conversions, and enslavements?

This chapter contextualizes Leander's kidnapping in the historical framework of the transcultural economy of abductions in the sixteenth-century Ottoman Mediterranean. I argue that the boy in abduction narratives is not just a classical prototype but is also a reflection of the boys who were actually abducted within imperial hierarchies in the early modern Mediterranean. Marlowe, I suggest, uses the classical figure of Ganymede to imprint on Leander's body an erotic-cultural history of these abducted boys. This history, I will show, is cross-cultural and interrelational, which becomes evident in accounts of England's geohistorical engagements with Mediterranean traffic. My pursuit of Leander in the Ottoman context thereby accentuates a connected history of homoerotic desire and imperial violence in English and Ottoman cultures that have been traditionally seen as incomparable. Accordingly, in what follows, I first attend to Marlowe's Hellespont for, as Anjali Arondekar reminds us, "the languages of the geopolitical matter to the articulation and meaning-making structures of sexuality."[3] Hence, the Hellespont as a generative site of homoerotic abductions, both in Marlowe's poem and in contemporary discourses, necessitates that we account for the Ottoman Mediterranean in exploring Leander's travel and abduction in this particular space. I subsequently swim to the other side of the Hellespont, to the Ottoman world, where abducted European boys appear as *ganimets*/Ganymedes and travel discursively beyond borders via European accounts. These travels reveal that the literary eroticization of abducted boys is informed by the Ottoman history of their enslavement situated in an eroto-imperial matrix. In this context, I finally return to *Hero and Leander* to trace the Ganymede effect in Leander's abduction as scripted by (and scripting) the cross-cultural Mediterranean traffic in boys.

The Hellespont and Boys

The Hellespont, the poem's first noun, is a gateway for the reader's entry to the poem and its world and to early modern Mediterranean relations: "On *Hellespont* guiltie of True-loves blood, / In view and opposit two citties stood, / Seaborderers, disjoin'd by *Neptune* might: / The one *Abydos*, the other *Sestos* hight" (1–4). The Hellespont is the very center of the disorderly world of erotics and crossings, "guilty of true love's blood." It establishes oppositions of places and persons—Abydos and Sestos, East and West, and Hero and Leander. It is a passage to desire, a passage in which desire is heightened. In Judith Haber's words, the poem "begins, preposterously, with its foregone conclusion."[4] Such a structural inversion in the first line reveals the interconnectedness of ekphrasis and desire, "enabling the poem to radically question the sexual and textual order upon which conventional sense depends."[5]

Indeed, a blend of the textual and the sexual is a feature of the English epyllion of the 1590s, the genre to which Marlowe's poem belongs. Scholars have long explored the epyllion as a literary reflection of local sites and personal memories: of the poet's humanist training at school and his literary display of rhetorical techniques, of *rites de passage* in the humanist grammar school, or of youthful sexual metamorphoses.[6] William P. Weaver, for instance, reads the epyllion as the representation of the *rites de passage* schema in the context of the humanist grammar school in his exploration of the formation of youths' subjectivity "locally" (that is, in England) and suggests that the Hellespont in the poem "symbolizes the threshold between the study of poetic narrative (grammar) and historical narrative (rhetoric)." The grammar school was "an in-between place for boys who had been separated from their homes and were destined to serve the Tudor monarchy as part of an elite corps of state administrators."[7] Miriam Jacobson, in contrast, has more recently reoriented the epyllion in "a new poetic economy" and locates *Hero and Leander* in a global mercantile context in which the use of foreign words and the imagery of imported goods "work alongside classical mythology and poetics ... placing the literary authority of the ancient Greco-Roman world on the same plane as late sixteenth-century global trade."[8] Yet for Jacobson, the emerging imagery of imported commodities such as pearls are mere verbal evocations in this new global poetics; they are pearls of rhetoric with little relation to the actual realities. She writes, "The space of the Hellespont is not populated by angry Turkish janissaries, renegados, or Barbary corsairs."[9] In addition to goods and words, however, boys circulated in this space from one man to another and from one side of the Hellespont to the other. While Jacobson's focus is on trade, my analysis pursues the boys. To repurpose Weaver's assertion about the Hellespont, what happens when we read the Hellespont as an in-between place for boys who had been separated from their homes and were destined to serve not the Tudor but the Ottoman monarchs as members of elite corps? When abduction plots such as Leander's are read with a focus on geospatial significations and practices, what do spatially oriented evocations of Eastern goods and imageries convey?

The Hellespont was the site of the Trojan War; it separated the Greeks from the Trojans. It was also where Ganymede's abduction took place. Significantly, for Marlowe, it is the site where the mythic Ganymede comes to life as Leander at a time when actual boys were abducted daily in the larger Mediterranean space. This location is associated not just with these mythical stories but also with the Ottoman Turks, as is evident in early modern travelogues such as George Sandys's *A Relation of a Journey* and Turk plays such as John Mason's *The Turke*, which associates Mulleasses the Turk with Leander when Timoclea says, "May I court Leander swimming in my arms, / And without pleasing motions mocke the seas / That rose and fell to wanton with his thighs: / Now ther's no Hellespont betwixt our loves."[10] In such mythological, ethnographic, and literary representations, the Hellespont is both a geographical place and an imaginary space. The Ganymede imagery woven into the abduction plot in this space thus reveals the absent presence of abducted boys and, I shall show, of janissaries, or "renegados" in the poem's world.

The emergence of the Elizabethan epyllion coincided with England's nascent investments in the global trade with the Ottomans in the Mediterranean, which the Turkey Company initiated in 1581, followed by the Levant Company in 1592. Mercantile and diplomatic Anglo-Ottoman interactions generated rich cultural cross-pollinations and a rich archive of the records of cross-cultural encounters. One prominent subject of these accounts is the circulation of bodies through travels, abductions, enslavements, captivities, and conversions that occurred in the Mediterranean.[11] As Alison Games notes, "The extent of Mediterranean captivity was considerable, equaling the Atlantic slave trade until the middle of the seventeenth century"; over one million Christians were captured along the Barbary Coast.[12] According to a recent estimation, at least three million people were captured and enslaved in the larger Mediterranean in the period 1450 to 1850.[13] England's entrance to this space as a trading partner made the English vulnerable to captivity, and as many as 12,000 English subjects were captured from the sixteenth century through the mid-seventeenth century.[14] Marlowe's Hellespont is thus not merely a mythic space but also a geographical zone of mutability in status and personages.

Before he plotted Leander's abduction, Marlowe had already contributed to producing this multicultural Mediterranean space and history on stage in his *Tamburlaine* plays, which led his contemporaries to characterize his language as outlandish and even "Turkish."[15] Specifically, he recast abducted Christian boys in this space. Bajazeth of *Tamburlaine I* describes his army: "As many circumcised Turks we have, / And warlike bands of Christians renied" (3.1.8–9). Christians "renied" refers to renegades or the converted janissaries (New Corps), whom Bajazeth later calls "janizaries of my guard" who "attend upon the person of your lord" (3.3.61–62). The janissaries were the boys who had been forcibly taken by the Ottomans to form an elite class of courtiers and soldiers under the *devşirme* (collecting) practice, which I further detail below. This institutionalized form of abduction and conversion was well known in Marlowe's England. Marlowe projects contemporaneous accounts about these boys onto the play's early fifteenth-century Ottoman army to render it an army of converts. Like Tamburlaine, these boys belong to Marlowe's late sixteenth-century world in which the Ottoman space of trade, diplomacy, travel, and war was imbued with abductions and conversions.

In this period, travelogues and chronicles about the Ottomans repeatedly linked Ottoman abductions of European boys with religious and sexual concerns about conversion, or "turning Turk."[16] *The Estate of Christians, living under the subjection of the Turke* (1595), for example, described this practice: "All the male children of Christians are written up at the day of their birth, and coming to ten or twelve yeres of their age, presented to the Turkes officers, who take all such as they find well made, and like to prove fit men in service in warre, from their parents, and convey them to the Turkes . . . to become Turkes, and enemies to God, and their own fathers and mothers, and kinsfolke, standing the Turke in more sted than his own natural people."[17] Abducted boys were transformed into new beings and became totally oblivious of the people of their native land. These "well made" boys became Turk and hence "enemies of God." This anonymous account is very much a retelling of previous accounts produced in Europe. As early as 1395, a sermon by the Metropolitan of Thessaloniki lamented that these boys "become a vessel of barbaric garb, speech, impiety and other contaminations."[18] What were those unspeakable "contaminations"?

Conversion to Islam, or "turning Turk," was often signified as sexual transgression associated with Ottoman decadence and perversion. Accordingly, concerns about abductions of Christian boys were linked with sexuality in English narratives that blended abduction practices with sodomy. John Rawlins, for example, mentioned the captivity of "a hundred handsome youths compelled to turn Turks, or made subject to more vile prostitution, and all English."[19] John Sanderson reported that a traveler was afraid that his twenty-one-year-old "beardlesse" son would be captured and sodomized by Turks during their travels into "Sodomiticall places." J. M. Gramaye reported that the Christian children captured by Mediterranean pirates were sent as presents to "Turke or his Bassas [to satisfy their] Sodomitical lusts for Boyes," and Thomas Coryat stated, "The Turkes are exceedingly given to Sodomie, and therefore divers keep prettie boyes to abuse them by preposterous venerie."[20] These accounts described the Ottomans as sodomites by means of their treatment of boys (who either were abducted or would be abducted) and described Ottoman lands as dangerous places for traveling boys.

Such sodomitical depictions have long been read as imaginary, stereotypical othering devices that shaped literary narratives that projected sexual transgressions onto the Mediterranean.[21] Importantly, when brought into proximity to the Ottomans' own discourses and cultural representations, such accounts also seem to have perceived and represented homoerotic relations and practices in Ottoman society as sodomitical. In early modern Ottoman society, male homoeroticism, mostly embodied in the beautiful boy, was prevalent in the poetic imagination, which shaped articulations of homoerotic relations in public, especially among the elite. As mapped out in the introduction, domestic and public relations and political power in the empire were structured around highly institutionalized, orderly homosocial male bonds, especially between adult men and boys. These included service, schooling, patronage, apprenticeship, friendship, and love.[22] In their anti-sex depictions of Ottoman society, English travelers and writers sometimes revealed suppressed forms of fascination with and desire for this sexual culture.

Jonathan Goldberg asserts that "to read for sodomy—for sodometries—is to read relationally," a process that reveals "relational structures precariously available to prevailing discourses."[23] Accordingly, in analyzing these accounts, a relational consideration of the Ottomans through their own voices, looking from the other side of the relations, uncovers intertwined cross-cultural mechanisms and routes in the production of sexual discourses in global contacts. It is thus essential to visit the Ottoman context, as I do in the next section, because it uncovers in global poetics the homoerotics of abductions that challenge the sodomitical matrix in England, in which homoerotic relations with boys were under scrutiny yet were possible. The Ottoman context also reveals Marlowe's playful erasure of the sodomitical paradigm in favor of homoerotic pleasure through the abduction of the beautiful boy in the Ottoman Mediterranean world of *Hero and Leander*.

The Imperial Homoerotics of Abductions

Ottoman accounts of abducted boys present the intricate interrelations between the representational and historical aspects of abductions. My focus will be the historical and literary abducted *devşirme* boys in the Ottoman context in order to trace the distinct histories they narrate while crossing boundaries between nations as captives and as beloveds. Developed in the fifteenth century, *devşirme* (collecting) was an institutionalized form of conscripting boys from conquered territories to serve the ruler of the empire. While the Ottomans—like the Abbasids, the Seljuks, the Byzantines, the Mamluks, and Italian city-states—used other forms of enslavement and recruitment to expand their military and governmental power, *devşirme* was a uniquely early modern Ottoman practice of recruiting, converting, and refashioning specifically Christian boys from the empire's territories in Southeast Europe to serve the royal household. According to one of the earliest Ottoman histories, Aşıkpaşazade's fifteenth-century chronicle *Manakıb u Tevarih-i Âl-i Osman* (The virtues and history of the house of Osman), the practice originated in the implementation of the divine license that permitted the Muslim sovereign to claim one-fifth of all war spoils. Initially, the vizier Çandarlı Halil, who came up with the idea, collected one-fifth of enslaved boys and presented them to Sultan Murad II, saying: "Let's give these boys to Turkish households so that they can learn Turkish; after they learn the Turkish language, we can bring them up as janissaries."[24] Separated from their kin and assimilated into the Ottoman imperial culture, these slaves would then become highly prized agents of empire; their loyalty would be not to their kin but to their sovereign alone.

Devşirme thus emerged as a new form of enslavement and assimilation in the structural, biopolitical organization of the empire through an adoption of older enslavement models and a rearrangement and exploitation of the Islamic *pençik* (one-fifth law). The *pençik* had allowed the Ottomans to capture people (male and female) of *harbi* status (non-Muslims living outside the empire or in the domain of war, called *daru'l harp*) since the formative years of the empire. However, *devşirme* evolved to incorporate the internal seizure of Christian boys among the imperial population, who should have been protected as subjects according to Islamic laws.[25] Those taken under *pençik* law were not subject to the same education and opportunities offered to *devşirme* boys and they did not have to convert or assimilate into the Muslim-Ottoman culture; they often maintained their native cultures and religions. In contrast, *devşirme* boys, most of whom were taken from Christian Balkan populations, including the Greeks, Hungarians, Bosnians, and Albanians, underwent a process of conversion, assimilation, education, training, and service. Under this unique practice, *devşirme* boys were forcibly taken from their families and were brought to the imperial capital and made the permanent slaves (*kul*) of the sultan.[26] As a class of European servants of the empire, the ruling elite, and the janissaries, *devşirme* boys formed an influential population ranging in size between 7,800 and 12,800 in the sixteenth century.[27]

The selection process for boys who would become part of such a crucial imperial unit was strictly regulated. Early modern accounts of these boys, especially such guidebooks for recruitment as *Kavanin-i Yeniçeriyan* (The janissary laws), clearly show that the body and beauty of *devşirme* boys were crucial factors in their abduction and enslavement. Christian boys who were chosen were mostly aged fourteen to eighteen.[28] They had to be good looking, uncircumcised, healthy, clever, and unmarried; boys who were deemed too tall or too short or those who had a squint would not be taken.[29] The collected boys were marked and dressed in a red robe and a hat (*kızıl aba ve külah*) in order to prevent kidnapping and escape during recruitment, as is evident in an anonymous miniature from Arifi's *Süleymanname* (fig. 1.1).

Following their arrival in Istanbul, these boys were stripped and screened for any bodily defects by the chief of the janissaries. Finally, they were circumcised, converted, and given a new Islamic name. Refashioned with a new identity, these boys were then assigned to particular spaces for certain roles based on their bodily perfection and merits. Those considered to be the more talented and handsome were sent to various palaces in Istanbul, while the rest remained in the army as *acemi oğlans* (novice boys) to do domestic, public, and military work. Those selected as palace boys received training in academic, administrative, and courtly matters with an emphasis on languages, literature, theology, and law. Every three to seven years, another selection would take place and the most talented among the palace boys would then be transferred to the imperial palace as pages for further courtly training in the highly coded palace culture and education system at Enderun (the Imperial Palace School), while the remaining few joined the elite army as *kapıkulu* (slaves of the Porte). According to a seventeenth-century source, "the *devşirme* boys would even be viewed by the sultan himself in the throne-room [*arz odası*] and those who looked 'good' [*eyü*] and intelligent would be chosen as pages."[30] Some palace boys advanced as high as becoming *vezir-i azam* (grand vizier), second only to the sultan in power.[31]

With their good looks and merits, these boys were often celebrated in homoerotic terms.[32] Aşıkpaşazade's history of *devşirme* concludes with two celebratory couplets, the last of which reads: "Know that they are the Sultan's rightful boy-properties, / No other soldiers can hereabouts be found, but the janissaries."[33] The editors of the modern Turkish edition of Aşıkpaşazade's *History*, Kemal Yavuz and Yekta Saraç, modernized the first line ("the Sultan's rightful boy-properties") as "the Sultan's *ganimet*": "They are taken out of *ganimet* for the Sultan."[34] Deriving from the Arabic word "*ghanīma*" (غَنِيمَة), "*ganimet*" refers to any sort of property, land, people, or goods gained from non-Muslim enemies.[35] The original term Aşıkpaşazade used is "*mal*," which refers to property, goods, and possessions. "*Ganimet*" aptly encompasses these significations, particularly considering that Aşıkpaşazade used "*mal*" and "*ganimet*" together and interchangeably throughout his account as "*mal u ganimet*."[36] Aşıkpaşazade's specification

FIGURE 1.1. Arifi, "Devşirme boys." In Arifi, *Süleymanname*, 1558. Walter Denny Collection, Fisher Fine Arts Library, University of Pennsylvania.

that these *ganimet*s were boy properties (*mal oglidur*) highlights the status and youthful appearance of boys as operative in their abductions.

The signification of "*ganimet*" as "spoils of war, booty" evokes an affinity with the iconic Ganymede, who was forcibly taken by Jove as booty of Troy. To be clear, despite closeness in spelling and meaning, there is no empirical evidence that I know of on the etymological connection between "*ganimet*" in Arabic and "Ganymede" in Greek. Yet, as I discuss later, there may have developed a closeness or overlap of words as a result of a mishearing by Europeans or Europeans' perception of a cognate. Their abduction as booty and the homoeroticism embedded in their abduction connects *ganimet* boys and Ganymede. Furthermore, early modern writers used "Ganymede" to refer to servant boys, as I discussed in the introduction, especially to abducted *ganimet* boys in the Ottoman court, which I discuss below. Considering such resemblances and conflations, I conceptually link *ganimet* and Ganymede in my contrapuntal exploration of the abducted boy.

Like the mythic boy Ganymede, abducted *ganimet* boys were ubiquitously represented in homoerotic figurations as beloveds, beautiful servants, or cupbearers. Arifi's ordering of the miniature of the *devşirme* boys in *Süleymanname*, one of the most important courtly accounts of the reign of Suleyman I (1520–66), for instance, illustrates the significance of their status while his poetic language eroticizes them as beloveds. The miniature, one of the sixty-five plates in *Süleymanname*, is the first plate after the scene of Suleyman's accession to the throne, showing their prominent position in the structure and rule of the empire. The lines in Persian surrounding the miniature celebrates the practice of *devşirme* and *devşirme* boys. The poem begins, "Those who have two beloved sons are saved from being needed by one of them," justifying the practice of abduction as helpful for parents.[37] The poem then describes how conscription is a result of a royal order that sends two officials to every European corner of the empire. As Arifi's line implies, whether due to the success stories of these boys or the poverty of rural households, some families requested the conscription of their sons. Yet the miniature shows how a janissary tries to console the people's grief as their boys are taken away in red clothes. In fact, there was great anxiety and resentment in these Christian lands of the empire, as is evident in sources such as a song from Epirus: "Be damned, Emperor, thrice be damned / For the evil you have done and the evil you do. / You catch and shackle the old and the archpriests, / In order to take the children as janissaries. / Their parents weep, their sisters and brothers, too / And I cry until it pains me; / As long as I live I shall cry, / For last year it was my son and this year my brother."[38] Historically, to prevent their sons from being recruited, some families hid their boys or had them married at an early age (married boys could not be taken), bribed the collectors, or had crosses tattooed on their foreheads. It was not rare for populations to leave their villages to protect their sons or to rebel against this practice.[39] Although the miniature illustrates the distress of the parents, the lines below it describe these boys in a celebratory tone: "Red roses, red dresses, more than green blossoms / Dresses in rose colors are layered like roses."[40] Arifi links the red color of their institutional garments with red roses, which metaphorically signify love in the Ottoman literary tradition (the rose and the nightingale stand for the beloved and the lover who sings his sufferings).[41] Each piece of the dress is a rose petal, and together the boys compose a rose garden. Singing his song to the rose like a nightingale, Arifi portrays these boys as the rose-like beloveds of the empire.

Other courtly miniatures portray the abducted boy as the cupbearer to the court. The miniatures of Selim II with his companions, for example, depict Selim with a handkerchief and a wine cup (a sign of kingship) in his hands and a *devşirme* boy as his youthful attendant behind him (fig. 1.2). Included in the next plate are poets, entertainers, and musicians with two young cupbearers in the middle (fig. 1.3). The abducted boy in such images follows the prevalent trope of the immortal youth as cupbearer in Islamicate literary and visual conventions, and in Ottoman chronicles, poets are often illustrated with their wine-serving boys (figs. 1.4–1.8).[42] The image of the youth as cupbearer for a wine party (which was usually located in a garden) recurs not only in Ottoman but also in Arabic, Persian, and Urdu traditions; and the imagery of the Islamic paradise itself is often a constitutive element of such representations.[43] The Islamic paradise, Jannah (which, like paradise, also means garden in a literal translation), is described in the Qur'an as a garden where rivers of wine flow and people, who are always happy and young, have luxurious clothes and are surrounded with gold, silver, and precious stones and eternally young boys serve cups of pure wine.[44] Literary images of gardens that were reminiscent of the heavenly garden were materialized through Ottoman gardens. As Gülru Necipoğlu notes, gardens became a constitutive component of Ottoman palaces and the imperial capital, marking these spaces as a paradise on earth hosting the absolute imperial power.[45] A garden becomes a paradise only when it is filled with beautiful boys. The fifteenth-century poet and courtier Ahmed Pasha, a favorite of Mehmed II, wrote a poem to the Topkapı Palace, for example, that compared the palace garden to paradise with "celestial" boys: "No House within the skies may be auspicious as thy roof / Nor any throne in Paradise high as the floor of thee ... / Yon Eden-bower fulfilled of houris and celestial youths / Meseems the most High Ka'ba 'tis, athrong with angelry."[46] The servant boys in such representations make the imperial palace a paradise for the sultan and his courtiers.

FIGURE 1.2. *Portrait of Sultan Selim II*, circa 1570. The Aga Khan Museum.

FIGURE 1.3. *Members of Court of Sultan Selim II*, Nigari, circa 1570. Los Angeles County Museum of Art.

FIGURE 1.4. *A Beautiful Boy with Wine cup*, artist unknown, seventeenth century. Topkapı Palace Museum, EH2836, *Album*, fol. 85a.

In the Ottoman literary imagination, these boys—whether as statesmen, soldiers, poets, or servants—stand out as beloved beauties. Specifically, the poetic tradition, especially ghazal, provides writers with the template of the beautiful servant boy for depicting the boy in homoerotic terms. In one poem, Ahmed Pasha grieved for one of the imperial pages who had been imprisoned by the sultan:[47] "Y-brent be earth! You Taper sweet and bland / A-weeping lieth,

FIGURE 1.5. *The Poet Figani with a Beautiful Cup-Bearer Boy in a Garden*, 1568. In Aşık Çelebi, *Meşa'irü'ş-Şu'ara*. Millet Yazma Eser Kütüphanesi.

bound with iron band / Would he but sell his Shiraz-comfit lip, / 'T would fetch Cairo, Bokhara, Samarcand."⁴⁸ Just as Ahmed Pasha made a connection between imperial realms through the boy's body, Hayali's poem for a beautiful cupbearer also evoked imperial language: "Passion for that magian boy / in Hayali's bosom lies / As dwells 'neath heaven's canopy / the monarch of the skies."⁴⁹ In a similar vein, the poet Yahya eroticized one janissary boy in his sixteenth-century *şehrengiz* (beauties of the city): "The janissary Safer too is one / His brow the moon, his face the world's sun / If golden headdress be this moon's attire / Its sun-like glow would set the earth afire / Wherefore is that distinguished eyebrow double? / Two nights to one moon's head is trouble."⁵⁰

FIGURE 1.6. *Poet Abdi with a Servant Boy*, 1568. In Aşık Çelebi, *Meşa'irü'ş-Şu'ara*. Millet Yazma Eser Kütüphanesi.

(It is worth noting that Hayali and Yahya replicated their own experiences; both poets were once a part of such an eroticized hierarchy as boys. Hayali was seduced and parted from his family by a dervish group and brought to Istanbul and Yahya was an abducted boy who became a janissary. Strikingly, they do not present the erotic component of abductions as traumatic.[51]) Further, Vasfi, a poet and a judge, explicitly declared his love for a janissary boy named Memi: "Don't praise the sun or moon to me saying they are loved / No beauties of this world do I love but Memi Shah."[52] These poetic representations

FIGURE 1.7. *Ulvi-i Salis with a European Boy*, 1568. In Aşık Çelebi, *Meşa'iru'ş-Şu'ara*. Millet Yazma Eser Kütüphanesi.

FIGURE 1.8. *Poet Hayali with His Servant Boy*, 1568. In Aşık Çelebi, *Meşa'iru'ş-Şu'ara*. Millet Yazma Eser Kütüphanesi.

adopted the literary trope of the beloved boy to express the poets' deep affection for recognizable servant boys.

Such literary and visual eroticization of serving *ganimet* boys also appears in nonfiction and in historical accounts. In them, abducted boys are depicted as the servants of the empire, reflecting the hierarchical superiority of their masters in the eroticized imperial matrix—a mastery over the subjugated boys who are destined to carry their master's cup. The literary boy comes to life as the servant boy of a distinct eroticized class in such accounts, in which class subordination elicits erotic desire and such hierarchically structured desire for boys has a racializing effect. For example, the famous courtier and historian Mustafa

Ali of Gallipoli's *Kava'idu'l-mecalis* (The rules of social gatherings; 1587) strikingly reveals the imperial erotics of religious and racial difference through the hierarchical ordering of these boys.[53]

Like Arifi, Mustafa Ali prioritized these boys in his depiction of imperial culture by devoting the first chapters of his book to them, beginning with a critique of the admission of "untrainable beauties" to the palace: "These types should not be accepted into palace service: spoiled, brazen youths; converts who run about in the service of lower types of people; those with waists as thin as hair, whose hidden treasure has fallen into the clutches of vipers and snakes, I mean to say, the infamous persons of the world who associate with the rogues and the rabble among the city boys and perhaps even frequent taverns to 'sell their wares.' One should prefer to keep one's distance from them rather than mingling with them.... A person of ill repute, head lowered in shame, looking like a drunkard, enters a palace staffed with many servants, and infects and corrupts the world of the bodies of the servant boys, who are under the spell of carnal desires" (31–32).[54] Mustafa Ali contrasted the sultan's servants, his boy slaves, with city boys, a group that included uneducated, adventurous youths (*levend*) and lower types (*evbaş*). He contended that palace boys were carefully selected with meticulous attention to physiognomy that required close inspection of their bodies but that the selection criteria were no longer morally upright. Indeed, in the late sixteenth century, the structure of *devşirme* and the janissary army began to change as the Ottoman expansion into Europe slowed down. The Muslim population began to be conscripted and janissaries were given the right to marry and to participate in trade. These changes would soon bring an end to the practice of conscripting only Christian European boys.[55] Mustafa Ali thus warned palace officials not to recruit certain boys who might ruin the harmony of "that paradise-like-place in which servants gather" (30).[56]

After sexualizing boys "whose hidden treasure has fallen into the clutches of vipers and snakes," Mustafa Ali protested that degenerate non-European boys were damaging the *devşirme* system; their inappropriate "mingling" with "a person of ill repute" "infects and corrupts" their bodies "under the spell of carnal desires." He attributed sexual agency to these boys, who sought sexual encounters with men. As he mentioned a common practice among the boys in the Palace Infirmary (*Hastalar Sarayı*) of the Imperial Palace, he wrote, "Whenever one of the Inner Palace boys feels himself burning with a kind of fever, he makes a pact with another servant who is feeling the same. The two of them ask the aga [supervising officer] for leave. If the servants are afflicted with an itch, they go to ask for an ointment; or the anxious patient who is in need of a purgative sets out to procure one" (36). Mustafa Ali implied one boy's burning desire and search for sex with another boy via the metaphors of "fever" and "itch," which evoke a phallic syringe (*hokna*) that was used to administer an enema to purge and help the boy. The feverish one and the one who sought treatment for his anal itch would hire a carriage in which they would satisfy their sexual desires (37). Such "corruptions," for the writer who would further his anal metaphors for the scandal of inappropriate relations, marked these boys as "the excrement of the palace" (35). While boys in such types of unions wasted and ruined their treasures, inappropriate boys introduced into "the ranks of purchased slaves" were "shameless catamites" (*hizek-ü bî'ar*) (208). These "catamites," or boys who sexually served other boys and men, were "destroying a rose garden by burying it under sticks and straw, or muddying a clear stream with rocks tossed into it by chuls" (207). Mustafa Ali evoked the rose imagery that Arifi used to celebrate *devşirme* boys. For him, neither dangerous liaisons nor boys who transformed their rosy treasures into excrement were uncommon; the palace was now infested with lustful boys who were sexual objects for men by "sell[ing] their wares" and pursuing a life of pleasure in taverns—be it in real life or in his fantasy (32).[57]

Mustafa Ali's sexual frameworks for describing these boys makes visible the homosocial structure they belonged to. As palace boys or as janissaries, these boys grew up together as abducted cohorts in a bond of fraternity. As Gülay Yılmaz notes regarding the janissaries, "sharing similar experiences in the early phase of their lives in Ottoman society, the boys developed special attachments to each other. This attachment was referred to as *ocakdaş* or *hocadaş*—being in the same regiment or trained under the same tutor. Every regiment had its own symbol, etched as a tattoo on every janissary's body."[58] This attachment did not always exclude erotic bonds; as Walter Andrews and Mehmet Kalpaklı assert, the army was a place "where young men developed romantic and sexual relations with each other."[59] The janissaries, all of whom were male and unmarried, were eroticized in the popular imagination (as we have seen in poems by Ahmed Pasha, Yahya, and Hayali), particularly because of their intimacy with one another and their proximity to the sultan as his slaves, servants, and guards. Mustafa Ali also noted such sexual activities in his suggestion for preventing the janissaries from debauchery: "If only the Janissary Corps were placed in special barracks and kept under the division commanders until they are old enough to grow beards.... They should not have the means to ruin their reputations and should not set out each night to rendezvous for whore-mongering" (34). In the early modern period, facial hair was a sign of adulthood and a mark of the impenetrable body; it determined sexual positionality and putatively released the boy from his status as a penetrable, receptive object of sex. Mustafa

Ali informs us elsewhere that some servants were dismissed from their secure positions as "beardless servant lads" because they had sprouted beards, thus losing their attractiveness (308).[60] Servants without beards were vulnerable to the sexual advances of other men, who "fondle and grope these boys, or subject them to ravishment." Some "fall prey to immoral men, and are used by them as a female animal, lose their status and their honor" (33). In his excursus on sexually active, beardless servant boys, Mustafa Ali thus portrayed them as sexual objects and sometimes as sexually active subjects who wandered about for the purpose of "whore-mongering."

Mustafa Ali's categorization of abducted boys in the class of "*sâde-rûyân*" or "*emred*" (beardless youths or servants) continued with ethnic and racial classifications and hierarchization in various chapters. Discarding "bastard" boys of Arabia and the illegitimate sons of Anatolian Turks as sexual objects who were "short of attractiveness and comeliness" (59), Mustafa Ali marked European boys as ideal servants in the empire: "The people of Rumelia, and the nations of various natural qualities along the shores of the Danube, are pure at heart and clean of disposition. In particular their beardless boys embody the perfection of courtesy, along with their beauty and attractiveness, for some twenty years; the appearance of the cheek down and fuzz when their beard begins to grow does not muddy the limpid water of their elegance and delicacy" (220). Rumelia refers to the Roman lands, the European territories taken by the Ottomans. The Danube was a natural boundary between the Ottoman lands in Europe and Hungary before 1526. And the bordering states were exposed to Ottoman raids that resulted in a flow of slaves, prisoners, and captives until central Hungary became an Ottoman province in 1541, after which Hungarian boys began to be taken as *devşirme*.[61] In praising Rumelian boys, Mustafa Ali evoked this history of Ottoman traffic in boys around the shores of the Danube, boys who were now elite Rumi administrators, soldiers, and intellectuals of the empire. In his erotic adoration, their youth and their attractive beardless faces made them legitimate objects of male desire.

Mustafa Ali's ethnographic epistemology and classification idealized whiteness in relation to location and ethnicity. He praised Christian boys for their cypress-like bodies and fair (read white) faces and celebrated the janissaries—those from Croatia in particular—who were so perfect in their beauty that they competed with Joseph, the paragon of male beauty in the Islamic tradition (61).[62] Among them, "the big and fierce-looking boys of Bosnia-Herzegovina" were gentle and "obedient"; their beauty lasted longer because they did not have facial hair even when they reach the age of thirty (59). (Again, the lack of facial hair in relation to penetrability is celebrated.) Albanian boys were impertinent and contentious but good lovers; Georgian, Russian, and Gurelian boys were "the excrement of the other harlots," most impure among those available for erotic pleasure (61). While "it is utterly impossible ... for a beardless page of Russian origin not to be a catamite," Slav boys were "disgraceful"; and Wallachian, Transylvanian, and Moldovian boys were beautiful and pleasing but "wicked" (217). The "nimbleness and quickness" of Hungarians should also be noted alongside the "cleanliness" of Slavic boys (218).

While such references to various ethnicities signal widespread abductions from the European territories of the empire and beyond, evocations of non-European boys as servants (gentle and feminine "virgin" boys of Abyssinia [Ethiopians], "degenerate" "black-faced Africans," and "impure" Kurds) evince the messiness of the traffic in boys and the emerging form of recruitment of Muslims and non-Europeans that the author complained about earlier (217–18). In this messiness, proximity to whiteness determined Mustafa Ali's hierarchization of the diverse spectrum of boys—Bosnians, Russians, Slavs, Hungarians, Albanians, Bulgarians, Georgians, Transylvanians, Africans, Arabs, Indians, Turks, Kurds, and Persians—based on their body, their ethnic lineage, their skin color, and their erotic disposition. In a racialization of bodies within dichotomies of white/superior versus black/inferior, Frank (European Christian) boys were at the center and all other boys were marginalized, as Mustafa Ali made most explicit in his concluding catalogue in verse: "Most [servants] are pure garbage; ... / And remember the Hungarian and Frank. / Take care to stay clear of others; / Do not incline toward wicked and malicious people" (219). European Christians were the ones who should be desired and possessed in the empire.[63]

Mustafa Ali's spatial-racial-erotic classification of boys reveals not only a multiethnic, homoerotic sexual culture but also a racializing imperial gaze. The sexual and the racial cooperated and were co-produced in the charting and marking of these boys as the objects of erotic desire. In fact, in his *Künh ül-ahbar* (The essence of history), his hierarchization of these boys instantiated his racial project of using European boys as breeding agents to whiten and beautify the population. Mustafa Ali celebrated Rumelians as "a select community and pure, pleasing people who, just as they are distinguished in the origins of their state, are singled out for their piety [*diyanet*], cleanliness [*nazafet*], and faith [*akidet*]."[64] When Muslim Ottomans intermingled with (converted) Europeans, it was "as if two different species of fruitbearing tree mingled and mated, with leaves and fruits; and the fruit of this union was large and filled with liquid, like a princely pearl. The best qualities of the progenitors were then manifested and gave distinction, either in physical beauty, or in spiritual wisdom."[65] For Mustafa Ali, Ottoman arrivals in Anatolia who mingled with lighter-skinned ("white") populations made possible a union of the religious/spiritual (Islamic) and the beautiful (Rumelian/Roman), and this mixture led to the production of a pious, intellectual, physically strong, attractive, and "pearl-like" Ottoman populace. As Cornell Fleischer notes, in Mustafa Ali's racial engineering, "Rum thus became a breeding ground for exceptionally fine, able, pious people; it was through the cultivation and encouragement of these, and by attracting learned men to Rum, that the Ottoman sultans had built up their state and made it 'the envy of the Arabs and Iranians.'"[66] Considering the role of *devşirme* in creating such heterogeneity by bringing Rumelian boys into Anatolia, the physiognomy and the look of these boys was of immense importance for Mustafa Ali's racial taxonomy. Eroticized as sexually submissive in their youth, in manhood, they came to be imagined as converted sexual agents of a whitening agenda. Hence, beautiful beardless white "bottoms" were at the top of the boy hierarchy in the eroto-imperial project.

Mustafa Ali's erotic gaze becomes most clear in his voyeuristic narrative, which emphasized the beauty of servant boys even when he criticized them: "When they are in the freshness of bloom, there are plenty of bidders for comely, smooth-cheeked lads and angelic-dispositioned, cheerful and pretty boys, just as there were for Joseph in Egypt" (306). He cast a connoisseur's eye over their bodies, describing in detail their youthful appearance, disposition, and prettiness, connecting them to the iconic, qur'anic, and poetic male beauty Joseph. Their beauty and the "desire exhibited toward them by a great personage" it generated facilitated a bright future for them: "Some intelligent youths among them, while still attractive objects of desire, make appropriate preparations for their future ... [and] by entering the service of a master of high prestige, some become notables with felicity and glory" (306, 308). Mustafa Ali did not seem to be critical of such widespread orderly homosocial relations in which the boy's strategic use of attractiveness for self-benefit was acceptable. The famous poet Hayali's biography supports Mustafa Ali's observation of how a boy could materially circulate from one space to another, from one group to another, and how his beauty and talents paved further career paths. Hayali was seduced and kidnapped by a dervish group in the European part of the empire and brought to Istanbul, where his good looks and literary talent helped him penetrate into the higher social circles, circulating from one patron to another as a successful poet, ending up at the court as a companion to the Sultan Suleyman himself.[67] And as an adult poet, Hayali wrote poems for boys. Mustafa Ali did not complain about such ascendancy. His main protestation occurred when lustful desire and inappropriate personality became the sole medium for arranging the relations of boys. He warned that "pages who are mischief-makers and gossips, even if they are as handsome as the servants of paradise, are not fit for service in the imperial palace" (33).[68] Yet still, in all-male wine gatherings, there must be "the sought-after and eager beardless boys, who are in service as the *saki* [cupbearer] and who keep an eye out for the needs of the guest at the banquet" (233). It was not just their service in wine gatherings but the companionship these boys offered that was celebrated.[69] Following the common poetic dispute over whether boys or women best represent love, Mustafa Ali noted the preference for and convenience of boys as love companions: "Friendship with young men is a door in the gate of companionship, both in secret and manifestly, and is both open and flung back. What is more, beardless youth can be a companion whether at home or on journeys" (58–59).[70]

Adopting the poetic prototypes of the paradisiacal youth and the cupbearer at wine gatherings, Mustafa Ali extended the metaphor to real-life figures, blurring the lines between representational beautiful boys and actual servant boys who become erotic objects of desire. While these boys, who would later become elite officers and ruling persons in the empire, were sometimes a target of the critical eyes of Turkish elites, other times, they were represented as beloveds of poets and sultans in literary and visual culture. In either case, the representations of these boys elucidated the homoerotics of power hierarchies ordered in an active/passive, master/servant matrix. Similar to Ganymede in the European accounts I explored in the introduction, these boys, as desirable *ganimets*, were the subject of debates about *amor spiritualis* versus *amor carnalis*. The classification and celebration of their bodies and beauty generated a racial hierarchy in which white boys with Euro-Christian origins were praised in accordance with the empire's westbound expansion into the Western Christian lands. (I further explore the boy's terrestrial signification in chapter 2.) The abducted beautiful boy in the form of the servant—as the beloved, the cupbearer, the sexual partner, or the ideal companion—thus unveils the entanglements of homoerotic desire, race, and imperial investments in the Ottoman world.

Boy-Companions of the Empire

Abducted boys appear in the narratives of and about the Ottomans. As I mentioned above, European accounts of these boys displayed great concerns about religion and sodomy. Yet like the Ottoman accounts, they portrayed the boys for the voyeuristic gaze of their readers. This discursive practice, as Goran Stanivukovic aptly observes, "allows sodomy to circulate in texts for English readers, making those texts outlets for pleasures proscribed in England."[71] Through such accounts, these boys discursively traveled into Western Europe and to England.

Paul Rycaut, the English secretary to the ambassador in Istanbul from 1660 to 1668, for instance, described the palace boys this way: "These youths must be of admirable features, and pleasing looks, well shaped in their bodies, and without any defect of nature; For it is conceived that a corrupt and sordid soul can scarcely inhabit in a serene and ingenuous Aspect; and I have observed, not only in the *Seraglio*, but also in the Courts of great men, their personal attendants have been of comely lusty youths, well habited, deporting themselves with singular modesty and respect in the presence of their masters: So that when a *Pascha*, *Aga*, or *Spahee* travels, he is always attended with a comely equipage, followed by flourishing Youths, well clothed, and mounted, in great numbers."[72] Rycaut's writing underscored their bodily perfection; in a single sentence, he listed "admirable feature," "pleasing look," "well shaped in their bodies," "comely," "lusty," and "well habited." His description relegated them to a subservient role: they were not just the servants of their masters but also the object of Rycaut's and his readers' gaze.

Positioning the boys as objects of observation and close analysis, Rycaut next described how they were educated. These youths studied romance, and what they learned "endues them with a kind of Platonick love each to other, which is accompanied with a true friendship amongst some few, and with as much gallantry as is exercised in any part of the world. But for their Amours to Women, the restraint and strictness of Discipline, makes them altogether strangers to that Sex; for want of conversation with them, they burn in lust one towards another, and the amorous disposition of youth wanting more natural objects of affection, is transported to a most passionate admiration of beauty wheresoever it finds it."[73] Highlighting "true friendship" in the platonic paradigm of spiritual love, Rycaut's use of "gallantry" blurs the implication the word suggests. While "gallantry" appears as a term of praise in the first sentence, considering the words in OED definitions ("fashionable people," "splendour," "bravery," "courtly characteristics"), the very next sentence, which moves to their "amorous" relations, makes explicit the term's signification of "amorous intercourse or intrigue."[74] By cataloguing their bodies and stressing the platonic nature of their love and friendship, Rycaut surprised his readers by connecting their "gallantry" not with women but with each other. For him, it was not the literary materials these boys were exposed to but the exclusively male social structure that created an environment in which same-sex sexual relations were possible.[75] As a result, Rycaut fantasized that these boys were more inclined to develop affection not for "natural objects" (i.e., women) but for one another.

Situating the relations between these boys in an "unnatural" matrix, Rycaut came back to "platonick love" only to show that the platonic had morphed into perversion in Constantinople: "The Doctrine of platonick love hath found

Disciples in the Schools of the *Turks*, that they call it a passion very laudable and virtuous, and a step to that perfect love of God, whereof mankind is only capable, proceeding by the way of love and admiration of his image and beauty enstamped on the creature." However, platonic love is only "the colour of virtue" that the palace boys "paint over the deformity, of their depraved inclinations." In reality, Rycaut claimed, "this love of theirs, is nothing but libidinous flames each to other, with which they burn so violently, that banishment and death have not been examples sufficient to deter them from making demonstrations of such like addresses, so that in their Chambers, though watched by their Eunuchs, they learn a certain language with the motion of their eyes, their gestures and their fingers, to express their amours; and this passion hath boiled sometimes to that heat, that jealousies and rivalries have broken forth in their Chambers without respect to the severity of their Guardians."[76] Alluding to the Sufi tradition that seeks to reach divine love via the beloved beautiful youth, Rycaut opined that this form of platonic love was just a cover for their "depraved inclination" in ways that were similar to discussions on misunderstandings of platonic love in seventeenth-century England. For instance, in a section devoted to "platonick love" in his *Collection of Miscellanies* (1687), John Norris noted that "platonick love is a thing in every bodies mouth; but I scarce find any that think or speak accurately of it. By platonick love seems generally to be meant, a love that terminates in itself... that does not proceed to the enjoyment of its object." A truly platonic lover "loves at a distance" and does not seek "fruitation of the object." For Norris, that kind of love was called "platonick" because it stemmed from the dialogues in which Plato treated love as "mystical and allegorical."[77] However, for the writer, a misunderstanding of this doctrine was so widespread in England that he devoted a section to reminding his audience of the spiritual aspect of this superior love. Rycaut made a similar claim, but for the Ottomans. Rycaut claimed to narrate what he had seen; his eyes were on the boys to unveil their sexual agency in seeking other boys with a certain body language they developed, their burning "libidinous flames each to other" and their use of "eyes, gestures, and fingers to express their amours." All of these "deformities" were conveyed under the veil of the "doctrine of Platonic love."

What is expected to be purely *amor spiritualis*, Rycaut noted, was *amor carnalis* in the Ottoman Empire—passionate, sensual, and sexual. And "Persons of eminent degree" were so much "enamored of these boys" that they became "Companion[s] of the Empire":

> Persons of eminent degree in the *Seraglio* become inveigled in this sort of love, watching occasions to have a sight of the young Pages that they fancy,

either at the Windows of their Chamber, or as they go to the Mosque, or to their washing or baths; offer them service and presents, and so engage them as to induce them to desire to be made of the retinue of him that uses Courtship towards them. . . . The great Signours themselves have also been slaves to this inordinate passion. For Sultan Murat became so enamoured of an Armenian boy called Musa. . . . At another time [he] fell in love with a boy from "Galata," promoted him to higher offices; and even a son of slave who became "his chief Favourite" he made him clothe like him, ride by his side, and commanded all to present and honor him, in the same manner as if he had made him Companion of the Empire.[78]

From this English perspective, men promoted beautiful boys and offered service or "presents" to win the boys' love. Recalling the figure of "the royal Favourite" in these Christian boys (one was Armenian and the other was from Galata, a neighborhood with a non-Muslim population of mostly Christians), Rycaut strikingly probed the subject/object dichotomy. Their love, their "inordinate passion," rendered the eminent masters "slaves" to these servant boys. These boys become the subjects according to which their lovers shaped their actions; they arranged what they would do by "watching occasions to have a sight of the young Pages that they fancy." Commencing his account by depicting the beauty of the boys and moving to their education and homosocial environment, Rycaut concluded that these boys were erotic objects at the center of the empire. All men, including the sultan, were enchanted by these boys: "these darts of Cupid are shot through all the Empire, especially *Constantinople*."[79]

Rycaut was not alone among the English in contributing to the cultural imagination of abducted boys as sexual objects of perverse love. Traveler Fynes Moryson reported that upon the death of Sultan Murad, "the new sultan sent out of the court all of his father's 'sodomeittical boyes.'"[80] George Sandys claimed that "eight hundred boyes & virgins, excelling the rest both in birth & beautie," were reserved for the seraglio in Constantinople and that these boys were abducted Christian youths who were "the most compleatly furnished by nature": "Jemoglans, who have their faces shaven (the token of servitude) wearing long coates and copped caps, not unlike to our idiots, [were] taken in their childhood . . . instructed in Mahometan religion (changing their names upon their circumcision)."[81] Sandys further claimed that "many of the children that the Turkes do buy (for these markets do afford of all ages), they castrate, making all smooth as the back of one hand." Just like the smooth cheeks of the boys in Seraglio, the purchased slaves were made smooth through castration with the suggestion that they were to be used sexually, for "sodomy [is] an ordinary crime, if esteemed a crime, in that nation."[82]

Displaying considerable knowledge of classical, particularly platonic ideas, such early modern accounts also revived and actualized Greco-Roman sexual culture and Ganymede in the Ottoman lands, in persons and practices. Thomas Gainsford recalled Greek pederasty, calling Turkish and Persian sodomy "that horrible corruption of the Grecians."[83] Likewise, Sir Henry Blount claimed that, apart from their wives, "each Basha hath as many, or likely more, Catamites, which are their serious loves; for their wives are used (as the Turkes themselves told me) but to dresse their meat, to launderesse, and for reputation."[84] Like ancient Greeks, the Ottomans had boys for love and wives for domestic and social concerns. As a corrupt form of Ganymede, "catamite" was, in Thomas Blount's definition, "a boy hired to be abused contrary to nature, a Ganymede."[85] The servant boy as Ganymede appeared more explicitly in Richard Knolles's story of the stay of the brother of Wladus Dracula in the court of Mehmed II: Wladus Junior "became his Ganimede, and was of him [for a] long time wonderfully both beloved and honoured."[86] Similarly, Michel Baudier noted that of "twenty Emperors which have carried the Turkish scepter, you shall hardly find two that were free from this vice" of "the love of men."[87] He later used the term "Ganimede" when he asserted that the Turks "abandon their affections to young Boyes, and desperately follow the allurements of their beauties. . . . This abominable vice is so ordinary in the Turks Court, as you shall hardly find one that is not miserably inclined toward it: It serves for an ordinary subject of entertainment among the greatest when they are together; they speak not but of the perfections of their *Ganimedes*."[88] Baudier reminds us of Mustafa Ali's narrative of the wine gatherings, at the center of which stands the servant boy. His use of "Ganimede" in reference to the conversations of men blurs the line between, indeed combines, *ganimet* and Ganymede in terms of sexuality, service, and property.

Mythical boys who were abducted in imaginary landscapes evoking a range of desires found their analogues in the histories of real boys who were abducted in sexual, social, and cultural economies. The abducted boys were *ganimets* of these men. At the same time, this descriptor may be read as Ganymede from a European perspective, just as Blount, Knolles, and Baudier, among others, beheld the iconic Ganymede in these boys. If we believe that Baudier witnessed their conversations, it is most probable that he conflated "*ganimet*" with "Ganymede," as becomes evident when he narrated the details of the conversation: "One sayes, they have brought me from Hungarie the most beautiful and accomplished Minion. . . . Another saith, I have lately bought a young Infant of Russia."[89] These "masters" might have referred to these boys as "ganimet," yet they appear in Baudier's and in Knolles's text as "*Ganimede*." This might stem from a mishearing or the crossed wires of homonymic likeness. In either case, such instances exemplify a sodomitical reading of Ganymede resuscitated in abducted boys in Ottoman lands. The beautiful boy, both a captive and an erotic beloved, stands as a multifaceted and dynamic erotic figure not just in Ottoman representations but also in European accounts about the Ottomans, recalling homoerotic relations, master/slave dynamics, and platonic ideals through Ganymede. To what extent, then, can such discourses be traced in Marlowe's imagery of the beautiful boy abducted in the Hellespont?

Leander in the Ottoman Mediterranean

It is in the Ottoman Mediterranean context, geography, and discursive space that Marlowe imagined the abduction of Leander as Ganymede, "beautiful and young" (51). Reported to have said that "all those who loved not Tobacco & Boys were fools," Marlowe located boys in a homoerotic frame in many of his plays and poems.[90] While the beautiful boy Ganymede figures as the playful boy in Marlowe's *Dido, Queen of Carthage* (1.1.1) and the favorite of the king in *Edward II* (1.4.180–81), he embodies the abducted boy in a Mediterranean space in *Hero and Leander*, evoking Bajazeth's janissaries. *Hero and Leander*, "the most openly licentious of Marlowe's poems," radiates a particular energetic homoeroticism.[91] It is, as Jeffrey Masten declares, Marlowe's "Orphic song" for boy-desire."[92] It is then no coincidence that the beloved Gaveston of *Edward II* imagines himself as "Leander" and the English Channel as the Hellespont upon receiving his lover Edward's letter: "Sweet prince, I come. These, these thy amorous lines / Might have enforced me to have swum from France, / And, like Leander, gasped upon the sand" (1.1.6–8). While the land is the premise of Gaveston's homoerotic vision, in *Hero and Leander* Marlowe makes central the passage, the travel itself, creating the homoerotic aura through the abduction of Leander as Ganymede in the Hellespont.

The reference to Ganymede is not incidental to the poem's world; it produces what I call the Ganymede effect, which functions as a metacommentary, generating abductions and illuminating the blurred line between the real and the mimetic. Ganymede is first evoked when the narrator compares Leander's beautiful body to Jove's cupbearer: "Jove might have sipped out nectar from his hand" (62). His hand not only carries the cup but also becomes the cup that is sensually felt through sipping. The narrator further invokes consuming his flesh in the next line: "Even as delicious meat is to the taste, / So was his neck in touching, and surpassed / The white of Pelop's shoulder" (63–65). Like gods tasting Pelop's body, the narrator intensifies the carnal erotics by portraying Leander's delicious white body as edible. The mythic Ganymede is subsequently followed by a visual illustration in Venus's glass temple in Sestos, underneath the radiant floor of which can be seen "gods in sundry shapes, / Committing heady riots, incest, rapes" and "Jove slyly stealing from his sister's bed, / To dally with Idalian Ganymede" (143–44, 147–48). In a sensual picture, the lines bring pederastic sex and geography together in a play of "dalliance" and "Idalian." Then comes the third evocation of Ganymede, this time as an illusion when he is recalled by Neptune, who, like the narrator earlier, fantasizes Ganymede in Leander, Leander as Ganymede: "Imagining that Ganymede, displeased, / Had left the heavens; therefore on him he seized" (641–42). These examples seem to follow the template of Ganymede not only to highlight and praise the beauty of the boy but also to emphasize his vulnerability to abduction and dalliance, that irresistible male desire to seize him in this space. Ganymede, who appears as a mythic allusion and visual illustration in the first two moments, is actualized in the third instance in the poem. He becomes a figure for Neptune, a representation of the representation pictured on crystal floors, obscuring distinct lines between the mythic, the aesthetic, and the real. Both the narrator's and Neptune's recasting of Ganymede contribute to the creation of a homoerotic world in which Leander *becomes* Ganymede during his swim to the other side of the Hellespont, an object of abduction, seduction, and possession.

The description of Leander as "shipwreck treasure" is reminiscent of the real-life boys abducted in this space because of their beauty—be it through captivity, piracy, kidnapping, or recruitment. Neptune, "the sapphire-visaged god," imbues Mediterranean abductions with a mythic intervention (639). He appears not only as embodied, penetrative, "wounding" waves but also as a mundane, "kingly" adult man (643; 650). At the moment of the abduction, in particular, the narrator mixes the mythical with the real, framing Neptune's pursuit of and interaction with Leander as an everyday encounter. Charmed by Leander, Neptune "puld him to the bottome, where the ground / Was strewd with pearle, and in low corrall groves, / Sweet singing Meremaids, sported with their loves / On heapes of heavie gold, and tooke great pleasure, / To spurne in carelesse sort, the shipwracke treasure. / For here the stately azure pallace stood / Where kingly *Neptune* and his traine abode" (644–50). The undersea world of the Hellespont is Neptune's realm, where pleasure covers treasure. In this space, which is not the unreachable realm of gods but a kingdom at "the bottom" of the Mediterranean Sea with shipwrecks, a palace, promised treasures, pearls, and gold, Neptune becomes "kingly" with his "traine," a worldly ruler Leander is not surprised to have encountered. In this dangerous zone, the lusty and kingly god Neptune replaces the corsairs and Turkish masters, abducting alluring boys.[93]

Moreover, "the bottom [of the sea] ... with pearle" locates the setting in the Mediterranean of the sixteenth century. The imagery of pearls, which appears multiple times in the poem (33; 297; 376; 389), is a sign of wealth for Lynn Enterline, who suggests that such images of riches, including pearls, gold, jasper, coral, amber, and diamonds, function to link wealth with rhetoric in the context of classical *copia*.[94] But Miriam Jacobson more specifically situates these pearls of rhetoric in the context of Mediterranean trade, as a result of which "pearl" emerged as a new word in connection with "the orient" in the sixteenth-century poetic imagination: the pearled Mediterranean is "the layered landscape of an Ottoman-inflected mythological Hellespont."[95] But what about "the orient" in Marlowe's orientation? From the fourteenth century onward, the "orient" signified the East and what was from the East.[96] Marlowe and his contemporaries associated pearls with the orient, from India to the Ottoman Mediterranean: Marlowe's Faustus envisions ordering spirits to "fly to India for gold / Ransack the ocean for orient pearl" (1.1. 84–85). In Marlowe's *The Jew of Malta*, Barabas talks about "pearl/ Orient and round" in his household (4.1.66). Similarly, Edmund Spenser uses "pure Orient perles" (2.12.78) in *The Faerie Queene* to depict the exotic seductress Acrasia in the Bower of Bliss. Gremio of Shakespeare's *The Taming of the Shrew* depicts his wealth through his "Turkey cushions boss'd with pearl" (2.1.346), and pearls in Ben Jonson's *Volpone* are "more orient / Than that the brave Egyptian queen caroused" (3.7. 191–92). In *Hero and Leander*, the narrator more pointedly uses "orient" to describe Leander's body and thus links his "oriental" or Eastern beauty with the space "strewd with pearle" (72–73).[97] In this way, Marlowe blends the Greco-Roman Mediterranean context into the Ottoman context, in which Leander's body is associated with and almost fused with the Mediterranean he swims in.

In his description of Leander's beauty, Marlowe erotically orients his readers' gaze toward the boy's body in this space.[98] While "orient" as a signifier for the East marks Abydos's Leander as culturally different from Sestos's Hero, it further signifies his pearl-like skin as in the "pearl of the orient." It eroticizes Leander's youthful and white body: "How smooth his breast was, and how white his belly" (66). It is at the very moment when Leander's oriental cheeks are mentioned that he is described as a boy-object of other men's gaze and desire, although the narrator claims that "his rude pen / Can hardly blazon forth the loves of men / Much less of powerful gods: let it suffice / That my slack Muse sings of Leander's eyes, / Those orient cheeks and lips, exceeding his / That leaped into the water for a kiss" (69–74). As Jacobson notes, "orient" could invoke the water associated with a pearl's luster: "In the early modern world, pearls were associated with dew, tears and seminal fluids as much as they represented the opposite, serving as emblems of chastity and sexual imperviousness."[99] In fact, in describing Hero, the narrator makes this signification clear: "as she spake, / Forth from those two traluscent cisterns brake / A stream of liquid pearl, which down her face / Made milk-white paths" (295–98). While Jacobson reads this watery image as a reference to the fluidity of the Mediterranean, the "oriental" liquidity in Leander's eyes, cheeks, and lips actually depicts Leander as watery. In the early modern Galenic humoral conceptualization of body, fluids in the body were considered to be determinative of the constitution of one's gender. In the humoral gender discourse, bodily liquids and wetness were associated with women and femininity. As Hero's "milk-white" fluids as a response to Leander's seductive rhetoric is a sign of her femininity, Leander's watery body indicates his raw, virgin youth (298). Leander, whose youth is stressed repeatedly, is distinctly a boy whose body is in a fluid, in-between phase and space.

Focusing on Leander's body, Bruce Smith proposes that the ambiguous gender and erotic allure of the boy was more appealing to Renaissance readers than those of definitively gendered heroes and heroines.[100] This is surely the case for Marlowe's narrator: Leander is "a maid in man's attire," as some "swore" (83). Leander's association with water and fluidity heightens his erotic allure as a boy in between, in the process of becoming. This fluid imagery reinforces the idea that he is in a state between being the dominant lover of Hero and the submissive beloved of Neptune. The virgin and vulnerable Leander, "rude and raw" at this point, is about to transform in the sea god's arms. His naked and swimming body unites with the body of Mediterranean water and becomes a site in which Neptune swims and through which boys—from Narcissus to cupbearers—are trafficked. With "orient" cheeks and lips, Leander the boy is not like Narcissus but "exceed[s]" him; he is not mythological but is beyond mythic beauty, a beauty that would convince "wild Hippolytus," who preferred hunting to love, of love (77). Framing this fantasy through mythic evocations, the narrator shifts to everyday life and positions Leander's white beauty in relation to "wild," "rude," "barbarous" followers: "His presence made the rudest peasant melt," and "the barbarous Thracian soldier, moved with nought, / Was moved with him, and for his favor sought" (79–82). "Amorous Leander, beautiful and young" whose "looks were all that men desire," further entices "adventurous Greek youths" (51, 84, 57). Nancy Vickers suggests that inherent in the Renaissance blazon is the violent appropriation of the objectified female through a close-up description. When it is men who are blazoned, a similar violent appropriation is in practice, where the male is "incongruously placed in a 'normalized' female position, that of a commodity in the traffic between men."[101] This "traffic" in the boy's case can specifically be seen through the all-male admirers listed in the poem: wild Hippolytus, the rude peasant, the barbarous Thracian soldier, and lusty Neptune. As the object of the erotic gaze and desire—on the part of the narrator, the reader, the sea god, and other men—he is not, however, violently appropriated in a normalized female position, for he assertively announces: "I am no woman, I."

Nor is he a silenced and submissive victim of abduction. Reminding us of Mustafa Ali's boys who actively search for amorous relations with other boys or Paul Rycaut's boys who use their "eyes, gestures, and fingers to express their amours," Marlowe's "amorous" Leander is not simply at the receptive end of desire. As Masten's queer philological focus on the use of "amorous" reveals, the term refers not only to a person actively inclined to love but also one who is passively loved; lovely, lovable. Amorous boys are, Masten proposes, "positioned as simultaneously active and passive: driven by desire (itself also of penetrative force through which they are enamoured); thus, subjects subject to the force and virtue of the loving look; themselves inciting or instigating desire (*himeroeis*); *and* often the object of such desire."[102] Hence, "amorous Leander is inclined from the beginning in both directions."[103] Leander, who asserts "I am no woman, I" as a response to Neptune's desire, resists appropriation by an adult male and pursues his own amorous interest, exemplifying not a fully submissive Ganymede but merely a Ganymede effect, in which allusions to and refigurations and reminiscences of the iconic Ganymede function to generate abductions inflected by an affective mode. This affective mode, as we see in Leander's abduction as Ganymede in a pederastic scenario, is loaded with both homoerotic pleasure and violence.

Following the desiring gaze on the beautiful youth as Ganymede, Leander's abduction materializes the boy as an object of exchange in an ephemeral, playful homoerotic fantasy. It is right after Neptune "seized" Leander that the narrator states, "The lusty god embraced him, called him love, / And swore he should never return to Jove" (651–52). Neptune not only steals the boy but also imagines mastery and ownership over him. Jove abducted Ganymede from Mount Ida as a spoil of war, and now Neptune kidnaps the boy as a shipwreck treasure and an object of pleasure. While this signals a shift in imperial power from warfare/conquest to mercantilism/sea trade, the abduction and eroticization of the beautiful boy is the common motif in both forms of mastery. Although soon after dragging him down to his kingdom at the bottom of the sea Neptune realizes the boy is not the already-transformed, immortalized cupbearer Ganymede, he nevertheless pursues him with "talk of love," swimming under, on, beside him, between his arms and legs, prying into his "breast, his thighs, and every limb" (666–75). The god tries to impress the boy by giving him "gaudy toys" and "Helle's bracelet." Yet the beautiful boy refuses to be his love toy, refuses to be trafficked between gods and men on the ground that he is "no woman." Although Leander is stolen, he soon gains his freedom thanks to feeling "guiltie of the lover's blood"; that is, feeling bad about the god's "fresh bleeding wound" after "darting" Leander with his phallic mace (697). With this moment of disrupted violence, Marlowe disallows a coercive homosexual intercourse in his poetic world. Leander's objectification, his temporary abduction in the middle of the Hellespont, and his eroticization for readerly pleasure locate him in a celebrated homoerotic world that differs from the violent heterosexual world where Hero is objectified, enjoyed, and silenced under Leander's gaze at the end of the poem.

The homoerotic dynamic in this moment is further reinforced through the transformation of Neptune into a shepherd. In Masten's words, the god becomes the "personification of boy-directed amorous admiration and desire"; a model of early modern pederastic structure in which "adult figures are always attempting to teach the boy, persuade the boy, to a desire of which they assume him fundamentally *to be capable*."[104] When Neptune's talk of love, intimate swimming moves, and gifts do not persuade the boy, he turns to a story to awaken Leander's desire. When Leander replies, "You are deceav'd, I am no woman, I," emphasizing not what he is (a man? a boy?) but what he is not (a woman), Neptune proffers a homoerotic pastoral story of a shepherd and a fair boy—a non-dichotomous, alternative sexual paradigm to that of cross-sex relations—to educate the boy in the business of love between men: "Thereat smiled *Neptune*, and then told a tale, / How that a sheapheard sitting in a vale, / Playd with a boy so faire and so kind, / As for his love, both earth and heaven pyn'd; / That of the cooling river durst not drinke, / Least water-nymphs should pull him from the brinke. / And when hee sported in the fragrant lawnes, / Gote-footed Satyrs, and up-staring Fawnes, / Would steale him thence" (677–85). Reminding us of Marlowe's "The Passionate Shepherd to His Love," this story puts the sea god in the position of the shepherd while transforming the Neptune/Leander relationship into a classical shepherd/boy homoerotic dynamic.[105] In fact, Neptune's interruption of Leander's visit to Hero also echoes Leander's father, who warns him about his love for Hero. It is as if both the father and the god see the orderly homosocial structure as more fitting for the boy, who is too young to be in an amorous heterosexual relation: "Leander's father knew where he had been / And for the same mildly rebuked his son, / Thinking to quench the sparkles new begun" (620–22). Yet like Shakespeare's Romeo, Leander leaves the homosocial masculine structure for an amorous bond with a woman, which ends tragically. Leander insists on an erotic mode that replaces classical, pastoral homoeroticism. In this pastoral world, the boy is available and vulnerable to others whenever he is alone. He has been abducted by Neptune (albeit briefly), and "water-nymphs, Gote-footed Satyrs and Fawnes" try to pull him into the water and "steale him thence" (682–83). The traveling boy is thus subjected to multiple "stealing" or abduction scenarios in erotic terms, which serves to engender and enhance the reader's desire to "seize" the boy.

The eroticization of Neptune's abduction of the beautiful boy in the Hellespont offers a celebratory alternative to the anxious sodomitical matrix offered by travel accounts about the Ottomans and the larger Mediterranean. James Bromley argues that Neptune's erotic play with Leander "on the nexus of eroticism and power pervasive in Marlowe's England" is a form of short-term, situational intimacy that does not necessitate a commitment or consumption. Neptune's play and his pursuit of Leander therefore is governed by the logic that "what happens in the Hellespont stays in the Hellespont."[106] Yet this erotic power dynamic, when read in relation to Mediterranean references and the trafficking in boys, is a reflection not only of Marlowe's England and the temporary and intimate cruising therein, but also of the Mediterranean. In the Mediterranean, "stealing" happened regularly. The stories of the experiences, relations, and travels in the Ottoman Mediterranean reached the banks of Thames through travelers' stories and were recreated again and again in poetic imaginations. What happened in the Hellespont did not actually stay in the Hellespont.

The abduction of the traveling boy emerges from Marlowe's reimagination of both classical works and the Mediterranean of his time. Marlowe's poetic queer touch regarding the abduction of boys exposes a space with erotic possibilities and, in contrast to anti-sex narratives about this transformative space, contests a strict boundary between East and West. The fluid waters of Hellespont do not separate the two sides but unite them as a lively and energetic passage populated with desiring and desired persons. The poem demonstrates how everyday realities and literary conventions coalesce politically and erotically around the beautiful boy. The traveling boy stands in water, uniting gazes and desires from all around, shaping the crossroads—real and imagined—between the eastern and western sides.

Marlowe's interest in the erotic boy figure as Ganymede in his *Dido, Queen of Carthage* or *Edward II* is here inflected more explicitly in a geohistorical engagement with Mediterranean traffic. The Hellespont with Ganymede has a function: performative power to generate Leander's abduction. As this chapter has argued, in the Ottoman Mediterranean context, the beautiful boy was subject to male desire—like Leander, he was "made for amorous play"—and, as a result, he was vulnerable to abduction like Ganymede. And wherever we see a Ganymede, there appears a Jove, or a man who wants to be and feel like Jove. Ottoman poets have their own *ganimets* sitting next to them in gardens and the Ottoman sultan has his own beautiful cupbearers. While poetic genres and conventions—be they ghazal or epyllion—made possible the depictions of homoerotic relations with boys, the abduction component of such representations in Ottoman and English writings were in dialogue with the historical context of violent real-life abductions. Marlowe's Leander, whose body embodies an appearance and history of Ganymede, blends the mythic boy with abducted beautiful boys appearing as ganymedes/*ganimets* in other accounts. Marlowe's poem is unfinished, leaving us with the conclusion that "*desunt nonnula*" (something is missing). We know the tragic end of the classical story of Hero and Leander and we know George Chapman's continuation of Marlowe's poem, but we do not know Marlowe's own ending.[107] Marlowe's poem thereby leaves us with alternatives, inviting us to imagine, or even fantasize about, "amorous" Leander's destiny with Neptune as he swims back to the eastern side, "on Hellespont."

2
———

Mapping Boys on the Horizon

While Marlowe portrayed the Hellespont as the site of the beautiful boy's abduction, the Ottoman courtier, judge, and poet Aşık Çelebi mapped the river Danube as a boy in his "Ode to the Danube" ("Tuna Kasidesi") in his biographical masterpiece, *Meşa'irü'ş-Şu'ara* (Biography of poets, ca. 1569).[1] In twenty-two couplets, each of which has a rhyme ending in "Danube," the poem deploys different metaphors to depict the river that marked the empire's western border in Europe. In the first couplet, the Danube is related to the poet's own heart and chest (*gönlüm/gögsüm*), sometimes flowing fast in excitement and at other times slowly in pain. From the fifth couplet onward, the river is variously personified as a lunatic, a Muslim, a lover, a ruler, a poet, and finally as a boy:

> He who hits his head on the rock, after leaping from the heights,
> Who is a crazy lover, is the naked mad Danube.
> He who culminates like the water, getting murky when it stops,[2]

> Who plays with dirt and dust, is the little boy Danube....
> He who flows from the infidel fields to the people of the Faith,
> Who faces the *qibla*, is the Muslim Danube.
> He who trails his chains, running free from infidel thralldom,
> Who comes to the Lord of Islam, is the man of faith Danube....
> He who gives all service prostrating himself on the ground,
> Who, like a servant boy, is the compliant Danube.
> He who throws cold gazes to his lovers, freezing they are,[3]
> Who yet melts the hearts of beauties, is the burning fire Danube.
> He who plays chest to chest with silver-toned bodies, yet
> Who is content with naked limbs, is the chaste[4] boy Danube.[5]

The river in these lines is first called a crazy lover running from one corner to another, flowing briskly, jumping from the heights and creating the waterfall. The river's energetic movement is next depicted through the imagery of a playful boy. In its orientation in flow, the Danube is facing the Ottoman Empire as its guide and final destination, its *qibla*, which refers to the direction in reference to the Ka'ba in Mecca that Muslims turn their bodies toward during prayer. The direction of the river is thus sacred; it runs wildly from the land of the infidels to the sultan's lands, from Germany toward the Ottoman Black Sea, from the Christian realm to the Islamic, and from slavery to freedom. This moving river, now free from chains, is represented as an obedient servant boy to the ruler to whom he submissively prostrates, lying on the ground on his face in respect, humility, and service. The subsequent two couplets further intensify the boy imagery by depicting the river not only as an enchanting lover but also as a chaste boy who enjoys other naked youths with lustrous, silver-like, light-skinned bodies that swim and bathe in "him." The river has an erotic mingling with the naked swimming youths, yet he is satisfied with merely enjoying the naked limbs, no more than that. Hence, he is chaste, pure, or uncontaminated.

Such an embodiment of the fluid Danube in the youthful male body with evocations of slavery and conversion is very much linked to the significance of the river in early modern contestations between Christianity and Islam, between the Ottoman and European powers. In the previous chapter, I considered the geopolitical significations in literary abduction plots by exploring them alongside historical boys abducted in the Mediterranean space. Specifically, the Hellespont in Marlowe's *Hero and Leander*, I argued, has performative power in generating the abduction of the beautiful boy as Ganymede. Here I continue to follow the boy in other cross-cultural sites. What kind of spaces are particularly marked with beautiful boys? What does the boy's body do in the representations of certain spaces?[6] In early modern England, besides the gendering of certain geographies (including the Mediterranean), such sites as houses, alehouses, theaters, markets, barbershops, and churches were frequently both gendered and sexualized.[7] Especially in colonial imaginations, land was almost axiomatically represented as female, and such "work of gender" in these imaginings, in Louis Montrose's formulation, reflected the colonial male desire for women by portraying the "virgin" territory as the female body to be cultivated. Hence, rape/penetration of this body stands for colonial mastery in discourses of discovery, exploration, exploitation, possession, and use of the land.[8] Figurations of the boy as an embodiment of territory, however, reveal not binary but plural gender dynamics in spatial representations. The work of the boy in relation to cross-cultural liminal borders thus challenges a conceptualization of space solely as the sexual-reproductive female body in a binary gender frame.

In this chapter, I trace spatial embodiments with a focus on boys who represent their native lands in the imagination of Ottoman poets and European mapmakers. Recounting the gendered work the eroticized boy performs in such representations of space in varied moments of cross-cultural encounters unveils the homoerotics of conversion—in sexual, temporal, or spatial forms—in imperial contestations between men. Aşık Çelebi's marking of the Danube as a boy to convey the imperial significance of the river is a recasting of the conventional trope of the beautiful Christian boy from Galata, the neighborhood adjacent to Istanbul that housed the Christian population of the empire and foreign diplomats, ambassadors, travelers, and merchants. In early modern literary and cartographic representations, Galata is the microcosmic Euro-Christian space of difference in the imperial capital and the Danube is the fluid border separating European Christendom from the world of the Ottomans. These two cross-cultural contact zones, I will argue, were converted to imaginary thresholds in poetic and cartographic imaginations that both generate and probe such dichotomies as self/other, Islam/Christian, Ottoman/European, and converter/converted. These works do so by creating a horizon on which the beautiful boy is located. I use the term "horizon" to refer to an imagined place that is anchored in a geographical location that is close enough, within eyesight, to promise the fulfillment of desire, yet is always unreachable.[9] This horizon orients and disorients its viewers. It calls up the idea of crossing, cruising, traveling, and contact and makes possible what seems impossible through heterogeneous significations. The horizon evokes a Ganymede effect generated by the beautiful boy under the gaze of the poet, the cartographer, and the viewer and thus engenders a homoerotic affect by inducing a desire to seize the boy. The figures of the boy of Galata and the "boy" of the Danube reflect competition between Ottomans and Europeans for imperial dominion. Subject to a homoerotic gaze with their ambiguous gender status, these boys expose the gendering and objectification of spaces for imperial agendas. Yet the boys as markers of their lands seem not yet fully submissive and tamed; at the horizon, they project a promise to reach for domination and conversion. In early modernity, this way of gendering boys challenged binaries of male/female, subject/object, pleasure/violence, and desire/anxiety in the frame of eroticized power plays between men.

The Boy of Galata

While the Danube was the geographical threshold that bordered the Ottoman lands in Europe, Galata was a liminal space at the heart of the empire. Located across from the Imperial Palace (Topkapı Sarayı) in the historical city of Istanbul, Galata (Pera) was a town where mostly non-Muslim Ottoman subjects, mainly Christian and Jewish communities, lived under their own laws and customs, a right granted by royal decree after Mehmed II conquered Constantinople in 1453. As a multicultural site adjacent to the capital, Galata was famous for its wineries and taverns. It housed European embassies and merchants, mystic Islamic circles, and some Ottoman elites who had villas there where they could entertain guests and host social gatherings. Galata was thus a place of daily cross-cultural, cross-religion interactions between various peoples.

Galata is frequently spatialized in the Ottoman poetic and cartographic imagination as the empire's European site, a distinctly transgressive yet desirable space that was inseparable from Istanbul. In a cartographic representation of Galata by Matrakçı Nasuh, an influential courtier and soldier in the court of Suleyman I, Galata and Istanbul, indivisibly pictured in the same colors, face one another (fig. 2.1).[10] On the left-hand side, Galata is the part around the tower; Istanbul stands on the other side of the Golden Horn, whose traffic and commercial significance is alluded to by multiple ships. On the upper left-hand edge of Istanbul is the imperial seat Topkapı Palace, built by Mehmed II's order after the conquest. In Nasuh's map, Galata is rendered not as a separate space but seems interwoven with Istanbul, set apart only by a thin margin of water. The horizon of Galata exists only in relation to (and by looking from) Istanbul. Strikingly, Nasuh portrays Galata with a paradisiacal garden lying behind the walls of the town that makes it almost equal in size with Istanbul. This picturesque map with such an inviting garden offers a symbolic representation that is reminiscent of the poetic tradition in which Galata, a site of earthly pleasures, extends into restrictive Istanbul.

Poetic representations of Galata, as Walter Andrews and Mehmet Kalpaklı have demonstrated, conjoin churches, wineries, bathhouses, and boy lovers in

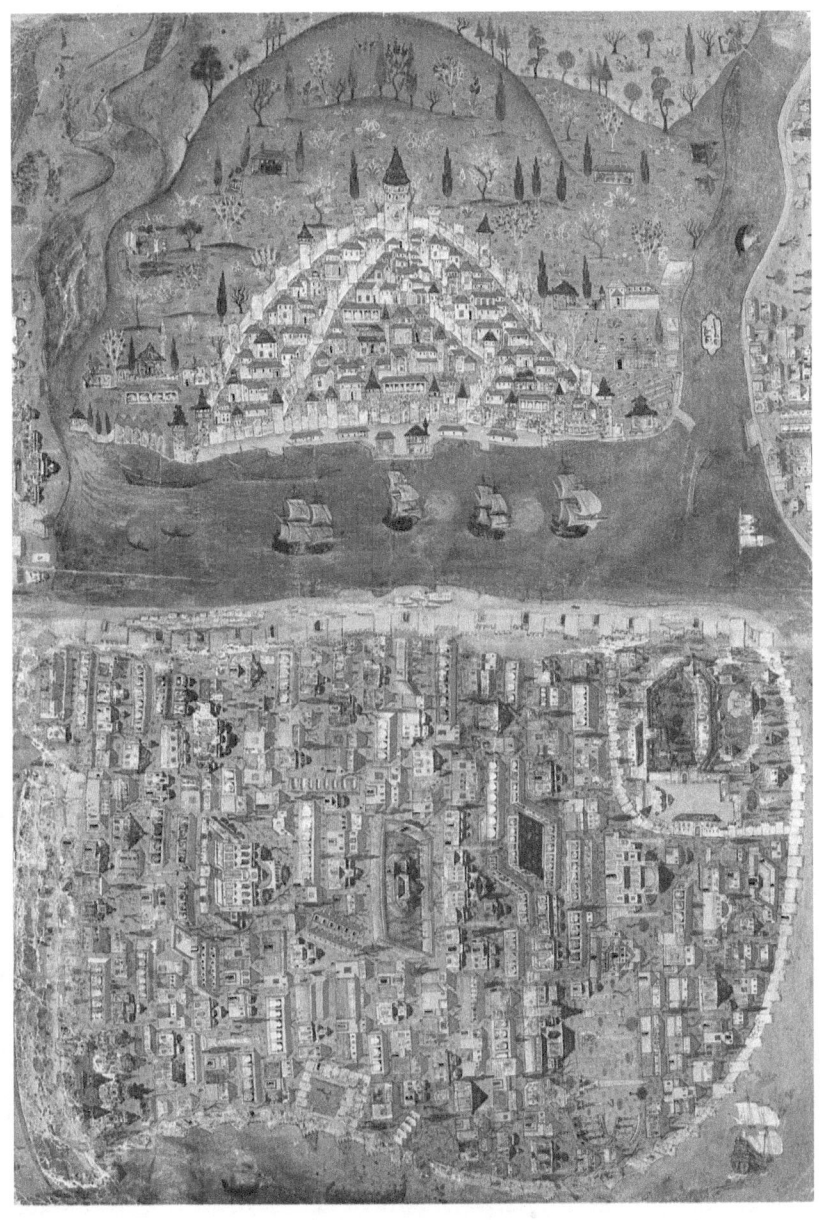

FIGURE 2.1. *Galata*, Matrakçı Nasuh, circa 1532. Topkapı Palace Museum.

this space.¹¹ The poet Latifi, in his sixteenth-century *Evsaf-ı Istanbul* (Description of Istanbul), for instance, depicted Galata in that way:

> For wine and beloveds [boys] it is without peer, and it is proverbial as a place of pleasure and amusement. Every corner of it glows like sunrise with moon-bright faces of Frankish [Euro-Christian] idols, yet its location and its every cranny are superior and preferable to a thousand Frankish realms.... This heart-captivating town is so generous with its pleasures and so stimulating that its merriment goes on without stopping; its pleasure gatherings are continual, and its wine parties in any other place would be forbidden. Because most of its people are of the community of Jesus and the nation of the Messiah, like the ancient Shah Cem, the wine cup never leaves their grip, and because they always have a goblet in hand, worries and dark thoughts never swarm about their heads. They are sensualists and wine bibbers, worshippers of the grape and sellers of wine.¹²

Latifi exoticizes Galata as a peerless place that exceeds all "Frankish" lands in Western Europe and at every corner of which stands a beautiful boy. The word "Frank" signifies Christian nations in Europe, particularly those west of the Mediterranean; "Frengi" (Frankish) refers to a person who has the dispositions of the Franks in terms of accent, dress, habits, and look.¹³ Latifi associates Galata, and thus its Frankish population, with sensuality, pleasure, and merriment, symbolized by the imagery of wine and boys. He blends his descriptions of Galata with poetic tropes; alongside wine, the beautiful boy, as the object of cross-religious desire, stands out as a distinct component of this space, generating desire and anxiety with his eroticized body and his religious difference.

The imagery of the Christian boy recycles the trope of cross-religious Muslim/Christian amorous encounters, which was a thematic hallmark of Arabic love poetry and the Persian ghazal tradition from the tenth century onward. In these representations, the Christian boy is usually a seductive wine server, specifically a cupbearer, seducing and corrupting the pretentious Muslims and diverting them from the right path of religion and thereby reducing them to abasement. Conversion from Islam to Christianity is associated with lust and shame in this tradition. As Franklin Lewis notes in his exploration of Islamicate tales and topoi of love for Christian boys, these narratives "may be said to explore the boundaries between god-fearing piety and the temptations of the flesh, but they also tend to undermine religio-didactic authority in favor of a situational morality, privileging some degree of tolerance for human nature over rigid adherence to social propriety."¹⁴ In such accounts, transgression lies not in homoerotic desire but in conversion itself. The Christian boy of Galata in Ottoman poetry, which I further trace below, displays common traits with this conventional Arabic-Persian trope, especially in evocations of conversion and common imageries of the sun, the moon, the cypress tree, the golden girdle, and the wine server.

In Ottoman poetry, this boy is almost always from Galata. One must note that Galata, the home of the iconic beautiful Christian boy of poetry from the fifteenth century to the sixteenth, was also a real place with Christian boys. The poetic voice in these poems usually speaks from Istanbul, gazing at Galata. This space is described through movements, actions, and topographical entities; it is distinct from Istanbul and has a border that must be crossed in order to access and experience life there. Whereas Nasuh's map borrows from the poetic imagery of Galata with paradisical gardens, the poetic language depicting Galata in these poems, like a cartographer's gaze, visualizes and dissects the place while gazing upon its boys. Andrews and Kalpaklı contend that the poetic desire for the boy in this literary convention very much mirrors historical homoerotic relations and especially the exchange of boys between men; the boy is not only a poetic metaphor, but also a real-life figure as an object of desire in the elite male culture of the empire.[15] So is the space. The Christian boy of Galata not only uncovers the homoerotic relations among elite Istanbulites, but also, I suggest, functions to reflect and produce larger spatial-imperial discourses and racial effects as a figure who is exoticized as the embodiment of European Christendom. The effect produced is a cross-religious desire for conquest and domination.

As early as the fifteenth century, the boy from Galata in these poems generates an erotic game that highlights a masculine imperial desire for political dominance over Christian lands. At that point, Mehmed II had already conquered Galata and made it a part of the Ottoman Empire. In that historical context, these Galata poems present the conquest not as a finalized act but as an ongoing process. Indeed, Mehmed II himself, the conqueror of Constantinople, penned poems that used Galata to create an imperial orientation. In the poem "Bir güneş yüzlü melek gördüm," Mehmed wrote about a beautiful Frank (Christian) boy from Galata who not only is a reflection of Jesus, whose lips "give life anew" yet whose "glance kills," but also embodies all Christendom:

A sun-faced angel, I saw,
    the moon of whom is the universe,
Dark hyacinth curls
    of whom are sighs of his lovers.
An alluring cypress
    like moon in black dress,

> Lure of whom alone
>   reigns in Frank realms.
> Whoever is not devoted
>   To his girdle's knots,
> No man of faith he is
>   but a heathen amidst his lovers.
> His lips give life anew to those
>   whom his glance kills,
> The faith this bestower of life follows, if any,
>   is the path of Jesus.
> Do not assume, O Avni,[16] to you
>   that beauty will submit,
> You are the lord of Istanbul,
>   he is the lord of Galata.[17]

The poem starts with the moment when the speaker, Avni, sees the sun-faced angel who brightens all other beauties of the universe and whose dark hyacinth curls are swirling, winding like sighs of his lovers. As a literary trope, the sigh *ah* refers to a lover's suffering from burning in the fire of love, and these sighs are metaphorically depicted through the black curls of the beloved. This beautiful boy becomes the object of Avni's first sight, his dissecting gaze, and for him, the boy's beauty is not only the angelic, solar, and lunar light of this world, it is also what reigns over Euro-Christians, or Franks.

Avni topographically associates the boy with the irresistible and incomparable beauty of the space he inhabits. Both the boy and Galata as religious others, however, are objects of desire and have the potential to destabilize the Islam/Christian bifurcation by generating conversions for love. The boy's "girdle knot" (*zünnar*) signifies the belt Christians and Jews of Galata had to wear as a marker of their religious difference. This belt then was a racializing demarcation, like the badge Jews had to wear in medieval Europe. This *zünnar* imagery follows Persian poetics of conversion, which influenced the Ottomans. In the *Divan* (Collected works) of the influential twelfth-century Persian poet Farid al-Din Attar, for example, the famous story of Shaykh San'an offers a conversion narrative through a Muslim man and a young Christian woman whose beauty threatens the man's piety: "She was a sun, but one that never sets ... / All who delved into the curls of that heart-ravisher / Chasing the image of her curls, tied on a *zünnar*."[18] In Mehmed's poem, instead of "a Christian girl," the Frank boy of the Galata is the radiant object of love with his golden girdle and dark hyacinth curls. His belt is metaphorically a knot of devotion for lovers; those who are not devoted to the boy's girdle knot are called heathens. This is paradoxical in terms of Islamic belief, since if a Muslim was devoted to the girdle knot that is Christianity, he would then lose his faith. What is more, the beautiful boy becomes Jesus himself through a reference to Jesus's miracle of bringing back the dead in the Islamic Sufi tradition.[19] Like Jesus, the boy's kiss has a life-bestowing, transformative power. The boy resurrects those who have been killed by his glances. Avni claims to recognize Christianity as the boy's religion only after he sees the similarities between the boy and Jesus, particularly between their life-giving lips/kisses. In Mehmed's poem, a Muslim man's desire for and encounters with the boy result in not reaching divine love but in diverting the man from it.[20] Instead of emphasizing the physical attraction for the religious other as a threat, Mehmed celebrates the adoration of the Christian boy, suggesting a conversion for love.

Following the boy/Jesus association, Avni moves to another comparison, one that is more explicitly political. He declares in the last couplet that this boy is the lord (şah) of Galata who will never submit to another lord, including the imperial lord of Istanbul. In these concluding lines, wherein the speaker addresses himself, the poem puts pressure on the trope of the Christian boy; it brings forth, through Galata, an imperial game of domination between the Ottoman Empire and Christian Europe. Using the second-person pronoun, Avni reveals his own identity as the ruler of Istanbul, making a connection between himself (the speaker) and the poet (Mehmed II). The conclusion, by using a reference to hierarchical political rule (i.e., şah/lord) and by separating the two spaces (Istanbul/Galata), emphasizes imperial and dominating motives after setting the territorial attachment of the boy to the Christian realm in the imperial capital. Avni surprisingly equates Galata with Istanbul by referring to both himself and the boy as "lord." The encounter or the first sight between the speaker and the boy in the first few lines is later described in terms of a religious encounter between a Muslim man and a Christian boy, which is finally depicted as an incommensurable, nonsubmissive, egalitarian encounter between rulers: an Ottoman man and a Frank boy. All of these three relations (personal, religious, political) in the poem are imagined through an erotic dynamic that is grounded in the boy's beauty, which is inseparably linked with his location, Galata.

The alluring Christian boy of Galata as a spatial embodiment appears in another poem by Mehmed, who this time inscribes Galata upon the body of the boy:

> Never would they desire paradise,
>   on Galata, those who lay eyes but once.

> Never would they praise a cypress,
>   on this pleasing hue, those who lay eyes once.
> I saw a Jesus, Frankish
>   he was to the ears and eyes,
> "Jesus anew" would say lips
>   of those who on him lay eyes once.
> How can they keep their mind and deed,
>   their faith and creed;
> They would turn heretic, O Muslims,
>   Those, on this Christian, lay eyes once.
> Never would they bethink of *kevser*,[21]
>   those who taste the pure wine he drinks;
> Never would they approach the mosque
>   those, on his church, lay eyes once.
> All those would know, Avni,
>   a heathen he was,
> On his girdle and cross
>   those who lay eyes but once.[22]

Avni begins by setting a dichotomy between Galata and the Islamic paradise (*firdevs*): those who see Galata but once would never again dream of paradise. In his comparison, Avni positions Galata and its resident, the Frankish boy, as superior to the Islamic paradise and its inhabitants. Further, the two contrasted spaces are gendered: *firdevs* as the space of houris (virgin women in paradise) and Galata as the space of boys. Although the poem begins with a focus on Galata, Mehmed quickly blends this space with the boy by suddenly shifting his poetic gaze from Galata toward the boy's pleasing body in the rest of the poem: those who see his pleasing form, so worthy of adoration, would not look for the paradisiacal cypress tree.

The poem scripts qualities of Galata upon the boy's body. His body, with its distinct clothes, looks, and accent is presented as, to use Henri Lefebvre's term, a "spatial body," a body with gestures, accents, clothing, fashion, and style that thus carries spatial markers. It is "a body so conceived, as produced and as the production of a space, [that it] is immediately subject to the determinants of that space."[23] The beautiful boy is not only a product of the space, he also produces that space, and through this transference and extension of the space to the body, he becomes the embodiment of a Christian space with churches, girdles, cross pendants, wine, and love; he becomes an alternative to the Islamic heaven. The slightest gaze upon his body would risk one's religious orientation because it dangerously contains all temptations. Those who see him or hear his beautiful voice and his Frengi accent would think the boy is Jesus himself or that Jesus the Prophet came to life with the kiss of this Jesus boy from Galata. Reminiscent of the Jesus/boy analogy in the previous poem, the beautiful boy in this poem is explicitly called Jesus (Isa). The poem leaves ambiguous whether the real name of this boy is Jesus (a common name in Islamicate cultures) or this is a metaphor to connect him to Jesus. Either way, his beauty, his life-giving lips, and his alluring body are all so irresistible that Muslims who see this beautiful boy but once would lose their religion, and those who drink from his cup would never dream of the *kevser* (holy fountain of wine in paradise). Besides his lips, his cup, and his wine, the church he attends has a converting power, as those who see "his church" would never go back to their mosque.

The last couplet actualizes this risk of conversion. One reading can be that those who saw the girdle around his waist and the cross around his neck would know that the boy was a Frankish heretic. Yet here the girdle (*zünnar*) and the cross (*çelipa*) can be attributed to the speaker Avni as well. The lack of gendered pronouns in the Turkish language adds double meaning to the couplet. Turkish is an inflectional language; the possessive meaning is conveyed through the personal endings, which are identical for the second- and third-person singular. It is thus not clear whose waist and neck are referred to in these lines (*belun u boynunda zünnar u çelipa*: girdle and cross on the waist and neck of his/yours): whether Avni refers to the girdle and the cross of the boy who is a heathen or refers to himself as the direct addressee in the second-person singular, wearing the girdle and the cross on his own waist and neck. In the case of addressing himself, Avni seems to have converted in the process of gazing upon and depicting the body of the boy, becoming precisely the Christian heathen he warned about throughout the poem. The conditionality and the gaze emphasized through repetition of *gören* (*gör*: to see; *gören*: one who sees) first makes the boy the object of the erotic gaze and then morphs Avni into the converted object of the gaze. The boy as the object of the poetic gaze has now become the subject who has converted the poet. Avni transgressed and transformed because he laid eyes on the boy but once!

Desiring and dominating the other runs the risk of changing the self. It is important to note that in both poems, Mehmed's poetic persona is not only that of a poet but also that of the sultan of the empire. As I explored elsewhere, he was often associated with Alexander the Great and Julius Caesar in both Ottoman and European writings, challenging the Ottoman/European binary of the early modern period.[24] After taking Constantinople, Mehmed declared himself the new Roman Emperor. He envisioned Istanbul as the Roman capital flourishing through both Eastern and Western institutions and architecture and as the place where Muslim, Christian, and Jewish communities would cohabit. He fashioned a polycultural, polyglot, polyreligious empire from a Roman model: he patronized Italian artists by bringing them to Istanbul; he designed Topkapı Palace, the new imperial seat, as a synthesis of Persian, Turkic, Byzantine, and Italian traditions; and he designed medals depicting him as a Roman emperor. (After Mehmed, whose reign marked the emergence of a polity bridging the so-called East and West, the Ottoman sultans claimed as their titles Caesar [*kayser*], emperor, and universal monarch to reflect their imperial dominance over both Asia and Europe, both Islamic and Christian worlds.) As a poet, Mehmed, the emperor and the ruler of "the promised city" Constantinople, illustrates how he imagines his domination over Christendom by depicting it through the body of a European Christian boy.[25] In his two Galata poems, the territory and the body become inseparable. While the poems express some anxiety about religious conversion as a result of adoration of the Christian boy, Mehmed's gaze upon Galata, his objectification of that space through its embodiment in the beautiful boy, orients his readers' desire, and his own, toward this space and the bodies that inhabit it. Obviously, for Mehmed, the conquest was not just a military domination, it was also a process that was carnal and imaginary.

Mehmed's representation of European lands through the beautiful boy, who both inhabits and represents Galata and tempts Istanbul to convert, became emblematic during the Ottoman expansion further into European territories in the following century, when Aşık Çelebi wrote his "Ode to the Danube." The famous sixteenth-century poet Revani also described Galata and its pleasures through the beautiful boy of Galata:

> Do not favor the bright wine cup, if you are joyous;
> But raise your cup towards Galata, if you are wise.
> Those who wish to see Frank lands in the Roman realm,
> On the city of two beauties, always lay your eyes.
> Were you to see those Frank boys but once, O Sufi,
> Never would you cast an eye on the houris in paradise.
> The new moon met Pleiades in the heavens, I say,
> When the beauties sail the skiffs set toward the sea.
> These beloved infidel boys despoil the faith;
> Beware, O Muslims, go not near the church.
> Heaven is that beauty's shining palace, wherein the sun
> Opens a window to the world to see the beauteous.
> Boys and girls, O Revani, at every corner eyes can see,
> Never do they desire Paradise, those who enter here but once.[26]

Revani's beloved boy from Galata is a Christian European youth who eclipses not only Muslim beloveds but also the beautiful houris: "Were you to see those Frank boys but once, O Sufi, / Never would you cast an eye on the houris in paradise." Like Mehmed's gendering of the two spaces, Revani also relates houris to the Islamic paradise and the beloved Frankish boy to the worldly space of Galata, which he depicts as an extension of Istanbul. Istanbul is "a rose with two colors" (*rana*), a city with two beauties, with two parts, the Ottoman and the European. One part is associated with the imperial palace, Muslims, and paradise populated with houris; the other part is where churches, Christians, and boys are accommodated. And like Mehmed, Revani orients his desiring gaze in the direction of Galata by putting the beautiful Frank boy at the center of its horizon. This orientation is most clear with the movement of "gazing" or "heading toward" in the lines ending with the rhyming "*yana*" (toward, to, on the side of): to "gaze," "lay eyes on," "look at" the direction of the city, houris, the world, and paradise (lines 2, 4, 10, 12); and to "go," "direct," "head to the direction of" the sea and the church (lines 6 and 8). In this sense, the poem creates a movement, a flow of desires, gazes, and bodies from Istanbul toward Galata on the horizon.

However, the horizon in these representations is tied up with anxiety about conquest and conversion. The boy is both the object of the poetic gaze and the potential subject who will master the poet or "despoil the faith." Similarly, the churches are both desirable structures that house the Christian boys and fear-inducing sites of religious conversion. The Sufi conception of love metaphorically conveyed through the boy as a pathway toward the divine and heavenly reward (as cupbearers in paradise alongside houris) is materialized through the celebratory appraisal of the boy of Galata. While the Christian boy generates desire, he is nevertheless a dangerous temptation on the path to the divine. In the Islamicate poetic tradition, such unconsummated passion for the boy is not a transgression, as Khaled El-Rouayheb points out through his analysis of early modern discussions of the saying attributed to the Prophet: "He who loves passionately and is chaste [variants add: 'and conceals his secret'] and dies, dies a martyr."[27] Platonic, chaste love for an unattainable boy therefore promises paradise immediately after death as a martyr. Yet the Galata boy in the abovementioned poems rather seems a medium that is too dangerous to figure as the resistible object of love because even gazing upon him makes one forget the Islamic paradise. Love for this boy, and therefore for Galata, may result in a heretical conversion, not the promised martyrdom. The encounter with the other is never pure; it is always infectious. The constitution of the self in opposition to the other necessarily risks adoring and becoming the other, ending up with a self that is the extension of the other. The cautionary tale in these poems thence goes astray through the voyeuristic depiction of the boy. In these poems, Galata with its beautiful boy complicates dichotomous pairings of the subject/object, self/other, desire/anxiety, metaphoric/material, Islam/Christian, and Ottoman/European.

The spatial nature of these poems also mirrors a political effect of the Ottoman Empire's orientation toward Europe, which is poetically framed as a desire to dominate Galata. Ottoman advancement, particularly from its foundation at the turn of the fourteenth century to the early seventeenth century, was mainly toward the West (alongside some eastern campaigns to guarantee domination in Asian and African territories); in the sixteenth century, Ottoman armies reached as far as Vienna in Europe. Istanbul was now in the East, compared to other western territories under Ottoman rule. Facing the West from Istanbul, the Ottoman literary-political gaze was on beautiful European boys, revealing the homoerotics of imperial expansion and religious conversion. European Christendom as the object of imperial desire and westbound ambitions was signified by Galata, the West in the East, the Frangistan in Istanbul. Galata became the horizon, the European destination toward which the Ottomans repetitively oriented their gaze. It was a horizon that brought together a mélange of desires and ambivalences, proximities and differences, hereness and thereness. Galata and its beautiful boys were, as Andrews and Kalpaklı have noted, geographically as close to Istanbul as a short boat ride, yet, in the eyes of poets, Galata was distant in character from the Muslim side of Istanbul; it was unreachable outside the lines of a poem. It teased with the promise of an erotic union and yet remained distant. It was a representation of what was far away, foreign, although it was a nearby neighborhood where boy love, pleasure, and wine was possible and promised. Its proximity, implicated in the very nature of desire, made it a paradise with boys on the horizon—an earthly paradise, a risky alternative, contesting a divine one in the shared imagination of Ottoman poets.

The Boy of the Danube

Aşık Çelebi imagined a similar horizon in his depiction of the river Danube as a boy under his eroto-imperial gaze. While Galata was located in the domestic imperial realm, the Danube was a threshold in Europe with the promise of conversion; it was a literal boundary yet to be crossed. The Danube was the northern border of the Ottoman presence in Europe for many centuries; it was a natural boundary between the Ottoman lands in Europe and Hungary before 1526 and thereby a space of Ottoman penetration into northern European territories. Many of the Euro-Ottoman wars, especially with the Austrian

Habsburgs—the Battle of Nicopolis (1396), the Battle of Mohács (1526), the Siege of Vienna (1529), the Battle of Vienna (1683), and the Great Turkish War (1683–1699)—took place around this river. The bordering states were exposed to Ottoman raids that resulted in the flow of slaves, prisoners, and captives into the Ottoman Empire. When central Hungary became an Ottoman province in 1541, a more institutionalized and regulated flow of boys into the empire as slaves began.[28] Aşık Çelebi's evocation of conquest, enslavement, conversion, and boys in this space refers to this history of abductions.

Aşık Çelebi was not alone in associating the Danube with boys in the early modern period. Writing two decades after Aşık Çelebi, Mustafa Ali of Gallipoli invoked the circulation of boys around the river in his cataloguing of servant boys based on their ethnic background (which I showed in chapter 1). Let us recall his remarks: "The people of Rumelia, and the nations of various natural qualities along the shores of the Danube, are pure at heart and clean of disposition. In particular, their beardless boys embody the perfection of courtesy, along with their beauty and attractiveness, for some twenty years; the appearance of the cheek down and fuzz when their beard begins to grow does not muddy the limpid water of their elegance and delicacy. Their natures are luminous."[29] Rumelia was a reference to the Roman (Byzantine) lands: that is, the European territories under Ottoman control. By praising Rumelian boys as ideal slaves, Mustafa Ali evoked the Ottoman enslavement of boys in European lands and around the shores of the Danube that had taken place since the mid-fifteenth century. As discussed in the previous chapter, Mustafa Ali idealized and eroticized the boys in spaces around the Danube, describing and generating a desire for this space through its submissive beardless boys. Likewise, in Aşık Çelebi's poem to the Danube, he represented the submission of the river as the submission of the boys. Danube is dynamic, out of control, and resisting; hence, it needs to be taken under control like a boy. It needs to be transformed from being a heretic to becoming a Muslim; it needs to submit to the Ottoman ruler.

The beautiful Christian boys of the Danube and of Galata reveal eroticized imperial politics as they become the embodiments of spaces that promise a future on the horizon. The Ottoman homoerotic imagination of the transformative spaces embodied in the boy guides us to recognize European spatial representations produced in a period that did not have a strictly stabilized binary sex/gender system. Thus, it is important to resist dichotomous analyses. Cartographic representations produced in Western Europe also evoked a history of boys in their representations of certain spaces through boys. In what follows, I extend Aşık Çelebi's imagination of the Danube and Ottoman poets' imagination of Galata to an exploration of such cartographic representations that visually map these spaces through youthful male bodies to be abducted, tamed, and possessed. Cartographic boys reflect ongoing imperial contestations in liminal spaces between men in which the boy is an object of voyeuristic pleasure and colonial domination who performs a particular work of gender. The embodiments of boys reveal the homoerotics of imperial imagining, expansion, and domination.

The projection of early modern Euro-Ottoman contests for territory through the poetic boys of the Danube is represented in maps that have putatively literal, factual claims. In maps, youthful male bodies operate more explicitly in geopolitical agendas, since maps and mapmaking are forms of cultural poetics that contribute to the making of subjects, cultures, histories, and nations.[30] Tracing gendered embodiments on early modern maps, Valerie Traub notes of cartographic bodies that "what seems to be a superfluous aesthetic convention conveys a strategy of spatialization that brings significantly new ethnographic, racial, and gendered relations of knowledge into view."[31] Revealing a universalizing domestic heterosexuality through their placement of male-female pairs on cartographic grids, such maps, Traub suggests, inform us about the shift in sexual discourses in relation to race in Europe. Similarly, the male bodies and boys on maps, I suggest, function not simply as ornamental embellishments but as erotic forms of embodiment that associate particular bodies with particular spaces in accordance with imperial trajectories. In tracing cartographic boys specifically, I ask: Why have male embodiments on maps been invisible to scholars while female personifications on maps have attracted scholarly attention? What do boys attached to certain spaces perform on maps or in the "theaters of the world"?[32]

The placement of male bodies on European maps goes back to at least medieval world maps such as *mappae mundi* (maps of the world) and T-O maps (premodern world maps designed with the letter T inside an O). In these maps, each continent is often linked to one of Noah's three sons, either through inscription of their names or through placement of their bodies (fig. 2.2). In the early modern period, the attachment of bodies to territories, including the allegorical visualization of continents, began to shift sharply from male to female. This of course does not mean a total elimination of male embodiments on maps. For example, Jean Rotz's *Book of Hydrography* (c. 1542), a cartographic text presented to Henry VIII, has no female images, only male embodiments of territories. In Paolo Farinati's *Allegory of America* (1595), America is represented as a half-naked man looking at, adoring, and almost embracing the half-naked crucified image of Jesus (fig. 2.3). Charles Le Brun's *Les différentes nations de l'Amérique* shows America as a well-proportioned half-naked masculine man whose confident and commanding look is directed outside the painting: the direction of his look does not meet the onlooker's gaze and his

FIGURE 2.2. *Mappa Mundi*, 1459–1463. In Jean Mansel, *La Fleur des Histoires*. The University of Michigan Library. Author's photo.

well-proportioned, almost naked upper body is highlighted as an enticing object on the horizon (fig. 2.4). Continental differences and contestations are sometimes imagined in the frame of male competition and sexual aggression in human or animal form, as one can see in the frontispiece of *Speculum Orbis Terrae* by Gerard de Jode (fig. 2.5): each continent is represented by an animal, and each animal exhibits different degrees of aggression or passivity. Europe is

FIGURE 2.3. *Allegory of America*, Paolo Farinati, 1595. Ackland Art Museum.

FIGURE 2.4. *Les différentes nations de l'Amérique*, Charles Le Brun, 1674. The University of Michigan Library. Author's photo.

FIGURE 2.5. *Speculum Orbis Terrae*, Gerarde de Jode, 1578. The University of Michigan Library. Author's photo.

a horse, rearing up in a display of aggressive virility with a charged and muscular body and raised head, while Asia is a feminine camel in a tame posture with a submissively lowered head and softly curved body lines. These representations maintain men as the generic representation of humankind, harkening back to classical personifications and biblical accounts of the then-known world, yet they also indicate a picture of contemporary contests between male-personified territories that are gendered and eroticized.

Many other early modern maps include naked male bodies on their margins such as those of Atlas, putti, cherubim, or cupids. In some cases, they depict all-male parties. In Frederik de Wit's map, satyrs, boys, and adult men partake in festivities. Mostly naked men lie on the ground, their lightly covered loins and buttocks inviting an erotic gaze (fig. 2.6). More strikingly, we see a cartographic image of erotically illustrated men along with river gods in a map of the Rhine River (*Rhenus Fluviorum Europae Celeberrimus*) dedicated to Andreae Bickero in Willem Blaeu's *Theatrum Orbis Terrarum* (fig. 2.7). In this map, a row of putti holds coats of arms of the regions surrounding the river on the top left-hand side,

MAPPING BOYS ON THE HORIZON 99

FIGURE 2.6. Detail of a map by Frederik de Wit, 1670. The University of Michigan Library. Author's photo.

positioned outside the map proper, above the scale, and thus on the margin, as is Lady Justice, who is positioned next to the dedication and a coat of arms (probably Bickero's). On the bottom right-hand side is a party of naked men, boys, and Bacchus with a wine cup, surrounding the title of the map. The image of Bacchus associates the river with wine while attributing, alongside the river gods, mythological and erotic qualities to the river Rhine. The older man is accompanied by a young boy and this pair is faced by a man whose deliciously revealed rear attracts the viewer's attention (fig. 2.8). In the older man/younger boy coupling, the older man's crown and beard, denoting his older age and hierarchical superiority, contrasts with the boy's tenderness and secondary position in a master/minion, god/cupbearer matrix. More strikingly, the muscular buttocks of the man facing them (and their frontal view) captures attention, as the angle of his rear and the angle of the bottom of the container are parallel and are in the same proximity to the viewer. The image reveals male bodies, particularly the buttocks, as compellingly subject to the viewer's gaze in the mapped space of the Rhine.

In alignment with such cartographic male personifications and river imagery, the map *Danubius*, which also was published in Willem Blaeu's *Theatrum Orbis Terrarum*, provides an image that invites a bolder gaze upon naked male bodies, especially youthful ones, in association with the fluid river space. While the Rhine map offers voyeuristic pleasure via a mythical pederastic couple and the buttocks of a seemingly adult man, the map of the Danube strikingly places on

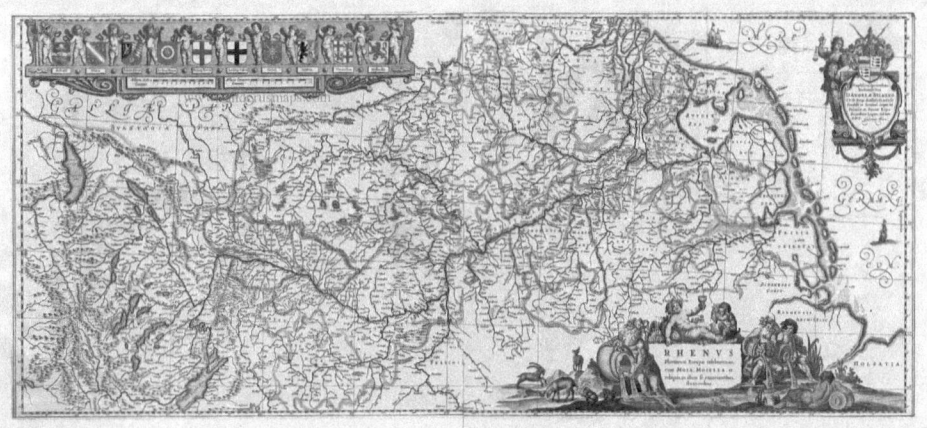

FIGURE 2.7. *Rhenus*, Willem Blaeu, 1635. In Blaeu, *Theatrum Orbis Terrarum*. The University of Michigan Library. Author's photo.

FIGURE 2.8. Detail from *Rhenus*.

FIGURE 2.9. *Danubius*, Willem Blaeu, 1636. In Blaeu, *Theatrum Orbis Terrarum*. The University of Michigan Library. Author's photo.

its horizon a bending youth as the object of not only erotic pleasure but also imperial contestation in the frame of the territorial contest between the Ottomans and Western Europeans over the Danube (fig. 2.9). The map shows the river Danube running from the Black Forest of southern Germany to the Black Sea. On the top right-hand side of the map is the title *Danubius, fluvius Europa maximus, a fontibus ad ostia, cum omnibus fluminibus, ab utroque latere, in illum defluentibus* (Danubius, Europe's prime river, from its source to its end, with all the rivers connecting with it from both sides). The title is inscribed between two couples. On the left is a Christian European couple, a king holding a sword and a woman holding a shield bearing the image of Jesus on the cross. On the right is an Ottoman couple, a turbaned sultan pointing his sword at the Europeans and a woman behind him who holds an incense burner as she steps on a cross (fig. 2.10). While the title of the map represents the map itself, the content of the map, inscribed as the most important and the largest (*maximus*) river of Europe and its surrounding territories, the drawn swords indicate that the river is the object of contestation between Christian Europeans and Ottomans. And like the Danube as a boy in Aşık Çelebi's poem, the boy as the Danube in this map is central to this territorial quarrel between men in projecting the homoerotics of abductions and conversions.

The map of the Danube highlights the significance of the river in the political and military struggles in the region from the fourteenth to the late eighteenth centuries, especially in the rivalry between the Ottomans and the Austrian Habsburgs for the control of the Danube. The locations represented on this map are the European Christian territories that were under Ottoman

FIGURE 2.10. Detail from *Danubius*.

threat, if they were not already dominated; they were the sites of multiple wars and flows of people as slaves and captives. The contemporary contestations and conflicts in this space are evident on other maps as well. For example, Jodocus Hondius's map of the river, *Maximi Totius Europae Fluminis Danubii*, includes a cartouche with the assertive Hungarian Empire pointing at "Maximi" while the Ottoman sultan looks at him defensively. The river itself is the very real border separating the Ottoman realm from Christendom. Asian/European, Islamic/Christian binaries are more evident in Blaeu's *Danibius*; the emperor and the sultan are accompanied by female personifications of the continents. The emperor on the map is probably the Habsburg Holy Roman emperor protecting Christian Europe, which is allegorized as female-personified Europe, while the Ottoman sultan has Asia on his side, even though his territories also extended into Europe. The Danube began to represent Europe in the sixteenth century (as Rose Marie San Juan highlights in her argument about river gods attached to continents) and thus instantiated an East/West, Islam/Christendom divide that applied to the extent of the Ottoman Empire across Eurasia.[33]

Within this divide, the river in Blaeu's map of the Danube is personified with the group of river gods and boys in the cartouche, who provoke the question of continental belonging: Is the river Danube European or Ottoman/Asian? Or does it stand for a liminal space in between? Positioned above the scale, on the bottom left-hand side of the map, a party of naked men creates a contrast between the fully dressed Europeans and Ottomans in the upper right-hand cartouche, as they are symbolically attached to the river and territories represented (fig. 2.9). The men with beards are river gods. Such images were quite popular in visual representations of spaces. In the sixteenth century, there was a revival of river gods. Images and statues of these gods were installed in and around buildings, fountains, gardens, festivities, political propaganda, and triumphal entries. In her exploration of personifications of cities and nature through these figures, Claudia Lazzaro suggests that "river gods became vehicles for contemporary notions about natural science, artistic creativity, and political hegemony.... Renaissance artists invented new river god types for local rivers, which allowed them to signify not just aspects of nature—gendered, animate, abundant—but also particular places and together with other personifications of nature, a region in microcosm.... Unlike characters charged with telling a story, river gods demonstrated artistic license, but artistic style was also inflected with place."[34] It is therefore not surprising to see the image of river gods on a map of a river that is personified through these images. In the map of the Danube, the river gods are accompanied not by nude female figures but by boys who mirror the territory the rivers flow through. The river gods are "inflected with" the Danube; the boys surround them as the embodiment of the territories represented, evoking a history of abduction, enslavement, and conversion of boys in this space.

By generating a gaze upon these bodies, the map objectifies not only the territory but also youthful male bodies. What is unique about this map is that at the center of the male party in the cartouche a boy is bending over, whose light-enhanced rear draws the viewer's attention. This particular boy, who we see only from behind, tells the story of the spaces and the territorial quarrel represented above. Water flows from a large container the river gods hold as the boy at the center holds another container. His rear and the O-shaped bottom of the container he holds are contrasted with the frontal view of the rest of the men. This positioning creates an analogy between body and vessel, between the bottom of the boy and the bottom of the vessel. As Patricia Rubin posits in her consideration of beautiful bottoms in visual representations and costume books, the buttocks of young men "provided striking silhouettes that could capture attention. They act to energize, if not also eroticize the act of beholding."[35] In fact, as the object of the viewer's gaze and voyeuristic pleasure, the boy in this map, with his peculiar charm and pose, eroticizes the act of beholding. Put into relation with the withdrawn phallic swords on the map, the bending boy with his penetrable bottom becomes an object of contestation between men for sexual and terrestrial domination.

Moreover, the naked party in the map is located at the Adriatic Sea, as if they are pouring the water of the sea that borders central Europe and Italy, a space that sodomy was attributed to in the early modern period.[36] Among them stands the bending vessel-bearing boy who reveals a distinct Ganymede effect. In his work on the Renaissance images of Ganymede, James Saslow shows that

FIGURE 2.11. *Ganymede Serving Nectar to the Gods*, Parmigianino, 1530–1540. Private Collection, London.

an increasing number of representations of the iconic boy portrayed Ganymede from the back. In Parmigianino's *Ganymede Serving Nectar to the Gods*, for example, a nude Ganymede holding a cup is viewed from the rear. The angle highlights Ganymede's buttocks, thighs, and back (fig. 2.11). As Saslow suggests, the image of Ganymede from the rear (*da tergo*) and Parmigianino's other drawings of nude men seen from behind became a prototype for many images.[37] *Danubius*'s cartographic boy, bending over naked, evokes this formal conception of naked Ganymede seen from behind among naked gods. Indeed, because of his service as cupbearer, Ganymede appears as the water-pouring cup carrier Aquarius and hence the constellation in astrological depictions.[38] The Latin writer Hyginus, for instance, noted in his *Fabulae* that "Ganymede, son of Assaracus, [was made] into Aquarius of the twelve signs."[39] Symbolized mostly with a water pitcher, Aquarius/Ganymede is therefore evident among the gods in this river imagery as a cupbearer or water-bearer to the gods who are pouring water into the river. By centering the boy who stands alone, the map uniquely transforms the myth into everyday reality, producing a Ganymede effect by blending mythical embodiments with the contemporary political contestations. Like Ganymede, this boy is to be seized.

Given that boys from the territories represented on this map were historically vulnerable to abduction, the cartographic boy of the Danube can be read as an expression of their vulnerabilities. The Ganymede-like boy of the map, the bending bottom, becomes implicated in the Euro-Christian and Ottoman wars upon European territories surrounding the river. Similar to the poetic boy of Galata who crosses East/West, Islam/Christian, metaphoric/material separations in the cross-cultural encounter, the cartographic boy of the Danube creates an ambiguous boundary between Europe and Asia, between the European and the Ottoman. Yet he simultaneously challenges this separation through the imaginary, mythic space of the flowing river. The river is a divisive border that separates spaces, yet it is also a connector making crossings possible, if not inevitable. The boundary it creates is thus artificial and malleable. The boy is attached to a fluid border and its surrounding territories represented on the map; as an embodiment of territory, he engenders an erotic gaze on the part of the viewer. From a Western European perspective, his centrality marks him as the object of the drawn swords between the European man and the Turk, as the very embodiment of the contested territory. The boy's naked body becomes a disputed terrain that the imperial cartographer charted to project the quarrel between Western Europe and the Ottomans. He is yet to be gained by one power. Will the white men save the white boy from the Muslim Ottomans?

Gazing Boys on the Horizon

These poetic and cartographic representations offer sexualized conceptions of territory and territorialized conceptions of sexuality by erotically associating beautiful boys with the spaces represented on the horizon—whether of the Danube or Galata. This sort of gendering challenges the conventional imagery of land as female that scholars who focus on European colonialism in the Americas have especially emphasized. A shift in perspective toward Mediterranean relations illuminates diverse forms of gendered embodiments in early modern imaginations. Here, by focusing on spatial representations that responded to Ottoman expansionism in Europe, I do not suggest that the boy as a metaphor for territory is a substitute for the virgin female who represents territory. Instead, I suggest that we need to consider further what a boy's body does differently from the embodiment of a female or an adult male. On the objectification of different genders and races in contemporary arts, Peggy Phelan proposes that "sexual objectification of men allows for an ascendancy toward 'power' while sexual objectification of women almost always implies a degradation. This is absolutely and crucially connected to how men and women are seen within a patriarchal ideology of heterosexuality and sexual difference."[40] How about when it is the boy—not a woman and not yet a man—who is objectified?

In exploring this, I find helpful to return to Michel Foucault's remarks on the ancient Greek aesthetics of the boy's body:

> In the sphere of sexual ethics, it was the juvenile body with its particular charm that was regularly suggested as the "right object" of pleasure. And it would be a mistake to think that traits were valued because of what they shared with feminine beauty. They were appreciated in themselves or in their juxtaposition with the signs and guarantees of a developing virility. Strength, endurance, and spirit also formed part of this beauty; hence it was good in fact if exercises, gymnastics, competitions, and hunting expeditions reinforced these qualities, guaranteeing that this gracefulness would not degenerate into softness and effeminization. The feminine ambiguity that would be perceived later (and already in the course of antiquity, even) as a component—more exactly, as the secret cause—of the adolescent's beauty, was, in the classical period, more something from which the boy needed to protect himself and be protected. Among the Greeks there was a whole moral aesthetics of the boy's body; it told of his personal merit and of that of the love one felt for him. Virility as a physical mark should be absent from it; but it should be present as a precocious form and as a promise of future behavior: already to conduct oneself as the man one has yet become.[41]

Foucault's proposal aligns with Phelan's argument in that it situates the celebration of the boyish bodies in the patriarchal ideology that associated woman and femininity with degradation. Masculine power is still the ideal in representations of the boy. Indeed, the boys in the spatial representations I have traced so far similarly suggest strength, endurance, and spirit in the manly, masculine realm of territorial conflicts. (Note the strikingly muscular body of the boy in *Danubius*.) While the boy in these representations was objectified, he points toward a promise of virility by actively converting the poet or by pouring water into the river as a companion to a god. While female personifications of territory such as America as a woman signified gendered forms of possessing and violating a passive land, the boy as a spatial metaphor highlights the dynamic masculine competition between men and a desire to own the space/boy in future. However, the boy's vulnerability withholds power and a degree of recognized presence. Just like the Danube or Galata, and unlike most female-gendered lands, the boy is not fully tamed, not fully domesticated, but shows signs of resistance to submission. He thereby stands for a future promise to be achieved: his possession depends on the one who will "win" the boy in the sense of both courtly love and imperial conquest and domination. Like the flowing water—of the Danube or the body of water that separates Galata from Istanbul—the boy as an object of voyeuristic pleasure and of future conversion thus reveals the cultural work and function of gender and sex by standing on the horizon of these cross-cultural, transformative spaces.

The boy of the Danube in Aşık Çelebi's poem or in Blaeu's atlas and of Galata in Mehmed's poems has an ephemeral, fleeting status in the fluid space of cross-cultural encounters. His juvenile body with its peculiar charm marks him as the "right object" of masculine pleasure—a pleasure that consists of imperial gazing and gaining. The spatial boy beckons from the horizon: the boy is there, yet he is mythical by virtue of his positioning among classical gods. As a territorial embodiment who affects the meaning-making of the space and as an object of homoerotic desire and gaze, the boy thus generates a desire to reach out and seize what is on the horizon. The conqueror of Istanbul, Sultan Mehmed II, objectified Galata, putting it on the horizon of the poem through the medium of the cypress-like Christian boy. He oriented the poet's and the reader's gaze and desire toward this specific space, Frangistan, a microcosmic Europe in Istanbul, by repeating the act of seeing. The Danube, the symbolic threshold in Europe, was also imagined through mythic beautiful boys giving life to it by feeding its waters. Ultimately, these two spaces necessitate an affective distant encounter: the boys on the spatial horizons are *there*—on the banks of the Danube or in Galata—yet they are never reachable; they always escape from a touch in these representational spaces through their racialized and mythic aspects (whether as a Christian infidel or a Ganymede). They slide between borders; they appear only through a gaze from a specific point and stance. That gaze, that desire, is still not independent from anxiety about conversion and submission, which are embedded in the boy's transforming, converting, yet-to-be-adult male body among imperial contestations between men.

What about the boy in literary or historical English abductions? While I have so far analyzed literary and visual examples in the historical context of Ottoman abductions of boys, in the next chapter I turn to abducted boys and their spatializations in England to put them in counterpoint to the Ottoman context of abduction practices, discourses, and representations. Hence, the concluding chapter to this part will trace shifts in abduction practices and in the figurations of abducted boys in a period when England began its relations with the Ottoman Empire, became a mercantile player in the Mediterranean, and moved toward establishing an empire.

3

(In)Visible Boys in English Abductions

Around the same time as the appearance of Marlowe's beautiful boy Leander, abducted in the Hellespont, another boy appeared who was abducted in the Mediterranean world: the Indian boy of Shakespeare's *A Midsummer Night's Dream* (ca. 1594–1596), a lovely "sweet" boy who was "stolen from an Indian king" and placed in the fairy site of the Athenian woodland (2.1.22–23). The Indian boy does not have a name or any lines to speak and there are no stage directions for him in either quarto (1600) or folio (1623) editions. Yet he is at the center of the dramatic conflict that engenders the topsy-turvy world of Shakespeare's *Dream* that starts by "stir[ring] up the Athenian youth to merriment" (1.1.13). This chapter revisits the beautiful abducted boy of Shakespeare's *Dream* in the cultural poetics of imagining the Mediterranean with beautiful youths and places this eroticized, exoticized, and racialized boy in the early modern context of abductions and conversions of boys in the Mediterranean.

In the previous chapters I traced Mediterranean abductions—both historical and representational—and suggested that the Ottoman practices and discourses of eroticizing, abducting, and refashioning the exotic boys find their resonances in English imaginaries, either in the form of anti-sex condemnations as in travelogues or in the form of celebratory homoerotic teasing such as Marlowe's. In this chapter, I argue that the portrayal on the English stage of an abducted Indian boy from the last decade of the sixteenth century not only recalls Ottoman abductions but also echoes English abductions of "other" boys. On the increasing number of representations of circulating children in early modern English sources, Joseph Campana notes that "perhaps it is no surprise that Shakespeare's drama, which was produced in an era fond of stories of changeling children, including boys, would find such interest in the mobility, transferability, and exchangeability of children."[1] Such "traffic in children," he suggests, mirrored the economy of the child, monetary and otherwise.[2] These transferences, however, were not limited to the local economy of children but included widespread global exchanges and trafficking.

Scholars have persuasively demonstrated that the Indian boy reveals dynamics of cross-cultural mercantilism and emergent racial and colonial discourses that were circulating in early modern England, but the homoeroticism embedded in such discourses often goes unacknowledged. Margo Hendricks's examination of the play, for example, suggests that the Indian boy and "the discursive space that is India" "[mark] the play's complicity in the racialist ideologies being created by early modern England's participation in imperialism."[3] For Ania Loomba, the boy "evokes the merchandise of the east, the riches plundered from the Americas, and the human traffic of Africa and the Indies."[4] The Indian boy is thus "both the commodity-form that enables, and the dream of colonial possession that signposts, the transition from feudalism to capitalism"; he is the "personification of colonial possession."[5] For Loomba, the otherness of the boy at the intersection of colonialism, mercantilism, gender, and familial structure serves to trace "fantasies of racial otherness" imprinted "on the relations between men and women."[6] These fantasies, I suggest, can also be traced through relations between men and boys framed in a hierarchical erotic matrix. As an object of desire, the Indian boy calls for an exploration of the homoerotics of colonial and racial fantasies.

Furthermore, while the Indian boy surely exhibits the racialist imperial ideologies at work in England's emerging relations in Asia, India is not the sole discursive space of exchanges in the play, as Hendricks proposed. The Indian boy emerged during England's increasing participation in cross-Mediterranean traffic. While scholars have made India, as one of the evoked settings in the play, contemporary, the Mediterranean setting remains frozen in time, specifically in the play's Greco-Roman context. What, then, is the role of the Mediterranean setting in the imaginary of the abduction of the Indian boy in Athens in Shakespeare's time? The Indian boy in fact undergoes two separate displacements: one by Titania, who, Puck alleges, stole the boy as a changeling from an Indian king before the dramatic action, and the other by the faery king Oberon, which occurs in the course of the play, not in the spicy air of India but in the wild forest of Athens in the broader Mediterranean. The Indian and Mediterranean settings that enable the two abductions suggest different interpretations. Titania's maternal, reproductive, mercantile language in depicting the boy's abduction in India is not to be conflated with Oberon's homoerotic motive in the Mediterranean, a space with a long history of being associated with pederastic homoeroticism. By taking seriously the setting of the play, which strictly speaking is in Athens and the surrounding woods, I ask: What is the role of the Indian boy in the play with regard to the Mediterranean politics of abducting boys and the erotic alternatives that this space offered to sexual regimes at home? In the play, all the parties come together to celebrate the coercive marriage between the ruler Theseus and the captured Hippolyta. The portrayal of the Indian boy in erotic terms in this larger Mediterranean space marks not only reproductive heteroerotics but also homoeroticism embedded in imperial objectifications and abductions.

Building on this Mediterranean context, in what follows, I begin by offering a history of transported boys in England within the eroticized master/servant power dynamics. In contextualizing the figuration of the Indian boy as a gendered, aestheticized, and eroticized template in a homoerotic matrix, my focus in the first part of the chapter is especially on the "other" boys in England—whether Indian, African, Native American, or Asian—who were abducted and transported from their native lands by Englishmen.[7] There was a long history of appropriating boys in England for particular kinds of servitude, such as medieval oblation, through which the monasteries took boys from their families. In the early modern period, boys were seized for cathedral choirs and play companies seized them for the stage. Masters also seized boys to become their apprentices.[8] Such coercive seizures of boys became a model for colonial assimilations in the New World, as Emily Bryan notes: "The Virginia Company looked to the English stage and the English university for methods of acculturation when subduing the native population."[9] In the early seventeenth century, theatrical and colonial warrants allowed Englishmen to abduct indigenous children from their homes to train them either for performance on stage or to be made English.[10] And some of these boys, like those abducted from Africa or South Asia, were brought to England. As I suggested before, while boyhood in the early modern period was an ephemeral social, erotic, gender category for English youth, it lingered permanently for "other" boys who would always be boys due to their racialized subservient status in the English hierarchy. After a brief history of these "other" boys brought to England, I return to Shakespeare's Indian boy to show how Shakespeare's imagining of the boy in a homoerotic Mediterranean matrix exemplifies, probes, and challenges English practices of abducting boys from foreign lands as commodities.

"Indian" Boys in England

The abduction plot in *A Midsummer Night's Dream* brings to the fore the presence of abducted boys in England shortly after the 1580s, when the Ottomans granted England trade privileges in the Mediterranean. By 1610, the English had begun to have substantial control over Mediterranean trade and piracy activities.[11] In fact, English piracy became a problem for the Ottomans, who in 1607 sent an emissary to London for the first time with a formal complaint about English corsairs. During the period of these cross-Mediterranean activities and England's well-documented investments in North America, Asia, and Africa, England also participated in the trafficking of exotic boys.[12] In *Black Lives in the English Archives*, Imtiaz Habib documented 448 records of individuals identified as black in legal, taxation, medical, and civic archives for the period 1500 to 1677. As he writes, these people first "started arriving initially as curiosities, the residue of their function as market commodities, through which they became items of miscellaneous consumption in the English domestic market."[13] During the late sixteenth and early seventeenth centuries, Oriental, Indian, Moor, African, and Saracen boys appeared in English representations and on the streets of London as servants, grooms, henchmen, pages, weavers, entertainers, and divers.[14]

Englishmen first carried off boys in order to train, convert, and assimilate them for future international policies and for personal service. A Guinean king's son, Dederj, for instance, was brought from West Africa to London and baptized as John in 1611 in order to strengthen trade relations.[15] This abduction was, as Habib notes, "the auspicious beginning of the training of an international African diplomat."[16] An increasing number of abducted, transported, and converted boys also appeared as household servants. Sir Walter Raleigh transported many boys—including an eleven-year-old Guyanese boy, Charles, and the Native American boys Leonard Ragapo, Harry Pedro, and Christopher, among others—from the New World to England as servants and exotic objects. The chaplain of the East India Company, Patrick Copland, brought a youth from India in 1614, who was later baptized with the name Peter Pope. Robert Cecil had a black servant named Fortunatus. In 1618, the Virginia Company got a government warrant to abduct Native American children to educate them. Englishmen captured "Moor" boys in order to convert them.[17] Since slavery was not recognized in English law until 1677, the year a London court declared Africans to be slaves for the first time, these people were legally unrecognized, hence rendered invisible in law, as Habib observes.[18] However, their nonwhite bodies were visible enough to cause trouble for the English, as is evident in the decrees of 1596 and 1601 of Elizabeth I that sought to expel black people from England because, as the 1596 decree stated, "there are of late divers Blackmoores brought into the realme, of which kinde of people there are all ready here to manie."[19] Yet royal decrees could not stop this circulation; colonial agents, aristocrats, and merchants continued to keep servants from other lands.

The abducted boys in London were both invisible in legal terms and visible enough to appear in representations, and they began to appear more frequently in literary works, in the theater, in paintings, and on bookshop signs.[20] As Kate Lowe states, their "arrival in Europe as slaves meant systematic erasure of all the more significant aspects of their past, starting with their names, their languages, their religions, their families and communities, and their cultural practices, but it did not erase their appearance."[21] Taking into consideration the appearance of black boys in particular, I ask: How were they selected?

Their youthful bodies seemed to have operated crucially in their abductions. An English ship, for instance, captured "two young Moors not above 13 or 14 yeares of age" in 1636 because of "tenderness of their years."[22] The director of the Royal Adventurers, a mercantile company that traded along the west coast of Africa, instructed the company's ship captains "to buy 15 or 20 lusty Negers of about 15 yeares of ages, bring them home with you for London."[23] What are the ramifications of "lusty Negers" being carried unwillingly to England? Why did the company want to have "lusty" young boys at the age of fifteen? Given one definition of "lusty" as "pleasing, pleasant" in terms of appearance or beauty, these boys clearly should be seen as beautiful and pleasing to the eye. "Lusty" in connection to "lustful" also refers to "full of desire" and "full of lust or sexual desire."[24] While these definitions signify the sexual and energetic character of the lusty boys referred in the account, another *OED* definition puts bodily strength at the center of the term, defining it as "full of healthy vigour."[25] Evoking this signification, in his 1578 *Thesaurus linguae Romanae & Britannicae*, Thomas Cooper used "strong, lusty: in health" as synonyms in his definition of the Latin word "*firmus*," and youthful energy and a healthy body were also implicated in his use of "lusty": "That beautie and that strength that was in youth they had lost: or they had lost all their valiant and lusty young man."[26] Following on these definitions, literary deployments of the term often emphasized

FIGURE 3.1. *Laura Dianti*, Titian, circa 1523. Collezione H. Kisters, Kreuzlingen. ARTstor.

the sexual signification. Marlowe's *Hero and Leander* used "lusty" to refer to not only Neptune's strength but also to his excessive desire for Leander: "The lusty god embrace'd him, called him 'love'" (651). Iago, evoking Othello's sexual energy in expressing his fear that he had been cuckolded by Emilia, suspects that "the lusty Moor / Hath leap'd into my seat" (2.1.282–83). Paul Rycaut called the beautiful servant boys in the Ottoman court "comely lusty youths" as he wrote about their erotic relations.[27] All of these significations—pleasing, energetic, youthful, strong, sexual, desirable, and desiring—indicate that the youthful *body* of "Negers of about 15 yeares of ages" mattered in their selection by the Englishmen.

One venue where their bodies are most detectable is visual culture, wherein the trope of the exotic boy became almost a subgenre in European portraiture of the early modern period. As England began to increasingly invest in economic expansion in Africa, the black servant role created in Dutch and Italian artworks such as Titian's *Laura Dianti* (c. 1523) and *Fabricius Salvaresius* (1558) migrated northward to England via Anthony van Dyck's *Marchesa Elena Grimaldi* (1623) and *Henrietta of Lorraine* (1634). They feature the form of a white female patron standing with a black servant (figs. 3.1 and 3.2).[28] These representations, as critics

FIGURE 3.2. *Henrietta of Lorraine*, Anthony van Dyck, 1634. Kenwood House. ARTstor.

have observed, visually reveal the commodification of black bodies for voyeuristic pleasure by portraying the black servant as exotic commodity objects that served to illuminate the white colonial mastery and wealth of their mistresses.[29]

Before moving to my analysis of *Dream*'s Indian boy in this historical and representational context, I would like to bring into attention two visual examples in which the exotic boy stands with a white male patron. These two paintings heighten the domineering figuration of the colonial male agent in the abduction of boys. Anthony Van Dyck's *William Fielding, First Earl of Denbigh* (1633), for instance, strikingly shows an Indian boy with local dress, almost recasting Oberon's Indian boy and his desire to trace the wild forest with him (fig. 3.3).[30] The portrait, which represented Fielding's 1631 expedition to India,

(IN)VISIBLE BOYS IN ENGLISH ABDUCTIONS 115

FIGURE 3.3. *William Fielding, First Earl of Denbigh*, Anthony Van Dyck, 1633. National Gallery.

creates a dominant/submissive bond between the white master and the Indian servant. The boy in Indian dress, standing in front of a coconut tree with a parrot in it, embodies oriental exoticism and space. As Kim F. Hall observes, in this portrait the boy "is subtly associated with foreign commodities.... [He] stands at the site of riches and seems to offer more."[31] Like Prospero's Caliban or (potentially) Oberon's future henchman, the boy guides Fielding to his native land, as is evident in his hand gesture. The Indian boy's turban and robe create a contrast with Fielding's English attire. Fielding's bulky body, his parted legs, and the frontal opening of his tunic and dangling girdle suggest his assertive masculinity. Fielding's masculine and military power, as symbolized by the phallic flintlock in his right hand, encompasses his dominance over the boy and the space he inhabits.

FIGURE 3.4. *Prince Rupert of the Rhine*, Daniel Mytens, circa 1658. Collection of the Duke of Brunswick-Lunebourg. WikiImages.

A similar, yet more explicit example of masterly authority over the exotic boy is evident in Daniel Mytens's portrait of Prince Rupert of the Rhine, who was the son of Elizabeth of Bohemia, hence the grandson of James I, the nephew of Charles I, and the cousin of Charles II. The prince was also the commander of the king's forces during the Civil War and was one of the founders of the Company of the Royal Adventurers of England Trading into Africa and of the Royal African Company. In Mytens's *Prince Rupert of the Rhine*, the prince stands with his black servant, who, according to Rupert's biographers, he captured when he commanded ships around Gambia and Guinea (fig. 3.4).[32] During one of his voyages, because of a conflict between Rupert's party and "a tribe of Mohammedan nomads," the boy's parents, who were presumably Muslim, left the boy behind and escaped the scene after Rupert's men shot their camel. Later, they demanded that the boy be returned, but the prince refused this request. Rupert considered this boy "as a New Yeares gift," according to a contemporary account of the incident, and kept "this little native hostage, who stayed with him until after his return to Europe."[33] This little boy, as Patrick Morrah notes, was not the only one the prince captured; Rupert brought other black boys home after his voyages. Evidently "his 'blackamores' added to the glamour of his reputation."[34] This glamorous reputation further contributed to the popularization of the practice of keeping black servants in England as the country was transforming into an empire. However, this little boy that Rupert abducted from his parents stands out as a special boy in the prince's life. Similar to Titania's maternal affection for her Indian boy, Rupert, some suggest, "treated him with an almost fatherly tenderness."[35] Rupert nevertheless disposed of the boy; he gave him to his cousin, who had him baptized and educated.[36] Obviously, these trafficked boys were easily transferable, despite their masters' and mistresses' claims of affection.

Interestingly, while the abducted African boy is highlighted in Rupert's biography, he had another "boy" in his life that finds more space and is referred to more often in the accounts about the prince: his dog, named Boy.[37] The dog was given to him by Lord Arundell, and according to an early account, "these dogs were so renowned that the Great Turk gave it in a particular instruction to his ambassador to endeavor the obliging of one of them."[38] The dog became an object of exchange like other boys, as his name also suggests, as though "boy" had become a reference term for exchanged goods, animals, and people.[39] During the Civil War, the prince's affection for Boy became a significant element of satirical pamphlets by the Puritan Roundheads (i.e., those fighting on the side of Parliament against the monarchy), who especially propagandized against Rupert by using his "unnaturally" close affection to Boy, which was ultimately killed during a battle in the Civil War.[40] Why was the dog named Boy? Srinivas Aravamudan argues that black servants and pets, particularly dogs, were equivalent displays of aristocratic splendor in seventeenth-century England and that "Africans seized for the slave trade were also transported to England and sold as pets and domestic servants."[41] In other words, boys were seen as domestic pets; they were dehumanized, thingified in the process of enslavement and put in a process of domestication. (In my discussion of the Indian boy below, I return to the imagery of the exotic boy-animal that also signals the roles of boys as grooms.) "Boy" is what united the stolen black child and the dog, which was an object of exchange, an object that even "the Great Turk" desired to own.

The dog's name thus signifies the boy as a transferable category, a circulating object, and as satirical pamphlets suggested, a subservient role that made him vulnerable to the master's sexual advances. One of the parliamentary pamphleteers described the relationship of Rupert and Boy in this way: "he [the dog] salutes and kisseth the Prince, as close as any Christian woman would, and the Prince salutes and kisseth him backe againe in favorily, as he would (I will not say any Alderman wife, but) any Court-Lady. . . . Then they lye perpetually, in one bed, sometimes the Prince upon the Dogg, and sometimes the Dogg upon the Prince."[42] As a once-favorite boy in the court of Charles I, the charismatic and handsome Prince Rupert, who never married, was attacked through an attribution to him of bestial sodomy.[43] Another pamphlet published in 1643, *An Exact Description of Prince Ruperts Malignant She-Monkey, a great Delinquent: Having approved herselfe a better servant, then his white Dog called* BOY, invoked a sexual relationship between the prince and a she-monkey who "was formerly some proud dame, that pulling up her cloathes, and setting her looking-glasse a good distance from her, would needs view her white belly in that imitating mirrour; whereupon the gods being angry at her obscene wantonnesse, did convert her into the shape of a lascivious she-monkey."[44] The pamphlet gives details of their relationship: "But let that passe, certain it is that the prince doth love this Monkey exceedingly; and the Monkey doth by all her gestures, and actions tempt the prince to lascivious desires ... and if he were anything effeminate as it is not to be doubted but he is foreward enough in expression of love as well as valour."[45] Similarly, in another pamphlet, the "effeminate" Rupert "had a minde to peep into the Monkeys black Art or Arse."[46]

Such accounts are part of the larger early modern discourse that linked sodomy and buggery. That is, transgressive sexual relations and bestiality were considered inseparable, as Edward Coke's title of a section makes it evident: "Of Buggery, or Sodomy," a section that includes same-sex intercourse, pederasty, and bestiality with a particular example of woman-baboon intercourse.[47] It is obvious in these accounts that Rupert's intimacy with the "white" dog Boy is sodomitical. So is his relationship with a she-monkey a form of buggery not only because of human-animal intercourse but also because of the blackness of the female monkey. Puritan reproach of female beauty, male effeminacy, anality, sodomy, and mimetic arts are all reflected in these pamphlets in relation to Rupert's "uncontrolled" lust during his time at Oxford.[48] These animals are called "servant" in the title, and their service is mainly to satisfy the sexual pleasures of the prince; the "BOY'" (scripted in capital letters) specifically evokes boy servants and sodomy. (The boy's replacement by a half-human, half-monkey creature in such accounts, furthermore, reminds us of the asinine Bottom, who replaces the Indian boy as an erotic focus for Titania in *Dream*, which I discuss below.) Although these writings were propaganda tools whose accusations cannot be taken at face value, the language they used is suggestive of the relationship between service and sexuality, slavery and dehumanization, race and animalization as they were mapped onto both animals and servant boys in the seventeenth century.

What does Rupert's touching of the boy in the portrait (fig. 3.4) suggest? While the image of the black boy being touched by female patrons was relatively common (as in the mistress's hand on the boy's shoulder in portraits by Titian or Van Dyck), to my knowledge, there is no other example of a white master/ black servant portrait that shows a physical, bodily connection in early modern English portraiture. This unique touch is significant for tracing further significations of the boy's body. While the boy's gaze at the level of Rupert's loins orients us toward Rupert, the baton Rupert holds urges the spectator to notice Rupert's grasp on the boy's head and the scenery outside the window, which offers a horizon of overseas trade and trafficking. The direction of the boy's adoring gaze contrasts with Rupert's confident look at the viewer. Rupert looks at our eyes; the boy, on the other hand, is dependent on Rupert. "The prince's dual gesture of one hand grasping the baton and one hand resting atop the black boy's head," Peter Erickson observes, "proclaims a dominance whose acceptance is signaled by the servant's adoring eyes."[49] Indeed, the boy's supplicating eyes mediate and direct the viewer's gaze toward the prince; in turn, Rupert's touch with an expansive grasp of the boy's head displays Rupert's recognition of and mastery over the boy. This offers, in Hall's words, "a standard colonial dynamic of dominant, powerful white with the submissive, even adoring, subaltern."[50]

The boy is the subjugated passive object not only of the viewer's gaze but also of Rupert's authority as signified by the commanding baton, his dominant hand, and his massive body size in comparison to the boy's small body. The conspicuous intimacy, the touching of the exotic, makes the boy more visible and induces a closer bodily proximity between the master and the servant. Rupert's hand on the boy's head (in contrast to white hands on black shoulders, as in other portraits) proclaims a controlling authority that is a parallel to the Armada portrait of Elizabeth I in which her hand rests on the globe (fig. 3.5). A similar hand gesture can be seen in Nicolaes Eliaszoon Pickenoy's *Man with a Celestial Globe* (1624), in which the man looks at the viewer while his hand confidently dominates the globe (fig. 3.6). A concurrent portrayal of the globe and the baton with similar sea imagery in the background can be seen in such portraits of admirals as Ferdinand Bol's *Lieutenant-Admiral Michiel Adriaenszoon de Ruyte* (1677), Bartholomeus van der Helst's *Aert van Nes, Lieutenant-Admiral*, and Ludolf Bakhuysen's *Portrait of Vice-Admiral Johan de Liefde* (1668) (figs. 3.7–3.9). Considering the function of the trio of the baton, the globe, and the scenic sea in portraiture, then in Mytens's portrait, the hand over the head evokes the hand over the globe of other portraits and the global engagements of trade and exploration suggested by the horizon in the background scenery. The prince's authority over the boy's body through his domineering hands conveys his transcontinental claims. The painting thereby offers a glimpse of figurative significations of the bodies of abducted boys as associated with the lands they were taken from; their bodies become spaces to be charted by princely hands.

FIGURE 3.5. *Portrait of Elizabeth I of England* (the Armada Portrait), artist unknown, 1588. Woburn Abbey.

FIGURE 3.6. *Man with a Celestial Globe*, Nicolaes Eliaszoon Pickenoy, 1624. The Metropolitan Museum of Art.

FIGURE 3.7. *Portrait of Lieutenant-Admiral Michiel Adriaenszoon de Ruyte*, Ferdinand Bol, 1677. Rijksmuseum, Amsterdam. ARTstor.

FIGURE 3.8. *Portrait of Aert van Nes, Lieutenant-Admiral,* Bartholomeus van der Helst, 1668. Rijksmuseum, Amsterdam.

FIGURE 3.9. *Portrait of Vice-Admiral Johan de Liefde*, Bartholomeus van der Helst, 1668. Rijksmuseum, Amsterdam.

Furthermore, the calm, stable scenery behind Rupert contrasts with the wilderness portrayed behind the boy, which is reminiscent of the wilderness depicted in the portrait of Fielding (fig. 3.3). This orientation of the spectator's gaze toward the background scenery and to Rupert's hand over the boy's head further equates Rupert's superiority over the boy with his domination over the wilderness. Additionally, the sea evokes the trade and piracy activities that brought the exotic boy into the prince's household. The boy's European dress indicates his appropriation and conversion, while pearls around his head and his pearl earring still manifest his exotic, oriental land, making him an embodiment of his native space and its material riches. In early modern England, pearls, as discussed in the first chapter, were associated with the Orient—from India to the Ottoman Mediterranean. The white pearls surrounding his head contrast with his black skin and offer an exotic identity, in contrast to Rupert's white adult English masculinity in armor. As Lowe notes, "For Europeans, wearing clothes was not a matter of choice but a sign of civility.... In Europe, material was directly related to status.... Once in Europe, Africans wore European clothing." In early modern images of black Africans in Europe, "Africans (even though usually slaves and servants) are often depicted wearing beautiful and expensive jewelry" to display the status of their masters.[51] While white servants do not appear with similar jewelry, exotic boys do, further illuminating not only the prosperous status of their master but also their master's mercantile and colonial investments in the boy's native land and the population therein. And while the boy's pearl jewelry exhibits his otherness, the style and color of his European dress (complete with white jabot) mirrors Rupert's clothing, almost a material extension of it, indicating that the boy belongs to the prince in the hierarchical matrix of the dominant, protective master and the submissive, needy boy. The boy is taken by and controlled under Rupert's wing-like arms and "phallic-militaristic authority."[52]

These visual representations of black servant boys make it possible to recognize the boy's existence, presence, look, and status. For Erickson, the servant boy in such portraits "is placed in an anomalous position." This anomaly results from the paradox of (in)visibility of the black servant: "The purpose of the role is display: hence the servant is a prominently visible object. Yet the display is simultaneously meant to signal a seen-but-not-heard subservience: hence the servant is invisible as subject." The boy is "secondary but nevertheless 'portrayed,'" and the visual dynamics "provide openings through which we glimpse the servant as a partially independent subject."[53] What can these images and the seen-but-not-heard subservience they signal tell us about the mentioned, (un)seen, not-heard Indian boy of Shakespeare's *Dream*?

Adopting Erickson's emphasis on shifting the perspective, which makes the invisible boy visible as a "partially independent subject," and queer historical work that has made visible the homoeroticism deemed invisible in master/servant relations, in what follows I examine the abduction and subordination of the Indian boy of *A Midsummer Night's Dream*. I will suggest that anticipating and probing the presence and representations of exotic boys in England before transatlantic slavery was fully established, the Indian boy of Shakespeare's *Dream* brings forth the Mediterranean space with its mythical and actual maritime associations with abducted boys—a space in which the English felt inferior and English boys were subject to abductions. In this space, Shakespeare puts at the center of the conflict between Oberon and Titania the desire for the "other" boy and thereby complicates the boy's status not only as a colonial object of exchange but also as an erotic subject desired by both of them. Their desire for the boy engenders climatic catastrophes, calamities, diseases, and transformations. As a result of the contestation between Titania and Oberon, the boy is ultimately put in a racialized homoerotic master/servant matrix that would imprison racialized boys in permanent subservience in the following decades. The literary, dramatic representation of the Indian boy, however, encompasses the boy's racial objectification, eroticization, and possession while also providing us with openings through which we can glimpse a partially independent subjectivity and project a possible futurity on him instead of a nonresistant passivity locked in a never-ending subjugated position. The boy in this sense figures as the (in)visible medium that enables and disables exchanges, subverts power hierarchies, and ultimately transforms most characters, including the queen, into objects of derision in the world of comedy.

The Indian Boy in Shakespeare's Mediterranean *Dream*

A Midsummer Night's Dream's Indian boy is exposed to two different abductions. While Titania's abduction of the boy takes place in India, the Athenian woods, which were part of the broader Ottoman Mediterranean world at the time of play's first performance, are where Oberon abducts the boy. This geography, like Marlowe's Hellespont or Tunis in Shakespeare's *The Tempest*, is a palimpsestic, multireferential space associated not only with classical world but also with the Ottomans as a part of their territorial empire; the Ottomans captured Athens in 1458. Early modern writers such as George Sandys carefully mapped greater Greece as a part of the Ottoman Empire and often associated Greek lands and people with Ottoman Turks.[54] Another traveler, William Lithgow, wrote, "this City [Athens] was the Mother & Well-spring of all liberall Arts and Sciences . . . but now altogether decayed." In his travels in Greek lands, he "could find nothing to answer the famous relations, given the ancient Authors, of the excellency of that land, but the name onely, the barbarousness of Turkes and Time."[55] As in these accounts, the classical Athens of the play is made contemporaneous. The forest is decorated with oriental riches: "orient pearls," "rubies," and "jewels from the deep" (4.1.51, 2.1.12, 3.1.140). Shakespeare's *Dream* amalgamates this Mediterranean setting with Indian and English ecologies and geographies of difference via the Indian boy and his putative displacements by the mythic fairy queen and king.[56] I will argue that whereas the first displacement of the boy is articulated in the language of trade, stealing, adoption, and changelings in exotic India, the second displacement operates in the homoerotic dynamics of abduction, transformation, and fluctuation as central to the dramatic conflict. In fact, Oberon's abduction is the only confirmable abduction of the Indian boy that occurs in the course of the play. Does the Mediterranean space itself produce or contribute to Oberon's desire to abduct the boy? How is the real geography related to this dream space that presents multiple sexual scenarios, from homoeroticism to bestiality?

As I noted in previous chapters, the abduction of boys was an integral component of historical and literary English accounts of this space, especially after English investments in the Mediterranean via the Turkey Company in 1581 and the Levant Company in 1592. About the same time that Shakespeare depicted the Indian boy's abduction on stage, Marlowe inserted the abduction of Leander through the iconic Ganymede in his rewriting of *Hero and Leander*. Likewise, in his romance *Menaphon*, Robert Greene imagined the abduction of the beautiful boy Pleusidippus as Ganymede on the shores of the Mediterranean. In this time period, whenever we see a beautiful boy in the Mediterranean space, a Jove-like man appears for the Ganymede. In the cultural imaginary of the period, the Mediterranean space presents boys as vulnerable to male abductions; as with Ganymede, the Indian boy is not exceptional.

From his first mention in the play, the Indian boy appears as an object of erotic desire to be abducted and owned.[57] The first account of his abduction comes from Puck:

> For Oberon is passing fell and wroth
> Because that she, as her attendant, hath
> A lovely boy stol'n from an Indian king.
> She never had so sweet a changeling;
> And jealous Oberon would have the child
> Knight of his train, to trace the forests wild.
> But she perforce withholds the lovèd boy,
> Crowns him with flowers, and makes him all her joy. (2.1.20–27)

Puck situates the "lovely boy" in an economy of exchange in which the Indian boy is circulated from one place to another, from one master to another. The boy, who may have been a prince or a page boy to an Indian king, is now a stolen object of possession, a changeling, and an attendant in the fairyland. This evokes the widespread practice of stealing boys from other lands in the early modern period, in particular boys who were kidnapped and circulated in Asia or shipped to Europe to be sold as slaves or servants, particularly on Portuguese ships.[58]

Differing from Puck's account, Titania's version of the boy's story, his adoption and possession, in the same scene offers a prehistory of the boy and calls up the Asian context of encounters, trade, voyages, and kidnappings as England's East India Company expanded in the region:

> His mother was a vot'ress of my order,
> And in the spicèd Indian air by night
> Full often hath she gossiped by my side,
> And sat with me on Neptune's yellow sands,
> Marking th' embarkèd traders on the flood,
> When we have laughed to see the sails conceive
> And grow big-bellied with the wanton wind,

Which she with pretty and with swimming gait
Following, her womb then rich with my young squire,
Would imitate, and sail upon the land
To fetch me trifles, and return again
As from a voyage, rich with merchandise.
But she, being mortal, of that boy did die.
And for her sake do I rear up her boy;
And for her sake I will not part with him. (2.1.123–137)

Set in an exotic space characterized by sensual intimacy and affection between women, Titania's narrative emphasizes maternal care as the generative cause of her desire to "rear up her boy." Instead of an act of stealing, as is the case in Puck's report, Titania claims a justified adoption framed in cross-cultural female solidarity and eroticism. The Indian mother, Titania's votaress, lies by her side and gossips with her in the spiced Indian air, sits with her on yellow sands, and fetched trifles for her. Titania claims the boy out of loyalty to her beloved servant. In this narrative, India becomes, in Hendricks's words, "the commodified space of racialized feminine eroticism."[59] Postcolonial readings of this scene have noted that Titania's narration of how the mother imitates the merchant's ship equates the boy with merchandise, linking him to England's overseas trade activities. Relating the boy to affairs of trade through exoticizing references (spiced Indian air, yellow sands, wanton winds) and mercantile metaphors (ship, voyage, trifle, traders, merchandise), Titania presents the boy as an exotic market object, a "commodity fetish," to borrow from Loomba, that circulates from one hand and land to another, from the mother to the queen, from India to fairyland, and finally from the queen to the king in the Athenian woods.[60]

While the story of the boy's origin differs in these two accounts, love for him brings the two stories into proximity. The repetition of love through "lovely boy" and "lovèd boy," which rhymes with "joy" in Puck's account, not only reveals Puck's own adoration of the boy but also emphasizes Titania's affective attachment to and pleasure in the boy. He is the "sweetest" changeling Titania ever had. (How many other changeling boys has she had?) The boy is loved and crowned with flowers. In Shirley Nelson Garner's words, "Titania's attachment to the boy is clearly erotic. She ... accord[s] him the same attentions as those she bestows on Bottom."[61] Indeed, Bottom's replacement of the boy makes Bottom a changeling. In the world of fairies, the term "changeling" often refers to the replacement of a child with an inferior substitute, usually a defective and monstrous one. Hence the only confirmable changeling in the play is the half-human, half-animal Bottom, who replaces the sweet Indian boy. The erotic nature of Titania's affection for the boy is, then, most explicitly reflected through Bottom's substitution for the boy and Titania's eroticization of Bottom.[62] Bottom's animalization reminds us of the accounts of Prince Rupert, who was attacked with claims that he had sexual relations with a dog who was a substitute for a black boy and with a she-monkey who used to be a woman. Here the Indian boy of Titania's joy is replaced by the asinine Bottom as a sign of Titania's sexual disorderliness.

Further, the erotic nature of Titania's bond with the Indian boy is hinted at by Puck's statement that Titania "never had so sweet a changeling." Remarkably, Titania calls Bottom "sweet love" more than once after he replaces the boy (4.1.25, 4.1.28). In his philologic exploration of "sweet" as an epithet in the early modern period, Jeffrey Masten persuasively unearths the erotics of sweetness in the language of affection between different genders.[63] The term "sweet" is frequently used as an erotic-affective term between lovers and intimates in Shakespeare's *Dream*; it appears more than forty times, marking *Dream* as a "sweet" play. Oberon calls the scene of Titania in bed with Bottom a "sweet sight," a sight that happens after she sought "sweet favors" for Bottom (4.1.43, 4.1.46). Oberon calls Titania "my sweet queen" (4.1.72). Demetrius calls his love Hermia "Sweet" (1.1.91). Helena calls her love Demetrius "sweet" (2.2.90). Lysander calls his love Hermia "sweet," and Hermina calls her love Lysander "sweet friend" (2.2.51, 2.2.66). Hermia calls Helena "sweet playfellow" right after she evokes their homoerotic past when they were "emptying our bosoms of their council sweet" (1.1.220, 1.1.216). And Theseus calls his new bride Hippolyta "gentle sweet" (5.1.87). The Indian boy's racial difference, however, makes him exceptionally "sweet" in this frame. As Hall reminds us, sweetness in relation to sugar was a feminized component of English colonial wealth and slavery.[64] The Indian boy as the sweetest of all changelings is the most valued, fetishized, delicious object of desire in the colonial economy of the play. Before Bottom appears, the Indian boy, "sweetest" of all, is "all" Titania's joy.

Titania's use of "my young squire" further suggests a possessive nonegalitarian erotic attachment to the sweet boy in a mistress/servant or mistress/lover relation, which layers onto the mother/son dynamic. She claims the boy before he is born, stating that the mother's womb was "rich with *my* young squire" (2.1.131, my italics). While we can recognize explicit homoerotic energy between Queen Titania and her votaress in the language of lesbian love and care in Titania's words and consider the boy as "their" child, Titania nevertheless uses the first person singular—"my" young squire—rather than saying that the child belonged to them together or to the birth mother. The Indian votaress thus serves as a medium, an enriched sailing vessel who delivers Titania's treasure. This statement also signals that Titania locates herself in a masculine knightly order; referring to the boy as her "squire" recasts the relationship of a servant to a knight in a feminine register. Or if we take into account the definition of the squire as "a man, esp. a young man, who attends upon, accompanies, or escorts a lady; a gallant or lover,"[65] the account once again puts "love" at the center as a driving motive for the conflicts around the boy for whom Titania left Oberon's bed, an act that makes her husband even more jealous. Considering that the juice of love creates changes in the erotic object of desire, the love potion applied to Titania's eyes clarifies that hers is more than merely maternal care for his Indian mother's sake; it is an erotic desire for the boy.

Titania's erotic attachment to the boy and his status as squire echoes the unseen and yet-to-be-accomplished erotic business between Oberon and the boy during the course of the play. Oberon "would have" the boy, and he demands that the boy trace the forest wild with him. In response, Titania "perforce withholds the loved boy" (2.1.26). Deriving etymologically from the French "*par force*," "perforce" signifies "by the application or threat of physical force or violence; forcibly, violently; by force." The *OED*'s example that is closest to Puck's deployment is the usage of the adverb in R. Fabyan's *New Cronycles Eng. & Fraunce* (1516): "They encountred the sayde people yt caryed the sayd Treasoure and stuffe, & parforce toke it from the knyghtes."[66] Likewise, the Indian boy is a treasure "perforce withheld" by Titania. In this vein, Puck's use of "the loved boy" clearly marks him as an object of Oberon's love; Oberon loves the boy and wants to "have" him as his company, but Titania keeps the boy by force. Garner suggests that "Oberon's wish to have the boy is consistent with the practice of taking boys from the nursery to the father's realm so that they can acquire the character and skills appropriate to manhood.... But Puck describes Oberon as 'jealous,' and his emphasis on the 'lovely boy,' the 'sweet' changeling, and the 'loved boy' suggests that Oberon, like Titania, is attracted to the child."[67] As far as we know, Oberon is not the boy's father, and his affection is not paternal (at least it is never stated explicitly in the way that Titania reveals her concerns for her "squire" as maternal). He claims a mastery over the boy not to move him from the nursery to the fatherly realm but to "make him all his joy" in a pederastic master/abducted boy paradigm.[68]

Oberon, according to Puck, wants to have the boy as "knight of his train, to trace the forests wild." Recalling Neptune of Marlowe's *Hero and Leander*, who abducts and takes the beautiful boy Leander down to the bottom of the sea to add him in his "traine" in the Hellespont (650), Oberon wants to have the boy in his "train" to trace deep into the wild forest around Athens with him. He desires him to be his desiring, wandering company, his knight in woods. (This also recalls Lysander, who, in love with Helena under a spell, vows to be her

FIGURE 3.10. *Charles I and Henrietta Maria Departing for the Chase*, Daniel Mytens, circa 1630–1632. Royal Collection Trust.

"knight" [2.2.150]). Oberon accordingly demands that Titania allow the boy to be his "henchman" (2.1.121). A compound of the Old English "*hengest*" (male horse) and "man," "henchman" etymologically "point[s] to the sense of 'attendant on a sumpter-horse'; perhaps the original meaning was simply 'attendant on a horse', 'groom.'" In this sense, the position of the boy as a henchman signifies a position of honor, reminiscent of young royal groomsmen in the early modern English court, as in "a squire, or page of honour to a prince or great man, who walked or rode beside him in processions, progresses, marches."[69] This status for the Indian boy anticipates the task of many black boys as grooms in ensuing decades, as is apparent in a number of seventeenth-century portraits. Daniel Mytens's *Charles I and Henrietta Maria Departing for the Chase* (ca. 1630–1632), for example, portrays the exotic servant as a groom in native costume holding the horse and places other animals such as dogs in the setting (fig. 3.10). Abraham van Diepenbeck's engraving *Machomilia en Turk* in William Cavendish's 1657 book *Methode et invention nouvelle de dresser les chevaux* (A New method and invention for dressing horses) shows the servant as a groom with a Turkish horse (fig. 3.11). Paul van Somer's portrait of Queen Anne of Denmark (1617), similarly, shows the black servant as a groom holding a horse with dogs surrounding Anne (fig. 3.12).[70] These images transform the subordinate, invisible status of the racialized boy into exotic signifiers for the animals they

FIGURE 3.11. *Machomilia en Turk*, Abraham van Diepenbeck. In William Cavendish, *Methode et invention nouvelle de dresser les chevaux*, 1657.

FIGURE 3.12. *Queen Anne of Denmark*, Paul van Somer, 1617. Royal Collection Trust.

attend. The many representations of black boys with animals link them together, pointing to the similar rank they shared as possessed and domesticated servants to the master. William Stepney's textbook *The Spanish Schoole-master* from 1591, for instance, includes a dialogue between a black stableboy and his master: "Negar, bring hither my horse / have you dressed him well? / Yea Sir, he did want nothing."[71] *A Midsummer Night's Dream* shows that black boys functioned as henchmen in the late sixteenth century.

In this frame, the play portrays Oberon's desire to take the boy from Titania's bower and add him to the homosocial order as a knight or a henchman in the forest in the structure of an idealized pederasty. The form of classical pastoral homoeroticism, which includes the training of the boy, appears as a corrective alternative to a mercantile, reproductive, domestic yet disorderly companionship between Titania and the boy. Recall that Neptune offers a pastoral alternative to prevent Leander from attending to amorous cross-sex relations with Hero, as I discussed in chapter 1. Shakespeare, likewise, in his *Venus and Adonis*, as Richard Rambuss has noted, portrays the wild space of forest as a preferable homoerotic alternative to Venus's heteroerotic space for the boy. Like the goddess Venus, Titania desires to put the boy in "female erotic domination."[72] For Oberon, under such erotic domination, the boy is disorderly and hence needs to be abducted and moved to the homosocial realm under his patriarchal mastery.

Oberon's desire to make the Indian boy his henchman is a reaffirmation of his hierarchical superiority, which potentially includes sexual mastery, given that sexual liaisons in early modern master/servant relationships were likely components of everyday life. In England, domestic and public relations, including political power, were organized and managed around orderly homoerotic male bonds that could include service, humanist schooling, patronage, apprenticeship, and/or friendship.[73] Jonathan Goldberg suggests that the legality or morality of sodomitical acts "emerge[d] into visibility only when those who are said to have done them also can be called traitors, heretics, or the like, at the very least, disturbers of the social order."[74] In this matrix, servants were positioned as passive partners in sexual acts with their masters who held hierarchical power. In Alan Sinfield's words, "The page, or other youthful minion, was understood as contributing to the erotic system of the household."[75] Laura Gowing asserts that "mastery in the household naturally carried with it authority over the household's bodies. . . . For at least some masters, apparently, sex was part of the master-servant contract."[76] Bruce Smith writes that "sexual desire took shape in the persons of master and minion; sexual energy found release in the power play between them because men define themselves *vis-à-vis* men above and below them."[77]

What none of these analyses note is the master/*racialized* servant relations that occurred in this homosocial structure. For example, Sinfield strikingly sees the iconic servant-cupbearer Ganymede embodied in the Indian boy, but Ganymede is not only an icon of homoerotic male desire but also an abducted figure in a relationship between those of different status and age, between a god and immortalized boy.[78] Hence, I ask: How does the boy's racial difference matter in the erotic master/servant paradigm? What difference does the interracial aspect of intergenerational relations make? While the boy status in the eroticized master/servant matrix was ephemeral for English boys, who might eventually become masters of their own households, slaves, mostly black boys, were imprisoned in this hierarchical matrix because of the permanency of their subservient status. Abducted boys, who were at the bottom of the household hierarchy, were vulnerable to their masters at the top. Lowe writes that "once in Europe, black African slaves were at the mercy of the sexual advances of their masters."[79] A codification of this hierarchy can be traced in the household books for the estate of Edward Stanley, the third Earl of Derby, who had several black servants. The household instruction sheet dated February 12, 1568, reads, "No Slaves nor boyes shall sitt in the Hall but in place therefore to be appoynted convenient" and "The Yeman of Horses and Gromes of the Stables shall not suffre anie boyes or Slaves to abyde about the Stables *nor lie in theym nor in any place aboute theym*."[80] Here, "theym" might be referring to "Stables," that is, the rule forbids boys to hang around the stables, lie in them (sleep there), or lie anywhere near there. Yet it is also possible that Stanley commanded a strict hierarchy that organized who could accommodate what where and was forbidding his hierarchically senior personnel to "lie" with his slaves and boys. Importantly, "slave" and "boy" are mentioned together as separate categories; neither can sit in the hall and both are under the threat of sexual exploitation in accordance with their subordinated status.[81] Since orderly sexual relations between masters and servant were rendered invisible, such exploitations would often be unrecognized in the legal realm as long as there was no social disturbance.

Racialized boys might have been considered as the threatening other for sodomizing English boys considering the common association of Muslim and black subjects with sodomy. Among the rare court accounts of sodomy in England is the case of Domingo Cassedon Drago, "a negro," who was put on trial on charges of committing "buggery" on "a poor boy named William Wraxal" in Essex in 1647.[82] Repeated references to Drago's blackness in the short entry in the Order Book explicitly link blackness to sodomy. Alan Bray notes that as a foreign element, he would invariably have "brought to mind the image of the sodomite."[83] Indeed, Muslim and black slaves were charged with sodomizing Christian youths in early modern Spain.[84] Sodomy, as Michael Warner has suggested, came from elsewhere; it is always there and never here. And when it is here, it is often committed by the "other." This case came to light because a (white) English boy had been penetrated by "a negro." Given our understanding of the hierarchies, it seems unlikely that the early moderns would have taken much legal notice of the abduction and rape of a black or Indian boy.[85]

In the nonegalitarian erotic matrix, the Indian boy was different in terms of gender, race, social status, and age. Given that his youth within the homoerotic frame of the play has baffled and troubled modern critics who link this early modern boy to the abused children of modernity—that is, seeing his exploitation as simply related to his status as a child—it is worth revisiting his age.[86] Shakespearean comedies offer rich catalogues of loving and loved boys, whether they were cross-dressed boy actors or desiring youths, but it is the *Indian* boy who has been consistently infantilized, objectified as a child, thingified, be it in a critic's essay or on stage. (I discuss this further in chapter 6.) Gary Jay Williams imagines the boy as a little child: "Titania's 'young squire' is almost certainly a small boy."[87] Louis Montrose suggests that he is about seven years old, when "he would be expected to move from infancy, dominated by women, to youth." For Sinfield, his age depends on "the local relevance" such as the age of Hamlet or the fair youth of the *Sonnets* who is called "lovely boy."[88] While I am more in agreement with Sinfield, I would add racial relevance in determining the age of the Indian boy. The elasticity of terms used in reference to the Indian boy's age, I propose, permits us to see an older person in this figure than what has been conventionally projected by modern critics.

I suggest that the Indian boy, as an object of desire and in a putative position of squire or henchman or knight in the play, is not a young child. The use of the terms "changeling" and "child" to describe the boy in the text of the play has complex significations worth considering. According to the definition of "changeling" in the OED, which takes Puck's usage as an example, it refers to "a child secretly substituted for another in infancy; a child supposedly left by fairies in exchange for one stolen." The term "changeling" was also "often used to refer to a child who is considered undesirable, or who does not resemble his or her family."[89] Titania never refers to the Indian boy as a changeling; Puck's use of "so sweet a changeling," and Oberon's "a little changeling boy" and "her changeling child" are the only moments when the term is deployed (2.1.23, 2.1.120, 4.1.56). In these instances, the boy is marked as one among Titania's many changelings, yet nowhere in the text do we see the Indian boy being exchanged for another child. As discussed earlier, the only exchange occurs when the adult Bottom replaces the boy, which highlights the erotic substitution, making the boy Oberon's changeling. Hence, from the perspective of Oberon and Puck, the changeling in these instances refers to a more vague history, to the past of the boy rather than to his present age.

The term "child" does not give us a definitive answer about the boy's age either, yet it reveals the categorical connection of his boyhood to service. Only three of twelve usages of "child" in the play refer to the Indian boy. Titania calls him "the child of me" (2.1.122), evoking maternal signification, which is also feminizing because "child" in this sense was "traditionally used more frequently (and longer) of a girl than a boy (Shakespeare nowhere uses 'my child' of or to a son, but frequently of or to a daughter)."[90] The word "child" has a similar feminine attribution when the Old Shepherd of *The Winter's Tale* asks when he finds the infant Perdita on a Bohemian seacoast: "A very pretty bairne. / A boy or a child, I wonder?" (3.3.67–68). In *Dream*, Aegeus's repetitive use of "my child" at the very beginning of the play to refer to his "daughter Hermia" follows this signification: "Against my child, my daughter Hermia" (1.1.23–30). Since she is of marriageable age, Hermia is obviously not a very young girl. Furthermore, references to Lysander as "child" with significations of contempt or to Cupid as a child probe the age dynamic in the use of the word and blur the child/boy distinction in a master/servant hierarchy. Titania's use of "child," therefore, seems to signify not the boy's infancy but his status as "a young person (in early use esp. a boy or young man) in service; an attendant; a page," which aligns with what Oberon calls the boy: "her page" (2.1.185).[91]

The other two instances where the word "child" is used to refer to the Indian boy (Puck's "jealous Oberon would have the child" and Oberon's "her changeling child") both point to his youthful boy status as a page. The boy, as I discussed in the introduction, first emerged in reference to a male servant, slave, or assistant and to a nonwhite servant or slave in early English, and it etymologically relates mainly to status, service, and racial and gender subordination in a power hierarchy rather than to age. As for the category of boy actors, some boys on Shakespeare's stage were in their early twenties. David Kathman has persuasively argued that on the pre-Restoration English stage, female roles were played by adolescent boy actors aged from twelve to the early twenties. If we entertain the idea that the Indian boy might have appeared on Shakespeare's stage, the projection of childhood on the Indian boy becomes even incredible. Also, if we consider the boys in the history of abductions—the aforementioned "lusty Negers of about 15 yeares of ages" the English desired or "two young Moors not above 13 or 14 yeares of age" the English ship captured because of the "tenderness of their years"—then the boyhood of the Indian boy is more due to his subservient status than to his age.[92]

In a hierarchical master/boy order, Oberon's abduction of the boy as his "henchman" in his "train" and his jealousy over the "sweetest, lovely and loved boy" are complementary. His homoerotic attachment comes into view in his adoration for the boy and his desire to place the boy within the master/servant hierarchy in which the sexual dominance of the master remains invisible even as it persists. The Indian boy is added to the powerful faery king's company as his "knight" in the happy ending of the comedy, which might not be happy for the modern reader or for all the characters (as is the case for the marriage of Athenian youths, including still-under-the-spell Demetrius whose marriage seems to take place without his sober consent, and for the Amazonian queen Hippolyta, whose defeat means reluctant [even forced] marriage to Theseus). Like Puck, the Indian boy is now made the loved servant to his master, but unlike Puck, he is not a fairy. He is reminiscent of the Ganymede boy abducted by the god and made a cupbearer. The homoerotic desire for the Indian boy therefore reveals both an intergenerational and a cross-cultural, cross-species, and interracial relationship—between the human-boy and a spirit of another sort, to use Oberon's self-definition: "But we are spirits of another sort" (3.2.389). Like Marlowe, Shakespeare, with a touch of homoerotic abduction, presents the Mediterranean space as characterized by pederasty (based on differences in age, gender roles, status, and race) alongside the emerging domestic heterosexuality based on companionship.[93] In this setting, the desire for the lovely, sweet, loved, and joyful Indian boy disrupts the established order, generating transformations in desire for humans and nonhumans. The representation of the boy from behind the curtain—and between the lines—offers a Ganymede effect that establishes a homoerotic order in addition to the heteronormative order projected on urban Athens in the play's social world.[94]

This nonegalitarian homoeroticism falls into what Mario DiGangi calls "the homoerotics of mastery," which in the early modern discourse of male service converges servitude and eroticism.[95] The master's homoerotic affection, DiGangi argues, normally subordinated the servant in the power dynamic. Yet in an affective hierarchy, the power of the master was open to subversion; the master could be subordinated by the servant, a dynamic that risked turning the orderly homoerotic dynamic into a disorderly sodomitical one. Likewise, Sinfield notes that nonegalitarian erotic relations "are at once imbricated into social power" but they risk "a subversive mode of asymmetrical reciprocity" in which the desired young person "may come to wield considerable power over the infatuated elder partner."[96] Perhaps considering the potential for such subversiveness, Sinfield speculates queerly about the Indian boy: "Perhaps the boy will enjoy the attentions of the king of the fairies, but we don't know."[97] Maybe he will enjoy the attentions or maybe he longs and will continue to long for his homeland with its spicy air. I stress the latter because the pederastic dynamic we see here is racially inflected. Yet this does not mean that the boy is a childish victim and can never deploy tactics for "creative survivance" or freedom in the racialized homoerotics of mastery.[98]

In the geographic and historical context and homoerotic structures previous chapters have explored, the racially and religiously marked boy is nevertheless sometimes imagined with power in literature. Like the captivating and transformative boys of previous chapters, the competing desires for the Indian boy from various directions signal the magnetic power his racially different body holds as an object of attraction. In the play's dramatic dynamics, the Indian boy's absent presence, his behind-the-scenes prominence in the dramatic conflict, marks him not only as the desired object but also as the invisible subject whose body, over which the king and queen contest, has orienting, transformative power during the course of the play. In this sense, as an erotic beloved, he aligns with Mehmed II's Christian boy who converts the objectifying Muslim subject; Marlowe's Leander, who resists Neptune's burning desire for him yet gains his favor; Shakespeare's silent fair youth whose love rules over his active lovers; or Richard Barnfield's beautiful boy, who controls the gaze and muse of the poet. While racially marked as Indian, his resemblance to other beloved boys makes possible speculation that the Indian boy will find the means for his survival in the new order where he is with Oberon but will also be surrounded by Titania. Will she continue to desire the boy when she comes back to her senses after the love potion wears off, enabling characters to go back to who they were in love with before? Will the boy use the king and queen's attractions for him to empower himself and make them fools of their infatuations? Like unresolved homoerotic plots in the happy endings of other comedies, including *Twelfth Night*, *The Merchant of Venice*, and *As You Like It*, Shakespeare's *Dream* drops the subject once the abduction is over and the boy is moved to Oberon's homosocial company, yet its queer effect lingers.

Evoking the global traffic in boys, the play renders the Indian boy central to the play's action by making him the invisible bullet of erotic, gender, and class conflicts. It portrays his abduction as motivated by a homoerotic desire that projects colonial mastery over the subservient in succeeding decades of structural slavery in which interracial desire was deemed unacceptable. As an abducted boy, the Indian boy embodies the "spiced Indian air" that English ships began to penetrate in the late sixteenth century. First associated with India and later equated with the fairyland ("Not for thy fairy kingdom"), the stolen boy becomes the signifier of the exotic space of India from which he was taken, most likely by force or coercive exchange. In the geography of the Mediterranean, he becomes the object of Oberon's homoerotic desire and later forceful abduction. The competition over the boy first disturbs social hierarchies, creating sodomitical disorderliness and transformations in desires and bodies, which are then corrected by moving the boy to the realm of the homoerotics of mastery. In depicting Oberon's motives, the play significantly does not recast Titania's mercantile language of adoption and theft as linked with India but presents a language of affective homosocial companionship, a pederastic kinship that moves the boy from Titania's immobile bower zone, an enclosure in which he is "perforce withheld" as a colonial trifle, to Oberon's moving space of "wild forests" as a knight or henchman that might allow an ascendancy in the homosocial imperial patriarchy.

In this sense, the Indian boy's abduction follows the literary deployment of homoerotic abductions in the cultural imaginary that associated the Mediterranean space with eroticized boys in alignment with historical abductions in this space. As I have noted, the only confirmable abduction happens in the transformative Mediterranean space in which English men and boys were themselves vulnerable to abduction and captivity. The Indian boy thus reminds us of the imperial desire of the Ottomans to capture and keep a multiethnic array of youthful boys, who were in turn imagined as having the power to convert their masters. The Indian boy's figuration also illuminates the Ganymede effect embedded in England's overseas investments, in which boys were abducted and carried off from one place to another as objects of imperial masculine desire. The Indian boy as object of desire and abduction anticipates other abducted boys who were eroticized and subjugated under a colonial spatial mastery, as is evident in portraiture of subsequent decades. The Indian boy therefore stands at the threshold of a shift in imperial imaginings of the *other* boy as England was becoming an international player in global politics, slavery, and trade.

The abducted boys I traced in the three chapters of this part of the book—poetic, cartographic, and dramatic—reveal the trajectory of transforming "other" boys within an imperial matrix that was generated by and generated homoerotic desire in the frame of early modern sexual regimes. What kind of transformation did the boy undergo? The chapters in the next part will trace bodily transformations; that is, the refashioning and regendering of abducted boys. The eroticization of boy abductions and the conversion of those boys echo in more material forms in the portrayals of abducted boys, specifically circumcised and castrated boys, in travelogues and in theatrical presentations of them, further illuminating the entanglements of sexuality, gender, and racial and religious difference in their mutual production, constitution, and reinforcement within imperial structures.

PART II

Boys Transformed

4

Refashioning Boys

Two English boys set out on a voyage into "Tripolis in Barbarie, in the yeere 1584, with a ship called the *Jesus*."[1] The Mediterranean waters were dangerous for traveling boys, as previous chapters have shown, so it is not surprising that in this space these two boys became objects of abduction, desire, and a coercive bodily transformation: circumcision. Thomas Sanders's account, which is included in Richard Hakluyt's *The Principal Navigations, Voyages, Traffiques, and Discoveries of the English Nation* (1589), describes minute details of the voyage, the crew, and their relations in the Mediterranean in this symbolically named vessel (192–200). After the *Jesus* arrived in "Tripolis" and the company achieved a profitable trade with the king there, a quarrel occurred between the crew of the *Jesus* and locals. As a result, the king, whom Sanders represented stereotypically as a despotic Muslim ruler, condemned the crew to slavery. At this point, Sanders's narrative digresses from the main plot of his own (adult) captivity to describe a particularly violent encounter that involved the two boys.

When the son of the ruler arrived in the town where the crew was being held, he saw the English party and "greatly fancied" the two young Englishmen of the crew. He became "very desirous to have them to turn Turks," but the two boys resisted conversion. The king's son, therefore, "violently used" them, and with the help of his men, circumcised them and forcibly "made [them] Turk" (197).

Sanders's narrative focuses on masculine tensions and competitions in cross-cultural encounters in the Mediterranean space through the forceful conversion of boys, elaborated with accounts of the scandal of circumcision. It emphasizes the mutability of boys in the process of encountering and interacting with "the Turks." This account is just one among many English accounts about the Ottomans in which circumcision emerges as a religious-cultural-racial mark on the youthful male body, which is gendered and sexualized. As Jonathan Burton observes, ubiquitous masculine anxieties in the West about "turning Turk" were conveyed through a matrix of conversion, circumcision, and castration.[2] In the early modern period, a man's conversion from Christianity to Islam meant losing both his religion and his penis (or at least part of it), his masculine embodiment according to Christian norms and habits. Thus, as Bindu Malieckal suggests, conversion itself was considered as a form of castration.[3] The conversion-circumcision-castration matrix, in Dennis Britton's words, imprinted "the body as a visible and accessible repository of religious faith."[4] These scholars have persuasively demonstrated the bodily aspects of conversion through circumcision, revealing the sexual discourses operating in the conversion narratives that frequently shaped Anglo-Ottoman encounters. Taking into consideration the focus on the youthful objects of enforced conversion and circumcision in Sanders's account, I ask: What is the specific role of figurations of boys in captivity and conversion narratives? Why is the bodily signification of conversion conveyed specifically through the boy's body? If circumcision narratives reveal religious, economic, and sexual anxieties in England, to what extent did those anxieties intersect with trepidation about traveling boys who were abducted, enslaved, and converted in the Mediterranean contact zone?

The premise of this chapter is that the youthful male bodies in such accounts appeared as sites of economic and religious conflicts imagined within a sodomitical matrix of exchanges and encounters. Sanders's story of the two boys who underwent conversion and circumcision against their will suggests that such a fate faced other English boys taken (or who might have been taken) captive in the era of Mediterranean trade and travel. Conveying the anxiety over such threats, Sanders's account is reminiscent of the abduction narratives I analyzed in chapter 1: of John Rawlins's tales about "a hundred handsome youths compelled to turn Turks, or made subject to more vile prostitution, and all English"; Thomas Coryat's account of the Turks who "are exceedingly given to Sodomie, and therefore divers keep prettie boyes to abuse them by preposterous venerie"; and John Sanderson's fear that his own twenty-one-year-old "beardless" son might be captured and sodomized by Turks during their travels into "Sodomiticall places."[5] Mirroring such accounts, Sanders's narrative further reflects great concerns over "cutting pricks" through the abduction and conversion of boys in the region, a nightmare for Englishmen that manifested itself most explicitly in circumcision narratives.[6]

It must be noted that circumcision, like abduction, was not solely an "othering" device in cultural imaginings; it was a social and cultural practice in the Ottoman Mediterranean. In what follows, I first contextualize the circumcision and conversion of boys in Sanders's account within the frame of discourses about circumcision in popular religious, ethnographic, and literary accounts in England and the Ottoman Empire. Whereas circumcision signified castration and emasculation in early modern England (and in the Christian West in general), it represented the opposite in Islamicate Ottoman society. Circumcision of boys, which was usually done after the age of six or seven, was (and still is in contemporary Turkey) considered the first step to adult masculinity, a rite of passage, and was thus celebrated with grandiose public festivities.[7] In Ottoman society, circumcision was thus a gendered practice, a religious rite, and a cultural performance. Its most elaborate celebration in courtly festivals involved political spectacle that was performed for both Turkish and European audiences. Such displays of masculine imperial power contributed to and shaped English concerns over "cutting pricks" that emerged in travelogues, medical treatises, and on stage. After showing English depictions of circumcision vis-à-vis Ottoman practices, I return to Sanders's account to further explore the role of youthful, boyish bodies in the connected histories of conversion narratives centered on bodily marks and transformations in both England and the Ottoman Empire.

"Magnificences of the Circumcision of the Turkish Princes"

For the Ottomans, circumcision signified more than the religious practice of cutting off the foreskin. In fact, as the Turkish term "*sünnet*" for circumcision implies, circumcision is not a religious obligation (*farz*) or a precondition for becoming a Muslim but a *sünnet* or *sunnah* (the Prophet's tradition) that is a social custom and practice in Islamic communities. Elaborating this practice with public celebrations marks circumcision as a performance that has gendered, sexual, and imperial significations in the Ottoman Empire. In particular, the grandeur of the courtly celebrations of the circumcision of *şehzades* (princes), which the sixteenth-century French traveler Michel Baudier described as "Magnificences of the Circumcision of the Turkish Princes," attracted all layers of society in festivities that lasted multiple days.[8] This had been the practice since the 1365 celebrations for the circumcision of Prince Bayezid, the son of Murad I.[9] In the emerging ceremonial culture of imperial displays in the sixteenth century, performance gained a specific importance for the ruling class. As Kaya Şahin points out, circumcision festivals replaced royal marriage celebrations as the ultimate public performance when the Ottomans gave up dynastic marriages and concubinage became the means of siring royal children.[10] In this new culture, the circumcision ceremony brought together the ruling class and the public in the same ceremonial space and, as Şahin comments regarding one of these celebrations, it "served an occasion for the public performance of political ideas, cultural ideals, and individual and communal identities. It offered new ways of being public, being present in public spaces, and experiencing various sights, sounds and tastes."[11] Royal circumcision festivities thus were not just an exhibition of religious commitment, they were also a public venue for exhibiting imperial power and political claims to an international audience.

One of the earliest records of such courtly celebrations is from Aşıkpaşazade's fifteenth-century chronicle *Manakıb u Tevarih-i Âl-i Osman* (The virtues and history of the house of Osman), which details the 1457 circumcision celebrations of the two sons of Mehmed II, princes Bayezid and Mustafa Çelebi.[12] The festivities, which took place in the former Ottoman capital of Edirne (Adrianople), lasted for three days. It was a grand event to which numerous lords, significant persons of every city, and the people of Edirne were all invited.[13] In the immediate aftermath of his conquest of Constantinople, Mehmed used the circumcision of his sons as a means of demonstrating his majestic power while reinforcing a hierarchical order of scholarly, religious, and governmental persons, as was evident in the dates of the invitations he issued. Scholars and higher administrators were hosted on the first day of the gathering, during which the sultan presented generous gifts to the attendees.[14] On the second day, the men of religion, dervishes, and members of Sufi orders were invited, and on the third day, statesmen, bureaucrats, and lords of other cities were hosted. These events, Aşıkpaşazade noted, were opportunities for sultans to demonstrate "their magnificent majesty" (*azamet-i şevket*).[15]

This 1457 event established a precedent for larger circumcision ceremonies in the following decades, most of which were celebrated in Istanbul and ranged in length from three weeks to almost two months. In 1582, for instance, Sultan Murad III ordered an illustrious ceremony for the circumcision of his son, Crown Prince Mehmed, which lasted for more than forty days in May through July. It is one of the most widely described events in Ottoman history; each

FIGURE 4.1. A scene of entertainment during the parade in the circumcision festival. In *Surname-i Humayun* (The book of the imperial festival), 1582.

day of the celebration was recorded by Imtiyazi in *Surname-i Humayun* (The book of the imperial festival, 1582), which depicts the festivities with more than 400 miniatures.[16] Starting with the sultan's procession into the Atmeydanı (the old Byzantium Hippodrome), the celebrations continued with parades of various classes, guilds, and international visitors, followed by public meals and performances such as games and mock battles; masques; wrestling; dances; singing; horse racing; shows by clowns, jugglers, and ropewalkers; and fireworks. While the religious aspect of circumcision was evoked by the parade of the Prophet's descendants (*seyyid*) on the first day, the political and imperial implications embedded in the ceremonies emerged in the parades of members of various trade guilds, Christian slaves, converts, Galata Christians, entertainers, and exotic animals from distant locales and in the staging of certain victories over other kingdoms (fig. 4.1). On the fortieth day, the prince was circumcised, and the festivity ended with a collective public circumcision of hundreds of other city boys.

The performances, the setting of the celebrations, and the audience that was targeted reveal how circumcision became a way for the Ottoman court to exhibit its state power and imperial claims. The space for the festivity was mainly the former Byzantium Hippodrome, an arena traditionally used by the (Eastern) Roman Empire to display its political power.[17] In addition to the selection of this symbolic setting, the festival itself was designed to blend Turkic-Islamic, Venetian, and Byzantine ceremonial conventions, mixing Islamic circumcision and recitations of the Qur'an with parades and artistic performances. The events included shows by Arab, Indian, Persian, Jewish, and European figures; ballet performances by Christian subjects; and the exhibition of models of conquered European castles and impressive architectural structures such as the newly built Suleymaniye Mosque completed by the guild of architects. Circumcision generated a venue for showcasing the multiethnic composition of the empire, which claimed domination over the East and the West as the new Roman Empire. Thus, the religious, the political, and purely sensational spectacles and agendas were intertwined during the celebration of the transition of the prince and other boys into the adult male world.

These varied displays of circumcision activities coalesced in their religious and political ambit the valorization of male homoeroticism. Centered on the bodily transformation of boys, these festivals brought together circumcised men, soon-to-be circumcised boys, and uncircumcised Christian boys in the same all-male space. Some events, for instance, included a procession of young Christian boys of Galata as Cupids with bows and arrows and as couples with cross-dressed boys. Ottoman chronicles of circumcision celebrations used the opportunity to eroticize Christian boys, who participated in parades, entertained, served, or simply attended the festivities. One account of the 1582 festival reads:

> A sweet voiced youth began to dance and thus graced the square:
> Couplet:
> In the way of Greeks, a Greek beloved lovely as sun,
> In the way of lovelocks, his locks' ringlets twisted every one.
> Rhyming Couplets:
> On every hair hung a thousand heart and souls;
> Every hyacinth was mussed, on account of his rose.
> Because of his lips, the ruby became mere stone,
> Because of his mouth, sugar was struck dumb.

A youth [was] of lovely countenance and smelling musk; a tall cypress and moon-lit face, sweet tongued and slender waisted. The Turks of Khitay [China] were bent and twisted [with envy] like hyacinths by the coils of his locks, and the [sweet] milk of Samarkand was distressed like lovers' hearts by desire for his riot-inducing sugar [lip]. The girdle of attachment to his locks was a bond to the soul, and the collar of attraction to his curls was fastened about the [neck of] the bride of the heart.[18]

Another chronicler described the procession and dance performances of the beautiful Euro-Christian boys in a tone of adoration: "Then came the Christians, European-born infidels of European mien who dwell in Galata, dressed in all sort of adornments and finery. Their young men, all prettied up, look like virgin girls. Their tousled locks and hair-thin waists, their delicacy, which had not a hair missing, [were] all in place, and they were such cruel infidels that they lacked any trace of true belief."[19] In these narratives, the parading Christian boys with their uncircumcised bodies became objects of heightened erotic gaze for the literati while also evidencing the homoerotic charge in processions of beautiful boys in front of an all-male audience.

With their religious, political, social, and erotic entanglements, circumcision festivals were carefully curated and choreographed spectacles that aimed to transgress the borders of the empire, as is evident in the inclusion of foreign rulers and their representatives in these events. In fact, almost all European countries sent representatives to attend these celebrations.[20] The *Surname-i Humayun*, for example, portrays foreign ambassadors being present every day of these events, watching the parades from the box reserved for them. Sitting in the first box on the left-hand side on the first floor in each miniature, these figures are easily recognizable by their costumes and hats as Europeans (kings, princes, ambassadors, or other diplomats) (fig. 4.1). Michel Baudier's account of the celebration observed that "in the third and lowest [row] they had made places for the Embassadours of Kings and Christian Princes.... That of the French Embassadour was in the first Ranke, the Emperours had the second, the Polonians the third, the Bailisse of Venice the fourth.... They were all in Cloth of Gold, and their Gentlemen in like manner."[21] The celebration's display of Ottoman power was thus directed not solely to Ottoman subjects but also to the larger world. Baudier wrote that during the first day of the royal procession, "all the wealth not only of the East, but of the whole World had beene transported to Constantinople"; he referred to the sultan "the most powerfull and rich Monarch of the Earth."[22] This reputation was what the Ottomans envisioned the circumcision festivals would do for them.

Numerous other European accounts describe these celebrations in detail in French, German, and Polish, including those by Nicholas von Haunolth, George Lebelski, Johannes Lewenklaw, Reinhold Lubenau, and Jean Palerne. European courts were attuned to these events. For example, right after the celebrations in 1582, an Italian named Le Vigne de Pera sent an account of the celebrations to the court of Elizabeth I.[23] Some of these firsthand accounts were later translated into English. George Lebelski's account in Polish was translated to English in 1585 under the title *A True Description of the Magnificall Tryumphes and Pastimes, represented at Constantinople, at the solemnizing of the Circumcision of the Soldan Mahumet, the sonne of Amurath, the third of that name, in the yeare of our Lorde God in 1582, in the Monethes Mai and June*. Passages from George Lebelski's account that refer to performances during the celebration were included in Edward Grimeston's translation of Simon Goulart's *Admirable and memorable histories*.[24] Grimeston's citation to "George Lebelski, a *Polonian in the discription of things done at Constantinople, at the Circumcision of Amuraths Sonne in the yeare* 1582" in Goulart's text shows that Lebelski's firsthand account in Polish was already in circulation under various titles.[25] Baudier's long description of these celebrations appeared in Grimeston's translation in 1635.

Such accounts demonstrate that grand circumcision celebrations such as the 1582 royal festival contributed to discourses about the Ottomans and circumcision outside the Ottoman realm. Circumcision thus became a threatening component of "turning Turk," associated with the moral and sexual threat the Ottoman power posed as its reputation reached the banks of the Thames. Thus, a complex picture emerges of the practices of circumcision in Ottoman society and the wide-ranging responses to them, from a fascinated curiosity to anxiety about changes in bodies and beliefs.

Circumcision, an Utterly Confused Category

While Western accounts often accurately represented these illustrious circumcision celebrations, they connected them with other discourses about religion, gender, sex, and race, imposing previous templates about Islam and circumcision onto the Ottomans' celebratory practices. Narratives about circumcision as a mark of cultural and ethnic difference go back to Herodotus's fifth-century description of Egyptian circumcision: "In this country also the manner is to circumcise and cut round about the skin from their privy parts, which none other use except those that have taken letter and learned the custom from the Egyptians."[26] In the early modern period, this mark of ethnic and cultural difference was combined with religious and racial difference, especially when no phenotypical trait of demarcation was visible. English narratives about circumcision display contradictory assessments of circumcision as baptism and as a form of gender and sexual perversion.

Circumcision as a threat was first and foremost characterized as a Jewish practice in England, but from the sixteenth century onward, it was often also transfigured as a "Mohamedan" perversion.[27] In almost any text about Islam and the Ottomans—including plays, travelogues, medical treatises, and poems—circumcision was specifically associated with Turks. James Shapiro reminds us that with some exceptions (including the circumcision of infants by radical Puritans and a few self-circumcizers in the early seventeenth century), "there is no evidence that circumcision took place in early modern England."[28] Writers of accounts of the operation often claimed to have witnessed the event elsewhere, usually in the Ottoman lands. Circumcision narratives that linked the practice to the Ottomans projected the Ottomans as threatening "others" whose male bodies bore the scar of circumcision. In Marlowe's *Tamburlaine*, for example, Bajazeth, referring to the Ottoman army, says, "As many circumcised Turks we have, / And warlike bands of Christians renied" (Part I, 3.1.8–9). While Tamburlaine's army was also circumcised, it was the Ottoman Turks to whom the practice was primarily attributed. The fear of circumcision was deeply linked to religious conversion and to the Ottomans' convert army, or "Christians renied" (renegades), as Bajazeth described them.

What is common to many English accounts, and to Western accounts in general, is the depiction of circumcision as opposed to a Christian identity and to normative sexual and gender roles. For example, in *The Order of the Greate Turckes courte* (translated from French in 1524), a comprehensive narrative of the circumcision ceremony, the rules for the ceremony, and the feasts that followed the operation, Antoine Geuffroy opined, "Instead of Baptisme they ben circumcised. . . . Their children are often five or seven yeres of age or more" before their circumcision, "at which they make a greate feaste and assemble."[29] Circumcision as a form of "baptism" was depicted in terms of a Christian analogy; it was a threshold that was crossed to gain a Muslim identity. According to Geuffroy, circumcision was also a moment of conversion, of becoming not only an adult man but also a Muslim.

Geuffroy also linked circumcision to masculinity and male superiority: "The women gooe not in to the churches wyth the menne, because they ben not circumcised. Wherefore they ben count unclean."[30] By noting the mosque as an all-male space that excluded women, he marked circumcision in the production of this gendered space.[31] Female bodies were unclean because they were uncircumcised (hence, unbaptized), he said. Within this gendered matrix, boys were brought in closer proximity to women, and circumcision enabled them to transition to the male world. Circumcision generated a hierarchy of bodies, at the bottom of which were not only women and boys but also Christians, who were inferior because of their uncircumcised bodies: "It is a great despyte amonge them when they call one *Sunet* that is uncircumcised."[32] Indeed, the Ottomans pejoratively referred to uncircumcised others, especially infidels, as *sünnetsiz* (the uncircumcised)—a term still in use in contemporary Turkey to refer to non-Muslims. Yet, Geuffroy asserted, although the Turks despised "uncircumcised" people, "they have the Italians in good estimation."[33] Whether this assessment was related to close trade relations between the Ottomans and the Venetians or to sexualization of the Italians as sodomites in early modern discourses (Italians were often associated with transgressive sexual practices, especially anal sex), the Ottomans and Italians were brought close in Geuffroy's translated account, a proximity delivered contradictorily through the confused lens of circumcision.[34]

Circumcision as gendered baptism reemerged in ensuing decades. *The Offspring of the House of Ottomanno* (1569) by Bartholomeus Georgieuiz described circumcision as the sole means of baptism to become a "Musulman": "They use circumcision called in their proper speech *Tsuneth*, not on the eight day, according to the custume of the Jews, but after the childes birth when he is in the age of seven or eight yeares, then skilefull in speaking their language: and that ceremony is observed amonge them at that time, for the words of confession, whiche are required before circumcision. . . . First of all their friends are called together at a bankete, for whom of dayntye dishes, ther are sufficient prepared, of all kyndes of fleshe, suche as they may lawfully feede upon. . . . [In the middle of the feast, the child is brought up and circumcised.] Thenceforth he shall be called Musulman, which is circumcised."[35] Claiming reliable authority, like Geuffroy, by deploying the authentic Turkish word "*tsuneth*" (*sünnet*), Georgieuiz also described circumcision using Christian terms and practices: circumcision as baptism combined with confession. Islamic circumcision, he stressed, was different from the Jewish practice; the boy needed to be articulate in order to confess during the circumcision performance. Only after the ceremony could the person be called a "Musulman" (the Turkish word for Muslim).[36]

George Sandys's account, *A Relation of a Journey* (1615), described circumcision in terms of baptism/conversion and gender hierarchies. Muslims do not circumcise women, he wrote, "nor circumcise they the males until they be able to answer the Priest, and promise for themselves: which is for most part at the age of eight. They are circumcised in the houses of their parents, as a festivall meeting, and in the midst of the assembly, the child holding up his forefinger, in a token that he is a Mohametan. As soon as cut, the priest washeth the wound in water and salt, and bindeth it in linen. Who changeth not his name but is from thenceforth called a *musselman*: which is a true believer.... Then they put him a white Turbant; and for returning with drums and hoboys, is with great solemnity conducted to the Mosque, and presented with gifts according to his quality."[37] These narratives—whether English translations of French accounts or firsthand accounts in which an author blends previous discourses with their own observations—describe circumcision by making an analogy with what is familiar. Islam does not have the notion of original sin. Everyone is born pure; hence no baptism. Yet in these accounts, circumcision becomes baptism in church-like mosques ordained by priest-like figures. In fact, in early modern writings, Islam was sometimes not considered as a separate religion but a deviation from Christianity, as is evident in the refusal of most Christian authors to use such terms as Islam and Muslim, instead using the term "Mohemmedans."[38] Georgieuiz and Sandys's deployments of the term "Musulman" are rare examples, but their descriptions put it in relation to Christianity and they use the term not to refer to Muslim persons but as a gendered signification that referred exclusively to a circumcised male. Therefore, women, who, according to these writers, were unclean because their bodies were uncircumcised, could never be truly Muslim and neither could boys before they were circumcised. Circumcision was perceived and presented as a transformative moment, particularly for boys, whose conversions to Islam would be marked on their bodies.

Accounts of circumcision in travelogues and chronicles contributed to the public discourse, as is evident in Christian church sermons. In 1628, two sermons were published together with the title *A Returne from Argier: A sermon Preached at Minhead in the County of Somerset the 16 March, 1627, at the re-admission of a relapsed Christian into our Church*. One of the sermons, a forty-five-page document penned by Edward Kellet, was devoted to circumcision in the context of conversion. The sermon described the reconversion of an Englishman who had "turned Turke" (converted to Islam) after he was captured by "Turkes" and had decided to "turne Christian" after being brought back to England by an "English Captaine." Marking this conversion moment, the sermon mainly noted how unchristian circumcision is and stated that from an English Christian perspective, it is a form of idolatry. Comparing it to Christian baptism, Kellet excitedly announced that choosing "the blood of circumcision" over the "crystal-clear water of baptisme" was worse than being a Jew and killing Christ or being Cain and killing Abel. "If you be circumcised," he declared, "Christ shall profit you nothing."[39]

Kellet condemned circumcision by calling Muhammad a false prophet who was adulterous, lustful, and a sodomite. Deploying popular medieval templates, he associated circumcision with the stereotype that Muhammad and Muslims in general were sexually aberrant. It is interesting that the man converting back to Christianity in Kellet's account was still wearing Turkish clothes. The preacher became angry with him because in his view, Turkish clothes were barbarous and dressing in them was a great sin. If this man really wanted to repent, first he had to change into Christian clothes because Turkish attire, particularly the turban, was "nastie," a term that evokes excessive affect with significations of "morally corrupt; indecent, obscene, lewd" in the early modern period.[40] To be Christian was to dress in a Christian way, to make the body stand out differently from those of non-Christians. As noted above, Sandys also remarked that right after a man was circumcised, "they put on him a white Turbant." In these accounts, the Ottomans are "circumcised Turkes" whose foreskin had been replaced by the "nastie" turban on the head. As Gerald MacLean and Nabil Matar note, the turban and circumcision usually appear together; English authors frequently described the turban as a symbol "of a diseased skin."[41] Indeed, in a well-worn image from Shakespeare's *Othello*, the "turbaned Turk" is equated with "a circumcised dog" (5.2.363–65). The poem "Lepanto," which King James VI and I of Scotland and England wrote in 1595 about the Ottoman defeat at the Battle of Lepanto, was republished when James was coronated in 1603 with additional references to "circumcised Turban'd Turkes" fighting against "the baptiz'd race."[42] Bodily practices and clothes were perceived or represented as closely related to religious and racial identity. They were also imbricated in sexual discourses, especially as regards feminized, castrated, sodomitical, and monstrous male bodies.

Circumcision was thus conceptualized as a sexualized practice that was frequently confused with castration and was associated with sodomy.[43] As the examples I have offered so far show, circumcision served to mark religious others as sexual others with different bodies, which were then racialized. Early modern physiognomy texts and medical pamphlets confirm such links between religious, bodily, racial, and sexual differences. In *Anthropometamorphosis: Man Transform'd: or, the Artificial Changeling*, a "corporal philosophie, being an Historical tract of the Use and Abuse of Parts," John Bulwer devoted a chapter to the ordering of private parts in "divers Nations," especially to circumcision as it was practiced in Egypt, Guinea, the Cape of Good Hope, and Arabia. He made explicit connections between circumcision, race, and sexuality, writing that circumcision was supposed to "help to bridle and restrain inordinate lust and concupiscence of the flesh; but the contrary doth appear; for no nation is more given to carnal lust than Egyptians, Saracens, and Turks that are circumcised."[44] Although he depicted circumcised men as more lustful, he noted that circumcision actually caused problems for them: "that part which hangeth over the end of the foreskin, is moved up and down in coition, that in this attrition it might gather more heat and increase the pleasure of the other sex; a contentation of which they are defrauded by this injurious invention.... Circumcision detracts somewhat from the delight of women, by lessening their titillation."[45] That was why "there commonly passeth opinions of invitement, that the Jewish women desire copulation with Christians rather than their own Nation, and affect Christian carnality before circumcised venery."[46] He further stated that circumcised Turks, Persians, and "most Orientall Nations" used opium to "extimulate them to venery."[47] It was because of circumcision, which resulted in premature ejaculation and failure to give pleasure to women, Bulwer claimed, that "Mahomet[,] well knowing this their beastly and inordinate affectation, promiseth them that the felicity of their paradise should consist in a jubilee of conjunctions, that is, a coition of one act prolonged into fifty years."[48] Bulwer's account blended the discourse of circumcision with common understandings of excessive sexual desire and failure in the cross-sex sexual relations attributed to Turks and Muslims in general.

The English framed religious conversions using sexual terms. In such depictions, circumcision, an outward, bodily sign, highlighted masculine anxieties about failure in heterosexual couplings. English writers attributed sodomitical dispositions and ostensible femininity to Ottoman men and to circumcised converts to Islam. Daniel Vitkus observes that "circumcision emphasized the sexual significance of the change in faith, imagined both as a kind of castration or emasculation."[49] Jane Degenhardt argues that "conversion [was] a matter of bodies and outward materiality" that was often imagined on stage in the context of sexual intercourse.[50] Dramatizing such complex associations between religion and sexuality, Robert Daborne's play *A Christian Turned Turk* (1612), for example, put circumcision at the very center of the religious and sexual conversion of the famous pirate John Ward. Daborne dramatized the scene in which Ward underwent circumcision as a dumb show because, as the chorus notes, the act was too horrible a deed to be acted on stage:

> Enter two bearing half-moons, one with a Mahomet's head following. After them, the Mufti, or chief priest, two meaner priests bearing his train. The Mufti seated, a confused noise of music, with a show. Enter two Turks, one bearing a turban with a half-moon in it, the other a robe, a sword: a third with a globe in one hand, an arrow in the other. Two knights follow. After them, Ward on an ass, in his Christian habit, bareheaded. The two knights, with low reverence, ascend, whisper the Mufti

FIGURE 4.2. *Circumcision*, Sabuncuoğlu Şerefeddin, 1465. In *Cerrahiyetü'l Haniyye*. Fatih National Library.

in the ear, draw their swords, and pull him off the ass. He [is] laid on his belly, the tables (by two inferior priests) offered him, he lifts his hand up, subscribes, is brought to his seat by the Mufti, who puts on his turban and robe, girds his sword, then swears him on the Mahomet's head, ungirts his sword, offers him a cup of wine by the hand of a Christian. He spurns at him and throws away the cup, is mounted on the ass, who is richly clad, and with a shout, they exit. (198)[51]

Turban, sword, robes: these were the three accessories a Christian man needed to become a Turk in English narratives of circumcision. The play thus suggests that to become a Turk/Muslim, one needed to be "baptized" in the Turkish way; that is, to denounce wine and become circumcised. And as noted in the introduction, "to turn" in the term "turning Turk" could mean to change, to transform, to convert, to pervert, to go back on one's word, or to turn through space. English writers often regarded the religious conversion as a form of sexual perversion.[52]

Here, Ward's circumcision became a presentation of such perversion. While Ward must be laid on his back during the circumcision (because it makes cutting more possible, as can be seen in figure 4.2), the dumb show exaggerates this scary act by having Ward "laid" on his belly (then probably bent forward for making the cutting happen), centralizing his rear for the gaze of others. This positioning evokes sodomy. Right after Ward converts, Rabshake, the Jewish character of the play, makes fun of Ward by implying that his circumcision has resulted in penetration: "Poor fellow, how he looks since Mahomet had the handling of him! He hath had a sore night at 'Who's that knocks at the backdoor?' Cry you mercy, I thought you were an Italian captain" (210). Rabshake describes circumcision as anal sex, "knocking at the backdoor." As Celia R. Daileader notes, anal sex was called "back door sex," and "the form of difference English Renaissance culture most frequently associated with back door sex was not gender (women, after all, have anuses too) but ethnicity." Anal sex was associated with the Italians, particularly considering that "Venice [was] acting as the geopolitical and mercantile door to the East."[53] (Geuffroy's account also implied Ottoman-Italian intimacies, as noted above.) Rabshake suggests that Ward, laid on his belly, was handled anally "by Mahomet": to be converted/circumcised was to be sexually dominated by Muhammad.

Later, Rabshake makes anal fun of Ward once more, stating, "the best is behind" (211). He conflates Jews and Muslims through their bodies, suggesting that religion shapes one's body and sexual abilities:

RABSHAKE: The newcome pirate is *a reasonable handsome man of a Christian*.

AGAR: Why? Doth religion move anything in the shapes of men?

RABSHAKE: Altogether! What's the reason else that the Turk and Jew is troubled (for the most) with the gouty legs and fiery nose? To express heartburning. (174, my italics)

Jews and Muslims were frequently connected in English representations of the Ottomans, as Jonathan Burton notes: "Both Jews and Muslims rejected the Trinity. Both practiced circumcision and claimed physical descent from Abraham. Both considered Semitic languages their sacred tongues and both dressed in *caftans*, or long robes, and turbans."[54] These similarities encouraged a linkage between Judaism and Islam that we can see in Marlowe's *The Jew of Malta*, in which the two villains, the Jew Barabas and his Turkish slave Ithamore, complement each other in evil. Theirs is a partnership created through circumcision, as Barabas notes: "We are villains both; Both circumcised, we hate Christians both" (2.3.216). Similarly, Rabshake's argument connects Jewish and Muslim men through their "gouty legs and fiery nose," essentializing and manifesting their religious aberrance and racial difference through their bodies.

The body of the circumcised man is made different and presented as an index of his sodomitical nature.[55] All the references to castration, anal sex, and related sexual permutations are suggestive of how religions mark bodies and how bodies are said to act in specific ways as a result of religious practices. Ania Loomba notes that "religious difference provides a vocabulary for the expression of racial difference."[56] For English writers, exteriority was a reflection of interior faith, and the "sickly," sodomitical body of the circumcised man contrasted with the body of the "reasonable handsome man of a Christian." In this context, circumcision was generative of bodily failures. In the case of Ward's circumcision, it is conflated with castration resulting in sexual inability. Right after Ward is circumcised, the Ottoman princess Voada, for whom he converts in the first place, suddenly loses interest in him. Reminiscent of allegations that Jewish and Muslim women prefer to have sex with Christians because circumcised men cannot sexually satisfy women, Voada leaves Ward for a handsome Christian man. It is worth remembering that Captain Ward was a real-life convert and was popular in England with lower-class audiences. A ballad titled "The Seaman's Song of Captain Ward" relates: "This wicked-gotten treasure / Doth him but little pleasure / The land consumes what they got by sea, / In drunkenness and letchery, / Filthy sins of sodomy, / these evil-gotten goods so waste away."[57] While Ward's sodomy is associated with piracy in the ballad, Daborne's Turk play conveys Ward's "filthy" sodomy through emasculation symbolized by his circumcision. Ward's conversion/circumcision generates a bodily, sexual, and romantic failure, in alignment with other circumcision narratives.

In another Turk play, Shakespeare's *Othello, The Moor of Venice* (ca. 1601–1603), it is not a Christian who turned Turk but the already-circumcised, racialized body of a "Moor" whose circumcision signals his failure in heterosexual coupling and his conversion to Christianity. Called black and Moor and entrapped in Iago's racist plot, Othello, after murdering his beloved wife Desdemona, requests that Venetians "Speak of me as I am" (5.2.351). In his penultimate speech, Othello presents himself in his multilayered identities of both Venetian and Ottoman, Christian and Turk via a reference to circumcision: "In Aleppo once, / Where a malignant and a turbaned Turk / Beat a Venetian and traduced the state, / I took by th' throat the circumcisèd dog / And smote him thus" (5.2.361–65). The speech ends with Othello destroying the Turkish figure he has created by stabbing himself, taking on the role of the murdered and the murderer at the same time. By this act, he (dis)identifies across Christian-Venetian/Muslim-Ottoman categories, which presents as much confusion as the confused category of circumcision I have depicted so far. Such self-identification puts pressure on the question of mutability in conversions. That is, to what extent did the racial, gender, and sexual difference of a circumcised body allow for successful religious conversion and amorous cross-sex union in a Christian society?

Although the editors of *The Norton Shakespeare* annotate "circumcisèd" as "an identification of Othello with Jews," Othello explicitly equates himself with the figure of a turbaned, circumcised Turk.[58] In aligning himself with a circumcised Turk in Aleppo, Othello insinuates that the destruction of his love and himself is an effect of his body marked by circumcision—a religious and racial mark. In Othello's account, circumcision is also a spatial mark within the play's Mediterranean context.[59] Othello links himself with Ottoman Mediterranean territories by evoking his travels and relations in the Black Sea, the Bosporus, the Dardanelles, Egypt, and Barbary throughout the play. His name itself, which is uttered for the first time by the duke during a meeting about the Ottoman threat, echoes "Ottoman": "Valiant Othello, we must straight employ you / Against the general enemy Ottoman" (1.2.48–49).[60] Othello's evocation of the Ottoman city Aleppo to express his difference at the end of the play once again calls into play the Ottoman Mediterranean as an operative context. The play's sources for the Ottoman Mediterranean context were early modern travelogues, chronicles, and ethnographic writings such as Richard Knolles's *The Generall Historie of the Turkes* and Leo Africanus's *Description of Africa*. Such accounts often offered complex factual and sometimes fictional depictions of sexual relations in the Mediterranean in a mode of disgust, fascination, confusion, and misunderstanding. In these accounts (as well as Sanders's narrative, which I explore in the next section), the Mediterranean was often represented as a sodomitical site. Travel into and within this space was perceived and presented as not only a promising prospect of wealth but also as a highly risky act that might put one at risk for sodomitical captivity, slavery, and conversion. Often, such trepidations were reflected through the religious and racial mark of circumcision. While Othello stages himself as an implicitly Christian traveler, he at the same time creates himself as Othello the Ottoman, inhabiting the travelogues' threatening figure of the turbaned and circumcised Turk of Aleppo.

Othello's self-presentation as "a turbaned Turk" and "circumcisèd dog" complements earlier moments when Othello's "Moorish" body and his sexual function as an extension of it is presented as a problem in Christian Venice. *Othello* starts with Iago's racist account of sex between black Othello and white Desdemona as a scandal of bestial sodomy: "an old black ram / Is tupping your white ewe" (1.1.88–89). Iago animalizes Othello as "a Barbary horse" and imagines his sexual performance as "making the beast with two backs" that would generate unnatural, monstrous children: "coursers for cousins and jennets for germans" (1.1.113, 1.1.118, 1.1.114). With his racial otherness, Othello is put in the complex matrix of sodomy in Iago's racist fantasy of interracial sex as bestial and unnatural and hence sodomitical. Othello's lodging in Venice, "the Sagittary," a reference to the mythic half-man, half-horse centaur, also suggests this type of conflation, evoking monstrosity and bestiality in relation to Othello's difference (1.1.159). In this space, Ian Smith argues, lines between queer and race blur in producing English racial and sexual norms.[61] Othello's use of "circumcisèd dog" as a curse to defamiliarize and dehumanize himself before his suicide not only reduces him to the level of disposable animals but reconnects his racial and sexual difference by conflating the circumcised man and castrated dog. As a circumcised body part, Othello's penis is a site of difference where, as Daniel Boyarin puts it, "sex(uality), religion, and race" intersect.[62]

As a sign of essential difference, circumcision in Othello's final words complements the abovementioned accounts that link the circumcised body in its imperfection and failure to sodomy, effeminacy, and castration. Earlier in the play, Othello announces himself as "defunct," lacking in sexual urges, in response to Desdemona's request to join him in Cyprus to have "the rites" of love: "Vouch with me heaven, I therefore beg it not / To please the palate of my appetite, / Nor to comply with heat—the young affects / In me defunct—and proper satisfaction, / But to be free and bounteous to her mind" (1.3.256, 1.3.260–264). Iago, too, mentions Othello's "weak function" in his gender-inverted relationship with Desdemona who, for Iago, is the active agent of the couple: "His soul is so enfetter'd to her love / That she may make, unmake, do what she list, / Even as her appetite shall play the god / With his weak function" (2.3.319-22). Iago's use of "function" is reminiscent of Othello's use of "defunct," as both terms are etymologically connected: "defunct" derives from the Latin "*dēfunctus*," meaning "discharged, deceased, dead" (prefix de+*fungi* [to perform, discharge]); and "function," from the Latin "*functiō*" (performance, execution), which also derives from *funct*—the past participle stem of "*fungi*."[63] Othello's "defunct" is echoed in Iago's "weak function" in a shortened form—"de-*funct*" as "*funct*-ion" cut short or circumcised.

Descriptions of Othello as defunct and with weak function implies that his body is dysfunctional during sex with Desdemona even though he is "enfetter'd" to her like a slave in chains. As we have seen, in English discourses, circumcision was often conflated with castration, and English authors frequently claimed it decreased sexual prowess and capacity even among the nations that were, in Bulwer's words, most "given to carnal lust ... Egyptians, Saracens and Turks that are circumcised." Circumcised men fail, in Bulwer's categorization, in "Christian venery," to which women married to circumcised men were attracted. On the one hand, Othello is depicted in the play as superior in his military power and as "lascivious," "valiant," "warlike," and "lusty" (1.1.127, 1.3.48, 2.1.28, 2.3.282). His threatening virility foreshadows the military threat the Ottomans pose from the very beginning of the play. On the other hand, such excess is contradictorily reduced to weakness and deficiency, which is connected not only to his age but also to his circumcised black body, which has no "heat [and] proper satisfaction." Othello's excessive affection for Desdemona is a sign of effeminacy (in the early modern sense of the term) within the militaristic masculine homosocial structure that demands a prioritization of male-male companionship.[64] Othello himself sees his immoderate love as a problem when he calls himself in the same speech "one that loved not wisely but too well" before piercing his body with a phallic weapon (5.2.353). Othello's reference to himself as "circumcisèd dog" therefore exposes his failure as the Moor of Venice to act like the white uncircumcised Christian men of Venice in the business of cross-sex love.[65] As in *A Christian Turned Turk*, in *Othello* circumcision is a gender and sexual problem in the masculinist and heterosexual economy.

In a larger sense, circumcision in these dramatic examples and in travel accounts and ethnographic narratives was embedded in what Michel Foucault calls the "utterly confused category" of sodomy.[66] As the examples above show, in English and European perception, circumcision itself was an utterly confused practice and it was often misrepresented as baptism, castration, failure, effeminacy, and sodomy. It is not simply a bodily difference; it was a confused signifier of overlapping religious, racial, and sexual demarcations shared by what Sandys called "effeminate Asians."[67] As Valerie Traub asserts, " Early modern travel accounts, in particular, contribute significantly to the construction of the contours and meanings of the early modern [Western] body."[68] The circumcised Ottoman men in such accounts function to construct the opposite: the intact Christian body as the perfect form.

English Boys Circumcised

While theatrical representations usually chose adult man to stage circumcision as the bodily aspect of conversion, travel accounts frequently used youthful bodies to produce and project concerns about religious and sexual conversions. Adult bodies were already complete or incomplete, but boyish bodies were still open to bodily changes. Baudier's account of the forementioned 1582 royal circumcision celebration, for instance, evoked the conversion of boys via circumcision:

> But if the description of this Royall Feast hath beene a pleasing diuersion vnto vs in the toile of this Historie, let vs end it according to the naturall course of pleasure, by the griefe which followes. Doubtlesse it will be great

enough to impart it to those which shall read the issue of this Chapter, where we obserue than during the spectacles of this solemnity, the wretched Grecian... troupes in this place to make themselues Mahometans: Some abandoned Christianitie to auoid the oppression of the Turkes, others for the hope of priuate profit: The youngest and most beautifull were sent into the Serrail, with the Ichioglans, and the rest among the Azamoglans: This hope of better fortune drew the Idlenesse of many young men, so as they could hardly find Masters enough to cut them: This detestable troupe of Rascals, went to shew themselues before the Grand Seigneur, their Bonnets vnder their feet, in signe that they did tread their law and honour vnder foot: There a Turkish Priest did cause them to lift vp the demonstratiue finger of the right hand, in signe that they did not beleeue but one God in one person, & to say with a loud voice, Laila ey lala alla Mehemer Rasoul alla; Then they led them into certaine Pauillions, which were erected expresly at the end of the place where they were circumcised: The number of these cast awayes was found to bee aboue foure thousand souls.[69]

Baudier could not resist connecting the circumcision of city boys to the circumcision of abducted *devşirme* boys in order to generate horror after his lengthy description of his fascination with the celebration in previous pages. Likewise, Bulwer's ethnomedical treatise recalled abducted boys in the context of depicting circumcision/castration: "The Turks that dwell in Europe and Asia do use the very same castration on such young boys as they can seize on in the Christian countries."[70]

Such descriptions reflect concerns about the Ottoman practices of abducting and enslaving Christian boys, who would then be imagined as forcibly violated, as in Thomas Sanders's account of the crew of the ship *Jesus* that I introduced earlier. The monstrous act of circumcision done on youthful English bodies raised the larger specter of abducted and sodomized boys in the Ottoman Mediterranean. In this section, I return to Sanders's story to highlight how it reflected contemporary anxieties about circumcision and abduction while making youthful bodies vulnerable objects of desire and transformation, both their own and those of others.

Sanders's narrative of the circumcised English boys of the *Jesus* belongs to and contributed to the abovementioned discourses.[71] It most explicitly located the circumcision of abducted boys in the Mediterranean economy of captivity and conversion. The voyage of the *Jesus*, Sanders notes, "was set foorth by the right worshipfull sir Edward Osborne knight, chiefe merchant of all the Turkish company" (192). It left for "Tripolis in Barbarie" from Portsmouth in 1583;

in Tripolis (Tripoli), the crew was "very well entertained by the king of that country" (192). However, despite emerging good relations and a profitable trade in oil with the king, the crew ended up in slavery after Romaine Sonnings, the French factor in the crew, quarreled with an Englishman from another trading ship. When the Frenchman Sonnings tried to help one of captives, Patrone Norado, escape, "who the year before had done this Sonnings some pleasure there" but "was indebted to the King," the king attacked the ship right after it left the shore (193). The twenty-three members of the crew of the *Jesus* fell into captivity and slavery and three, including the captain, were killed. After this point, Sanders's account of the English trade turned into a conventional story of captivity devised with the trope of Turkish tyranny over Christian slaves and a conversion tale with a religious moral mediated through English boys.

In this narrative of "miserable bondage and slavery" of the Englishmen and of other slavery practices such as Spanish human trafficking in Africa "to steal negroes," English boys figure to convey the horrors of bondage and conversion (195). Yet Sanders mentioned an English boy on another ship who converted voluntarily. When an English ship called the *Green Dragon* arrived at "an Island called Gerbi . . . six score miles from Tripolis" that was ruled by the king's son, "a very unhappy boy in that ship, and understanding that whosoever would turne Turke should be well enterteined of the kings sonne, this boy did runne a shoare, and voluntarily turned Turke" (197). Without explaining why the boy was unhappy, Sanders recognized the probable lure of the Mediterranean world for some boys, who would willingly leave their crew and convert. Some early modern European reports also noted that some Christian men voluntarily converted to Islam, seeking wealth and sexual freedom in their pursuit of same-sex relations or to avoid punishment from local Christian authorities when they were caught practicing same-sex sexual relations in the Mediterranean. Some accounts reported that boys in European vessels would have been instructed not to leave the ship by themselves because of the threat of sodomitical Turks who kidnapped and exploited boys.[72] We don't know exactly why this "very unhappy boy" of the *Green Dragon* escaped from the English party. However, his deliberate escape and immediate conversion to join the boy harem of the king's son implies that boys among English crews were instructed about the sexual habits of Turks. Despite this information, or perhaps because of it, some boys wanted to become Muslim and live in Muslim households. Sanders's use of "unhappy" in reference to the boy also makes it possible to entertain the probability that the boy ran to "voluntarily turn Turk" for unspeakable erotic reasons, considering that in early modern English, "unhappy" signified "causing or involving trouble or mischief; objectionable, evil; naughty."[73] Accordingly, unhappiness and sadness appear in literature as linked to intense same-sex desire among men within the social norms of procreative heteronormativity.[74] Hence, in the Mediterranean, what was taught to be transgressive and unacceptable could actually be tempting for others, especially the "very unhappy" ones.

Leaving this unhappy boy aside, Sanders quickly moves to a more detailed story of the two heroic English boys of his own ship the *Jesus* to narrate the horrors of Mediterranean captivity through boys taken and forcefully converted:

> Shortly after the kings sonne came to Tripolis to visit his father, and seeing our company, hee greatly *fancied* Richard Burges our Purser, and James Smith: they were both yong men, therefore he was very desirous to have them to turne Turkes, but they would not yeeld to his desire, saying: We are your fathers slaves, and as slaves wee will serve him. Then his father the king sent for them, and asked them if they would turne Turkes? And they saide: If it please your highnesse, Christians we were borne, and so we will remaine, and beseeched the king that they might not bee inforced thereunto. The king had there before in his house a sonne of a yeoman of our Queenes guard, whom the kings sonne had inforced to turne Turke, his name was John Nelson: him the king caused to be brought to these yong men, and then said unto them: Wil not you beare this your countreyman company, and be Turke as hee is? And they saide, that they would not yeeld thereunto during life. (197)

The king's son's house appears as a harem with young English men, including the "unhappy boy" of the *Green Dragon* and the youthful son of a yeoman of the queen's guard, John Nelson. Recounting these incidents of conversion and foreshadowing what would follow, Sanders's use of the term "fancy" hints at the homoerotics of the conversion economy. As the OED defines the term, "fancy" means "to take a fancy to; to entertain a liking for; to be pleased with; to like" while in its early usage in the sixteenth century, the verb followed by a personal object signified "to be or fall in love with."[75] The word appears as a motive for erotic attraction to circumcising boys in Thomas Gainsford's *The Glory of England*. Gainsford narrated the story of "Scanderbeg, or *George Castriot*," an Albanian *devşirme* boy who later becomes a military commander who leads a rebellion against the Ottomans. The sultan kills the king of Epirus and his sons after taking Epirus, Serbia, Bulgaria, and Albania, "except the youngest named *George*, whom he so fancied in his infancie, that he presently circumcised him, instructed him in the Law of *Mahomet*, and kept him secure in his owne palace."[76] Gainsford later voyeuristically described a wrestling duello in which the boy took part "starknaked," noting that he was "not fully 18. yeere old, and without procrastinating the matter, stripped himselfe before them, and made them as much amazed at the beautifulnes... and comelinesse of his person as greatnesse of courage."[77] Likewise, Sanders's use of "fancy" with the adverb "greatly" to refer to the feelings of the king's son ("greatly *fancied* Richard Burges our Purser, and James Smith") hints at the son's intense erotic desire for English boys. Sanders had already prepared the reader with his description of the son's famous entertainments with and his fancy for beautiful English boys. His desire for two English youths further emphasizes the son's amorous drives, which he sought to fulfill through forceful circumcision and conversion.

In Sanders's narrative of the conversion process, circumcision became a means of gaining control over the bodies of these boys. The two Christian boys, Richard and James, resisted conversion and the son's "desire"; they preferred slavery to "turning Turk." However, the king's son could not control his attraction to these two boys, whom he carried to his home in Gerbi. In their letter to Sanders, the two boys stated that they "were violently used" there and forced to convert. When the two resisted conversion a second time, the son used "force" on them: "Then the kings sonne very angerly said unto him [Richard]: By Mahomet thou shalt presently be made Turke. Then called he for his men, and commanded them to make him Turke, and they did so, and *circumcised him*, and would have had him speake the wordes that thereunto belonged, but he answered them stoutly that he would not: and although they had put on him the habite of a Turke, yet sayd he, A Christian I was borne, and so I will remaine, though you force me to doe otherwise" (197, my italics). The son used the same force with John as well, and both boys were forcibly "made Turk." As Sanders's language ("force," "violently used") implies, the boys were physically tortured with sodomitical violence.[78] The conversion in this scene emerges, in Burton's words, as a picture of "male-male rape," or what one could call circumcised-uncircumcised rape.[79] That is, the encounter between the English youths and the king's son is imagined through a circumcised Turk's coercive masculine domination over uncircumcised boys. This language, in Patricia Parker's terms, "combines the territorial threat of Turkish conquest with sodomitical invasion of which circumcision functions as the outward bodily sign."[80]

Yet the divine intervention that Sanders saw as operating in English relations in the Mediterranean disrupted the tyrannous domination of the king and his son. Sanders wrote, "Here may all true Christian hearts see the wonderfull workes of God shewed upon such infidels, blasphemers, whoremasters, and renegate Christians, and so you shall reade in the ende of this booke, of the like upon the unfaithfull king and all his children" (195). God's will and the English queen's care for her subjects would finally liberate the English party, even though half of them were dead by the time Sanders was writing. Sanders claimed to have written a letter to his father in Devonshire that was delivered to the queen. Upon her intervention, the party was set free, thanks to the English ambassador in Constantinople, who was reported to have used the commission he got from the Ottoman court to liberate it. The freed English group demanded the freedom of the two boys, since they were not "infidels, blasphemers, whoremasters, and renegate Christians" who willingly converted; they had been forced to convert. It was necessary to save them as an example of God's will and of Christians who became "renegate." But the king refused the freed sailors' demand, saying that "it was against their law to deliver them, for they were turned Turkes" (198).

Although the English party was "set at liberty" in 1585, Sanders did not stop there; he continued to tell the story of the boys after the liberation of their shipmates. In Tripolis, a plague occurred and the king's own soldiers killed him. As a result, "the kings sonne, according to the custome there, went to Constantinople, to surrender up all his father's treasure, goods, captives, and concubines, unto the great Turke, and tooke with him our saide Purser Richard Burges, and James Smith, and also the other two Englishmen, which he the said kings sonne had inforced to become Turkes" (198). Reminiscent of J. M. Gramaye's report that Christian children captured by pirates were sent as presents to "Turke or his Bassas [to satisfy their] Sodomitical lusts for Boyes," the two English boys become objects who were circulated from one space to another, from one master to another.

Yet these boys did not become ganymedes/*ganimets* again. On the journey to Constantinople, the four English youths on board heroically organized an uprising to kill the king's son. However, they failed, and as a result, "Master Blonkets boy was killed, and the sayde James Smith, and our Purser Richard Burges, and the other Englishman, were taken and bound into chaines, to be hanged at their arrivall in Constantinople." But with intervention of some Venetians, the boys were soon saved:

> As the Lordes will was, about two dayes after, passing through the gulfe of Venice, at an Island called Cephalonia, they met with two of the duke of Venice his Gallies, which tooke that Galley, and killed the kings sonne, and his mother, and all the Turkes that were there, in number 150, and they saved the Christian captives, and would have killed the two Englishmen because they were circumcised, and become Turkes, had not the other Christian captives excused them, saying, that they were inforced to be Turkes, by the kings sonne, and shewed the Venetians also, how they did

enterprise at sea to fight against all the Turks, and that their two fellowes were slaine in that fight. Then the Venetians saved them, and they, with all the residue of the said captives, had their libertie, which were in number 150 or thereabouts, and the saide Gallie, and all the Turkes treasure was confiscated to the use of the state of Venice. And from thence our two Englishmen travelled homeward by land. (198–99)

In the Mediterranean economy of captivity, the Venetians captured the Ottoman ship, intending to kill all "circumcised" men. Thus, circumcision was a mark that liberated or enslaved men, or even brought their death, depending on how and by whom it was perceived. Sanders's account nevertheless probes a simplistic discourse of the circumcised body as heretical by highlighting how certain bodies could be changed and branded without their consent. The two English boys had been circumcised against their will. They were innocent of this non-Christian stain on their body, and as a result, they were saved instead of being killed by the Christian Venetians. Sanders did not leave his reader with curiosity about the fate of these boys. He later assured that "within two monethts after our arrivall at London, our said Purser Richard Burges, and his fellow came home also" (199). As "the Lord's will was," Richard and James were free in England, yet they carried a irrecoverable mark of circumcision on their body.

The anxiety over circumcision that Sanders's account reveals is embedded in the Ottoman threat and in European and English men's fear that they would be captured, abducted, and converted by Turks in the Mediterranean space. The story of the *Jesus* suggests that Mediterranean trade relations were not free from risks of captivity, enslavement, and death in the hands of cruel rulers. Yet it has a happy ending despite the struggles it relates. Sanders noted that "we are bound to praise Almightie God, during our lives, and as duetie bindeth us, to pray for the preservation of our most gracious Queene, for the great care her Majestie had over us, her poore Subjects." In Sanders's narrative, the queen always cares for her subjects and saves them when they are in need. The account thus ends not only with the moral of Christianity winning over tyrannous Islam but also with a pragmatic, nationalist twist that encouraged further relations in the Mediterranean space.[81]

In fact, Queen Elizabeth I was very involved in this conflict. In 1584, she sent a letter to Sultan Murad III requesting "the restitution of the shippe called *Jesus*, and the English captives detained in Tripolie in Barbarie, and for certaine other prisoners." The letter, which was included in Hakluyt's *The Principal Navigations*, shows that trade and traffic in the Mediterranean involved troubles. "Most noble and puissant Emperor," the queen wrote,

> about two yeeres nowe passed, wee wrote unto your Imperiall Majestie, that our welbeloved servant, William Hareborne, a man of great reputation and honour, might be received under your high authoritie, for our Ambassadour in Constantinople, and other places, under the obedience of your Empire of Musulman: And also that the Englishmen, being our Subjects, might exercise entercourse and marchandize in all those Provinces, no lesse freely then the French, Polonians, Venetians, Germanes, and other your confederats, which traveile through divers of the East parts: endevouring that by mutuall trafique, the East may be joyned and knit to the West.[82]

Evoking the trade privileges the Ottomans had given to Englishmen to freely engage in commerce in the Mediterranean under Ottoman control, Elizabeth noted that some of her subjects had been ill treated in "Tripolis in Barbarie, and at Algiers," adding, "wee doe friendly and lovingly desire your Imperiall Majestie, that you will understand their causes by our Ambassadour, and afterward give commaundement to the Lieutenants and Presidents of those Provinces, that our people may henceforth freely, without any violence, or injurie, traveile, and do their businesse in those places."[83] The Ottomans heard the queen: in Sanders's account, the Ottoman administration actually took action for the liberty of the captured sailors, and confirming this, Hakluyt said that right after the Ottoman court in Constantinople received the queen's letter, the sultan commanded the ruler of Tripolis to release the Englishmen.[84] Hakluyt's insertion of the letter exchange between English and Ottoman rulers following Sanders's account thus encouraged Englishmen to participate in Mediterranean trade despite risk factors. Such encouragement motivated by the queen's support signals how England had begun to assert its relative power in the Mediterranean through Ottoman privileges that had been earned through intense diplomatic exchanges.

What is striking in Elizabeth's letter is her hope that "by mutuall trafique the East may be joyned and knit to the West." When the East and the West joined through interactions in the Mediterranean, imbricated in those relations were enforced bodily transformations of boys in an imperial economy that marked youthful penises. In the Mediterranean space, boys and their bodies mattered in religious, economic, and political relations. Circumcision of boys—whether it was celebrated or condemned—was not simply related to the removal of the foreskin. Rather, it had various and shifting religious, racial, sexual, and political connotations for both the Ottomans and the English. It was a practice that English writers condemned as foreign, non-Christian, heretical, barbarous, sodomitical, and feminine, while at the same time these writers expressed both curiosity about and fascination with circumcision festivities. The Ottomans celebrated the practice, and Ottoman poets used those celebrations as a moment not only to acclaim Ottoman imperial power but also to praise the beauty of uncircumcised European boys.

Viewed through the prism of circumcision, the boy, with his youthful and vulnerable body, makes clear the mutability of bodies in religious and sexual conversions as a part of imperial politics of domination. Conversion signified by the convertibility of his body was what the Ottomans desired, "fancied" in erotic terms, braiding together homoeroticism and religion, and erotics and domination. The boy's body and his ephemeral youth not only made it possible to entertain the possibility of shifts in religious orientation but also revealed power-inflected erotic possibilities in gender and racial hierarchies in the imperial structure. The traveling boy became an object of an erotic gaze and desire that was materialized through a mark on his body. Perhaps this mark was no more prominent and apparent elsewhere than in the regendered bodies of "castrated boys" or eunuchs, the subject of next chapter.

5
―――

Regendering Boys

One dark side of early modern Mediterranean relations that has usually been invisible is the systematic castration of black African boys. These black boys, who were often younger than fifteen, were abducted and enslaved mostly from south of the Sahara and transported into upper Egypt, where they were castrated to serve empires as eunuchs. Castrated abducted boys engendered similar concerns as the circumcision of abducted boys did in England. In addition, on the English stage, they also became racialized objects of fascination and exoticism. In one of Shakespeare's Mediterranean plays, *Anthony and Cleopatra* (ca. 1606–1607), for instance, eunuchs are on stage to mark the oriental Egyptian setting of the play. The play opens with Philo mentioning that Anthony's heart "reneges all temper, / And is become the bellows and the fan / To cool a gipsy's lust" (1.1.8–10). As if responding to the invoking of "fans," Cleopatra emerges on stage in majesty, facilitated, as stage direction marks, by a group of "eunuchs fanning her" (1.1.10). The simultaneous materialization of the fanning Anthony as the fanning eunuchs walk in forces the audience to gaze upon the eunuchs and recognize them as a crucial part of the play. What might be considered textually an insignificant detail—the presentation of eunuchs—is, as Michael Neill observes, in fact crucial in performance, for it initiates the grandiose theatricality of the Egyptian queen for whom Anthony gives up the empire.[1] Later these fanning eunuchs would become "pretty dimpled boys, like smiling Cupids, / With divers-colour'd fans" (2.2.208–209), bringing abducted boys made into eunuchs and servant boys together in Cleopatra's court. Like abducted boys, the exotic eunuch is an object of curiosity and desire, as is evident in Cleopatra's question whether eunuchs have "affection" (1.5.12). Cleopatra has been a voluminously studied character in explorations of early modern gender and race, while eunuchs are often ignored in such scholarship, even though they are almost always standing next to the black queen in the play.[2] Who are these eunuchs? Why did an increasing interest in staging eunuchs on stage emerge? What work does their presence do? What histories do these differently embodied once-boy-now-eunuch figures reveal?

The emergence and popularity of such theatrical eunuchs have long been connected to both classical and Christian traditions, including Terence's Roman play *The Eunuch* and the biblical allusions to an Ethiopian eunuch and to "eunuchs who have made themselves eunuchs for the sake of the kingdom of heaven."[3] In his exploration of eunuchs, Anston Bosman uncovers the pairing of eunuch and black characters and notes "the broader context in which this pairing of eunuch and blackamoor recurs—the powerful and protean culture of empire, where these two figures share a political history grounded in two millennia of travel and conquest, enslavement and exile."[4] Considering the import of geopolitics in shaping the representation of eunuchs, my focus will be on the early modern Mediterranean, since during the period when the eunuch became an established theatrical figure, an exotic signifier in early modern culture, and an inevitable trope in Orientalist arts, the figure was associated with the Ottoman Mediterranean in most cases.[5] Hence, such representations are not merely inheritors of Christian and Greco-Roman conventions but also are deeply interlinked with and very much shaped by contemporaneous practices and discourses on a global scale, specifically regarding black boys captured in the African slave trade.

This chapter concerns abducted boys who were deprived of their boyhood through castration—their current and future perceived gender identity and their future reproductive capacity—and imprisoned in a new gender category in the Ottoman Empire. These boys, who often were castrated at the ages of seven, nine, or older, served no longer as boys but as eunuchs. Their bodies were refigured, reinscribed, resignified, re-formed, and regendered. In contrast to the white boys with Euro-Christian origins whose abductions were legitimated by religious difference, these black boys, whose systematic abductions were justified by antiblack sentiments, mediated an emergent racial vocabulary that was inflected by gender and sexuality. Uniquely, early modern Ottomans marked and distinguished eunuchs as black and white. This racialization, I will argue, was a crucial—albeit underanalyzed—component of the way these figures were depicted in Ottoman treatises, which reveal an emerging race-making process that constituted blackness as inextricably interlinked with nonnormative somatic, gender, and sexual significations. Specifically, some of these tracts conflated being black with being a eunuch. Furthermore, the historical boys remade as eunuchs traveled to England figuratively via their depiction in travelogues, chronicles, and diplomatic accounts. As a result, they appeared on the English stage as a distinctly racialized gender template loaded with Mediterranean discourses.

In what follows, therefore, I first trace eunuchs of the Ottoman court, a court that maintained and promoted the visibility of these figures and shaped the proliferation of eunuch imagery in early modern Europe. I subsequently shift my focus to England to catalogue and frame English representations of eunuchs in this Ottoman context in order to highlight how abducted black boys and their abductions operated in a cross-cultural matrix that contributed to the revival of such figurations in literature, anatomy texts, travelogues, and plays. This juxtaposition helps explain why "wherever we find a eunuch" in the early modern English imaginary, "we nearly always find a black character."[6] Abducted as boys and made into eunuchs, these black figures, with their distance from whiteness and from a putatively complete manhood, were invariably distanced historically and geographically from white boys and from nonblack populations, both in the Ottoman Empire and in the English imaginary.[7]

Eunuchs in the Ottoman Court

Although eunuchs were mainly associated with the Ottomans in early modern Europe, they were not an Ottoman invention. The Ottoman use of eunuchs was built on a long cross-cultural history. The fifth-century BCE historian Herodotus wrote that the victorious Persians conquered places and "picked the best-looking boys and castrated them, cutting off their testicles and turning them into eunuchs."[8] As early as the tenth century BCE, eunuchs were employed in the courts of the empires of ancient Mesopotamia, Egypt, and China, and in the medieval period they were employed by the Abbasids, the Byzantines, the Sassanians, the Mamluks, and the Seljuks. In Europe, some medieval towns such as Prague or Verdun were popular places for producing eunuchs and selling them to Muslims in Spain and elsewhere.⁹ Eunuchs served at royal courts as harem guardians, tutors for princes, and pleasure companions for the rulers.¹⁰

By the fifteenth century, eunuchs had become an important part of the administrative apparatus of the Ottoman Empire. The practice of employing eunuchs began alongside the implementation of the *devşirme* system, which, as the first chapter discussed, involved the systematic abduction of white Christian youths from the Balkans to serve in the military and administrative posts of the empire. While many of the *devşirme* boys were trained for positions outside the imperial household and only a few were made into eunuchs, from the mid-sixteenth century onward, black eunuchs were trained exclusively for gender-segregated domestic service in the harem (the private royal household) or became part of the powerful corps of eunuchs in the court.

Ottoman eunuchs were elite, high-status slaves who belonged to the sultan's household. This status carried with it privileges such as education, courtly training, and proximity to the sultan and his family. More specifically, eunuchs were responsible for supervising the women in the harem, mediating between the sultan and his family members, guarding access to the interiors of the palace and to the sultan's private chamber, and overseeing the early training and education of princes. As Jateen Lad notes, "If we view the harem as a diagram of power, then the eunuchs were its principal upholders, ensuring that the Ottoman obsession with status and hierarchy emanated from its core."¹¹ The chief harem eunuch was one of the most powerful positions in the empire. Some court eunuchs rose to even higher positions such as Suleyman Pasha, the Bosnian Hadım Ali Pasha, the Bulgarian Hadım Mesih Pasha, and the Albanian Hadım Hasan Pasha, who became grand viziers, a most influential position, second only to the sultan himself. (It is worth noting that no black person—eunuch or not—was ever promoted to this position.) Others, such as the Albanian Ali Pasha, became important military commanders, and still others, including Beshir Agha, contributed greatly to the empire's intellectual culture.¹²

Eunuchs had a very particular place in the highly gendered space of the Ottoman court. Topkapı Palace, the main residence of the Ottoman sultans, was composed of three different court spaces: the first was open to the public; the second was an administrative space used for meetings among courtiers, soldiers, bureaucrats, ambassadors, and the imperial council; and the third was the innermost courtyard that was the space of the royal household, known also as *harem-i humayun* (the imperial harem) or *enderun-i humayun* (the imperial interior). Access to this space was limited to eunuchs, select servant boys who were being trained for imperial service, and, of course, the sultan and his family. As Leslie Peirce states, "Only the sultan could freely cross the boundary isolat-

FIGURE 5.1. *The Funeral of Nur Banu Sultan*. In *Shahan-Shah-Namah-i Lokhmann*, 1592. The three courtyards of the palace and the corps of black eunuchs in the innermost gate are clearly visible in this miniature.

ing the inner courtyard, but when he did, he was surrounded by its eunuchs and 'youths of the interior.'"[13] Moreover, the imperial harem included two private spaces that were even more strictly protected: first, a male space for boys, young men, dwarves, and mutes; and second, the family harem for women and the children of the sultan.[14] Eunuchs guarded the interior boundaries between the family harem and the sultan's chamber and the gate to the third courtyard, which was known as the Gate of Felicity (fig. 5.1).

Beyond this third gate, the sultan was the only adult man in the imperial harem. Perceived as nonmen, the eunuchs were distinguished by their large, beardless faces, high-pitched voices, and distinctive facial features and stature. (The serving boys who worked in this space were also forbidden to grow beards, which signaled not only their youth or boyhood but also that they were not yet capable of sexual activity or reproduction.) The imperial harem was thus a highly gendered space with strict rituals for and restrictions on movement and bodies, all under the protection of eunuchs. The eunuchs' movement between the different spaces of the court clearly indicated that they existed outside the boundaries of adult male masculinity and even beyond the gender binary altogether. Their free movement across and between the rigidly gendered spaces of the harem as castrated, nonreproductive slaves suggests that they were perceived as neither masculine nor feminine, or both masculine and feminine.[15]

While this unique status made these eunuchs useful and valuable for the Ottoman rulers and afforded a few some power, their gender ambiguity was sometimes attacked, especially after the strict separation of black and white eunuchs. When the women's harem was constructed as a part of the Topkapı Palace during the reign of Suleyman I, black eunuchs were assigned to the innermost spaces behind the third gate, while white eunuchs of Caucasian, Balkan, and Slavic origin became the gatekeepers of the third courtyard. (It must be noted that most women in the harem had also been abducted, making the Ottoman palace an abduction hub.) These two groups of eunuchs were at first loosely separated in terms of their assigned spaces and duties. After Sultan Murad III implemented the office of the Agha of the Gate of Felicity (Ağa-yı Darüssaade, or Darüssaade Ağası) under the authority of a black chief eunuch in 1575, this segregation was strictly enshrined and codified. Around this time, the majority of eunuchs became black: of about 1,000 to 1,200 eunuchs in the palace, 600 to 800 were black eunuchs under the supervision of the chief harem eunuch.[16]

This division has long elicited scholars' curiosity. In his influential work on the harem, N. M. Penzer opines that "white eunuchs—Georgians and Circassians—were given jobs that would never bring them into close touch with the women, as in most cases their castration was incomplete. But as regards the negroes, the highest prices were paid for those who, besides being entirely *rasé*, possessed the ugliest and most revolting faces, it being imagined (correctly or not) that this was a further guard against any profligacy on the part of the women."[17] Drawing evidence from European travelogues on the putative ugliness of black eunuchs, Penzer specifies that black eunuchs were "entirely *rasé*," meaning both their testicles and penises had been removed. Fully castrated black eunuchs were seen as not posing a sexual threat to the women of the harem, and in this sense, they were unlike white eunuchs, who had only had their testicles removed. For Penzer, this must have been the reason for this separation.[18]

Yet even as we can assume that fear of sex between harem women and men impacted these decisions, we do not know if this explanation regarding different castration methods is historically accurate. Additionally, seeing the penis as the site of manliness is a more recent modern idea. As in Europe, in the early modern Ottoman Empire, the discourses around embodiment, gender, and sexuality were tightly bound to Galenic humoral ideals before the shift from "the regime of the scrotum" to "the regime of the penis."[19] The early modern model of manliness did not privilege the penis or pleasure but rather the testicles and reproduction as the constitutive sites of manhood. As Gary Taylor shows, the post-Enlightenment decline of eunuchs in the West coincided with the rise, so to speak, of the power of the penis. Rebecca Ann Bach likewise sees a testicular model that "value[d] breeding" developing at the end of the seventeenth century into a new sexual pleasure based on masculinity, one that focused on acts.[20] Will Fisher, who traced the tensions between these co-temporal regimes in early modern England by examining phallic and scrotal codpieces, confirms "a gradual erosion of the cultural centrality of the testicles over the course of the early modern period."[21] The testicles—as the principal part of the body, edging out even the heart, for Galen[22]—were gradually replaced by the penis as the principal organ that separated men from women. Indeed, in his *Anthropometamorphosis*, John Bulwer wrote that "Galen ... doth constitute the testicles to be next to the heart, a fountain of heat and strength; so that the testicles cut out, not only the other fountain destroyed, but the heat of the very Heart is lessened and debilitated.... The Voice and very forme becommeth womanish."[23] That is why eunuchs were "smooth and produce not a Beard, the signe of virility and therein not men."[24] Earlier in the second half of the sixteenth century, Bartholomeus Cocles in his physiognomy book had declared that eunuchs "are very much changed from the nature of menne, into the nature of women."[25] Bulwer's example for such practices was the Ottoman court as described in travel accounts. He copied Robert Withers's account, published in Samuel Purchas's 1625 compilation: "But the eunuchs in the Great Turk's seraglio, who are in number about two hundred, they are all of them not only gelt, but have their yards also clean cut off, and are chosen of those renagadi youths which are presented from time to time to the Grand Signior."[26] The idea that white eunuchs were separated from black eunuchs because they still had penises suggests the emergence of a penis-based reproduction and gender epistemology in the Ottoman Empire in the sixteenth century. However, such a probable shift in the valuation of genital morphology can only partially explain the reason for the separation of white from black eunuchs.

Besides the import of medical discourses regarding gender and reproduction, cultural ideologies that were emerging and at work in relation to the rise of the black African population in the empire suggest that the spatial division of white and black eunuchs may have also been based on a racial hierarchy. A similar hierarchy seems to have operated among the women of the harem: black women of African descent were given the hardest work such as cleaning walls, floors, and passageways while white women did lighter work.[27] Were black eunuchs fully castrated because they were thought to be "natural slaves"? Or because they were considered more highly sexual and thus in need of greater means of control? Were their white counterparts thought to be less masculine and thus less in need of castration? Or was the black body imagined to cross genders more easily and smoothly?

I propose that racial difference operated crucially in the separation of black and white eunuchs in the gendered hierarchies that idealized white masculinity. Early modern gender and racial discourses, as I will argue below, were intertwined in the figure of the black eunuch, who was distinguished from their white counterpart in the articulation, management, and structuring of human difference in the empire. Using racial context and analytics to explore depictions of black eunuchs does not mean the universalization of the modern concept of race. Rather, I highlight a genealogy of race in the past that positions it as inextricably interlinked with and articulated through the infrastructures of slavery and gendered power hierarchies.[28] In her historical exploration of the chief eunuch Beshir Agha, Jane Hathaway has examined this black/white separation and argues that "we must discard the notion that the division is entirely understandable in terms of modern-day racial attitudes."[29] Because the Ottoman imperial harem was also composed predominantly of white women from the north and from the western regions the Ottomans had conquered or otherwise controlled and because of "the sheer 'otherness' of African eunuchs in the eyes of these women from the Caucasus and Balkans," Hathaway suggests, "employing African eunuchs to guard them may have made sexual contact between the harem women and their guardians seem relatively unlikely."[30] Yet how can one ascertain information about the perception of harem women's attitudes toward Africans or whether white women would reject black sexual partners? In her more recent work on black eunuchs, Hathaway revisits the question and calls attention to "a kind of 'indigenous racism' that shaped the experiences of enslaved Africans," not putatively in the eyes of harem women but in the actions of white administrators and works of intellectuals in Ottoman society who differentiated among the geographies of the empire.[31] She suggests that "Ottoman attitudes toward different peoples and toward skin color were heavily influenced by the fact that before the mid-seventeenth century, the empire was administered by a Rumi elite—that is, an elite with roots in the empire's central lands," the Balkans and adjacent regions from which the empire drew its royal concubines and mother queens.[32] In the accounts of these elites, the Rumi became the ideal standard, as in Mustafa Ali's *Description of Cairo* (1599), in which he "disparages the locals, whom he calls evlad-ı 'Arab ('sons of the Arabs/blacks'), in contradistinction to Rum oğlanı ('sons of the Rumis'), whom he obviously considers superior."[33]

Indeed, as I also explored in previous chapters, there was an idealization of whiteness in such accounts and in literary representations, and as I shall show below, black eunuchs were often called ugly. Yet still, Hathaway proposes "view[ing] Ottoman attitudes toward 'black' East Africans in the context of... overarching ethno-regional chauvinism" as simply a result of the "'shock' of... exposure to a diverse spectrum of peoples" instead of viewing it in the context of racial attitude.[34] Comparing race and racism as we might know it today to a prior model of "shock" or phobia regarding the unfamiliar that is attributed to racisms in the past (in other words, a rational and scientific modern notion of racism versus irrational and xenophobic fears in the past) blurs how discourses, ideologies, and practices in the past affect and shape those in the present. Setting and maintaining a strict separation between past and present essentialisms also reduces the impact of superficial demarcations on certain bodies. After all, to recall Kim F. Hall's remarks, race *"was then* (as it *is now*) a social construct that is fundamentally more about power and culture than about biological difference."[35]

Making of a Racialized Gender

Racial ideologies based on skin color had become prevalent in Arab-Islamicate regions by the seventeenth century.[36] Historical race studies scholars have suggested that earlier forms of ethnocentrism based on differences in language, geography, climate, and religion evolved into a new racialized paradigm based on essentialized differences, including skin color, as a result of imperial expansion, conquest, an increase in slavery, and a more globalized slave trade. The adoption of Galenic humoral theory and theological renderings of the Hamitic curse served to establish vocabularies for articulating human difference, albeit ambiguously. As early as the ninth century, Ibn Qutayba claimed that heat overcooked Africans in the womb and curled their hair; and Al-Jahiz of Basra wrote, "If the country is cold, they are undercooked in the womb; if the country is hot, they are burnt in the womb."[37] Ibn al-Faqih mapped out this humoral theory more elaborately. Noting that people with pale brown skin such as the people of Iraq had the most proper color, he explained, "They are the ones who are done to a turn in the womb. They do not come out with something between blond, buff, blanched and leprous coloring, such as the Slavs and others of similar light complexion; nor are they overdone in the womb until they are burnt, so that the child comes out something between black and murky, malodorous, stinking, woolly-haired, with uneven limbs, deficient mind and depraved passions, such as the Zanj, the Ethiopians, and other blacks who resemble them. The Iraqis are neither half-baked dough nor burnt crust, but between the two."[38] Al-Masudi quoted Galen, who "mentions ten specific attributes of the black man, which are all found in him and in no other; frizzy hair, thin eyebrows, broad nostrils, thick lips, pointed teeth, smelly skin, black eyes, furrowed hands and feet, a long penis, and great merriment. Galen says that merriment dominates the black man because of his defective brain, whence also the weakness of his intelligence."[39]

Drawing from this long tradition, Ibn Khaldun, the influential historian and social thinker of medieval Islam, also proposed the geohumoral climatic theory as his etiology for black skin while simultaneously refuting the Hamitic curse.[40] He nevertheless remarked that "the Negro nations are, as a rule, submissive to slavery, because Negroes have little that is essentially human and have attributes that are quite similar to those of dumb animals."[41] Even those like Ibn Khaldun who did not accept the Hamitic curse found other explanations to justify the enslavement of sub-Saharan Africans. Such racial assertions prepared the path that the early modern period took to naturalize black Africans as inferior (and similar to animals), hence natural slaves.[42] In his exploration of slavery, race, and Islam in early modern Morocco, Chouki El Hamel shows that "the expansion and racialization of black slavery in Morocco and in the adjacent Atlantic world was taking place at the same time ... from common roots in a Mediterranean concept of slavery and Abrahamic traditions."[43] El Hamel convincingly demonstrates that with the rise of the new slavery practices that ignored the Islamic prohibition on enslaving Muslims, black Muslim Africans were increasingly seen as natural slaves. It is not surprising that in the Moroccan court of Mawlay Ismail, who legitimized the enslavement of all black Africans, there were 2,200 black eunuchs.[44] Abduction of boys intended to be made into eunuch slaves was a significant component of Mediterranean slavery, and the beliefs of those who ordered the castration of those boys cannot be considered to be free from these developing ideas of seeing black bodies as inferior.[45]

Influenced by such Arab-Islamicate racial discourses, Ottoman intellectuals circulated similar ideas as the Ottoman empire invested in Africa and the black population in Istanbul increased. The Ottoman categorization of these slaves was simultaneously simplistic and messy, with terms as "*zenci*" or "*zangi*" (Ethiopian or Negro), "*siyah*" (black or dark), "Arab" (black Arab, black African, or Ethiopian), and "Habeşi" (Ethiopian). Hakan Erdem notes that "Ottomans were less sensitive about the ethnic and geographic origins of slaves from Africa than the British consular offices were; they simply labelled them as *zenci* (black) or Arab although they usually respected the difference between them and the

Abyssinians (Habeş). On the other hand, it can be said that the Ottomans were more informed about the origins of white slaves. They not only observed the difference among various whiter groups but also differentiated between related tribes, as in the case of the Circassians."[46]

Early modern texts, especially those written by white writers under the patronage of white elites, put black Africans at the bottom of an established racial hierarchy that marked whiteness as the ideal. This seems to have been especially true during the period after the conquest of the Mamluks in 1516–1517, when the Ottomans intensified the transportation of African eunuchs (Abyssinians and eastern Africans) to the court, a process that continued from the second half of the sixteenth century.[47] Depictions of black eunuchs in particular show that on the one hand, black eunuchs and white courtiers were in constant competition for power and both had the potential to advance their careers in an imperial structure that prioritized slaves of European Christian descent, while on the other hand, an essentializing antiblack racism emerged that was grounded in previous antiblack templates, including those in the abovementioned medieval sources.[48] These intellectual discourses not only signaled a racial vocabulary and ideas blended with gender and sexual deviance, they also reveal how the idealized white beauty we see in Ottoman literature, as explored in previous chapters, functioned to construct somatic norms. That is, whiteness was being produced via antiblack discourses and images and antiblack racism was being structured on the grounds of already-established white ideals.

In this context, I revisit Mustafa Ali of Gallipoli's *Kava'idu'l-mecalis* (The rules of social gatherings; 1587), which, as I showed in the first chapter, categorized slaves based on their ethnic background. Here my focus shifts to the figuration of black African bodies as debased. In one section of his treatise, Mustafa Ali attacked the chief black eunuch Mehmed Agha as "the ugly and offensive Arab/black" (*zişt-rû dürüşt-hû 'Arab*), and a "black-faced man" (*felâ cerem siyeh-rûy-i*). This phrase connoted not only outward blackness but also unworthiness and innate evil character. He extended his racially inflected depiction by calling the Agha "a black misfortune" (*belâ-yı sihay*) and "a loathsome crow" (*gurab-i şâmit*).[49] And he complained about the promotion of Mehmed Agha:

> How is it possible that an uncultivated boor deficient in intelligence, an offensive brute who is but a black-faced slave [*abd-ı siyeh-ru*], could fly with the *huma* bird, all the while roosting with the crows and the kites? How is it that the raven, flying about in the loftiest melodic range, could be in harmony with the sweet-sounding parrot, and in refinement of song and melody be the equal of the sweet-tongued nightingale? Since one is forced

to feel revulsion at his scowling countenance [*vech-i abûsundan*], and repulsion at his black face [*sûret-i siyah-i hindden istikrah etmek*], and to feel not love for his conversation but rather nausea at it, how is it possible that this unavoidable black misfortune [*savulmaz belay-i siyah*] has become an imperial companion, how it is possible for him, when on a journey or in the capital, to utter pearls of royal wisdom in his bejeweled speech?[50]

Mehmed Agha, an Ethiopian, became the first chief black eunuch of the Ottoman Empire in 1575 during the reign of Murad III. Mustafa Ali dared to write this account (as full of invective as Iago's words about Othello) under the patronage of the influential white eunuch Gazanfer Agha, who had willingly become a eunuch as an adult in order to be close to the previous sultan, Selim II. In contrast to Mustafa Ali's dehumanization of the black Mehmed Agha as a black monster and a raven, he praised his white eunuch patron as "the lion of the forest of greatness, patron of the eloquent."[51]

Mustafa Ali's attacks on Mehmed Agha cannot be easily dismissed as resulting from a competition between two eunuchs. His antiblack insults were not limited to one particular individual: he also attacked black professors and youthful slaves of African descent. Thus, a racist ideology was at work in his writing. In a section where he mapped out the manners of slaves of African descent, for instance, Mustafa Ali wrote about "the domesticity and friendliness of Abyssinians (Ethiopians)" who display "womanish behavior in making up and spreading out bedding, and of their familiarity with gentleness, like virgins."[52] He wrote that other black Africans had "wicked characters, warped temperaments, and various foul and repellent qualities."[53] Mustafa Ali also complained that a judge and scholar named Mullah Ali, an "inwardly black-faced man of Nubian descent, the blackness of whose stupidity was luminous, and whose compound ignorance inwardly and outwardly was manifest, had penetrated the ranks of the *medrese* instructors."[54] For Mustafa Ali, the appointment of a black instructor to the highest education circles was similar to making "a black monster (*kara cânvar*) lie down on the carpet of the noble Shari'a [laws] . . . [in order to] favor . . . his fellows, the black eunuchs of the imperial harem."[55] Such attacks on this prominent black judge offer a glimpse of the racialized view of Africans and the nature of race and racisms in the Ottoman world.[56]

Mustafa Ali was not alone in directing racist attacks against the black judge Mullah Ali, whose fame and notoriety (based on his blackness) eventually extended beyond the Ottoman realm and reached audiences in Western Europe. Mullah Ali was not a eunuch. He entered the empire as a slave boy after he had been sold in slavery several times. His life changed when he was presented to Mehmed Agha, who supported Mullah Ali's education, which eventually enabled him to become a member of the ulema (educational-judicial) class, a status that was usually open only to select elite families.[57] After the death of Mehmed Agha in 1591, Mullah Ali continued to receive support and protection from other chief black eunuchs. As a result of this black solidarity, he managed to rise in his career to reach peak positions: the top teaching position at the Suleymaniye College, judgeship of Galata, chief judgeship of the capital, and finally chief judgeship of the Asian provinces, which in 1621 likely made him the first black member of the imperial council. He eventually became the chief judge of the Ottoman Empire's European provinces, the second-highest position a scholar could attain (the highest was *Şeyhülislam*, the qadi of Istanbul).

While such impressive advancement of a black slave might give the impression of racial equality in the imperial structure, Mullah Ali's experience was extraordinary because "the Ottoman central administration did not usually provide employment opportunities for Africans" apart from roles as eunuchs in the private compounds of the imperial palace.[58] Mullah Ali succeeded *despite* his blackness, and he was often subject to racist assaults, not only in writing or verbally but also physically. Baki Tezcan describes how when Mullah Ali was the judge in Edirne, he was attacked by a large crowd and his residence and belongings were pillaged. While some natives of the city attributed this anger to Mullah Ali's adamant nature, the reference to his blackness (*yüz karalığı*) suggests that this incident was inflected with racial animus. Also, while sons of judges in the higher ranks typically ascended easily in their careers, Mullah Ali's only son, Abdurrahman, did not move up in the ulema hierarchy.

Mullah Ali's skin color and his affiliation with black eunuchs also rendered him a target of antiblack attacks from his white elite peers. They referred to him as Sünbül (Hyacinth) Ali, a derogatory epithet often used for black eunuchs. Attacks on Mullah Ali's masculinity and blackness demonstrate how blackness and eunuchism were mutually imbricated in depicting black figures, even figures who were not actually eunuchs. Bostanzade Yahya, for instance, described him as a "black-faced and most wicked one ... known for ignorance and dissipation by mankind, called Sünbül, an ugly Negro." Karaçelebizade Abdulaziz wrote, "Sünbül Ali ... got an education [barely] enough to make him able to distinguish white and black, and perfected the science of reading (*sevad-h'anlik*; literally "reading the black [ink]") according to his own standards." He insisted that without the "ethnic/racial solidarity (*bi-hükm-i cinsiyet*)" of black eunuchs, "Sünbül" Ali would not have moved up the hierarchical ranks, as "he was [simply] a black slave."[59] Tezcan suggests that the use of the gendered epithet Sünbül instead of respectful titles such as "Mullah," "el-Mevla," and "Efendi" (references to "master" used for persons of high status) stemmed from competitive jealousy within the patronage system. He writes, "What calling Mullah Ali Sünbül Ali, or Ali the Hyacinth, did was to make the main line of the attack against him an allusion to castrated sexuality rather than to blackness," even though the precise signification of "Sünbül" in the seventeenth century would be hard to decode.[60] Although Tezcan recognizes that the ulema's use of the epithet "Sünbül" put Ali in the same category as black eunuchs, for the term had begun to particularly refer to black eunuchs, his reading nevertheless separates gender from race and argues that gender is the reference point of these attacks. This separation is also evident in Tezcan's analysis of Karaçelebizade's use of "*cinsiyet*" in the above-quoted reference to Sünbül's impressive advancement through the ranks of the scholarly hierarchy via "ethnic/racial solidarity" (*bi-hukm-i cinsiyet*). What Tezcan translates as "ethnic/racial" in the quotation becomes "sexual/gender" in his analysis. In other words, "*cinsiyet*" in Tezcan's translation refers to solidarity based on Ali's racial background. However, in his argument, it turns out to refer to solidarity among black eunuchs based on their shared gender.

Making race and gender into entirely separate categories in this case overlooks the way the two—black *and* eunuch—worked as mutually constitutive and operating dynamics. The word "*cins/cinsiyet*" derives from the Latin root "genus" (lineage, family, gender, class, tribe, nation, race, kind, sort, order, species) and could refer, in Ottoman Turkish, to both race and gender and to other types of "sort" or "kind."[61] Whereas Mustafa Ali, for example, used "*cins*" to refer to the class of enslaved Christian boys from Europe (*kul cinsi*), it was often deployed to signify different "races."[62] I suggest that marking Mullah Ali as a black eunuch by naming him Sünbül and placing him in the *cinsiyet* of black eunuchs connects gender and race inseparably in marking not only black eunuchs but also all black men and boys. Hence, in Karaçelebizade's reference, "*cinsiyet*" brings together blackness, eunuchism, race, and gender (since it can refer to demarcations and communal solidarity based on both skin color and gendered embodiment), which is consistent with other early modern usages. The Romans used "*genus*" to refer to eunuchs as a gender type invented for slavery, as in Claudian Claudianus's description of eunuchs as a "genus [race, class, kind] artificially invented" (*hoc genus inventum est*). That invention had a particular purpose: "This race is made for slavery" (*hoc genus inventum est ut serviat*). (Writing on the eunuch Eutropius, Claudian called eunuchs the "other sex" [*alter . . . sexus*]).[63] About 1,600 years later, the Ottoman ulema—people of law—transformed the classical eunuch as a gender type into a racialized gender classification that all black men—including non-eunuchs such as Mullah Ali—belonged to. (Not surprisingly, in the nineteenth and twentieth centuries, "*cins*" gained another demarcating signification when it began to be used to mean "sex" and "sexuality," as *"cinsiyet"* and *"cinsellik."*) What was othered in this new discourse, then, was not simply the eunuchs' castrated bodies but specifically their castrated *black* bodies.

Europeans picked up and used these connections. In a 1621 account, the French ambassador described Mullah Ali as a eunuch: "a black eunuch now rules the empire."[64] Likewise, English writers deployed racial terms that had gender and sexual connotations in their depictions of Mullah Ali. The ambassador Paul Pindar called Ali "a black Moore"; Edward Grimston referred to him as "Cadi [Judge] Negro"; and Paul Rycaut, the secretary to the English ambassador, assumed that eunuchs in general were of "that African race."[65] Mullah Ali, a black Ottoman judge and father to a son, was marked as a black eunuch because eunuch as a gender category had become inseparable from the black body, which was always in need of being emasculated. As a black man, he was associated with both castrated eunuchs *and* the black community that strove to promote him.

In dialogue with such accounts, Mustafa Ali's misogynist and antiblack language was most explicit when he wrote about the black eunuchs he associated with the black judge. He specifically warned the sultan not to spend time with women and eunuchs: "Admitting women to the presence of kings brings about a deficient intelligence. Tongueless persons in their presence results in their constant reduction to silence and bewilderment. In the same way, consorting with dwarfs lessens the majesty of a sovereign, just as sitting together and conversing with eunuchs diminishes his manliness."[66] Mustafa Ali thus linked women, mutes, dwarves, and eunuchs as inferior beings that a true "man" should eschew. (We will see these figures presented together on the English stage, as I detail below.)

Moreover, in his chapter on "Unseemly Affairs of the Ağas in the Inner Palace," he wrote, in verse, "Tutors in the harem nowadays are fornicators with the eunuchs. / Though it is a great offense for eunuchs to maintain contact with the outside, / Today those powerful people perpetrate reprehensible deeds. / Look at the strangers in the palace!"[67] Mustafa Ali directly attacked the black eunuchs of the palace, whose effeminacy he claimed could destroy another man's manliness. Because black eunuchs, women, and other bodies considered "deformed" were linked in their inferiority, it is not surprising to find them sharing the same space in the Ottoman court. When these ideas were combined with the Galenic formation of sex as variations along a spectrum measured against the adult male, we can see how black male bodies and white female bodies were brought in proximity and perceived to share common humors and hence were distanced from the default white male body.

Mustafa Ali's condemnation of black persons contrasted with his celebration of the "white" beauty of European servant boys, which I traced in the first chapter. For him, proximity to whiteness engendered beauty. Indeed, because of Europeans' physical beauty, he encouraged "minglings" with non-Muslim westerners in order to create an ideal Ottoman population rooted in Western beauty and Eastern intellect in his *Künh ül-ahbar* (The essence of history). In this racialized social engineering, there was no place for black Africans. Framed in this context and when read alongside other accounts of black Africans in the empire, Mustafa Ali's language suggests an essential hierarchy between white and black persons. Despite the fact that that they shared the same religion, skin color erased the equality Islam was supposed to enable. Such sixteenth-century accounts of blackness led to a more naturalized racist language that targeted black people via black eunuchs in the early eighteenth century while also attributing all sorts of sexual deviance to black people. One account of the affairs of black eunuchs, for instance, attributed to Ham's offspring (black Africans) such dispositions as lust, carnal desire, incest, nakedness, shameless sexuality, bestiality, antiwhite animosity, too-fertile female sexuality, and cannibalism.[68] This treatise also included a story about two palace servants who divorced their wives only one week after marriage because their wives told them that they were less sexually satisfying to them than the eunuchs with whom they had had pleasure while serving at the palace before they married. Using this anecdotal evidence, the writer proposed that black eunuchs were not devoid of sexual desire and the ability to give pleasure, and because of this they were a threat to the social order and should be expelled from the palace.[69]

Remarkably, one of the first pieces of writing that struck back at such attacks by praising blackness came from the black judge Mullah Ali. His 1612 treatise *Rafi'ü'l-gubûş fî fezayili'l-hubûş* (Dispelling the darkness on the merits of Ethiopians) was a celebration of black people in Islamic history that aimed to challenge antiblack discourses circulating in Ottoman intellectual circles.[70] While this treatise followed the templates that responded to antiblack attacks in the Arab-Islamic context by praising blackness, it departed from them by refuting both the Hamitic curse and geoclimatic theories of racial difference, showing a new understanding of skin color as an essential part of human difference that was divinely ordained and immutable—"among [other] signs of [God] in the creation of the heavens and the earth, and the variety of your languages and of your colors"—based on evidence in the Qur'an.[71] Connecting skin color to an essential divine ordinance, Mullah Ali attempted to equalize blackness and whiteness in a society that marked blacks as inferior and attached blackness to eunuchism. With five chapters exclusively devoted to celebrating eunuchs and their histories, Mullah

Ali's treatise offered a counterhistory and an alternative intellectual lineage to those of white elites, who rendered historical black subjects invisible. It was a rigorous response to the normative values projected by the ulema, to accounts such as Mustafa Ali's, and to Ottoman society in general. He wrote, "[God] said 'the noblest one among you in the eyes of God is the most pious'; He did not say 'the most good-looking, the most handsome, and the whitest.'"[72] This was a clear challenge to the creation of an Ottoman elite class via the *devşirme* system that abducted good-looking white boys from the European territories of the empire and promoted the whitest and most handsome of them.

These accounts from the sixteenth to early seventeenth centuries blended discourses from earlier Arab-Islamicate sources, which had been inflected by biblical myths and their later explications (i.e., the story of Ham) and geoclimatic theories with discourses previously used for religious difference that licensed the abduction of boys. The race-making of Ottoman writers reveals that early modern race was an amalgam of contradictory, unstable, and evolving ideas that operated to serve the changing imperial structure. As we have seen, especially after the Ottoman invention of separating black eunuchs from white eunuchs (often of Slavic or European origins) and assigning blacks to the interior feminine spaces, blackness and eunuchism began to be conflated with one another, especially in discourses produced by elites who saw the emerging black community in the capital of the empire as a threat to their privileges. These accounts contributed to an established antiblack racist language in the following century that continued to target black people—and black eunuchs specifically—and coincided with an increase in the number of African boys who were abducted, enslaved, and castrated. While one black boy such as Ali who was abducted and enslaved multiple times was able to become an Ottoman elite despite his blackness, he was still, along with the majority of others who were made into eunuchs, targeted by his white peers, while the "most handsome, most beautiful, most white" ones were normalized, idealized, and rewarded. The systematic separation of white and black eunuchs and the discursive conflation of blackness and eunuchism illustrate how gender and race were inextricably interconnected in the Ottoman Empire in producing imperial hierarchies for the management of the population.

Black Eunuchs in England

Black boys who were abducted and made into eunuchs fascinated English travelers on account of their nonconforming bodies, which writers regularly "othered" by marking them as beyond the bounds of gender and racial normativity. In the context of intense Anglo-Ottoman encounters in the 1580s as a result of England's participation in Mediterranean trade, the figure of the eunuch emerged as an integral, Orientalist component of travelogues and stage plays and as a means of signaling Ottoman and Mediterranean otherness. Early travel narratives such as Antoine Geuffroy's *The order of the greate Turckes courte* (translated from French in 1524) rarely referred to eunuchs, but from the late-sixteenth century onward, the eunuch was an ever-present figure in accounts of cross-cultural encounters and began to appear on the English stage more frequently. Gary Taylor notes that the noun "eunuch" appeared "at least 240 times in at least 78 different plays written between 1580 and the closing of the theaters in 1642," and eunuchs figured as speaking characters in more than twenty-five dramatic texts written in the period 1600 to 1640.[73] (Relatedly, "castrate" [usually as a verb] appears more than 150 times.[74]) In what follows, I catalogue and summarize the ways that eunuchs frequently appeared in English discourses about the Ottomans.[75] I put into dialogue with the Ottoman context a wide array of figurations of the eunuch, including in Shakespeare's *Anthony and Cleopatra* and *Twelfth Night*, to emphasize cross-cultural linkages and the impact of the Ottomans in engendering such representations. This wide focus aims to enable a contextual shift in our understanding of these figures, unearthing how Mediterranean practices and discourses matter for exploring the English imaginary in making gendered and racialized bodies via abducted boys.

One of the earliest eyewitness English accounts of Ottoman eunuchs is from the diary of Thomas Dallam, whom Queen Elizabeth I sent to Istanbul to deliver the gift of an organ clock to Sultan Murad III.[76] Dallam's account noted that in Murad's court, there were "neageres or blackamoor" eunuchs who guarded the sultan's harem and punished any transgressors. In fact, he mentioned that he was almost killed by these black eunuchs because he did not realize that the harem women were entering the imperial apartments he was working near: "I runn as faste as my legs would carrie me aftere and 4 neageres or blacka-moors cam running towards me with their semetaries [scimatars] drawne; yf they could have catche me theye would have hewed me all in peeces with these semeteris."[77] A more detailed account of Ottoman eunuchs appears in George Sandys's *A Relation of a Journey*: "Many of the children that the Turkes do buy ... they castrate, making [them] all smooth as the back of the hand, (whereof divers do die in the cutting)."[78] The smoothness or softness that was often attributed to their skins associates eunuchs with sodomy, as softness and sodomy appear together in both Roman and medieval Christian discourses of eunuchs.[79] Sandys noted that this practice of making all smooth—that is, the removal of both the penis and the testicles—was relatively new. He explained: "In times past, they did but only geld them: but being admitted to the free converse of their women, it was observed by some, that [the women] more than befittingly delighted in their societies." He then informed his readers about the duties of eunuchs: "They are here in great repute with their masters, trusted with their states, the government of their women, and houses in their absence."[80] Robert Burton discussed these figures at greater length in *The Anatomy of Melancholy*: "The Turks have I know not how many black, deformed eunuchs (for the white serve for other ministries) to this purpose sent commonly from Egypt, deprived in their childhood of all their privities, and brought up in the seraglio at Constantinople to keep their wives."[81] Burton acknowledged the existence of both white and black eunuchs and noted the different duties they had in the Ottoman court.

The Ottomans' striking demarcation of white and black eunuchs enabled European writers to project their own racialized ideologies onto black eunuchs, associating gender nonconformity with racial otherness. The English translation of Michel Baudier's French account, for instance, reads:

> [The] Men that serue them [harem women] are blacke Eunuches, from whom they haue taken all.... These Eunuches are all blacke, to distinguish them from those of the *Sultans Serrail* [inner palace]: and their perfection consists in their deformitie, for the most hideous are the fairest: For being neare vnto those beauties so perfectly accomplished, they serue for a lustre.... They giue them names fitter for their handsomenesse than for their *Moorish* deformity. For to some Boyes which haue flat Noses, wide Mouthes, thicke Lips, Eyes almost out of their heads, great Eares, their Haire curled like Wooll, and their Face fearefully blacke, so as there is no white to be seene but their Eyes, and Teeth: They call them Hycinthe, Narcissus, Rose and Gilliflowre. Doubtlesse such flowres are soone withered and vnable to fructifie.[82]

Baudier maintained that all of the eunuchs who accompanied the beautiful, white, and "perfectly accomplished" women in the sultan's harem were fully castrated ("they have taken all"). Like Burton, Baudier also coded their black bodies as "deformed," adding that this "deformitie" encompassed not only their castration but also their physical appearance—their "flat Noses, wide Mouthes, [and] thicke Lips" and their "curled" hair and "fearefully blacke" faces. Thus, the eunuchs' bodies were strategically chosen to contrast starkly with the white female bodies they surrounded. Ironically, the black eunuchs' "deformities" and imperfections generated their "perfection" for service (an idea that would be echoed on stage, as we shall see below).[83] Baudier later claimed that eunuchs "are cut or mutilated with their owne consent, and not by force, the which would indanger

FIGURE 5.2. *The Chief Black Eunuch*. In Paul Rycaut, *The Present State of the Ottoman Empire*, 1668.

their liues. . . . For in time they attaine to the greatnesse of Turkey."[84] Likewise, Paul Rycaut, whose account included a visual image of the chief black eunuch, observed that many eunuchs were "not only castrated but black, chosen with the worst features that are to be found among the most hard-favoured of that African race" (fig. 5.2).[85] Such formulations constructed a racialized hierarchy of beauty in which blackness was denigrated along with gender nonconformity.

Coinciding with such accounts, eunuchs begin to appear with some regularity on the English stage beginning in the late sixteenth century. By the end of the seventeenth century, they had become well-known oriental figures. Shakespeare's deployment of the eunuch is typical: he often evokes eunuchs along with other oriental curiosities and exotic or weakened bodies and in contexts that emphasize gender inversion, ambiguity, or feminization. In *All's Well That Ends Well*, Lafeu mentions punishing youths by "send[ing] them to th' Turk, to make eunuchs of" (2.3.83). Coriolanus envisions his own throat turned "into a pipe / Small as an eunuch" (3.2.113–14), while in *Love Labor's Lost*, the "eunuch" is the guardian Argos (3.1.184).[86] In *Anthony and Cleopatra*, eunuchs appear on the stage conjured as exoticized signifiers of gendered, racial, and corporeal otherness.[87]

Anthony and Cleopatra begins with Philo's speech that stresses the transformation Anthony underwent in Cleopatra's court: "Now bend, now turn / The office and devotion of their view / Upon a tawny front. His captain's heart ... / reneges all temper / And is become the bellows and the fan / To cool a gipsy's lust (1.1.4–9). Upon this speech Cleopatra appears on the stage alongside Anthony and eunuchs that include her chief eunuch, Mardian. Fanning Cleopatra during her grand entrance, these eunuchs signify Anthony's emasculation in his fanning and cooling of the gypsy queen's lust. Ania Loomba has noted that such references as "gipsy, black, moor" locate the play's Roman story in early modern history and an early modern imperial context.[88] Egypt, after all, was under Ottoman control and it was where enslaved black boys were often castrated. In the Mediterranean setting, then, the fanning eunuchs elicited contemporaneous anxieties about conversion in connection with circumcision and castration.

Philo's deployment of "turn" and "renege" right before declaring that Anthony had "transformed / Into a strumpet's fool" puts his transformation in the frame of a conversion narrative (1.1.12–13). To turn, as in "turning Turk," was used to refer to religious conversion to Islam with implications of sexual and gender transgressions. Anthony "turned," and his heart "reneges all temper." A borrowing from Latin (*re + negāre* = deny, reject, renounce), "renege" signified "to abandon, become an apostate to (one's faith)" in sixteenth-century English.[89] In the Spanish past participle form, *"renegado"* particularly referred to a Christian who had converted to Islam, a popular figure on the English stage.[90] Like theatrical and historical *renegados*, converted/circumcised/castrated Christians in the Mediterranean, Anthony "reneges all temper," "turns" or converts from being the warrior Mars into "the fan" the castrated eunuchs use to cool the "tawny" queen. Considering the early modern usage of "neger" in reference to black Africans and "Moors," the word "renege" includes a racist play on blackness.[91] Anthony's transformation is symbolically connected to the black eunuch's castration, as is evident in Anthony's own invocation of the loss of his "sword" (manhood) in his interaction with the eunuch Mardian: "O thy vile lady, / She has robbed me of my sword!" (4.15.23–24). This recalls what Cleopatra says earlier in the play: "I drunk him to his bed, / Then put my tires and mantles on him, whilst / I wore his sword Philippan" (2.5.21–23). The martial, masculine Anthony, lost in exotic luxury in the East where his "pleasure lies," becomes effeminate, distanced from whiteness and associated with eunuchs (2.3.38).

Cleopatra's chief eunuch Mardian, named after the nomadic Mardian tribe of Persia, orientalizes and racializes Cleopatra's court throughout the play. Mardian is present in almost every scene, from the first to the final act.[92] This presence suggests that Cleopatra *is* Egypt when the eunuch surrounds her. Indeed, in Plutarch's *Lives*, one of Shakespeare's sources for the play, Caesar also associates Egypt not with Cleopatra alone but with those who "ruled all the affairs" of her empire—and on the top of the list is the eunuch Mardian. If Cleopatra is racialized as a gypsy, a tawny Egyptian, then she is so racialized by means of her association with Mardian the eunuch.[93] (Productions of *Anthony and Cleopatra* from the twentieth and twenty-first centuries also racialize Cleopatra's court via eunuchs, especially Mardian, who is almost always black even when Cleopatra is white.[94])

Mardian is first cast by Cleopatra in reference to their singing voice—an attribution of not Roman but early modern eunuchs. Mardian's figuration further evokes accounts of Ottoman eunuchs, typically about their erotic lives, their loyalty, and their mediating powers between different spaces. In Cleopatra's oriental court, the first time we hear Mardian speak, it is to express their role of serving and pleasing the queen: "What is your highness' pleasure?" Yet Cleopatra "take[s] no pleasure / In aught an eunuch has," emphasizing their lack of functional genitalia (1.5.8–10). Mardian has nothing. Nevertheless, Cleopatra continues to make the eunuch's sexuality a point of curiosity and titillation by asking Mardian whether eunuchs have "affections" (1.5.12). Mardian replies: "Not in deed madam, for I can do nothing / But what indeed is honest to be done. / Yet have I fierce affections, and think / What Venus did with Mars" (1.5.15–18). While Mardian notes his lack in "deed," he nonetheless offers a fantasy that marks eunuchs as desiring, active, and powerfully feminine by giving a subject position to Venus—what Venus *did* with Mars—and identifying not only with Mars but also with Venus. Perhaps even more transgressively, it associates them with Cleopatra as Venus, since Anthony from the very beginning of the play is called Mars. As mentioned earlier, eunuchs were sometimes noted as Egyptian in travelogues, and Egypt was often associated with gender reversals; Henry Blount wrote that Egypt under the Turks was a nation "made effeminate and disarmed."[95] Here the eunuch Mardian further challenges gender norms as their fantasy includes being Venus/Cleopatra, who actually dominates Mars/Anthony, who in turn becomes like fanning eunuchs.

These are Mardian's fantasies, and in the play, they cannot be actualized by a eunuch. The play nonetheless continues to tease the audience with the eunuch's erotic desire. As Ellis Hanson argues, Mardian, "unseminared" in a testicular sense, is "obscene by virtue of his imagination"; indeed, they are "unsexed and thereby oversexed, so sexually overdetermined that in this play of phallic jesting and jousting, his marginality cannot help but to feel central."[96] Later the queen once again brings to the fore the eunuch's desirability while noting their gender ambiguity. She would like to "play" with Mardian "As well a woman with an eunuch played / As with a woman" (2.5.5–6). Mardian agrees to play "as well as I can," "though't come too short" for the queen—that is, Mardian's penis is not functional or sizeable enough. Thus, instead, the queen desires to go fishing for more adventure (2.5.7–9). This dysfunctionality in turn makes them loyal; their "deformity" makes them perfect for service (in alignment with the abovementioned accounts of the eunuch). Cleopatra responds to Mardian's unsatisfiable affections: "'Tis well for thee / That, being unseminared, thy freer thoughts / May not fly forth of Egypt" (1.5.10–12.). Because they are castrated, they will be loyal, the queen suggests.

Finally, Mardian interacts with Anthony when they deliver him the news of Cleopatra's feigned death, to which Anthony responds by calling them a "saucy eunuch" (4.15.25). This reference also points at eunuchs' sexuality, considering that "saucy" signifies not only insolence and disrespect, as editors usually annotate it, but also "wanton, lascivious." For example, Anthony describes Tributaries as getting "so saucy" with Cleopatra's hands (3.13.98). Racializing Cleopatra's court and complementing Cleopatra's racial difference, the eunuchs of *Anthony and Cleopatra* are saucy erotic subjects, standing next to "pretty dimpled boys" who are later described as standing on each side of the queen "like smiling Cupids, / With divers-colour'd fans whose wind did seem / To glow the delicate cheeks which they did cool, / And what they undid did" (2.2.208–11). Now it is pretty dimpled boys who are fanning and cooling the queen. These depictions, which mingle eunuchs and Cupid-like boys, are not unlike descriptions of the Ottoman court that included beautiful Ganymede-like servant boys and black eunuchs. They tease the audience with multiple erotic and gender variants infused with a sense of eroticized racial difference. The eunuchs of *Anthony and Cleopatra* thereby help mark Mediterranean courts—in contrast to putatively masculine Roman and English ones—as replete with nonnormative desires, embodiments, and genders.

In another Shakespearean play set in the Mediterranean, *Twelfth Night* (1601), the eunuch is evoked in association with gender ambiguity and other exotic figures in the court. At the very beginning of the play, Viola wants to disguise herself as a eunuch in order to gain access to the court of Illyria: "I'll serve this duke. / Thou shalt present me as an eunuch to him. / It may be worth thy pains, for I can sing / And speak to him in many sorts of music / That will allow me very worth his service" (1.2.51–55). The Captain wants to be Viola's "mute" when she presents herself to Orsino "as an eunuch": "Be you his eunuch, and your mute I'll be" (1.2.58). The pairing of eunuch and mute as the means of accessing the Illyrian court recalls the eunuchs and mutes of the Ottoman court. Why does Viola prefer to be a eunuch but not a page boy? Keir Elam suggests that "she is to play the part of not a boy but of a castrate."[97] Elam reads "eunuch" in terms of binaristic cross-dressing: "She must dress as a man, albeit an imperfect or 'castrated' man; her male disguise itself represents the self-punishing bridling of her sexuality."[98] Instead of cross-dressing as a page boy or a man, as was typical in Shakespeare's comedies, Viola evokes a transition into a distinct gender among other genders, the eunuch, an identity that is reinforced with the name Cesario, a name that is related to cutting and castration.[99] While this figuration of the disguised eunuch might evoke Terence's comedy *The Eunuchs*, the suggestion of singing brings this deployment of the eunuch closer to the early modern eunuchs, since the early moderns (rather than the Romans) attributed a beautiful voice to eunuchs. In this Mediterranean setting, therefore, it is not Terence's eunuch, a figure who is typically a man in disguise entering all-women spaces, but a woman who seeks to become a eunuch to enter Orsino's manly court. Moreover, we do not see Cesario singing as a castrate but, like Ottoman eunuchs, mainly mediating between two gendered spaces: Orsino's masculine court and Olivia's house while being under their attraction.

Furthermore, Malvolio's depiction of Viola-as-Cesario suggests an ambiguous yet distinct gender category beyond man, woman, and boy: "Not yet old enough for a man, nor young enough for a boy; as a squash is before 'tis a peascod, or a codling when 'tis almost an apple: 'Tis with him in standing water between boy and man" (1.5.139–42). One apparent reading of these lines is that the ripe peascod is suggestive of codpieces, while the squash refers to an unripe pea pod. (This coupling of "squash" and "peascod" also reminds us of Bottom's allusion in *A Midsummer Night's Dream* to "Mistress Squash" as mother and "Master Peascod" as father to Peaseblossom in Titania's Bower [3.1.168–70]). Malvolio's description of Cesario through their penis size, more squash than a majestic codpiece, is further stressed by locating him "in standing water," as water at the turn of the tide, fluid and distinctly between two genders. Jeffrey Masten's revelatory reading of this scene aptly suggests that "in standing water" actually signifies "a stagnant or standing pool or pond, a swamp between the states of land and water."[100] The term then refers not to a temporal stage of boyhood but a distinct, categorical one. In this case, one can suggest, it is categorically the eunuch whose "small pipe / Is as the maiden's organ, shrill and sound,

/ And all is semblative a woman's part" (1.4.31–33). The eunuch in *Twelfth Night* then probes the gender binary and offers gender ambiguity and plurality in the context of the Mediterranean.

Such eunuch effects in producing genders and racialized spaces and bodies in Shakespeare's drama lingered in many other early modern plays. Shakespeare's pairing of the eunuch and the tawny gypsy queen in *Anthony and Cleopatra* and the eunuch and the mute in *Twelfth Night* is mirrored by contemporaneous accounts that consistently surround eunuchs with other exoticized figures such as mutes, dwarves, and hermaphrodites. The linkages between these transformed curiosities are apparent in Ben Jonson's *Volpone, or the Fox*, in which Castrone, the eunuch, is coupled with Androgyno, the hermaphrodite, and Nano, the dwarf. These characters are all outlandish members of Volpone's Venetian household. They are, as the parasite servant Mosca puts it, Volpone's children whom "he begot on beggars, / Gipsies, and Jews, and black-moors" (1.5.44–45). This formulation significantly suggests that these gender-nonconforming figures were often racially othered, deformed bastards whose monstrosity is the effect of interracial and cross-class minglings. Hermaphrodites were, in fact, often associated with Muslim and Jewish interbreeding and were depicted among the monstrous races of Asia and Africa in the medieval imaginary, as is evident in the Hereford Mappa Mundi and other maps of the world and in *Mandeville's Travels*.[101] Jonson's pairing of the eunuch with the hermaphrodite/androgynous and the dwarf suggests that he may have meant Volpone's household to evoke the Turkish court if we recall that the first private quarter in the Ottoman imperial harem included beardless servant boys, eunuchs, dwarves, and mutes. This seems even more likely when we consider that in Jonson's *Epicene*, Morose mentions the ubiquitous accounts of the Turkish court in which the sultan is said to live with his eunuchs, mutes, and boy pages.[102] Appearing in a turban, what Corinne Zeman refers to as "sultanic drag," Volpone further *turkifies* himself and his household when he fantasizes about transforming Celia into a one-woman multiethnic harem: "Then I will have thee in more modern forms, / Attired like some sprightly dame of France, / Brave Tuscan lady, or proud Sophy's wife; / Or the Grand Signior's mistress; and, for change, / To one of our most artful courtesans, / Or some quick Negro, or cold Russian" (3.7.225–31). Volpone's Mediterranean world is thus a space of fantasized interracial couplings that generate outlandish bodies of different shapes, races, and genders—women, eunuchs, hermaphrodites, mutes, and dwarves.

The eunuch was a component of imagery of the Mediterranean that was frequently presented on the English stage as a space of crossings and turnings—gender, racial, religious, economic, or otherwise—especially in the rich repertoire of popular Turk plays. While Bajazet of *Selimus, Emperor of the Turks* (attributed to Robert Greene) depicts eunuchs simply as musicians at the imperial court, Philip Massinger's *The Renegado* gives the audience more information about the eunuch's function via the character Carazie, an English eunuch: "In the day, I wait on my lady when she eats / Carry her pantofles, bear up her train; / Sing her asleep at night, and when she pleases / I am her bedfellow" (3.4.45–48). The eunuch's evocation of being her bedfellow ("when she pleases") titillatingly plies the line between erotically active and reproductively incapable. And in Thomas Heywood's *The Fair Maid of West*, eunuchism is announced as "Moorish preferment . . . to rob a man of his best jewels" (5.2.126–27). Finally, it is in the most famous rewriting of *Anthony and Cleopatra*, John Dryden's *All for Love*, that a eunuch gives one of the longest speeches given by a eunuch on the early modern English stage. The eunuch Alexas reminds the audience of their abduction; the tale of their "ravishment," bringing to the fore the violence done to their boyish body for the pleasure of others; and the greater power bestowed upon a few of them: "The luxury of others robbed my cradle / And ravished then the promise of a man / Cast out from Nature, disinherited / Of what her meanest children claim by kind, / Yet greatness kept me from contempt" (3.1.436–440).[103] These dramatic examples establish that the eunuch was a recognizable historical figure drawn from the Mediterranean world and a racialized object of contempt, fascination, ravishment, and sympathy, reflecting the convergence of violence, sexual desire, bodily transformations, and loyalty in service.[104]

The eunuch in both the Ottoman and English contexts, then, was a multifaceted figure that was both private and public. Their figuration circulated throughout the early modern Mediterranean. With their surgically altered bodies and nonbinary gender signification, they not only operated in the Ottoman court and society but traveled across the pages and stages of Europe. The history of the eunuch harkens back to the abduction and enslavement of black African boys. For this reason, the early modern eunuch on the English stage must be read via the black boys abducted from Africa and remade into eunuchs for the Ottomans. I further propose that early modern eunuchs probably appeared on stage often in oriental costumes and blackface unless they were specified as white, as, for instance, the English eunuch Carazie of Massinger's *The Renegado*.

Such a recentering of a violent and racist history disrupts the Eurocentric nation-state framework, showing how Mediterranean practices have undergirded and shaped English representations. In the history of Mediterranean slavery, the eunuch's nonconforming body is not free from racial signification. Because of the corporal ambiguity of eunuchs, their association with foreignness and deformity, and their ability to move between gendered spaces, these figures both challenged and contributed to making what Valerie Traub calls "the fantasy of a new global body [that was] increasingly classifiable according to race and ethnicity, yet nonetheless unified by normative gender and erotic arrangements."[105] In this new cultural fantasy, black eunuchs were consistently pushed outside the boundaries of normality, often due to their intersecting gender and racial difference. In the early modern period, the eunuch was thus always already "there," together with the other, the heretic, the slave, and the foreigner, operating to help construct normative bodies "here"—wherever here might be. In their movement away from an unchosen starting place to an unchosen role and category and to an unchosen nonnormative gender identity and embodiment, black eunuchs thereby encapsulated fusions of multiple, multilayered histories and ideologies. Abducted as boys and re-formed into a new and specialized gender, eunuchs reveal a history of the making of gender and race out of boyish bodies in the early modern world.

Within this history, African eunuchs figured beyond the theatrical stage and became a popular iconographic motif of conversion in the visual arts of the sixteenth and seventeenth centuries.[106] In nineteenth-century modernity, the black eunuch became a well-established racial trope standing for Eastern sensuality in portrayals of harems in Orientalist art.[107] The eunuch's desire and sexuality was a part of Ottoman representations in modernity as well, as in the story of a chief black eunuch who was killed by a snake hiding in their dildo box.[108] The black eunuchs of the past, who were initially abducted as boys, offer a genealogy of an imperial assemblage of race and sexuality in modernity. In the next part, therefore, I conclude the book by deploying a transhistorical approach in order to elicit changing discourses regarding abducted boys and explore how early modernity reappeared in modern entanglements of sexuality, race, and empire.

PART III

Boys in Modernity, East and West

6
———

Staging Boys, 1690–1990

I have explored the abducted boy synchronically in various sites in the early modern context over five chapters. This chapter traces the remnants of this historical context of sexuality, race, and empire in modernity by revisiting the Indian boy of *A Midsummer Night's Dream*. In my discussion of the text of the play in chapter 3, I analyzed the Indian boy in the context of English abductions of boys from other places and suggested that the play differentiates Titania's abduction of the boy in India from Oberon's pederastic abduction of him in the Mediterranean. By making the desire for the boy the cause of and resolution of dramatic conflicts, the play marks Oberon's homoerotic abduction as a corrective to Titania's transgressive possession of the boy. In this chapter, I extend, in a transhistorical direction, my argument that Shakespeare exposed, with a single adjective that qualified the boy as Indian, transcultural interactions, abductions, exchanges, and intergenerational and interracial desire. I focus on the performative aspect of the Indian boy in the historical context of the (in)visible abducted boys I have examined so far. Tracing Shakespeare's sexually and racially marked boy in various figurations on and off stage from early modern to postmodern productions, I present the changing history of sexuality in relation to race and empire. Mainly, the staging history of the Indian boy, the object of love and abduction in the play, reveals that in the process of the colonial expansion of the British Empire in the East from the eighteenth century onward, the transnational early modern Mediterranean context of the play was replaced by colonial and imperial spaces. And in the West, with the rise of new sexual regimes in colonial modernity, the eroticization of boys was erased as conventional pederasty began to be conflated with pedophilia and associated with the so-called Orient.

The Indian boy stands out as strikingly different in Shakespeare's rich poetic and dramatic catalogue of beautiful boys. Yet with his exotic difference, the Indian boy is among Shakespeare's racialized others evoked or represented on stage, including Othello, the Prince of Morocco, Cleopatra, Shylock, Aaron, Caliban, Sycorax, and the black woman of the sonnets. What is more, his ambiguous absent presence in the play brings him close to Desdemona's invisible black maid Barbary, whose song pervades the affective aura of her marriage and her murder bed; or Othello's absent mother, whose handkerchief prophecy permeates Othello's tragedy; or the black woman impregnated by Launcelot, who adds layers to the racial and sexual politics of slavery in *The Merchant of Venice*. The Indian boy's racial embodiment and his very present impact on the play's plot through his abduction, engendering the actions of other characters, makes his (in)visibility on stage a critical concern. While Gary Jay Williams claims that the Indian boy appeared on Shakespeare's stage, proposing that "it seems unlikely that an Elizabethan theater company would have missed the opportunity to use an attractive child, at least in an early scene," we do not know whether such a child appeared on stage in its initial productions.[1] We do have clear evidence, however, that the boy appeared on stage in the 1692 adaptation, and since then, he has emerged on stage as a little boy, a girl, an adult man, an orientalized teen, an African American youth, or even a puppet, as in the 2016 Globe Theatre production.

What are we to make of the abducted Indian boy on stage—past and present? How did theater-makers (re)imagine the Indian boy of the sixteenth century in their own sociopolitical contexts and concerns? How to do things with abducted boys on stage, or not to? As with the staging of Shakespeare's other racially marked characters, the staging of the Indian boy deserves a specific contextual approach rather than an essentially set parameter.[2] In my particular focus on the Anglo-American genealogy of the staging of the Indian boy, I shall demonstrate that this history is one of infantilizing, silencing, thingifying, othering, objectifying, sexing, and eroticizing the boy. In exploring this history,

I pay attention to the boy as a distinct category that is often misread or misrepresented as a child. Theatrical transformations in the boy's characterization on and off stage are bound to past and present concerns about boys as objects of intergenerational and interracial desire.

The Indian boy's Indianness and youth have long been explored separately in relation to his (in)visibility, which renders the boy a medium for multiple fantasies. In Marjorie Garber's reading of the Indian boy as a changeling, the boy "is an idea that can never be realized or possessed"; he is "the fantasy child," "the ultimate 'transvestite effect,' the figure that comes between demand and desire."[3] Echoing Garber, who notes that "if it were there, it would not be what is desired" ("it?"), Madhavi Menon more recently described him as the wall between desire and embodiment, an invisible, nonbodily metaphor of "human desire."[4] Earlier psychoanalytical analyses read different sorts of desire and subjectivity into the boy, missing his racial difference. He is Shakespeare's younger brother displaced;[5] "a little girl's fantasy of stealing mother's baby and killing the mother";[6] neither human nor fairy but an in-between symbol of indeterminacy of love;[7] a child's post-traumatic fantasy of being taken away from his mother;[8] a promise of future potentiality;[9] or "a problem with homosexual overtones, ... the problem of achieving sexual identity."[10] As the embodiment of desire, a colonial possession, an oriental prop, a universal figuration of human psyche, or Shakespeare's younger brother, the Indian boy's eroticism and his exoticism are rarely analyzed together in scholarly explorations.

In both early modern and modern contexts, an examination of both the Indianness and the youth of this boy reveals changing racial and sexual dynamics that have scripted and been scripted by his embodiment in performance. In what follows, after mapping out the history of the Indian boy on stage, I will closely examine one particular production, one that was the subject of Margo Hendricks's game-changing exploration of early modern racial politics through the visibility of the Indian boy on stage: the Shakespeare Santa Cruz (SSC) production directed by Danny Scheie in 1991. In this production, the boy was in his early twenties, six feet tall, tanned, and almost naked except for a tiny and nicely fit gold lamé loincloth, a majestic turban complete with feather, Turkish slippers, and a jeweled dagger.[11] In this conspicuous figuration on stage, the boy, Hendricks suggests, was culturally and racially marked; this presentation was "instrumental in reaffirming an aspect of orientalist ideology," Hendricks argues, and "like the odalisque who became a favorite topos of Impressionist painting, the Indian boy of SSC's production silently conjured the template of eroticism and exoticism adumbrated in the West's vision of India and the East."[12] Without acknowledging "the complex and varied images of race in Shakespeare's play," productions of *Dream*, Hendricks suggests, "may be destined to rehearse endlessly a racial fantasy engendered as part of imperialist ideology: the fantasy of a silent, accepting native who neither speaks nor resists."[13] One can add a sexual fantasy to the shaping fantasy of race in imperial imaginings. Hence, I emphasize the nonnormative, transgressive sexual trajectories that this staged boy intersectionally entertained in the 1990s. In addition, interrogating the politics of giving voice, I argue that resistance to oppression may appear in various forms, including being silent.

This chapter thus puts into dialogue Hendricks's compelling race analytics with queer explorations of the Indian boy, which have often prioritized a sexual agenda over racial analysis. Noting that Hendricks's analysis does not credit Titania or Oberon with the same licentious appreciation of the boy, Alan Sinfield, for instance, highlights Oberon's desire for the boy as a moving and vigorous plot in the patriarchal oppression emblemized by Oberon's power to dominate the boy and Titania. "Only acute sexual infatuation," he proposes, "may plausibly move these great fairies to jeopardize the entire creation."[14] He locates this sexual infatuation in the traffic in boys: "Everywhere in the early modern period, we see a casual traffic in boys who, because they are less significant, are moved around the employment-patronage system more fluently than women. Patriarchy determined the lives of young, lower-class and outsider men, as well as women."[15] Recognizing that "Oberon's seizing of the boy is a victory for patriarchy, not a challenge to it," Sinfield further fantasizes being a director and having "Hippolyta led on in a cage, like the emperor Bajazeth defeated by Tamburlaine, and Oberon in bed with the lovely boy."[16] This queer reading, however, overlooks the racialized body of the boy, who is not an English boy but an Indian abducted boy. The relationship between Oberon and the boy and between Titania and the boy are not only cross-generational but also cross-racial. As I have argued in previous chapters, historical circulations of not only domestic boys but especially exotic, foreign boys and their difference informed literary and dramatic abduction plots. Hence, the Indian boy's racial otherness is not a coincidental factor in his abduction. The Indian boy is not moving from one master to another until he is a free adult man; he is not in a localized system of employment and patronage. Rather, he is a captive boy taken up from another land. He is a boy transported and transposed, and his racialized difference matters in the complex erotic entanglements his figuration engenders.

Both Hendricks's feminist-postcolonial analysis and Sinfield's queer intervention, like the SSC production itself, stem from the cultural and intellectual politics and investments of the last decade of the twentieth century, when the increased yet divergent attention to racial and sexual politics appeared in compartmentalized forms in early modern studies. However, as I have discussed so far, sexual and racial discourses were inextricably interlinked in the early modern period, as they are today, and an intersectional lens is necessary in order to grasp the ideological work early modern cultural representations did. The boy is, as Hendricks argues, exotic, but also, as Sinfield claims, erotic. The exotic and the erotic can be the two sides of the same coin; they are relational and supplementary to each other. Connecting Hendricks's emphasis on racial politics with Sinfield's stress on the sexual, in what follows I trace an Anglo-American genealogy of the Indian boy on stage to highlight ruptures, dissonances, and continuities between early modern and modern notions of cross-generational and cross-racial homoerotic desire in performance. This history reveals co-productions, crossings, and intersections of race and sexuality in the past and the present and changing sexual discourses regarding conventional pederasty. The visibility of the Indian boy matters. Erasing the Indian boy involves erasing histories: the history of intergenerational interracial relations as well as the history of the abduction and circulation of boys in a period before institutionalized Orientalism and before modern, pathologized sexuality. The Santa Cruz production in the 1990s spoke to these histories. It deployed and embodied the Indian boy on stage to convey queer liberation agendas. This production challenged the long history of the Indian boy as invisible and insignificant; it presented an Indian boy with a potential to signify, to subversively and creatively survive in oppressive structures. Nevertheless, while utilizing and idealizing Shakespearean homoeroticism for contemporary sexual liberation, the production detached erotic desire for the racially different and subservient boy from colonial violence and thereby ignored the violence embedded in the eroticization of abduction—a coercive component of the homoeroticism of the early modern period in which the play was written.

The Indian Boy in Performance

Although Williams has claimed that the Indian boy probably appeared on Shakespeare's own stage, the earliest evidence of his staging is Thomas Betterton and Henry Purcell's 1692 operatic adaptation of the play, *The Fairy-Queen*. In this adaptation, set in an exoticized East with a Chinese garden and an antimasque of monkeys, Oberon's pursuit of the boy was dramatically emphasized, as is evident in the stage direction: Titania enters "leading the Indian boy" and when Oberon comes, "He [the boy] sinks," disappearing probably via a trap door.[17] Bringing the boy to the fore, this production eliminated many passages, including Titania's description of the Indian boy's mother ("His Mother was a vot'ress of my order..."

FIGURE 6.1. The frontispiece of the promptbook of Colman and Garrick's 1734 production of *A Midsummer Night's Dream*. The Folger Shakespeare Library.

[2.1.124–37]), and therefore, Titania's maternal concerns. This, more aligned with Puck's and Oberon's depictions of the boy's history in the text, marks the boy as a changeling or an object stolen from an Indian king.

Following this operatic staging, the Indian boy waned in eighteenth-century productions that were often partial adaptations, yet his absent presence in these early adaptations, which influenced the gender frameworks of nineteenth-century productions, was a major concern.[18] The frontispiece of Nicholas Rowe's 1709 edition of the play in *Works of Shakespeare* (vol. 2) portrayed Titania's party as all female and Oberon's as all male, reflecting more the eighteenth-century use of the stage and perception of gendered fairy courts than what the play-text presents. The frontispiece of the promptbook for David Garrick and George Colman's 1734 adaptation (fig. 6.1) used a similar template of gender difference, and the adaptation itself set the gender difference in the play as blurring the Indian boy's story in Titania's narrative by deleting the line following "her womb then rich with my young squire" (2.1.124). Based on this Garrick-Colman version, the 1763 promptbook for the Drury Lane performance, which John Philip Kemble used for the 1816 Covent Garden production, eliminated Titania's love for the boy mentioned in Puck's narrative ("But she perforce withholds the lovèd boy / Crowns him with flowers, and makes him all her joy" [2.1.26–27]). As a result, Titania's putative "love" for and "joy" with the boy and her version of the boy's history, including his mother's pregnancy, partially vanished in most Victorian and early twentieth-century productions—whether because of the inappropriateness of the image of a pregnant unmarried woman or as a means of dehumanizing a colonial subject.[19] This exclusion also aligned the boy's history with Puck's version and eliminated the female homoeroticism on Indian shores in Titania's version that challenges domestic heterosexuality and highlights merchant riches and goods over persons.

Remarkably, Frederic Reynolds's book for the operatic staging of *Dream* at the Theatre Royal, Covent Garden in 1816 made the mother's pregnancy more visible by changing "grow big-bellied with the wanton wind" to "grow all pregnant."[20] This version explicitly addressed the invisibility of the Indian boy in earlier acts. Reynolds, it seems, saw the absence of the boy as a problem and tried to solve this by adding two lines right after Titania's narrative of the boy's story: Oberon asks "where is the youthful treasure?" and Titania replies that he is "still hid in India, far, far from Oberon's power."[21] Reynolds's decision to add new lines instead of introducing the boy at this point serves to tease the audience with a delayed possibility of having access to the boy, of seeing the boy. The shift from the Mediterranean as the setting of the abduction in the text to an Indian space is also striking. Emphasizing "India" even more as "far from Oberon's power," Reynolds depicted Oberon's abduction of the Indian boy in an elaborate scenic spectacle, creating a movement from England to India for the transference of the boy. In Williams's words, this "pictorial and musical elaboration on the return of the Indian boy, with Titania's galley sailing to England from India's shores, reproduced the very familiar discourse of colonial conquest. The spectacle narrates the mastering of the disobedient Titania and oriental India, combining colonialism and sexual domination in a familiar manner."[22] The Indian boy thus became a colonial object to be transported from India to the empire as a power move. The desire for him became the desire for Indian goods and spaces and persons to dominate and own.

Following Purcell's oriental spectacle and Reynolds's imperial scenery, in the nineteenth century *Dream* was a colonial dream with classical decor and costumes; India replaced the Mediterranean Athens as the space of abduction. And in this century-long dream, the Indian boy became a fixture on stage.[23] Productions including those of Charles Kean (1856–1859), Augustin Daly (1888), F. R. Benson (1889–1916), and Herbert Beerbohm Tree (1900) consistently made the Indian boy visible on the English stage. So too did American productions shortly after the play's first performance at the Park Theatre on Broadway in 1826. William E. Burton's production at Burton's Theatre in New York in 1854, a model for Daly's 1888 production, self-consciously explained the decision to stage the Indian boy in this way: "The *'lovely boy, stolen from an Indian king'*, never before placed on the stage, although undoubtedly intended to be personated, is costumed from an ancient print, and is believed, both in beauty and apparel, to be worthy the love of a Fairy Queen."[24] This Indian boy was Sally Holman, probably cross-dressed, because one critic for the *Morning Courier and New York Enquirer* (whose review is included in this promptbook) called her "Prince" with no mention of a change in gender: "Even that cause of fierce dispute, that dainty scrap of mortality, the Indian prince—who, by the way, is the manager's well-thought addition to the dramatic personae—was not forgotten."[25] Five years later, Laura Keene's 1859 *Dream* at Laura Keene's Theater in New York cast Mary Jane Bullock as the Indian boy, whose costume is depicted as "Indian tunic—feather head-dress."[26] Additionally, in *A Midsummer Night's Dream in Three Acts* by Samuel French in 1853, the Indian boy entered the stage in a chariot, standing by Titania; and the 1915 production at the Repertory Theater of Boston by Henry Jewett placed the Indian boy next to Titania, who, on the center stage, held the boy and later kissed him.

It is not clear what the Indian boy exactly looked like in most of these productions. His portrayal in visual arts and drawings from the late eighteenth century onward offer only ambiguous representations. Yet one common thread is the infantilizing of the boy as very young and small in size. The drawing attributed to John Hoppner illustrates the Indian boy as a little child standing next to Titania, dressed in a voluminous gown at the moment of Oberon's demand that she release him (fig. 6.2). The boy is situated in a gendered conflict between Oberon's party, which includes a slightly older boy in a chariot pulled by tigers, and Titania's feminine group with peacocks. In George Romney's *Study for Titania, Puck and the Changeling* for Lady Hamilton (1793), the Indian boy is an infant (fig. 6.3).[27] Frank Howard's *Illustrations of Shakespeare's Midsummer Night's Dream* of the 1820s exhibits a little Indian boy in two outline plates: one represents the moment

FIGURE 6.2. *Midsummer Night's Dream, Oberon, Titania and the Fairies*, John Höppner, 1888. The Folger Shakespeare Library.

of abduction of the boy as Titania sleeps in her oriental bedchamber in the company of sleeping servants in turbans, while the other captures Oberon's demand for the boy (figs. 6.4 and 6.5). In Washington Allston's unfinished large-scale canvas, *Titania's Fairie Court* (1836), the boy is a young Native American in a feather skirt, headband, and armbands serving Titania as her cupbearer, her Ganymede (fig. 6.6). In a drawing of *Scenes and Characters from Midsummer Night's Dream*, probably modeled on a production from the late nineteenth or early twentieth century, the "little Indian boy" is in a tunic and a turban and is racialized in terms of skin color (fig. 6.7). Arthur Rackham's illustrations for a rare collection in 1908 include two images of the boy: one portrays him as a brown boy sitting next to Titania, who crowns him with flowers; the other one depicts him being transported on the shoulder of a fairy to Oberon's bower, evoking Ganymede's abduction and flight by the eagle (figs. 6.8 and 6.9). In all these images, with the exception of Allston's, the Indian boy is made prepubescent, if not infantile.

FIGURE 6.3. *Lady Hamilton as Titania with Puck and Changeling*, George Romney, 1793. The Folger Shakespeare Library.

FIGURE 6.4. *Illustrations of Shakespeare's Midsummer Night's Dream*, Frank Howard, 1820s. The Folger Shakespeare Library.

FIGURE 6.5. *Illustrations of Shakespeare's Midsummer Night's Dream*, Frank Howard, 1833. The Folger Shakespeare Library.

FIGURE 6.6. *Titania's Fairie Court*, Washington Allston, 1836. The Francis Loeb Art Center, Vassar College.

FIGURE 6.7. "Little Indian Boy." In *Scenes and Characters from Midsummer Night's Dream*, artist unknown, late nineteenth or early twentieth century. The Folger Shakespeare Library.

FIGURE 6.8. "Titania and the Indian Boy." Arthur Rackham, *Illustrations for A Midsummer Night's Dream*, 1908. The Folger Shakespeare Library.

The Indian boy as an infant or little child became prominent in the twentieth century, when the boy "made intermittent but largely unremarked appearances" in productions by Nevill Coghill (1945), Michael Langham (1960), Ron Daniels (1981), Bill Alexander (1986), and John Caird (1989).[28] This century also introduced the Indian boy on screen with filmic adaptations. In the 1909 silent movie version, directed by James Stuart Blackton and Charles Kent and produced in the United States, the Indian boy causes a conflict not between Oberon and Titania but between two women, Titania and a woman named Penelope.[29] The boy's dusky oriental costume in this film anticipates Max Reinhardt and William Dieterle's 1935 influential movie in which the Indian boy is in a shiny oriental costume and turban standing out exotically among Titania's fairy children. The movie presents the boy in the process of transitioning from the maternal world to the world of adult men (albeit not without the implication of erotic intimacy, as highlighted by the zoom in on Bottom's replacement of the boy—Titania takes the flower crown off the boy's turban and puts it on Bottom's ass head, which makes the boy cry).[30] Paternal concerns mark

FIGURE 6.9. "The Indian Boy." Arthur Rackham, *Illustrations for A Midsummer Night's Dream*, 1908. The Folger Shakespeare Library.

the more recent filmic examples, including Michael Hoffman's 1999 movie, in which the little Indian boy with long hair dressed in nomadic Asian costume (and a blue face evoking Krishna) appears only once, and Adrian Noble's 1994 Royal Shakespeare Company version, a little white boy's dream in which the boy imagines himself as the abducted turbaned Indian boy.

While these filmic examples put the Indian boy in a maternal/paternal realm, the operatic and theatrical stage in the second half of the century brought the homoerotic dynamics to the fore more forcefully in parallel to the changing sexual discourses and rising gay liberation movements. As Purcell's opera had done four centuries earlier, Benjamin Britten broke ground in 1960 with an operatic adaptation that unabashedly highlighted the pederastic homoeroticism embedded in Oberon's motive for abducting the boy.[31] Casting Oberon as a countertenor, Britten's *Dream* associates the fairy king, through his vocal range, with effeminate homosexuality. In an era of increased surveillance of and public hysteria against homosexuals, Britten, in Sue-Ellen Case's words, "almost single-handedly created a space for homosexuality" with his version on the British stage, where any implication of homosexuality was strictly controlled until 1958 and plays had to be licensed until 1968.[32] The subsequent Royal Opera House adaptations of Britten's opera included the Indian boy in the 1960s. For example, in the 1961 production, Johaar Mosaval (one of the first ballet dancers of color in the United Kingdom) appeared as the Indian boy at the age of thirty-one. But then the Royal Opera House exiled the boy from productions in the 1970s and 1980s. Following these moments of relative homoerotic liberation on stage, the 1968 production of the play by John Hirsch and Jean Gascon at the Stratford Shakespeare Festival in Ontario staged the Indian boy as an African American in his late teens, who both Titania and Oberon longed for erotically and lustfully.[33] Likewise, David Pountney's 1995 production of Henry Purcell's *The Fairy-Queen* for the English National Opera queered *Dream* with the Indian boy, a stereotypically South Asian–looking young man in a loincloth who erotically danced between Titania and Oberon, who were both infatuated with the boy. As Williams notes, "Not in the history of the play or of this opera in particular had an overt homosexual reading of Oberon been thinkable until this time; in the 1990s, after a decade of increasing public awareness of homosexuality in the wake of the AIDS epidemic, it was, perhaps, inevitable."[34]

The *Dream* had become a dream of sexual liberation and its Indian boy a medium for expressing homoerotic desire on stage. Yet such sexual liberation with boys faced resistance with accusations of pedophilia. Indeed, pederasty and pedophilia have often been erroneously conflated. Pederasty, understood as a conventional, historically ordinary cross-generational erotic mode with power differentials in age, generation, or status, refers to adult desire for adolescent boys (as discussed in the introduction). Pedophilia, defined as adult desire for prepubescent children, on the other hand, is a modern Western category that does not apply to early modern cross-generational desire for boys whose boyhood was related to both age and status. New sexual moral codes of Western modernity found it hard to accept pederasty as an inevitable component of the Shakespearean world and repertoire. So when in the 1990s Oberon's desire for the Indian boy became a means of displaying homosexuality on stage, it risked being branded as a display of pedophilia partly because of the unacceptability of staging cross-generational desire and partly for being associated with Britten, whose real-life pederastic homosexuality was already under public scrutiny. In the 1996 production of Britten's *Dream* at the Metropolitan Opera, for instance, Oberon was overtly homosexual. Williams notes of this production: "As to pederasty, it is likely that the scores of stories in the press had sensitized the public to the covert sexual abuse of children and made the Indian boy sadly problematic."[35] Indeed, reviews such as Anthony Tommasini's for the *New York Times* reflected this concern: "For all the opera's fantastical exuberance, the earlier acts, with romantic couples drugged into disloyalty, a fairy king with a base need for young boys, and a depiction of dream states both lulling and disorienting, are genuinely disturbing."[36] He, of course, does not forget to remind his readers that Britten himself "formed strong attachments to a series of young, sometimes very young, men. And he did not have to contort Shakespeare much to uncover this implicit theme." Fifteen years later, in 2011, when the English National Opera production set the play in a school setting where fairies and the Indian boy were objects of their teachers' (Oberon and Titania) desire, Michael White, in a review for the *Telegraph*, similarly wrote: "Poor Britten. Poor, poor Britten. The vicarious, armchair thrill of picking over evidence of his (no longer hidden) sexuality in the minutiae of his work goes ever on; and I've rarely seen a nastier, more gratuitous example than the new *A Midsummer Night's Dream*."[37] White seems to have been traumatized by Puck's homosexual childhood trauma of being "groomed, abused and then abandoned (in favour of the 'little changeling boy') by Oberon." Nor did White forget to remind his readers of "Britten's own unfortunate habit of attachment to small boys." But "in fairness," he confesses, "it's extremely interesting, profoundly disturbing, and for the most part well done by a wonderful cast. But it's also perverse. And cruel." The cruelty mainly comes from "the identification between Oberon the stealthy pedophile and Britten the boy-lover." While it is not clear if the production actually made this identification, the reviewer's association later dictated a moral lesson: "No one would suggest that falling in love with boys is a good idea; and Britten[,] who in most respects was a man of high moral principle, knew it wasn't a good idea. That was his tragedy, and it's why the theme of corrupted innocence figures so largely in his work. It clawed at his mind." Yet the reviewer ends with a mixed feeling, still haunted by Britten: "As a piece of work it's brilliantly conceived. But hateful."[38] Interesting, brilliantly conceived, well done with a wonderful cast and yet perverse, cruel, and hateful. The reviewer is confused.

In the emerging sexual norms of the 1990s, reviewers seemed to not know what to make of Shakespeare's pederasts and desiring boys when staged in modern times. Their confusion and discomfort with facing the age-differentiated homoeroticism of *Dream*, presented on stage via Britten's visionary adaptation, reflects the increasing sex panics that particularly targeted adult man/adolescent boy relations with the accusation of pedophilia. However, the figure of the pedophile—an abnormal, violent, and harmful psychiatric type with uncontrollable sexual attraction to prepubescent children—is a specific modern category that emerged in the West. As Gillian Harkins notes, "In 1978, the idea that all adults who have sex with children are pedophiles and that all pedophiles are moral predators, was barely emerging. Only a decade later, all adults who have sex with children would become popularly (and at times legally) defined as pedophiles, all pedophiles would be depicted as predatory and 'children' considered naturally vulnerable might be as old as eighteen."[39] Joseph J. Fischel observes that "sometimes public anxiety about pedophiles masquerades [sic] homophobia; sometimes homophobic political leaders or opportunists affiliate homosexuals with pedophiles or child recruiters; sometimes self-proclaimed pedophiles liken their social and political struggles to those of homosexuals."[40] Such attachments often connected pederasty with pedophilia under a general rubric of homosexuality.

As previous chapters have shown, historically, pederastic cross-generational relations were common, and sometimes normative, forms of eroticism. With modernity, however, we see a turn that deems the pederastic erotics of Shakespeare's *Dream* unacceptable. Indeed, in this modern age of idealizing an egalitarian and liberal framework for "good homosexuals," as Kadji Amin notes, pederasty was not included in the assimilation of gay relationships. Hence, "pederasty was precipitously *made retrograde* between the 1970s and '90s"; now associated with "homosexual self-loathing [rather] than with contemporary sex radicalism," it was "assimilated to the 'then' of a vaguely defined pre-Stonewall history and the 'there' of an equally vaguely defined Arab-Islamic culture."[41] In its modern reconceptualization, pederasty was built on a fantasy of temporal, racial, and geospatial differences attributed to twentieth-century prisons, the Arab-Islamic world, and Renaissance Italy.[42] With the constitution of clearly defined, knowable, assimilable sexual identities in Western modernity, the pederastic mode of homoeroticism of earlier times became aberrant, unspeakable, anachronistic and pedophilic, attributed to temporal, geographic, and racial otherness. Modern pederasty is thus a racialized sexuality of imperialism. Yet even in such attributions, Western modernity is haunted by its pederastic past. On the one hand, pederasty is attributed to others, and on the other hand, as Eng-Beng Lim, Joseph Boone, and Hiram Pérez, among others, have shown, the homoerotics of modern Orientalism in the West is itself pederastic; that is, white men fantasizing about and saving the brown boy from his despotic oriental master.[43]

Pederastic concerns in modern times recognize Britten's and other queer productions as radically challenging while indicating it as the source of the troubles of Shakespearean critics and reviewers when they see that this form of love dares to speak its name. As Amin reminds us, Oscar Wilde's "love that dare not speak its name" was a specific form of homosexuality: an age-differentiated one that now goes by the name of pederasty. Wilde wrote that the "love that dare not speak its name" was "such a great affection of an elder for a younger man as there was between David and Jonathan, such as Plato made the very basis of his philosophy, and such as you find in the sonnets of Michelangelo and Shakespeare."[44] Wilde's "love that dare not speak its name" involves boys, just like the premodern "sin not fit to be named" often referred to sexual relations between adult men and boys.[45] While early modern pederasty and Shakespeare's fair youth were Wilde's medium for speaking of homoeroticism, his Indian boy became such a medium for the theater makers at the dawn of the twentieth century. Yet as idealizing as the homoeroticism of the past was for contemporary sexual liberation, one must also face the fact that pederastic erotics was inflected with possessive abductions, imperial imaginings, violent hierarchies, and exploitation in the early modern period.

Desiring the Indian Boy

Speaking to this long performance history as deeply interlinked with colonial, racial, and sexual histories, the 1991 Shakespeare Santa Cruz production enables a dialogue between Hendricks's focus on race and Sinfield's queer analytics to show that the Indian boy, as Sinfield has fantasized, may very well be a desiring boy in the arms of another man desiring him, "enjoy[ing] the attentions of the king of the fairies."[46] Furthermore, on stage, he may very well be silent, turbaned, and sexual, yet partially empowered. This vision presents race and sexuality in performance as mutually constitutive even when challenging the heteronormative hegemonic imaginings of Shakespeare's *Dream*. The SSC production radically transformed the Indian boy into a sexy youth in his twenties who was energetic, confident, active, and attractive, mobilizing others' desires and catching and moving their eyes—a figuration that clearly departed from the conventional infantilized embodiments of the boy. Whereas with such a figuration the production avoided the pedophilic matrix of modernity in which pederastic relations have been put, it nonetheless sanitized the historical violence and power differentials in the nonegalitarian homoeroticism of the past.

First, was the director Danny Scheie's decision to cast such an Indian boy in his twenties a radical departure from the text of the play? As I discussed in chapter 3 with a focus on the boy as a specific, historical category, Shakespeare's Indian boy was often misread or misrepresented as a little child. Neither "changeling" nor "child" in reference to the boy determines the boy's age clearly. In fact, the category of the boy refers not merely to age but also to status, service, and race in master/servant, master/slave dynamics in early modernity. In alignment with this historical context, Scheie's choice of a sexy adolescent

Indian boy thereby avoids as well as challenges the theatrical convention of putting desire for the boy in a pedophilic frame—and he does so without refraining from highlighting cross-generational erotics.

Within an erotically charged matrix, the production further blurred the lines between classes, genders, and races with the boy. Although the Indian boy was silent, not unlike other prominent youthful objects of desire in Shakespeare's comedies, from Rosalind/Ganymede of *As You Like It* to Viola/Cesario of *Twelfth Night*, he was given an active status in this queer version of the topsy-turvy world of *Dream* in order to subvert established orders and hierarchies. Highlighting the homoerotic dynamic through the boy, who generates the dramatic conflict, Scheie recognized his cultural and racial difference in his wholesale reimagining of the play. The boy was in a turban throughout, Titania was a black man in drag, while Oberon was acted by a cross-dressed white woman. Upsetting the conventional Theseus-Hippolyta/Oberon-Titania doubling that had prevailed since Peter Brook's 1970 Royal Shakespeare Company production, Scheie perverted the doubling by transforming Theseus into Titania and Hippolyta into Oberon. This radical shift in genders and races and in the embodiment of the Indian boy can be seen as a modern queer intervention in the sexual and racial politics of the 1990s. Titania's campy queer court of fairies were all adults in drag who performed drag shows to lull Titania to sleep (with the Indian boy in her arms). Oberon's party was composed of racially mixed, age-differentiated fairies that included white, Asian, and black persons. These fairies almost recast the American "fairies" of the early twentieth century who were now put in racial diversity, if we remember George Chauncey's note that "fairy" has been a term used for homosexuals since then.[47]

In this already racially mixed, radically queer world, the Indian boy appeared with his attractive body, becoming not only an object of Titania and Oberon's desire but also the object of the audience's gaze, orienting their eyes and bodies by moving from one side of the stage to the other. On the embodiment of the Indian boy on stage, Menon writes, "No matter whether he is big or small, fully-dressed or naked, the embodied Indian boy is necessarily spectacular because he has nothing to do other than *be*, nothing to offer other than be *seen*."[48] For Menon, subjectivity is related to signification and thus to speaking, and hence, the silence of the boy is the elimination of any agency related to his erotic and exotic presence. Menon does not consider that this boy's racially marked body might actively work by centrally vectoring the gazes and desires of others. Cannot the boy on stage do things without words? Does the boy have to speak to perform or get what he really wants or turn the world of fairies and lovers upside down with his desired body? Is speaking the sole universal medium for claiming agency and showing resistance? In Jonathon Glassman's exploration of the contradictory consciousness of slave resistance on the Swahili coast, he reminds us that language, autonomy, and revolt were not the sole mediums of the slaves' resistance and survival. Following Antonio Gramsci's concept of hegemony and contradictory popular consciousness, Glassman stresses that cultural contexts, ideological components of a given culture, and threads of cultural idiom must be taken into account in order to avoid the assumption that the "slave population had fully internalized the ideologies of the masters" just because not many slaves "consistently and uniformly rejected the ideological constructs of their masters."[49] Keeping in mind Glassman's insights on the possibility that the consciousness of the exploited might be contradictory, I consider it significant whether the Indian boy enacts some agency, whether he makes a decision. If decisiveness of the subaltern is evident, then it necessitates attention to his decision-making in a given circumstance. The Indian boy of the SSC production exemplified similar contradictions and ambiguities of the silent yet empowered decision-making subject not only by not being infantilized but also by making possible his mobility on stage via smooth movements and dances through which he confidently claimed and took pleasure in his own body. This boy thus showed signs of being a desiring subject, even as he was a body caught between multiple worlds.

With his alluring body that called for voyeuristic attention, the Indian boy of this production was queerly provocative. Despite his silence, or perhaps because of it, the boy's desiring body for both man and woman, black and white, and everything in between transformed him into a partially active agent with some capacity to decide, please, and have pleasure. The boy as an object of erotic desire and abduction was not thereby reduced into continuous marginality nor was he pushed to the edges of the stage or behind the curtain. Rather, this Indian boy with his delicious body was the visible object of desire for all: Titania, Oberon, and the audience. In addition to Oberon's homoerotic desire, Titania eroticized her relationship with the Indian boy as she narrated his "vot'ress" mother's story by approaching the boy, touching his body erotically, then climaxing in a sexual tone behind the boy, finishing: "I rear up the boy." This caused the audience to laugh as if releasing their own tensions under the intense erotic energy of the scene. Oberon pursued a similar erotic move when he successfully kidnapped the boy, saying, "Now I have the boy," then planting a passionate kiss on his lips. While the boy may be expected to be a passive object of their desires, Jamie Paglia as the Indian boy probed the simplistic paradigm of passivity in silence with a smile. The Indian boy did not resist, nor did he show any sign of having been forcibly taken up into a nonconsensual intimacy. Strikingly, in previous scenes when Titania and Oberon had their destructive debates, the boy seductively smiled at both of them, as if enjoying being at the center of the attention and conflict that destroyed the harmony in fairyland. In return for Oberon's kiss, the boy smiled with confidence and *decided* to join Oberon's "train." In the final scene, the Indian boy stood next to Titania, giving the impression that his move back to Titania's queer court was the happy ending, a harmony returned to fairyland. Or in the ideal dream, perhaps the boy freely and consciously and decisively moves between the two worlds without being possessed by anyone. While earlier productions reflect the imperial and colonial politics of the nineteenth and early twentieth century, Scheie's staging spoke back to the social context of sex panics, homophobia, and homosexual liberation agendas of the 1980s and 1990s. By putting sexual, racial, and gender identities in performance and centering them on the desire for the Indian boy, the SSC production blurred racial, cultural, and sexual differences in its reimagining of a modern Western culture that actually regards with suspicion sex across differences in age, race, status, and class.

It must also be noted that characterizing an adolescent Indian boy in a feathered turban is not merely an Orientalist fantasy but also an anachronistically creative portrayal and wishful dream of the boy as one who has not been fully assimilated, transformed, converted, or remade but exists with his cultural difference, in stark contrast to the historical boys who were abducted, refashioned, and regendered. This staged queer dream of finding pleasure and agency in oppression did not face historical violence and oppression and thereby disassociated the racially marked boy from the violence of eroticized hierarchies of the past. Visiting the past, specifically Shakespearean repertoire to find and claim homoeroticism and to remake and demonstrate progressive and liberatory racial and sexual meanings in the present risks idealizing a homoeroticism that historically also has less than ideal, messy, discomforting aspects. As I have discussed in previous chapters, orderly, age-differentiated homoeroticism was a component of normative homosociality in premodern times. The boys in nonegalitarian, pederastic relations were considered as seductive beneficiaries of these relations in the frame of patriarchy, not as victims. Early modern homoeroticism was troubled by hierarchies of gender, age, race, status, and religious difference in imperial structures, and such homoeroticism was often deployed in a colonial imaginary that eroticized violent abductions, exploitations, assimilations, and conversions. Therefore, the erotic modes of the past are not always ideal alternatives for contesting today's oppressions. While theatrical artistic license allows directors to dream a future by reenvisioning the past or Shakespeare's *Dream*, such reimaginings are often historically distorted, burying messy parts of queer history and literature.

The (in)visibility of the Indian boy on stage, to conclude, projects often-dynamic, intersectional histories and trajectories, crossings and interrelations of empire, race, gender, and cross-racial and cross-generational desire—in both Shakespeare's age and ours. As I discussed in chapter 3, the portrayal of the Indian boy of exceptional beauty in the last decade of the sixteenth century echoed and anticipated the homoerotics of the abduction of boys in colonial England, when the East India Company and the Turkey Company began their overseas investments. An exploration of his staging across time demonstrates how the erotic and the exotic inextricably blended into one other in contingent hierarchical structures of gender, age, class, race as England became an imperial power. Later, in modernity, the boy's social and racial status that made him an object of exploitation was replaced by solely his age as the unacceptable aspect of being an erotic object of adult desire. In the changing sexual norms from the early modern period to modernity, the boy as the object of adoration slowly disappeared, not only in England but, as the next chapter shows, in the Ottoman Empire as well.

7

The Orientalization of Boy Love

A CONCLUSION

The seventeenth-century Ottoman poet Nev'izade Atayi narrated the story of two youthful friends in *Heft Han* (Seven stories).[1] As young boys, Tayyib and Tahir pursue love, wine, and music in the taverns of Istanbul and spend their nights in pleasure with other city boys. As a result of their profligate lifestyle, they find themselves in poverty and decide to join a Sufi order in Egypt in order to develop self-discipline. During their sea voyage, the two friends are captured by an infidel ship and sold as slaves to two handsome European noblemen, Sir John and Sir Janno. Brought to European lands, Tayyib and Tahir, whose "hearts consumed with flames of passion," fall in love with their masters, and "bonds of affection grew among the four" in beautiful European gardens. Soon, gossip about erotic relations between the four begins to circulate in the town, and they suffer at the hands of the authorities. Christian Europeans, the poem suggests, cannot comprehend the beauty of love among these men. Now separated, Sir John and Sir Janno are imprisoned by the town's police commander, "a raving infidel," and Tayyib and Tahir are condemned to slavery at the oar of a galley, which is later attacked by Muslim galleys. This fortunate attack liberates the two Muslim friends. In the meantime, the imprisoned John and Janno convert to Islam, an act that miraculously unlocks the gates of the prison and frees them. Soon they find themselves at sea and are magnetically drawn to Tayyib and Tahir. Now in Istanbul, they all live happily ever after before passing "from this world accompanied by their pure love."

Atayi's story highlights abduction, slavery, and conversion practices operating in the Mediterranean and, quite strikingly, in both Islamic and Christian contexts. It suggests that the abduction of boys was a common practice in which Ottomans were also objects of abduction, captivity, and enslavement by Europeans in the global trafficking in the Mediterranean—though perhaps not always in equal measure. The story also eroticizes power relations whereby mastery and service as well as Christianity and Islam are hierarchically ordered. Tayyib and Tahir actively pursue other boys in Istanbul, yet they become objects of love once they are slaves in the Christian lands, where love between them and their masters is not welcome. It is only when John and Janno convert to Islam that all four are happily reunited as equals.

In the preceding chapters, I have located such expressions of homoeroticism prevalent in multiple genres, including romances and dramas that included abducted boys, travelogues with stories of sexual captivity on voyages and after shipwrecks, and ghazal and epyllion that featured beautiful beloved boys, in the early modern historical context of abductions. I have demonstrated how Ottomans used various ways, particularly *devşirme*, to abduct Euro-Christian boys, who appeared as eroticized servants in literary and cultural imaginaries. Similarly, Englishmen brought boys from Africa, India, and the Americas to England, where they were categorized as both exotic and alien and enslaved in lives of service. I have explored such historical abductions in tandem with the rising literary trope of the abducted boy and the imagery of Ganymede the cupbearer as the eroticized servant boy by highlighting both the convergences and tensions between violent historical practices and the literary aestheticization of abducted boys.

In concluding my readings from a powerful empire on the eastern side of Europe and an emerging one from the western periphery of Europe, I mark some differences in the historical shift from a homoerotic order to an heteroerotic one. While orderly homoeroticism was crucial in organizing homosocial structures and in producing racial difference and hierarchizations in both societies, the intensity and openness in the expression of homoeroticism changed in parallel with changing economic and sociopolitical arrangements and emerging legal regulations. In pre-Reformation England, religious jurisdiction handled sodomy as a sin through confession and penance in Church courts. After the

Reformation, the implementation of sodomy statutes as part of canon law in 1533 under Henry VIII made sodomy a statutory felony punishable by hanging. While the law was interrupted briefly under Queen Mary I, Elizabethan rule reverted back to the Henriad laws, noting that "divers evil disposed persons have been the more bold to commit the said most horrible and detestable vice of buggery."[2] Of course, as Alan Bray, Bruce Smith, Jonathan Goldberg, and Mario DiGangi, among others, have shown, theological and legal regulations, which were capacious and contradictory and were rarely enforced, cover but one small part of homosexual relations and their expressions in the early modern period. In stark contrast to theological and legal refusals of sodomy, most domestic and public relations as well as political power were organized around orderly homoerotic bonds and hierarchies, in service, during schooling, in patronage relationships, during apprenticeship, and in friendship. On the early modern stage, where boys acted women's roles, homoerotic energy circulated even as it was attacked by Puritans. Yet as household structures changed, urbanization intensified, capitalism and the mercantile economy expanded, and new class dynamics emerged in England toward the end of the seventeenth century, what Valerie Traub calls "domestic heterosexuality" emerged as the ideal, characterized by an amorous cross-sex companionship that necessitated reordering and often stigmatizing homoerotic bonds, which were now deemed particularly oriental.[3]

Around the same time that heterosexualization started to dominate English colonial modernity more visibly, puritanical attacks such as the Kadızadeli movement against homoerotic expressions and rituals emerged in the seventeenth-century Ottoman Empire. Yet homoeroticism lingered well into the late eighteenth and early nineteenth centuries as a prominent mode of erotic representations in the empire.[4] Soon after, however, intolerance for same-sex love, which the story of Tayyib and Tahir in *Heft Han* attributed to Christian European lands, began to circulate in the lands of the westernizing empire. Homoeroticism began to be considered as a sign of backwardness, something that was anachronistic in modern times. In this epilogue, I end my contrapuntal exploration of boys and boy-lovers via three cases from different times to rethink the history of sexuality in a transhistorical, transregional, and transcultural mode. In particular, I briefly chart changes in sexual discourses to indicate how modern sexuality as it appeared in Europe penetrated Ottoman culture and society.

The 1480s. An Ottoman prince poeticizes beautiful Christian boys he adores during his exile years in a French city. After an unsuccessful contest with his brother Bayezid for the throne upon the death of their father, Sultan Mehmed II, in 1481, Prince Jem (Cem/Djem) took up residence in Euro-Christian realms to secure his life and gain support for his ongoing claim to the Ottoman throne.[5] In Baldassare Castiglione's *The Book of the Courtier* (1528), Prince Jem appears as an ideal courtier, as an anecdote narrates: "Djem Othman, brother to the Grand Turk, being a captive at Rome, said that jousting as we practise it in Italy seemed to him too great a matter for play and too paltry for earnest. And on being told how agile and active King Ferdinand the Younger was in running, leaping, vaulting, and the like—he said that in his country slaves practised these exercises, while gentlemen studied the liberal arts from boyhood, and prided themselves thereon."[6] In Castiglione's account, the Ottoman prince is an exemplar for Christian princes, not the cultural other. During his seven-year stay in the French city of Nice (1482–1489), this ideal prince penned his "European Eulogy," which describes his daily social life and presents a particular unnamed French prince as the subject of his erotic admiration and pleasure:

> Drain, O Jem, thy Jemshid-cup;[7] here in Frankish land are we! . . .
> Look thou lose not the occasion; make thou merry with all cheer;
> Fortune bideth aye with no man, fleeting is the World, ah me!
> Make thou merry in this city of the French Prince,
> For that he's a wondrous lovesome chieftain of the fair and free.
> Cypress-figured, silver-bodied, fair the Frankish beauty is;
> Dazed for love of his bright beauty, sun and moon reel giddily!
> That with all this grace he offers thee the wine-filled beaker, Prince,
> China's throne is, Yemen's kingdom, yea, or Persia's empery![8]

Reminiscent of his father Sultan Mehmed's poetic imagination of his imperial majesty in relation to a beautiful Christian boy (analyzed in chapter 2), Prince Jem celebrates the French nobleman whose exceptional beauty makes the sun and moon drunk. He idealizes the white body of this Ganymede-like cupbearer youth who is "fair" and "silver bodied." This prince is not the sole object of the poet's gaze; later in the poem, he lists other beautiful boys, including "vassals," "sons of high noblemen," "twelve sons of European nobles," and "dancing boys" who entertain him. They all bring to life paradisiacal boys in this French city: "Kingship can be naught beyond this, O Prince Jem, I tell thee true, / Drain the bowl and glad thy spirit, 'tis the revelers' feast of glee." Spending a night with these beauties is worth a kingdom, Jem announces: "O thou youthful Prince, O Jem, to pass one joyous night with those / Midst of fair delice were sweeter than aught else on earth to thee."[9]

The 1620s. Philip Massinger's *The Renegado* is on the English stage. Vitelli, a Venetian gentleman disguised as a merchant, rents a shop in the Tunisian marketplace to sell, in his servant Gazet's words, "your choice of China dishes, your pure Venetian crystal of all sorts, of all neat and new fashions, from mirror of the madam to the private utensil her chambermaid, and curious pictures of the rarest beauties of Europa" (1.3.1–5).[10] Set in Tunis, the play puts "Turks" at its center; it stages Ottoman spaces, politics, characters, and customs, especially after the appearance of the Ottoman princess Donusa in this scene. Like other early modern English accounts about the Ottomans, *The Renegado* offers revealing intertextual deployments in its representation of the Turks. Its probable sources include Robert Daborne's *A Christian Turned Turk* (1612), Cervantes's *Don Quixote* (1605) and "Liberal Lover" (1613), George Sandys's *A Relation of a Journey* (1615), and Richard Knolles's *The Generall Historie of the Turkes* (1603).[11] Such an amalgamation of Spanish, English, and French sources (numerous accounts about the Ottomans were translations from French), which depict Italian, North African, and Turkish characters in the Mediterranean world of the play, uncovers the transcultural nature of the "Turkish" world as imagined on the English stage. The play's Ottoman marketplace includes various cultural artifacts. What are these "curious pictures" and "rarest beauties of Europa" that Gazet mystifies as objects that would attract customers in the transcultural Mediterranean world?

While in the same scene Gazet simply advertises the items as "China dishes, clear crystal glasses, a dumb mistress to make love to" (33–34), Vitelli poetically details these "rare beauties" as he presents his inventory to Donusa. After showing her a mirror "that Narcissus might / (And never grow enamored of himself) / View his fair feature in it" (1.3.112–13), Vitelli displays other pieces from "the Christian world":

> Here crystal glasses, such as *Ganymede*
> Did fill with Nectar to the Thunderer
> When he drank to *Alcides*, and received him
> In the fellowship of the *gods*: true to the owners.
> Corinthian plate studded with Diamonds,
> Concealed oft deadly poison....
> Here's a picture, madam;
> The masterpiece of Michaelangelo,
> Our great Italian workman; here's another
> So perfect at all parts that had Pygmalion
> Seen this, his prayers had been made to Venus,
> To have given it life, and his carved ivory image
> By poets ne'er remembered. They are indeed

> The rarest beauties of the Christian world
> And no where to be equaled. (1.3.115–36)

The "curious pictures of the rarest beauties" are revealed by Vitelli as not of "Europa," as mysteriously evoked by Gazet earlier, but of "the Christian world": a mirror that makes the beholder feel like Narcissus, a crystal glass comparable to Ganymede's wine cup, a Corinthian plate, one of Michelangelo's works, and a sculpture that generates passions like Pygmalion's. In other words, Vitelli uses famous Greco-Roman icons to sell "the rarest beauties" in the Ottoman world. Strikingly, in Massinger's imagination, the Ottoman princess Donusa does not show any unfamiliarity with Vitelli's references to these mythic characters who are presumably from a different world. While the non-Christian characters from diverse nations mark this Ottoman market as an exotic space of religious difference (as suggested by Vitelli's use of "the Christian world"), the Greco-Roman references challenge religious binaries. The play thus offers a world of not only incomprehension (i.e., Gazet's incomprehension of eunuchism) but also of crossings, exchanges, and common cultural ground between the English and the Ottoman, the Christian and the Islamic.

The artifacts in this marketplace, "toys and trifles," are described with references to mythic boys who symbolically mediate exchanges between the merchant and the customer: Narcissus, Ganymede, Alcides, Pygmalion, well-known representative figures of youthful beauty and love (1.3.104). Vitelli evokes these youthful male beauties to make his elite Ottoman customers desire the objects in this mostly male marketplace. We are told earlier by Gazet that Vitelli "studies speeches for each piece / And, in a thrifty tone, to sell them off" on a street near the bazaar (1.1.6–7). Hence his evocation of these youths is not impromptu but a part of well-studied and memorized rhetoric in his strategy for selling items, a rhetoric prepared before he even comes to this place.

By doing so, he evokes commonplace discourses that attribute homoeroticism and sodomy to the Ottoman space through youthful boys. The play further alludes to "catamites" and "eunuchs" in this space, figures that appear in other plays in relation to the Ottomans (2.5.13, 3.4.43). When the play generates a gaze upon these characters on stage alongside cross-dressed boy actors and refers to mythic and historical figures, it inevitably brings to the fore tales and images of beautiful boys of not only Greco-Roman but also Ottoman worlds—boys who were desired, abducted, and made into lovers.

The 1820s. A young Egyptian scholar, Rifai'ah al-Tahta'wi, spends the years 1826–1831 in Paris as part of a scientific delegation sent by the modernizing ruler of

Egypt, Muhammad Ali Pasha. Tahta'wi produces a description of the manners and customs of the Parisians, where, as Khaled El-Rouayheb uncovers, Tahta'wi was surprised to find that the French were not inclined to youths and considered a man's love for a boy disgraceful: "In the French language a man cannot say: I loved a youth [*ghulam*], for that would be an unacceptable and awkward wording, so therefore, if one of them translates one of our books he avoids this by changing the wording, so saying in the translation: I loved a young girl [*ghulamah*] or a person [*dhatan*]."[12] As Tahta'wi is facing this surprise in Paris, the British Orientalist Edward Lane is in Egypt, considering pederasty to be an unmentionable vice as he reports that in his translations of Arabic poetry, he "substituted the feminine for the masculine pronoun; for in the original, the former is meant, though the latter is used, as is commonly the case in similar compositions of the Egyptians."[13] In the same period, the English Orientalist translator of Ottoman poetry E. J. W. Gibb is busy silently deploying the pronouns "she/her" in reference to the beloved boy of Turkish poetry in his translations in order to straighten or blur homoerotic couplings. Love for youthful men now dares not speak its name or have it spoken in poetry. At the same time, the English Orientalist Richard Burton, a good reader of Lane, is marking the Mediterranean, especially Turkish and Arabic locales, as geographies of boy love or abominations in his formulation of the "Sotadic Zone," contributing to the homoerotics of Orientalism, that is, to homoerotic desire and homophobic contempt.[14]

Around the same time as the Egyptian traveler wrote his observations, a remarkable turn took place in Ottoman sexual culture in congruence with what Foucault called the emergent *scientia sexualis* in Western Europe.[15] This coincided with the abolition in 1826 of the Janissary Corps—the corps that began in the fifteenth century with abductions of Euro-Christian boys—as part of Sultan Mahmud II's westernization policies. As Ezgi Sarıtaş notes, the abolition of these corps impacted homoerotic and homosocial structures. Spaces associated with homoeroticism such as coffeehouses, bathhouses, or male brothels were either demolished or reconfigured in discreet ways following this abolition.[16] In the long nineteenth century, the Ottomans began to adopt the Western conceptualization of homosexuality as perversion, and, as Dror Ze'evi has shown, they attempted to repress the homoerotic component of literary and social life as part of the westernization of the empire. Within the new Western sexual discourses, which dissected and identified sexual acts and desires, "the homosexual" soon emerged as a pathologized identity.

Thus, remarkably, after a long acceptance of the expression of male homoeroticism, heteroeroticism with a touch of homophobia began to emerge as the norm in the modernizing Ottoman Empire. Ahmed Cevdet Paşa, a leader of the nineteenth-century reforms, for example, in the autobiographical *Maruzat* he wrote for Sultan Abdulhamid II, reported the salient changes taking place in the 1850s: "As the number of women-lovers increased, that of boy-lovers decreased. It is as if the people of Sodom disappeared off the face of the earth. The well-known love for and relationships with the young men in Istanbul has transformed to young women as the natural order of things.... We don't see people like Kamil or Ali Pasha or those similar to them who were well known as boy-lovers in the higher offices. Yet Ali Pasha had always tried to hide his love for boys because of the disapproval of the foreigners."[17] Cevdet Paşa acknowledged a shift in the sexual conduct of people in Istanbul, a move from same-sex relations to cross-sex ones, from homoeroticism to heteroeroticism, in accordance with "the natural order of things" (*hali tabii*). Cevdet Paşa's use of this phrase set forth a categorization of sexualities by declaring procreative sex as natural and normative, hence identifying all nonprocreative sexual inclinations as unnatural and deviant. This nineteenth-century paradigm shift in sexual discourse generated a selective integration of certain Western discourses (sexual, gendered, racial) into the discourses of the westernizing state at the height of European colonialism.

As the preceding chapters have shown, early modern Ottoman writers wrote unabashedly about beautiful boys—be it in the form of expressing carnal desire for them or the aesthetic celebration of chaste love. Writers such as Mustafa Ali, Aşık Çelebi, and Evliya Çelebi charted taverns, coffeehouses, bathhouses, and parks as sites for pursuing boys. *Şehrengiz* writers described cities by cataloguing their beautiful boys. Biographers of poets such as Aşık Çelebi categorized poets as boy-lovers or woman-lovers. Jurists discussed whether beautiful boys' faces had to be veiled because their beauty might exceed the beauty of women or whether it was appropriate for beautiful boys to pray in the front row since the prostrating boy could distract men who were seeing him from behind.[18] Whereas religious authorities frowned upon the potential threat of alluring boys to tempt men in all-male gatherings, Sufi mystics found the impression of God in the beauty of the beardless boy and did not avoid celebrating beautiful boys.

By the nineteenth century, representations of and references to homosexual relations were censored in textual materials including interpretations of dreams, medical and legal texts, and literary and dramatic works.[19] As marriage and family became idealized forms of companionship and as the emphasis on heteronormativity intensified, literary representations promoted monogamous, amorous heterosexual companionships.[20] Heteroerotic representations veiled and replaced conventional expressions of homoerotic friendship, affection, and love in the cultural and literary imagination. These changes suggest a desire not only *to be like* westerners but also *to be liked and approved by* westerners, as the second part of Cevdet Paşa's account strikingly shows: "Ali Pasha had always tried to hide his love for boys because of the disapproval of the foreigners." Ali Pasha's attempt to have his homoerotic affairs remain secret in order to avoid the criticism and disapproval of (Western) foreigners—travelers, diplomats, ambassadors—indicates how the change from a homoerotic to a heteroerotic matrix included a certain level of collective self-fashioning as a result of interactions with homophobic Europeans.

While early modern representations of the Ottomans by European travelers and authors presented a combination of fascination and awe, fact and fantasy, admiration and moral repugnance, nineteenth-century Orientalism, which saw the now-falling Ottomans not as a threat but as a target for colonizing, stabilized preexisting templates in the image of the despotic, feminine, lustful, sodomitical Turk. Conventional homoeroticism in the Ottoman Empire as well as the sodomitical template produced by early Western European travelogues were now used as ways of engendering and controlling knowledge production and justifying racialized human hierarchizations in systematic Orientalist thought. Considering the colonial European narratives that attributed sodomy and all other forms of sexual deviance to the Ottomans from the sixteenth century onward, we recognize how nineteenth-century Ottomans were well aware of these stereotypical representations and kept their guard up under the European gaze in order to prove the foreigners wrong about their presumed sexual practices. This exemplifies the influence of Europe on Ottoman society in the nineteenth century, which took place "whether by force of intellectual inspiration and imperialist aura or on the ground in the form of colonial administrators, missionaries, commercial agents, governesses, young Muslims returning from European educations, and so on."[21] In this colonial modernity, instead of a predominantly direct colonial imposition by the West, the history of changing sexual discourses in the Ottoman Empire suggests that the shifts taking place were also self-imposed and were consistent and concurrent with changing cultural and social trends and internal dynamics in what Sarıtaş terms "Ottoman sexual modernity."[22]

This self-transformation and auto-correction to avoid Orientalist European critique became even more visible in the new Turkish republic of the twentieth century, which defined itself strictly as a Western, civilized, modern, unified, secular nation-state in contrast to its supposedly Eastern, backward, multiethnic, Islamic Ottoman past. Nineteenth-century Ottomans adopted Western homophobia in order to fight the Western Islamophobia that had marked Muslims as sodomites. The twentieth-century republic instrumentalized both homophobia and Islamophobia to mark the Ottomans as Muslim perverts in its efforts to create a secular

European nation-state, framed in the idealized heteronormative family with reproductive, amorous companionship. A westernizing republic, now strictly non-Islamic, needed to catch up with the norms of secular Western modernity, which did not bring sexual freedom for all, but only for heterosexuals in a heteronormative structure. Within this republican condemnation of Ottomans as perverts, Ismet Zeki Eyüboğlu's 1968 *Divan Şiirinde Sapık Sevgi* (Pervert love in divan poetry), one of the earliest explorations of Ottoman homosexuality, unveiled the homoerotic nature of the Ottoman literary tradition in order to claim the boy-loving Ottomans as deviants who were outside the norms of the new secular, moral, and heterosexual republic (the title of the book is unironic). The modern project of heterosexualization reached its peak with the newly born Turkish republic's nationalist discourses of sexuality, which attributed all nonnormative sexualities to the imperial "perverted" "boy-lover" Ottomans, in a manner similar to Orientalist European discourses.

My queer historicist cross-readings of English and Ottoman discourses and representations in the preceding pages offer and perform a culturally and geographically intersectional genealogy. In doing so, this book's contrapuntal analysis of the two cultural contexts broadens the genealogical methods of charting earlier structures and categories in relation to modernity and the production of modern sexual notions and identities.[23] As I have argued elsewhere, while in Western Europe the older categories of sodomite, catamite, or effeminate man reemerged in the formation of the abnormal, pathologized homosexual identity ("the unrationalized coexistence of different models," in Eve Kosofsky Sedgwick's terms), Turkish discourses produced homosexuality as a new category that blended with and often included older, traditional sexual subjects (i.e., *gulampare, ubna*) while simultaneously disowning homosexuality as European "immorality."[24] Thus, ironically, and in a peculiar twist of definitions, the deployment of the Western-originating categories of gay, lesbian, homosexual, and transgender to refer to all queer and nonbinary subjects sometimes risks their demarcation as westernized, immoral perverts by the Turkish state and some conservative groups and authorities. I propose, regarding future studies, that carefully studying older categories and their historical changes in literature—for example, the abducted boy, the *gulampare* (boy-lover), the *emred* (boy), the *güzeşte* (man with a beard), the *levend* (adventurous young man), the *luti* (sodomite), the *mukhannes* (passive/bottom sexual partner), the *ubna* (catamite), the *köçek* (androgynous dancer), the beautiful man, the effeminate, the androgynous person, the eunuch, the hermaphrodite, the masculine woman, the unmarried woman, the dildo-using woman, the intimate friend—will not only limn a strong literary history of and for sexually and racially marginalized people and their expressions of desires but will also help us chart the historical complexities, if not the messiness, of queer relations and representations.

Mapping traveling sexual discourses while carefully and responsibly tracing diverse and distinct modes and forms of the eroticization of boys, the preceding chapters provide a sense of the varieties of cross-generational, cross-religious, cross-cultural, and cross-racial erotic representations and encounters that the early moderns imagined and pursued. In part, I did so by highlighting the historical and literary figure of the boy located in the adult man/boy erotic hierarchy that was common to the classical world and was recovered by the English and Ottoman renaissances. I particularly explored the abducted boy as a site in order to understand not only the erotics of youth but also the erotics of slavery, race, religion, and promotion, since boys were enslaved, converted, made cupbearers, and sometimes promoted. A specific focus on the abducted boy reveals the adult man/abducted boy dyad as an important component of early modern erotic modes in English and Ottoman imperial contexts.

This cultural history challenges modern colonial conceptualizations of sexuality that attribute pederasty only to the Islamicate world or the so-called oriental cultures. Recent critical work on pederastic cross-cultural erotics and sexual practices and their temporal and geographical imaginaries have highlighted how pederastic discourses operate in modern colonial representations. Exploring eroticized native boys in the colonial Asian context, Eng-Beng Lim argues that Asia is cast as an actual and conceptual native boy. An eroticized native boy is a component of "a pedophiliac Western modernity bearing the homoerotics of orientalism," awaiting a civilizing Euro-North American white savior.[25] Confronting ambiguities in the disavowal of pederasty in a Euro-North American context, I offer the early modern period as a rich context for pursuing continuities and ruptures between the past and the present by showing native boys who were abducted, exchanged, and circulated as a part of larger imperial and nascent colonial practices throughout Europe, including the Ottoman territories. The homoerotics of this pederastic modern European imperialism, I conclude, was anticipated by early modern Ottoman and English representations of the *other* boy who was eroticized and abducted, which I traced as Ganymede effects.

By paying attention to cultural and historical specificities in my pursuit of boys and Ganymede effects, the previous chapters also examined probable connections between the two cultural contexts in more general terms in order to map larger conceptual, critical, and operative discourses in the period. I offered early modern Ottoman texts not simply to diversify our archives but to mark their voices, their epistemes as crucial for exploring early modern and modern formations of sexuality, race, and empire. I hope that this book, which connects the Ottoman and English texts and contexts as well as critical insights from studies of sexuality, race, postcoloniality, and globality in the early modern period, will open new paths for further intersectional, cross-lingual, transnational, and transregional historical investigations.

In both English and Ottoman accounts, the early modern homoerotic matrix reflects and informs colonial and cross-cultural imaginings through the figure of the boy, who reveals the eroticization of mobile social, imperial, and racial hierarchies. Anglo-Ottoman encounters were first formed with the prospect of, in Queen Elizabeth I's words, the possibility of "mutuall trafique, [that] the East may be joyned and knit to the West."[26] For better or worse, in this book it is the abducted boys whose representations joined the two realms in my reassessment of the imperial histories of the so-called East and West and my exploration of the homoerotics of empire and race. These boys were desired, abducted, and forced to cross borders. They joined and knitted each to each with and in eroticism and violence.

Notes

INTRODUCTION

1. Since Philippe Ariès's study of childhood as a historically constructed category, studies on childhood and boys have formed a rich subfield in historical, literary, anthropological, and gender studies that reveal boyhood to be an ephemeral status shaped by moral, astrological, medicinal, pedagogical, religious, anatomical, philosophical, and political discourses and factors. Among these, on European boys, are Ben-Amos, *Adolescence and Youth in Early Modern England*; Griffiths, *Youth and Authority*; Miller and Yavneh, *Gender and Early Modern Constructions of Childhood*; Higginbotham, *The Girlhood of Shakespeare's Sisters*; and Karras, *From Boys to Men*. On the Ottoman context, see Araz, *16. Yüzyıldan 19. Yüzyıl Başlarına*.

2. On Galenic foundations of the premodern gender/sex spectrum and the humoral body, see Laqueur, *Making Sex*; and Paster, *The Body Embarrassed*.

3. On the boy as a gender and erotic category in the Ottoman context, see Andrews and Kalpaklı, *The Age of Beloveds*; Kuru, "Naming the Beloved in Ottoman Turkish Gazel"; Araz, *16. Yüzyıldan 19. Yüzyıl Başlarına*; Peirce, "Seniority, Sexuality, and Social Order"; and Ze'evi, *Producing Desire*. In the English context, see Fisher, *Materializing Gender*; Jardine, *Reading Shakespeare*; Howard, *The Stage and Social Struggle in Early Modern England* and *Theater of a City*; Levine, *Men in Women's Clothing*; Bloom, "'Thy Voice Squeaks'"; Orgel, *Impersonations*; Masten, *Queer Philologies*; Smith, *Homosexual Desire in Shakespeare's England*; DiGangi, *The Homoerotics of Early Modern Drama* and *Sexual Types*; Bly, *Queer Virgins and Virgin Queans on the Early Modern Stage*; Goldberg, *Sodometries*; Stallybrass, "Transvestism and the 'Body Beneath'"; and Garber, *Vested Interests*. On boys in the theater and other cultural venues, see McCarthy, *Boy Actors in Early Modern England*; Shapiro, *Children of the Revels*; Lamb, *Performing Childhood in the Early Modern Theatre*; Rutter, *Shakespeare and Child's Play*; Low, *Manhood and the Duel*; Levine, *Men in Women's Clothing*; Kathman, "How Old Were Shakespeare's Boy Actors?"; Knowles, *Shakespeare's Boys*; and Chedgzoy, Greenhalgh, and Shaughnessy, *Shakespeare and Childhood*. On boys in school, see Enterline, *Shakespeare's Schoolroom*; and Stewart, *Close Readers*.

4. *Oxford English Dictionary* (hereafter OED), s.v. "boy," n., 1a, 1b, 2. Similarly, "lad" in Middle English denoted a "serving-man, attendant; man of low birth and position" (*OED*, s.v. "lad," n., *1*).

5. OED, s.v. "boy," n., 3.

6. For more on these terms and historical emergence of such categories in English context, see Sasser, "Shakespeare and Boyhood"; Higginbotham, *The Girlhood of Shakespeare's Sisters*; and Ben-Amos, *Adolescence and Youth in Early Modern England*. In the Ottoman context, see Peirce, "Seniority, Sexuality, and Social Order"; and Araz, *16. Yüzyıldan 19. Yüzyıl Başlarına*, 87–99.

7. Munro shows that the word "boy" carried significations of low-class status and sodomitic behavior ("Coriolanus and the Little Eyases," 91). On the beard and body hair in relation to adulthood, see Fisher, *Materializing Gender*; and Simons, *The Sex of Men in Premodern Europe*. On marriage and the transition to adulthood in the Ottoman context, see Peirce, "Seniority, Sexuality, and Social Order"; and Araz, *16. Yüzyıldan 19. Yüzyıl Başlarına*.

8. Smith shows that boys aged five to sixteen appeared in seventeenth-century sodomy trials. In a 1624 legal case, the "boy" in question was "aged 29 years or thereabouts" (*Homosexual Desire in Shakespeare's England*, 51). Of the word "boy," he writes, "age has little if anything to do with it" since the word "elaborates a distinction in power vis-à-vis a social or moral superior" (194–95).

9. Shakespeare's Anthony, for instance, insults Caesar as a boy, and Caesar compares Anthony to boys who "being mature in knowledge / Pawn their experience to their present pleasure, / And so rebel to judgment" (*Anthony and Cleopatra* 4.1.1, 1.4. 31–33). All Shakespeare references throughout the book are from Greenblatt et al., *The Norton Shakespeare*.

10. "Boy" as subservient category would later lead to the racist use of the term in a dehumanizing, emasculating pejorative sense for Black slaves and for African American men.

11. My formulation of traffic in boys draws on the conceptualization in Rubin's "The Traffic in Women" and Sedgwick's *Between Men*. On women as objects of exchange, exploration, possession, and enslavement in the early modern period, see Hall, *Things of Darkness* and "Object into Object?"; Newman, "Directing Traffic"; Matar, "Wives, Captives, Husbands, and Turks"; Andrea, *The Lives of Girls and Women from the Islamic World*; and Malieckal, "Slavery, Sex, and the Seraglio." On captive women in Ottoman harems, see Peirce, *The Imperial Harem* and "Abduction with (Dis)honor"; and Zilfi, *Women and Slavery in the Late Ottoman Empire*. On the traffic in local boys in England, see Campana, "Shakespeare's Children."

12. OED, s.v. "abduct," v., etym., and "abduction," n., etym.

13. On changing norms of beauty, see Najmabadi, *Women with Mustaches*.

14. Masten, *Textual Intercourse*, 6–7. On cruising and outing as historical agendas, see Pittenger, "To Serve the Queere." Bromley uses term "cruisy historicism" in reference to not only his exploration of historical representations of cruising but also a queer methodology that is informed by those representations ("Cruisy Historicism," 21–58). Stanivukovic titles his essay on erotic travels in the Mediterranean "Cruising the Mediterranean."

15. Muñoz, *Cruising Utopia*, 18.

16. OED, s.v. "cruise," v., etym. According to the OED, "cruise" also corresponds to Spanish *cruzar*, Portuguese *cruzar*, and French *croiser*, all signifying "to cross."

17. *OED*, s.v. "cross," v., 8; Shakespeare, *Two Gentlemen of Verona*, 1.1.22.

18. *OED*, s.v. "cruise," v., 1a and 1d.

19. Smith, "The Queer Moor," 191.

20. Vitkus, *Turning Turk*, 84.

21. Dinshaw, "Got Medieval?" 203.

22. Amin, *Disturbing Attachments*, 4. On the silence in queer studies regarding pederasty, see Sinfield, *On Sexuality and Power*, 113.

23. Cleves, *Unspeakable*, 10. Cleves's book offers a compelling argument on the necessity for the historian of sexuality to explore pederasty in historical context. On exploitation in pederastic relations, see Elliott, *The Corrupter of Boys*.

24. On pedophilia as a modern category, see Fischel, *Sex and Harm in the Age of Consent*.

25. Halperin, *How to Do the History of Homosexuality*, 115.

26. Halperin, *How to Do the History of Homosexuality*, 139. On sex and various power differentials including gender, age, class, and race, see Sinfield, *On Sexuality and Power*.

27. Amin, *Disturbing Attachments*, 35.

28. The early modern use of the term "economy" connects household management and domestic, state, and global economies, which highlights the intricate interrelation between the domestic and the global across trans-spatial exchanges. I use "economy" to signify not merely domestic and commercial aspects but also various other notions of exchange, including military, political, colonial, and discursive. Thus, economy refers to both material and libidinal practices, which I suggest play out in English and Ottoman cultural scenarios. For more on the interrelations between domestic and global economies, see Deng, "Global Œconomy," 245–63.

29. Loomba, "Race and the Possibilities of Comparative Critique," 501, 518.

30. Ortiz, *Cuban Counterpoint*, 55–62, 98–103.

31. Said, *Culture and Imperialism*, 51.

32. Said, *Culture and Imperialism*, 318.

33. Said, *Culture and Imperialism*, 52.

34. Greene, *Greene's Arcadia*, 91. For more on homoeroticism in romance narratives, see Smith, *Homosexual Desire in Shakespeare's England*; and Stanivukovic, "Cruising the Mediterranean" and *Knights in Arms*.

35. On these traditions, see Barkan, *Transuming Passion*; and Saslow, *Ganymede in the Renaissance*.

36. Homer, *The Iliad*, xx:230.

37. Qtd. in Barkan, *Transuming Passion*, 35.

38. Plato, *Laws*, 636d.

39. During the Christianization of the myth in the Middle Ages, the figure of Ganymede transformed from a character in a transcendental love story into a mundane, worldly person, as is evident in the fourteenth-century *Ovide moralisé*, in which Jove, as a warrior with an eagle, seizes Ganymede as a war prize. Divine love is embedded in this version, which equates Jove's symbolic eagle with Jesus and Ganymede with St. John the Evangelist. Yet Ganymede continued to figure in many medieval Latin homoerotic poems; see Boswell, *Christianity, Social Tolerance, and Homosexuality*, 243–66. For more on Ganymede imagery in the Middle Ages, especially representations evoking the role of pederasty in medieval clerical culture, see Mills, *Seeing Sodomy in the Middle Ages*.

40. Rambuss argues that the myth's association with "spiritual ravishment" continues in early modern English interpretations through the figure of Ganymede in devotional poems by male poets ("Symposium"). On other spiritual associations, such as the poetic desire to be like Ganymede and Jesus as Ganymede, see Rambuss, *Closet Devotions*, 11–72.

41. For more in-depth discussions of these associations, see Barkan, *Transuming Passion*, 19–20; Scott, "Queer Rapture," 2–4; and Saslow, *Ganymede in the Renaissance*, 25.

42. Golding, *The xv bookes of P. Ouidius Naso, entytuled Metamorphosis*, X.157–67. On the influence of Golding's 1567 translation on Renaissance writers, see Lyne, "Ovid in English Translation," 252–54.

43. Golding, *The xv bookes of P. Ouidius Naso, entytuled Metamorphosis*, 62, 65.

44. Similar copies after Michelangelo's 1532 drawing are Nicolas Beatrizet's 1542 *The Rape of Ganymede* at the Metropolitan Museum of Art, and Giulio Clovio's 1540 drawing at the Royal Collection Trust.

45. Barkan, *Transuming Passion*, 89.

46. On conflations of boys, see Saslow, *Ganymede in the Renaissance*, 97–141.

47. Brown, "The Boyhood of Shakespeare's Heroines," 251.

48. Florio's 1611 Italian/English dictionary translates "*catamito*" as "one hired to sin against nature, an ingle, a ganymede" (*Queen Anna's New World of Words*, 88). See OED, "catamite," n., etym. For more on the link between the term catamite and Ganymede, see Saslow, *Ganymede in the Renaissance*, 29; and Bredbeck, *Sodomy and Interpretation*, 18.

49. In Marlowe's *Dido, Queen of Carthage*, which begins with "Jupiter dandling Ganymede upon his knee" (1.1), Ganymede is the object of Jupiter's attraction; he is enjoying Jupiter's gifts, which his beauty and allure purchase. In *Edward II*, Marlowe links Ganymede with the royal favorite of the play through Queen Isabella's protestations: "For never doted Jove on Ganymede / So much as he on cursed Gaveston" (1.4.180–81). Richard Barnfield sees Ganymede in his beloved boy in the pastoral world of his sonnets (i.e., *The Complete Poems*, sonnets 4, 10, 15). Ganymede appears as Sir Beauteous Ganymede, a companion to gender-nonconforming Molly in Thomas Middleton and Thomas Dekker's play *The Roaring Girl*. On Ganymede and male homoeroticism in literature, see Smith, *Homosexual Desire in Shakespeare's England*; DiGangi, *The Homoerotics of Early Modern Drama*; Bredbeck, *Sodomy and Interpretation*; Orgel, "Tobacco and Boys"; and MacDonald, "Marlowe's Ganymede." On Ganymede and female eroticism, see Carter, *Ovidian Myth and Sexual Deviance*.

50. On premodern boys considered to be seducers in pederastic relations, see Elliott, *The Corrupter of Boys*.

51. Marston, *The Metamorphosis of Pigmalion's Image and Certaine Satyres*, 48, 52.

52. For more on Ganymede in initial letters in print, see Masten, *Queer Philologies*, 131–49. For the bookseller's sign, see Masten, "Ben Jonson's Head," 163.

53. See Barkan, *Transuming Passion*; Saslow, *Ganymede in the Renaissance*; Smith, *Homosexual Desire in Shakespeare's England*; and DiGangi, *The Homoerotics of Early Modern Drama*.

54. Goffe, *The Couragious Turke, or, Amurath the First*, C3r.

55. Massinger, *The Renegado*, 1.3.115.

56. Baudier, *The history of the imperiall estate of the grand seigneurs*, 162.

57. Herbert, *Travels in Persia*, 155.

58. Adolphus Slade's nineteenth-century account narrates the moment he was entertained by the grand vizier of Adrianople while a boy was attending to their pleasures: "with such an apparatus [smoking pipe], presented by a youth á la Ganymede, you may imagine you are inhaling the spirit of nectar" (*Records of Travels in Turkey, Greece, etc.*, 168). In 1883, the colonial agent Ernst Haeckel in Ceylon described his servant boy as a "beautifully naked, brown figure" who made the learned scientist think of "Ganymede, for the favorite of Jove himself could not have been more finely made, or have had limbs more beautifully proportioned and moulded" (*A Visit to Ceylon*, 265). The servant boys are Ganymede not only because they are beautiful but also because they make men feel like Jove; it is the Orientalist phallic power fantasy of being the god to the servant boy in the Orient. For more on Haeckel's relationship with this boy, see Aldrich, *Colonialism*, 287–90.

59. Aşıkpaşazade, *Manakib u Tevarih-u Al-i Osman*, 282–83.

60. While I use Istanbul and Constantinople interchangeably throughout the book, I usually use Constantinople to refer to the city before its conquest in 1453 and Istanbul for after that date. Istanbul, which was how Greeks referred to Constantinople, did not become the standard name for the city until the 1930s. The Ottomans used Constantinople, Kostantiniyye, Istanbul, or Islambol to refer to the city.

61. Qtd. in Bryan, "In the Company of Boys," 264.

62. Here I follow Marjorie Garber's term "transvestite effect," which, she suggests, is "an underlying psychosocial, and not merely a local or historical, effect.... Nobody gets 'Cesario' (or 'Ganymede'), but 'Cesario' (or 'Ganymede') is necessary to falling in love. The transvestite on the Renaissance stage, in fact, is not merely a signifier, but also a function" (*Vested Interests*, 36–37).

63. On the potentiality of pederasty, see Cleves, *Unspeakable*; and Delany, *Times Square Red, Times Square Blue*. On pederastic abuses and the long history of exploitation of boys, see Elliott, *The Corrupter of Boys*.

64. Amin, *Disturbing Attachments*, 44.

65. Stoler, *Race and the Education of Desire*, 7. Scholars of sexuality in the twenty-first century have stressed the significance of a transnational approach to sexuality studies and the effects of globalization on indigenous sexual cultures, while others, deploying postcolonial perspectives, have pointed at imperialist and neocolonial motivations operative in globalizing sexualities as a new form of cultural imperialism. See, for example, Povinelli and Chauncey, "Thinking Sexuality Transnationally"; Inderpal and Kaplan, "Global Identities"; Eng, Halberstam, and Muñoz, "What's Queer about Queer Studies Now?"; Lowe, *The Intimacies of Four Continents*; Povinelli, *The Empire of Love*; Spurlin, *Imperialism within the Margins*; McClintock, *Imperial Leather*; and Arondekar, "The Voyage Out." For a critique of some transnational approaches, see Massad, *Desiring Arabs*; and for responses to such critiques, see Traub, "The Past Is a Foreign Country?"; Spurlin, "Shifting Geopolitical Borders/Shifting Sexual Borders"; Atshan, *Queer Palestine and the Empire of Critique*; Boone, *The Homoerotics of Orientalism*; Arvas, "Queers In-Between"; and Çakırlar and Delice, *Cinsellik Muammasi*.

66. Bray, *Homosexuality in Renaissance England*, 19. On sodomy and marking religious difference in the Middle Ages, see DeVun, *The Shape of Sex*. On sodomy in relation to geographical and climactic theorization of race in the eighteenth century, see LaFleur, *The Natural History of Sexuality in Early America*.

67. *OED*, s.v. "bugger," n. 1, etym.

68. Nixon, *The Three English Brothers*, H4.

69. Lithgow, *The Totall Discourse of the Rare Adventures, and Painefull Peregrinations*, 163.

70. Sandys, *A Relation of a Journey*, 69.

71. For a list of examples of sodomy as a trope, see Matar, *Turks, Moors, and Englishmen in the Age of Discovery*. Matar adopts a defensive strategy by suggesting that sodomy is simply a stereotyping derogative term and that it was strictly prohibited in the Islamic lands: no sodomites in the East, according to Matar. He argues that sodomitical discourses in the New World were transported to the East. All indicators, however, suggest the opposite: American Indians were called Moors or sodomites probably because of preexisting discourses attributing sodomy to Turks and Muslims. See Goldberg, *Sodometries*, for a more theoretically and historically grounded discussion of sodomy in the New World. Also, scholars of cross-cultural encounters (e.g., Vitkus, Burton, Matar, Degenhardt, and Nocentelli) have emphasized the sexualization of the Ottomans in dramatic representations of heterosexual interracial relations between Christians and Muslims in the larger Mediterranean, which, as Stanivukovic (*Knights in Arms*) has demonstrated, was also a space for homoerotic imaginary in romance tradition.

As Bray asserts, feeling a "reluctance to recognize homosexual behavior, the English were quick to find it among people, like Turks and renegades, whose actions were considered heretical and disruptive of the Christian heterosexual social order" (*Homosexuality in Renaissance England*, 76). Bredbeck reminds us that in the 1631 preface to the trial of Mervin Touchet, the Earl of Castlehaven, sodomy was described as "this sin being now Translated from the Sodomitical Original, or from *the Turkish* and Italian Copies into English" (*Sodomy and Interpretation*, 5–6). Warner likewise explores sodomy as related to geography and exoticism in his work on New England, noting that "the topic of sodomy was linked primarily to the topic of national judgement" ("New English Sodomy," 21). DiGangi also notes that "the sodomite was devil, heretic, New World savage, cannibal, Turk, African, papist, Italian" (*The Homoerotics of Early Modern Drama*, 13). Traub has explored how Europeans projected deviant acts upon foreign women, especially Turkish women, in travelogues and medical accounts in order to control female sexuality at home (*The Renaissance of Lesbianism in Early Modern England*).

72. My reference is to Goldberg's field-initiating 1993 collection *Queering the Renaissance*.

73. Considering the Mediterranean not as a fixed geographical place but as a conceptual space to think with performatively, Sharon Kinoshita has demonstrated how the Mediterranean forces us to think with such concepts as contact, interaction, and circulation (instead of a vocabulary of origins, development, and expansion) as a result of its millennia-long history of migration, commerce, warfare, and diplomacy and demands that we privilege routes over roots and the pragmatism of acts over fixity of identities. See Kinoshita's "Locating the Medieval Mediterranean," "Romance in/and Medieval Mediterranean," and "Medieval Mediterranean Literature."

74. Subrahmanyam, "Connected Histories," 302. On connected history, see also Subrahmanyam, "On World Historians in the Sixteenth Century," "A Tale of Three Empires," and *Explorations in Connected History*.

75. Singh, *A Companion to The Global Renaissance*, 6. Some of the exemplary critical works on cross-cultural encounters are Vitkus, *Turning Turk*; Burton, *Traffic and Turn-*

ing; Matar, *Turks, Moors, and Englishmen in the Age of Discovery*; MacLean, *Looking East and The Rise of Oriental Travel*; McJannet, *The Sultan Speaks*; Andrea and McJannet, *Early Modern England and Islamic Worlds*; and Brotton, *The Renaissance Bazaar* and *Trading Territories*.

76. Hakluyt, *The Principal Navigations*, 200.

77. On the circulation of Ottoman portraiture, carpets, objects, and fashion, see MacLean, *Looking East*; Jardine and Brotton, *Global Interests*; and MacLean and Matar, *Britain and the Islamic World*. On letter exchanges between Elizabeth I and Safiye Sultan, see Andrea, *Women and Islam in Early Modern English Literature*. On captivities, conversions, and crossings, see Vitkus, *Turning Turk*; Burton, *Traffic and Turning*; Degenhardt, *Islamic Conversion and Christian Resistance on the Early Modern Stage*; Matar, *Turks, Moors, and Englishmen in the Age of Discovery*; and Clines, *A Jewish Jesuit in the Eastern Mediterranean*.

78. On Turks on stage, see Vitkus, *Three Turk Plays from Early Modern England*; Robinson, "Harry and Amurath"; McJannet, *The Sultan Speaks*; and Dimmock, *New Turkes*. For a list of these plays, see Burton, *Traffic and Turning*, 257–58; and Hutchings, *Turks, Repertories, and the Early Modern English Stage*, 203–18.

79. As Goffman reminds us, "the early modern Ottoman Empire constituted an integral component of Europe," and neither the Ottoman polity nor Europe makes sense without the other (*The Ottoman Empire and Early Modern Europe*, 7). Brotton suggests that early modern studies should "orient an understanding of early modern Europe and its boundaries [by placing] the Ottomans as central, rather than peripheral, to the political and intellectual preoccupations of the period" (*Trading Territories*, 91). Similarly, in *Early Modern England and Islamic Worlds*, Andrea and McJannet note the long-held lack of interest in the Ottomans and call for centering the Ottomans in any exploration of early modern European literature and culture.

80. Arvas, "The Ottomans in and of Europe."

81. Gibb, *A History of Ottoman Poetry*, 1:447.

82. Gibb, *A History of Ottoman Poetry*, 1:446.

83. Andrews, "Suppressed Renaissance," 17.

84. Andrews, "Suppressed Renaissance," 31.

85. On parallel shifts in bureaucratic establishments, diplomatic relations, military and mercantile patterns and technologies, and education, see Kafadar, "The Ottomans and Europe." For more on changes and Euro-Ottoman exchanges in military technologies in the emerging state-building process, see Aksan, "Locating the Ottomans among Early Modern Empires." On shared imperial structures, see Faroqhi, *The Ottoman Empire and the World around It*; Tezcan, *The Second Ottoman Empire*; and Şahin, *Empire and Power in the Reign of Süleyman*. On multiethnic cooperation and commercial settlements, see Brummett, *Ottoman Seapower and Levantine Diplomacy in the Age of Discovery*; and Fleet, *European and Islamic Trade in the Early Ottoman State*. On the circulation of cartographic technologies, see Casale, *The Ottoman Age of Exploration*; and Emiralioğlu, *Geographical Knowledge and Imperial Culture in the Early Modern Ottoman Empire*. On the common religious discourses, see Bulliet, *The Case for Islamo-Christian Civilization*; Fleischer, "The Lawgiver as Messiah"; and Krstić, *Contested Conversions to Islam*. On shifting gender dynamics, see Dursteler, *Renegade Women*; Zilfi, *Women and Slavery in the Late Ottoman Empire*; Peirce, *The Imperial Harem*; and Ortega, "'Pleading for Help.'"

On shared sexual discourses, see Andrews and Kalpaklı, *The Age of Beloveds*; and Artan and Schick, "Ottomanizing Pornotopia."

86. Qtd. in Malcolm, "Positive Views of Islam and Ottoman Rule in the Sixteenth Century," 212.

87. While on the one hand, the Ottomans were represented as non-Christian others, on the other hand, they were linked with Trojans in contemporary European chronicles from the fifteenth century onward. Some chronicles report that Mehmed II called himself a Trojan when he visited Troy as Caesar, as Kafadar notes in his account of this moment: "He seems to have been aware of the explanation of Ottoman successes by the theory, upheld by some in Europe, that Turks were, like the Romans before them, vengeful Trojans paying back the Greeks" (*Between Two Worlds*, 11). On the notion of Turks as Trojans in Europe, see Spencer, "Turks and Trojans in the Renaissance"; MacMaster, "The Origin of the Origins"; and Harper, "Turks as Trojans, Trojans as Turks." For a humanist reworking of the Turkish identity through classical terms and through the East/West division, see Bisaha, *Creating East and West*.

88. For more on the cartographic construction of Europe, see Wintle, *The Image of Europe*. On the Ottomans in European cartography, see Brummett, *Ottoman Seapower and Levantine Diplomacy in the Age of Discovery*.

89. Casale, "Seeing the Past," 83.

90. Casale, "Seeing the Past," 85.

91. Casale, "Seeing the Past," 85.

92. Terms like "Turk," "Turkey," and "Turkish" were less Ottoman terms than highly ethnicized European references. The Ottomans did not use these terms to identify themselves or their subject populations, but used "Rumi" or "the Romans" in the early modern period (Kafadar, "A Rome of One's Own"). Kunt also notes that "though in Europe the [Ottoman] empire was often referred to as 'Turkey,' such a term itself—either as a political or geographical entity—was totally unknown in the Ottoman Turkish language or in any of the many languages spoken by its subjects within its order" ("State Sultan up to the Age of Suleyman," 4). In fact, the term "Turk" itself referred to "peasant-like, barbarous, warlock, savage, wild" in the early modern Ottoman culture (Sılay, *Nedim and the Poetics of the Ottoman Court*, 19).

93. Foxe, *Second Volume of the Ecclesiasticall History Containing the Acts and Monuments of Martyrs*, 964.

94. Rycaut, *The Present State of the Ottoman Empire*, 79, Rycaut's italics.

95. Qtd. in Kafadar, "A Rome of One's Own," 14.

96. Amer, *Crossing Borders*, xi.

97. On tales from Islamic lands, see Schleck, *Telling True Tales of Islamic Lands*. On Turkish history in early modern England, see Ingram, *Writing the Ottomans*.

98. Hendricks reminds us that knowledge from other lands "would have come orally, from seamen who served on the merchant and fighting ships traversing the Atlantic and Indian oceans" ("'Obscured by dreams,'" 45). On Hakluyt's public lectures, see Hendricks, 45 fn.16.

99. Dimmock notes that "by the late sixteenth century English readers and audiences could encounter an Ottoman voice in a number of different places.... English men and women read speeches in chronicle histories; they copied the letters of the 'Grand Signor'

into their commonplace books; some were even able to hear a 'Turk' publicly express his desire to be baptized into the English Church.... The voice of the 'Turk' was commonly heard in late Elizabethan London" ("Tudor Turks," 335). On Ottoman voices in England, see also McJannet, *The Sultan Speaks*; and Arvas, "The Ottomans in and of Europe."

100. I borrow "provincialize" from Dipesh Chakrabarty's *Provincializing Europe*, which challenges the concept of Europe as the original site of modernity and seeks to "find out how and in what sense European ideas that were also, at one and the same time, drawn from very particular intellectual and historical traditions that could not claim any universal validity" (xiii).

101. From eleventh century onward, Aristotle and Galen emerged in England via Arabic translations, as did Ibn Sina's synthesis and reconceptualization of sex and gender difference as suggested by them. On Ibn Sina's (Avicenna) influence in the Ottoman Empire, see Ze'evi, *Producing Desire*. For his influence in England and Europe, see Cadden, *The Meanings of Sex Difference in the Middle Ages*; and DeVun, *The Shape of Sex*.

102. It is only in the last two decades that literary scholars and historians such as Ze'evi, Kuru, and Andrews and Kalpaklı have begun to explore diverse sexualities and sexual discourses in the Ottoman Empire, in contrast to earlier criticism, which read homoerotic representations in Ottoman poetry as either a form of Ottoman perversion or a purely metaphoric and transcendental convention. Two names exemplify those views on metaphorical readings: Zeki Eyüboğlu (*Divan Şiirinde Sapık Sevgi*) declares that the Ottomans were perverts, while Atilla Şentürk ("Osmanlı Şiirinde Aşka Dair") ignores the gender of the beloved to point out that it is love not the beloved that matters. According to him, all such representations seek a unity with God by divorcing love strictly from sex. English Orientalist Gibb (*A History of Ottoman Poetry*) sees these figurations of boys in poetry as a part of Persian tradition while he silently changes the personal pronoun "he" to "she" in reference to the object of love in poems in his translations, which would become a model for later translators including Andrews and Kalpaklı's earlier translations which, as they regretfully expressed, "translate the gender of the beloved as *she* when every indication is that the beloved of this poetry was most often a *he*" (*The Age of Beloveds*, 19).

103. *Şehrengiz*, which is mostly an erotic genre of obscene catalogues of beautiful men of the cities, is borrowed from Persian models. It evolved to include different countries as the empire expanded its boundaries. For more on the genre, see Levend, *Türk Edebiyatında Şehrengizler ve Şehrengizlerde İstanbul*; Stewart-Robinson, "A Neglected Ottoman Poem"; Öztekin, "Şehrengizler ve Bursa: Edebiyat ve Eşcinsel Eğilim"; and Tuğcu, "Şehrengizler ve Ayine-i Huban-I Bursa." On how European modernist artists transformed this genre into a visual catalogue, see Boone, "Modernist Re-Orientations." *Bahnames* (books of libido), or medico-erotic treatises, were famous examples of erotic literature from thirteenth century onward. See Bardakçı, *Osmanlı'da Seks*, for representative passages from *bahnames*. Some other genres that observe such representations are the highly obscene shadow theater (*karagöz*), jokes (*nasreddin hoca*), songs (*mani, şarkı*), texts about bathhouses (*hamamiye*), and biographies of poets. For an overview of sexuality and gender in Ottoman-Turkish literature from medieval to contemporary, see Schick, "Representation of Gender and Sexuality in Ottoman and Turkish Erotic Literature."

104. It took more than a decade for the Turkish translation of this work to appear. In their preface to this edition, Andrews and Kalpaklı ask readers to keep in mind that the

book was mainly written for readers in the West and Western scholars in Euro-American academia in order to introduce Ottoman literature and culture as a part of ongoing debates around early modern sexualities (*Sevgililer Çağı*, 9). My project is in conversation with theirs in terms of a change in positionality; that is, I am looking at English texts from the Ottoman lands.

105. Indeed, the beloved boy's name was often explicitly stated in this literature. Certain poetic catalogues—*şehrengiz* (city thrillers)—describe the disposition and physical beauty of certain popular boys. For more on real-life boys, see Andrews and Kalpaklı, *The Age of Beloveds*, 38–43, 95–106. On naming the beloved in poetry, see Kuru, "Scholar and Author in the Sixteenth-Century Ottoman Empire." On boys as objects of love in the Ottoman Empire, see also Ze'evi, *Producing Desire*; and El-Rouayheb, *Before Homosexuality in the Arabic-Islamic World*.

106. Andrews and Kalpaklı, *The Age of Beloveds*, 158–60.

107. As the flourishing field of premodern critical race studies (following earlier work by Eldred Jones, Elliot H. Tokson, and Anthony Barthelemy) has demonstrated, early modern English racialization, which was based on somatic, geo-humoral, climactic, astrological, theological, and class differences, was always related to gender, sexuality, religion, class, empire, and colonialism. For exemplary intersectional feminist explorations of the ways gender difference shapes and was shaped by the emerging racial formations in early modern England, see Loomba, *Shakespeare, Race, Colonialism* and *Gender, Race, Renaissance Drama*; Hall, *Things of Darkness*; Hendricks and Parker, *Women, Race, and Writing in Early Modern England*; Hendricks, "'Obscured by dreams'"; Callaghan, "What Is an Audience?"; MacDonald, *Women and Race in Early Modern Texts*; Andrea, *Women and Islam in Early Modern English Literature*; and Loomba and Sanchez, *Rethinking Feminism in Early Modern Studies*. On sexuality and race, see Little, *Shakespeare Jungle Fever*; Nocentelli, *Empires of Love*; Smith, "The Queer Moor"; Goldberg, *Sodometries*; Burton, "Western Encounters with Sex and Bodies in Non-European Cultures"; Traub, "Sexuality"; and Loomba, "Identities and Bodies in Early Modern Studies." On race, empire, and colonialism, see Loomba, *Shakespeare, Race, Colonialism*; and Singh, *Colonial Narratives/Cultural Dialogues*. On race and class, see Chakravarty, *Fictions of Consent*; Akhimie, *Shakespeare and the Cultivation of Difference*; and Feerick, *Strangers in Blood*. On race and religion, see Britton, *Becoming Christian*; and Andrea, *The Lives of Girls and Women from the Islamic World*. On staging race, see Grier, *Inkface*; Ndiaye, *Scripts of Blackness*; and Weissbourd, *Bad Blood*.

108. See, for instance, Barbour, *Before Orientalism*; Cirakman, *From the "Terror of the World" to the "Sick Man of Europe"*; Bisaha, *Creating East and West*; Burton, *Traffic and Turning*; Dimmock, *New Turkes*; Vitkus, *Turning Turk*; and Matar, *Turks, Moors, and Englishmen in the Age of Discovery*.

109. On various forms of Orientalism, see Aravamudan, *Enlightenment Orientalism*.

110. On genealogy as method, see Foucault, "Nietzsche, Genealogy, History." As Halperin explicates, genealogy traces "separate histories [of the historical accumulation of discontinuous notions] as well as the process of the interrelations, their crossings, and, eventually, their unstable convergence in the present day" (*How to Do the History of Homosexuality*, 107).

111. "Orientalism" has become a free-floating term in contexts like contemporary Turkey, where conservatives deploy the term to debase anyone who is critical of the

Ottoman or Islamic past. Said's *Orientalism*, which surely does not apply any critique of non-Western contexts, clearly defines who or what is Orientalist.

112. Loomba, "Introduction," 26.

113. Burton, "Race," 213.

114. Burton, "Race," 208–209.

115. See, for example, Ortaylı, *Osmanlı Barışı*; and Çiçek, *Pax Ottomana*. Reading conquest and domination as "extending the benefit of citizenship" might unintentionally serve imperial-nationalist discourses of the Pax Ottomanica, which has become "a myth the way it is understood, especially by conservative masses, and utilized by populist and neo-Ottomanist demagogues" in their nostalgia regarding conquering the world (Karateke, Çıpa, and Anetshofer, *Disliking Others*, xi–xii). Other scholars have questioned such glorifications; see Barkey, *Empire of Difference*; and Krstić, *Contested Conversions to Islam*.

116. See Yermolenko, "Tartar-Turkish Captivity and Conversion in Early Modern Ukrainian Songs," and Kursar, "Ambiguous Subjects and Uneasy Neighbors," on such traumas and resentments.

117. Bosnia was an exception. Muslim boys were also recruited from there due to a special license granted by Mehmed II.

118. For more on peculiarities of Ottoman slavery, see Toledano, "The Concept of Slavery in Ottoman and Other Muslim Societies"; Kunt, *The Sultan's Servants* and "Kulların Kulları"; Erdem, *Slavery in the Ottoman Empire and Its Demise*; and Sobers-Khan, *Slaves without Shackles*. For more on the emergence of the practice of *devşirme*, see Imber, *The Ottoman Empire*, 116–30. On women slaves and their rights, see Zilfi, *Women and Slavery in the Late Ottoman Empire*.

119. Ibrahim Pasha's well-known biography mirrors the paradigm of desire/anxiety as a part of the lives of abducted boys. Enslaved at a young age, Ibrahim become the intimate friend, chief chamberlain, and grand vizier to the sultan. He was killed one night by the sultan's order and is now posthumously known as The Favorite and the Slain (Makbul ve Maktul). On slavery and death, see Patterson, *Slavery and Social Death*.

120. Qtd. in Çıpa, "Changing Perceptions about Christian-Born Ottomans," 9.

121. El Hamel, *Black Morocco*, 9.

122. Historians Karateke, Çıpa, and Anetshofer, for example, separate the "rhetoric of dislike and actions of hate as two separate analytical categories" in their edited volume *Disliking Others: Loathing, Hostility, and Distrust in Pre-Modern Ottoman Culture*, which initiated long-due conversations about race in the early modern Ottoman Empire (xiii). Instead, the editors as well as all the authors of thirteen essays on various "others" such as converts, black Africans, Jews, and the Romani use terms such as "phobia," "prejudice," "social antipathy," and "disliking." Only Tezcan raises the issue of race explicitly in his cogent analysis of antiblack and pro-black treatises, in which he calls the former something that "could have called blatantly racist had it been written today," and the latter "the Bible of the 'black is beautiful' movement if it had been published in the 1960s" ("*Dispelling the Darkness* of the *Halberdier's Treatise*," 44).

123. Heng, *The Invention of Race in the European Middle Ages*, 4.

124. Gomez, *African Dominion*, 56.

125. Heng, *The Invention of Race in the European Middle Ages*, 3, Heng's italics. Tracing multiple sites and forms of race-making, Heng demonstrates that racial significations—

including gens, nation, blood, stock, and kind—have no singular or stable referent. She convincingly conceptualizes race as a cultural production, and hence seeks not the origin but perpetual inventions and reinventions of race: moments and instances of how race is made, how it operates in the premodern world, and how it extends into the sociopolitical and biopolitical aspects of modern race. Erickson and Hall note that contemporary race formations are also not "stable, deliberate, and without contradictions" ("A New Scholarly Song," 10). After all, as Hall asserts, race "was then (as it is now) a social construct that is fundamentally more about power and culture than about biological difference" (*Things of Darkness*, 6).

126. See Goldenberg, *The Curse of Ham*; Lewis, *Race and Slavery in the Middle East* and *Race and Color in Islam*; Walz and Cuno, *Race and Slavery in the Middle East*; El Hamel, *Black Morocco*; Gratien, "Race, Slavery, and Islamic Law in the Early Modern Atlantic"; and Gomez, *African Dominion*. While Lewis and Goldenberg's works have instances of essentializing Islam and Islamic discourses, they provide valuable primary materials for a sustained analysis of race.

127. El Hamel, *Black Morocco*, 58.

128. On biographies of black Ottomans, see Tezcan, "*Dispelling the Darkness* of the Halberdier's Treatise" and "*Dispelling the Darkness*: The Politics of 'Race' in the Early Seventeenth Century Ottoman Empire."

129. Qtd. in Tezcan, "*Dispelling the Darkness*: The Politics of 'Race' in the Early Seventeenth Century Ottoman Empire," 93.

130. Nocentelli, *Empires of Love*, 116.

131. Race as an inevitable component of queer embodiment has yet to be fully attended to in early modern studies. An exception from the early 2000s is Little's *Shakespeare Jungle Fever*, which analyzes Shakespeare's queer representations from a critical race perspective. Goldberg's *Sodometries* brought to the fore colonial encounters in shaping sodomitical discourses in early modern England. More recent edited collections and individual articles have successfully and deliberately connected gender, sexual, and racial difference. See Chakravarty, "More than Kin, Less than Kind." Loomba and Sanchez's *Rethinking Feminism in Early Modern Studies* and Traub's *The Oxford Handbook of Shakespeare and Embodiment* skillfully weave together work on race, gender, and sexuality among many intersections. Such collaborations offer a model pushing against scholarly compartmentalization while generating creative and political alliances in exploring the past more fully to question and deliberate on our present-day issues.

132. Erickson and Hall, "A New Scholarly Song," 12.

133. Smith, "The Queer Moor," 200.

134. For the queer of color turn, see, among others, Muñoz, *Disidentifications*; Manalansan, *Global Divas*; Musser, *Sensational Flesh*; Ferguson, *Aberrations in Black*; Somerville, *Queering the Color Line*; Holland, *The Erotic Life of Racism*; Snorton, *Black on Both Sides*; Rodriguez, *Queer Latinidad*; and Eng, *Racial Castration*.

135. Nash, *The Black Body in Ecstasy*, 150. See Holland, *The Erotic Life of Racism*, on how erotic desire is deeply embedded in quotidian racism and its operations.

136. Traub, "Sexuality," 148.

137. Andrea, *The Lives of Girls and Women from the Islamic World*, 4.

138. Traub, "Sexuality," 174.

139. As Bernstein reminds us via her historicization of "racial innocence" in the late eighteenth and early nineteenth centuries, a new view of children emerged as innocent, "sinless, absent of sexual feelings, and oblivious to serious concerns" (*Racial Innocence*, 4). And even this innocence, she persuasively shows, was racialized and attributed to white children. On the emergence of the sexless, innocent child with modernity, see Jackson, *Child Sexual Abuse in Victorian England*; Kincaid, *Child-Loving*; and Stockton, *The Queer Child*.

140. On such differences, Cleves argues that "contemporary definitions of consent do little to help historians differentiate the sexual landscape of the past, which was defined by inequalities, and at the same time capacitated a wide range of interactions from violent assault through enthusiastic mutuality" (*Unspeakable*, 151).

141. Bryan traces various figurations of Cupid as an active boy from Ovid to Marlowe and suggests that in different subject positions, from the master to the boy, or occasionally in between, the boy Cupid appears as commanding, authoritative, weak, dominated, alluring, and seductive ("In the Company of Boys," 93–158). One can add Rosalind, who does not want to be a man but the boy Ganymede and as Ganymede actively arranges relations and shapes desires in *As You Like It*. See also the exchange between Rackin and Shapiro ("Boy Heroines") about how to approach boy actors that is careful not to sentimentalize but instead historicizes and recognizes their dependency and sometimes agency in power hierarchies.

142. Masten, *Queer Philologies*, 166, Masten's italics.

143. Scholars have reassessed the relation between sexuality and power by noting how the modern detachment of sexual desire from youth and age egalitarianism have been used to manage adult sexuality. See Stockton, *The Queer Child*; Edelman, *No Future*; Kincaid, *Child-Loving*; Higonnet, *Pictures of Innocence*; Steedman, *Strange Dislocations*; Jackson, *Child Sexual Abuse in Victorian England*; and Cleves, *Unspeakable*.

144. Not until the twentieth century were boys under sixteen considered victims of abuse in legal terms rather than complicit in sexual encounters with men as traditionally conceived. In his study of medieval pederasty in clerical settings, Elliott shows that children were thought of as corrupt individuals with undisciplined minds and a tendency to sin: "it was generally the victimized child who was singled out for blame as opposed to the older predator" (*The Corrupter of Boys*, 37). Even when we see some defenders of children, they are never motivated by "the welfare of children" but are invested in condemning same-sex relations (5).

CHAPTER 1. TRAVELING BOYS IN THE MEDITERRANEAN

An article version of chapter 1 appeared as "Leander in the Ottoman Mediterranean: The Homoerotics of Abduction in the Global Renaissance," *English Literary Renaissance* 51, no. 1 (2021): 31–62, https://www.journals.uchicago.edu/doi/abs/10.1086/711601?journalCode=elr.

1. All references to *Hero and Leander* are from Cheney and Striar, *The Collected Poems of Christopher Marlowe*. Subsequent references appear parenthetically in the text, citing line numbers.

2. For more on abducted boys as a classical trope, see Smith, *Homosexual Desire in Shakespeare's England*, 117–59.

3. Arondekar, "The Voyage Out," 339.

4. Haber, *Desire and Dramatic Form in Early Modern England*, 39.

5. Haber, *Desire and Dramatic Form in Early Modern England*, 39.

6. On rhetoric, see Enterline, "Elizabethan Minor Epics." On metamorphosis, see Ellis, *Sexuality and Citizenship*. For more on epyllia, Ovid, and humanist pedagogy, see Enterline, *Shakespeare's Schoolroom* and *The Rhetoric of the Body from Ovid to Shakespeare*; Keach, *Elizabethan Erotic Narratives*; Hulse, *Metamorphic Verse*; Brown, *Redefining Elizabethan Literature*; Dolven, *Scenes of Instruction in Renaissance Romance*; and Wallace, *Virgil's Schoolboys*.

7. Weaver, *Untutored Lines*, 64, 3–4.

8. Jacobson, *Barbarous Antiquity*, 186–87.

9. Jacobson, *Barbarous Antiquity*, 185.

10. Mason, *The Turke*, sig. H3v. On the Hellespont as an Ottoman space in travelogues, see Jacobson, *Barbarous Antiquity*, 153–62.

11. On captivities and examples of captivity texts, see the essays in Vitkus, *Piracy, Slavery, and Redemption*

12. Games, *The Web of Empire*, 68.

13. Hershenzon, *The Captive Sea*, 2.

14. While Games estimates 8,000 (*The Web of Empire*, 69), Colley notes that in the period 1600 to 1640, about 12,000 English subjects may have been enslaved in North Africa and other parts of the Ottoman Empire and that 800 English, Scottish, Welsh, and Irish vessels were seized (*Captives*, 43–44).

15. Qtd. in Nicholson, *Uncommon Tongues*, 1. For more on Marlowe's influence, especially that of his *Tamburlaine* plays, on the discourses of Turks and the Mediterranean relations, as well as his sources, see Dimmock, *New Turkes*; McJannet, *The Sultan Speaks*; Bartels, *Spectacles of Strangeness*; Burton, *Traffic and Turning*; Vitkus, *Turning Turk*; and Barbour, *Before Orientalism*.

16. For more on conversion/perversion paradigm, see Vitkus, *Turning Turk*; Burton, *Traffic and Turning*; and Parker, "Preposterous Conversions."

17. Anonymous, *The Estate of Christians, living under the subjection of the Turke*, A2–A3.

18. Qtd. in Imber, *The Ottoman Empire*, 122.

19. Rawlins, *The famous and wonderfull recoverie of a ship of Bristoll*, B1–B1v 4.

20. Purchas, *Hakluytus Posthumus*, 9:483, 9:281, 10:425.

21. See Stanivukovic, "Cruising the Mediterranean"; Matar, *Turks, Moors, and Englishmen in the Age of Discovery*; Vitkus, *Turning Turk*; Burton, *Traffic and Turning*.

22. On orderly homoeroticism in the homosocial structure of the Ottoman Empire, see Andrews and Kalpaklı, who note that "sexual or erotic relations between men and men and boys were seldom punished, especially if they were carried on in private" (*The Age of Beloveds*, 80). My separation of orderly homoeroticism from disorderly sodomy owes to DiGangi's *The Homoerotics of Early Modern Drama*, which frames homoeroticism as distinct from the legal and theological conceptualization of sodomy.

23. Goldberg, *Sodometries*, 23, 20.

24. "*Bunları Türke virelüm Türkçe ögrensünler, sonra Türkçe bilicek getürelüm yiniçeri olsun*" (Aşıkpaşazade, *Manakib u Tevarih-u Al-i Osman*, 382–83). All translations of Aşıkpaşazade from Turkish are my own.

25. See Imber, *The Ottoman Empire*, 121.

26. For more on *kul* and some distinct characteristics of Ottoman slavery, see the introduction.

27. For more on the emergence of *devşirme*, see Imber, *The Ottoman Empire*, 116–30. On differences between *pençik* and *devşirme* boys, see Yılmaz, "Becoming a *Devşirme*," 119–34.

28. Yılmaz notes that the boy had to have reached puberty to be taken and that this was usually after the age of twelve. The average age of recruited boys in the late fifteenth and early sixteenth centuries was thirteen or fourteen. In early seventeenth century, most recruited boys were aged sixteen to twenty, the average age being sixteen or seventeen ("The Devshirme System and the Levied Children of Bursa," 924).

29. It was forbidden to conscript the only son of a family or more than one boy from the same family or from less than every forty households. Recruitments generally took place every three or four years. More details and rituals of abduction are described in *Kavanin-ı Yeniçeriyan* [The janissary laws], written by an anonymous veteran janissary in order to criticize contemporary changes in the system. For the facsimile and transliteration, see Akgündüz, *Osmanlı Kanunnameleri ve Hukuk Tahlilleri*, 128–34. For more on how the boys were selected, see Yılmaz, "The Devshirme System and the Levied Children of Bursa"; for more on the *devşirme* system, janissaries, and military structure, see Imber, *The Ottoman Empire*, 116–30; Yılmaz, "Becoming a *Devşirme*"; Uzuncarşılı, *Osmanlı Devleti*; Kunt, *The Sultan's Servants*; Kafadar, "On the Purity and Corruption of the Janissaries"; Inalcik, "Military and Fiscal Transformation in the Ottoman Empire"; and Menage, "Some Notes on Devşirme."

30. Erdem, *Slavery in the Ottoman Empire and Its Demise*, 8.

31. Thirty-three of the forty-eight grand viziers of the Ottoman sultans in the period 1453 to 1623 were *devşirme* boys (Braudel, *The Mediterranean and the Mediterranean World in the Age of Philip II*, 159).

32. In many other instances these *kuls* were exposed to constant attacks as unreliable converts, mainly due to their non-Muslim lineage. For anti-*kul* sentiments and perceptions about converts, see Çıpa, "Changing Perceptions about Christian-Born Ottomans."

33. "*Bunlar mal oglıdur hanlarına bil / Irakdur gayrı çeri bil ha bu da.*" Aşıkpaşazade, *Manakib u Tevarih-u Al-i Osman*, 383.

34. "*Hükümdarları için ganimetten alınmışlardır.*" Aşıkpaşazade, *Manakib u Tevarih-u Al-i Osman*, 115.

35. For the definition and the Arabic etymology of "*ganimet*," see the entry in *Türk Dil Kurumu Sözlüğü* (Turkish Language Institution Dictionary) online. For Arabic derivations, see the entry in Ibn Manzur, *Lisan al-Arab*. For more on "ganimet" in religious discourse as a motivating drive for the Ottoman army, see Ertaş, "Evliya Çelebi'nin Seyahatnamesi'nde Gaza."

36. Aşıkpaşazade, *Manakib u Tevarih-u Al-i Osman*, 333, 346, 458.

37. "*İki sevgili evladı olan, birine muhtaç olmaktan kurtulur.*" I thank Nagehan Gür for her help in translating these lines from Persian to Turkish. The English translation is mine.

38. Qtd. in Vakalopoulos, *The Greek Nation*, 36–37.

39. Yılmaz, "The Devshirme System and the Levied Children of Bursa," 911.

40. "*Kırmızı güller, al fistanlar, yeşil fidan yapraklarından daha çok / Gül renkli abalar dikilmiş, gül gibi içi içe katlanmış.*"

41. For a brief survey of the rose imagery in Ottoman literature, see the entry *"gül"* in *Türkiye Diyanet Vakfı İslâm Ansiklopedisi*, 14:219–22.

42. On wine parties with immortal boys in the Qur'an and Arabic poetry, see Stetkevych, "Intoxication and Immortality." For a general overview of the tradition in Ottoman, Persian, Urdu, and Arabic literatures, see Andrews and Kalpaklı, *The Age of Beloveds*, 156–62. For boys in premodern Sufi traditions, see Ze'evi, *Producing Desire*; and El-Rouayheb, "The Love of Boys."

43. Andrews and Kalpaklı, *The Age of Beloveds*, 156–57.

44. Qur'an 56:10–24. For other descriptions of paradise in the Qur'an, see 3:133–36, 13:23–35, 18:31, 107, 38:49–54, 35:33–35, 52:17–27, and 56:10–24. References to the Qur'an are from Abdullah Yusuf Ali's translation.

45. Necipoğlu, *Architecture, Ceremonial, and Power*. On the garden and garden parties, see Andrews, *Poetry's Voice, Society's Song*.

46. Qtd. in Gibb, *A History of Ottoman Poetry*, 2:59–61.

47. For more on Ahmed Pasha's poetry, and his attachment to the page-boy, which was widely recorded in in contemporary accounts, see Gibb, *A History of Ottoman Poetry*, 2:41–46; and Babinger, *Mehmed the Conqueror and His Time*, 474–76.

48. Gibb, *A History of Ottoman Poetry*, 2:42.

49. Qtd. in Andrews and Kalpaklı, *The Age of Beloveds*, 158.

50. Qtd. in Andrews and Kalpaklı, *The Age of Beloveds*, 42.

51. On Hayali's abduction and eroticization, see Andrews and Kalpaklı, *The Age of Beloveds*, 138–40.

52. Qtd. in Andrews and Kalpaklı, *The Age of Beloveds*, 104.

53. All translations of Mustafa Ali's text are from Brookes's translation, "The Ottoman Gentleman of the Sixteenth Century," with some corrective changes that I mention in endnotes. Subsequent references appear parenthetically in the text. For the modern Turkish transcription of the text, see Şeker, *Gelibolulu Mustafa Ali ve Meva'idu'n-nefais fi-kava'idi'l-mecalis*.

54. I changed the translation of "peasants" to "converts" in agreement with Şeker's annotation of the original *"potur"* as *"dönme"* (convert); "wispy things" to "those with waists as thin as hair" because *"mû-miyān"* signifies those whose waists are as thin as a hair; "town boys" to "city boys," a more common translation of the original *"şehir oğlanları"*; "the world of servants" to "the world of the bodies of the servant boys" because the original *"vücudları 'âlemine"* means the world of their bodies, hence reinforcing the connotation of corruption and destruction signified by *"ihtilali fena vire"* as the verb of the sentence (273).

55. For more on changes in army structure, see Kunt, *The Sultan's Servants*.

56. Koçi Bey also criticizes the change in recruitments in the 1630s, noting that "city boys of unknown religion, Turks, Gypsies, Tats, Kurds, outsiders, Lazes, Turcomans, muleteers and camel-drivers, porters and confectioners, highway men and pickpockets, and other people of various sorts" have been recruited since 1620 (qtd. in Imber, *The Ottoman Empire*, 129).

57. In a section on taverns, Mustafa Ali notes that there were mainly two prominent groups in wine taverns. One was the group of prominent young men, eloquent speakers, successful businessmen, artisans, and government officials, who came to the tavern with their beloveds to eat, drink, and "make their way over to the tavern's private room.

According to the demands of their lust, they extract milk from the sugar cane" (272). The other group consisted of black Arabs and lowborn Russians who wasted their lives in taverns. These men arranged their sexual lives so they would have sex with women on Thursday nights and with beardless servant youths on Friday nights (272–73). While Mustafa Ali seems to be critical of the elite men who did not pursue a moral life away from taverns, he holds officers responsible for the moral decay in the empire rather than the promiscuous slave boys, and he is against the publicity of such relations. He writes, "To every servant all things are forgiven except the public commission of sin" (273). Besides taverns, bathhouses were a popular space for erotic contact. Some janissary boys, as Delice shows through the records of bathhouses (*hamam*), provided sexual services as shampoo boys in bathhouses alongside boys from other lands ("The Janissaries and Their Bedfellows"). The accounts of Aşık Çelebi and Evliya Çelebi also mention homoerotic happenstances in bathhouses. Aşık Çelebi describes his and other poets' visits to bathhouses to flirt with and watch beautiful young men. In Evliya Çelebi's travelogue, he also mentions the erotic atmosphere in the bathhouses and how lovers and beloveds enjoyed each other's company in the warm waters. Some of the other sexual spaces these writers discuss are Tophane and Galata taverns such as Efe Meyhanesi and Yani Meyhanesi, the banks of Bosphorus and Marmara, gardens, coffeehouses, and picnic areas such as Göksu and Kağıthane. On such sexualized spaces, see Andrews and Kalpaklı, *The Age of Beloveds*, 63–84.

58. Yılmaz, "Becoming a *Devşirme*," 124.

59. Andrews and Kalpaklı, *The Age of Beloveds*, 138.

60. Body hair, especially facial hair, as a sign of transition from boyhood to adulthood and from a submissive to a dominant role is well established in ancient Greek pederasty. Similarly, body hair marks a new stage in a boy's identity and putatively sexual unavailability in Ottoman discourses. For the relationship between body hair, facial hair, masculinity, and sexual availability in Islamicate societies, see El-Rouayheb, *Before Homosexuality in the Arab-Islamic World*; Najmabadi, *Women with Mustaches and Men without Beards*; Ze'evi, *Producing Desire*; Peirce, "Seniority, Sexuality, and Social Order"; Andrews and Kalpaklı, *The Age of Beloveds*. For similar arguments about how facial hair determines masculinity in Europe, see Fisher, *Materializing Gender in Early Modern English Literature and Culture* and "The Renaissance Beard."

61. Imber, *The Ottoman Empire*, 121.

62. Joseph stands for the ideal male beauty in Islamicate traditions, particularly in Persian and Ottoman representations. The story of Joseph is the subject of the surah Yusuf in the Qur'an.

63. I address emergent discourses on blackness further in chapter 5.

64. Qtd. in Fleischer, *Bureaucrat and Intellectual in the Ottoman Empire*, 254.

65. Qtd. in Fleischer, *Bureaucrat and Intellectual in the Ottoman Empire*, 254.

66. Fleischer, *Bureaucrat and Intellectual in the Ottoman Empire*, 254–55.

67. Aşık Çelebi, *Meşa'irü'ş-Şu'ara*, 368–70.

68. On similar anxieties about sex with boys under the influence of alcohol in the English context, see DiGangi, *Sexual Types*, 51–52.

69. Mustafa Ali's celebration of the companionship of boys uses the misogynistic discourse that defines woman as inferior. The inequality between sexes is an underlying component of these discourses that go back to Greek ideas of male friendship and homosociality

(i.e., Ganymede in Plato's *Symposium*, who signifies the best form of companionship: ideal same-sex friendship that increases masculine bonds). The prominent sixteenth-century scholar and courtier Deli Birader Gazali provides an example for the superiority of the boy in companionship in his erotic text *Dâfi'ü'l-gumûm ve Râfi'ü'l-humûm* [Repeller of sorrows and removers of cares]. On similar poetic disputes about the preference of boys over women as ideal objects of love in Arabic tradition, see El-Rouayheb, "The Love of Boys." On similar discourses of same-sex male friendship and masculinity in the English context, see Sinfield, "Cultural Materialism and Intertextuality"; Bray, *The Friend*; and DiGangi, *The Homoerotics of Early Modern Drama*. On similar medieval discourses, see Zeikowitz, *Homoeroticism and Chivalry*.

70. *Tezkire* (biographies of poets) is a particular genre in which disputes between woman-lovers and boy-lovers are a commonplace. The early modern biographer Aşık Çelebi stresses a poet's boy-loving or woman-loving disposition when describing him, illustrating that erotic preference was something worthy to record about poets. For example, the famous poet Fevri writes: "The man of [true] love doesn't look at the women of this world / Does an accomplished man conform to one 'deficient in reason and faith?'" Similarly, Yahya Bey expresses his distaste for traditional narrative poems about female-lovers (i.e., *Hüsrev u Shirin*, and *Layla vu Menjun*) in his own *mesnevi* (narrative poem) *Şah u Geda*, stating, "Those, woman-chasing, lacking taste / These, suffering, cure-less, and chaste / What do they know of love's mystery / Of the rapture of love and its ecstasy" (qtd. in Andrews and Kalpaklı, *The Age of Beloveds*, 135, 56).

71. Stanivukovic, "Cruising the Mediterranean," 66.

72. Rycaut, *The Present State of the Ottoman Empire*, 25–26. While the recruitment of Christian European boys was almost obsolete by the time Rycaut was writing, it is still significant to realize the extent to which such accounts build on and circulate the previous discourses while producing new ones, presenting an intertextual play between travelogues, literary representations, and historical narratives in the depiction of these boys.

73. Rycaut, *The Present State of the Ottoman Empire*, 31.

74. *OED*, s.v. "gallantry," n., 1, 2a, 3a, 5a, 8a.

75. As I discuss elsewhere, Rycaut's reasoning that gender segregation—lack of women in the social sphere—generated homoerotic attachments and same-sex sexual relations is a discourse that was reborn in nineteenth-century Ottoman studies by Orientalists who sought to find the reason for this common "perversion." Interestingly, critics who define the Ottomans as backward to celebrate western, republican ideas convey the same reasoning as Rycaut's. More recent post-Foucauldian explorations still ask the same question—"Why homosexuality?"—as if there needs to be a good reason for homoeroticism/homosexuality to be socially acceptable and common in a society. (They hardly ask "why heterosexuality?" for other contexts.) For a critique of questions that naturalize heterosexuality in approaching early modern Ottoman literature, see Arvas, "From the Pervert Back to the Beloved."

76. Rycaut, *The Present State of the Ottoman Empire*, 33.

77. Norris, *A Collection of Miscellanies*, 305–306.

78. Rycaut, *The Present State of the Ottoman Empire*, 33–34. In fact, Murad IV had an intimate, close courtier named Musa who was killed by the janissaries during an armed uprising against the sultan.

79. Rycaut, *The Present State of the Ottoman Empire*, 34.
80. Qtd. in Stanivukovic, "Cruising the Mediterranean," 65.
81. Sandys, *A Relation of a Journey*, 17, 47.
82. Sandys, *A Relation of a Journey*, 70, 73.
83. Gainsford, *The Glory of England*, 25.
84. Blount, *A Voyage into the Levant*, 14
85. See "catamite" in the OED for the etymology. For more on the link between the concept of a catamite and Ganymede, see Saslow, *Ganymede in the Renaissance*, 29; Bredbeck, *Sodomy and Interpretation*, 18.
86. Knolles, *The Generall Historie of the Turkes*, 363.
87. Baudier, *The history of the imperiall estate of the grand seigneurs*, 156. I refer to Edward Grimeston's 1635 English translation of Sandy's 1626 text since my focus is on discourses in England.
88. Baudier, *The history of the imperiall estate of the grand seigneurs*, 162, my italics.
89. Baudier, *The history of the imperiall estate of the grand seigneurs*, 162.
90. Qtd. in DiGangi, *The Homoerotics of Early Modern Drama*, 18. For more on this saying attributed to Marlowe, and Marlowe's sexuality, see Goldberg, "Sodomy and Society"; and Orgel, "Tobacco and Boys."
91. Orgel, "Tobacco and Boys," 576. The homoeroticism in the poem was noted in the early twentieth century. J. B. Steane, for example, reads Neptune's amorous advances as "the nightmare intrusion of the homosexual into a normal man's life" (qtd. in Darcy, "Under my hands . . . a double duty," 45). Bredbeck notes that earlier criticism "re-read" the homoerotic scene and generated allegorical readings (*Sodomy and Interpretation*, 131–32n70). In the late nineteenth century, Minto and Saintsbury read the rupture in the poem as conflicting drives between ideal and sensual love. See Cheney, "The Passionate Shepherd to His Love," for a brief history of the poem's reception. Ellis (*Sexuality and Citizenship*), Bredbeck (*Sodomy and Interpretation*), Smith (*Homosexual Desire in Shakespeare's England*), Bromley (*Intimacy and Sexuality in the Age of Shakespeare*), Haber (*Desire and Dramatic Form in Early Modern England*), and most recently Masten (*Queer Philologies*) have highlighted erotic significations in the poem.
92. Masten, *Queer Philologies*, 160.
93. Jacobson notes that "like Marlowe's Neptune, the pearly sea-god in the late Elizabethan Canning Jewel (in the collection of the Victoria and Albert Museum) holds a 'saphyr-visaged' shield in his left hand, brandishing a scimitar-shaped knife in his right that calls to mind a marauding Turkish pirate" (*Barbarous Antiquity*, 243n52).
94. Enterline, "Elizabethan Minor Epics," 260.
95. Jacobson, *Barbarous Antiquity*, 166.
96. OED, s.v. "orient," n. and adj., 1, 2.
97. He later uses "orient cloud" (804) to refer to the eastern light.
98. On the description of Leander's body as exemplary of the Renaissance blazon that conventionally concerns the female body, see Bredbeck, who discusses how the depiction of Leander's body follows the female blazon without assigning him femaleness (*Sodomy and Interpretation*, 110–15).
99. Jacobson, *Barbarous Antiquity*, 165. Oberon of Shakespeare's *A Midsummer Night's Dream* uses "orient pearl" in this sense of a lustrous and watery amalgam to refer to

Titania's eyes: "And that same dew which sometime on the buds / Was wont to swell like round and orient pearls / Stood now within the pretty flow'rets' eyes" (4.1.50–52).

100. Smith, *Homosexual Desire in Shakespeare's England*, 136.

101. Vickers, "'The blazon of sweet beauty's best,'" 97.

102. Masten, *Queer Philologies*, 167, Masten's italics.

103. Masten, *Queer Philologies*, 157.

104. Masten, *Queer Philologies*, 166–67, Masten's italics.

105. For more on pastoral and homoeroticism, see Bredbeck, *Sodomy and Interpretation*, 187–232; and Smith, *Homosexual Desire in Shakespeare's England*, 79–116. For a homoerotic sexual paradigm in this scene in particular, see Bredbeck, *Sodomy and Interpretation*, 132–34; and Smith, *Homosexual Desire in Shakespeare's England*, 132–36.

106. Bromley, *Intimacy and Sexuality in the Age of Shakespeare*, 43.

107. Marlowe's poem was published with George Chapman's continuation of it in a second edition in 1598, and it was mostly reprinted as such thereafter. Others, including Henry Petowe (1598), wrote continuations to the poem. We do not know if Marlowe ever intended to finish the poem or if he wrote it knowing that Chapman or others would continue it. I focus on the abduction plot as imagined in Marlowe's poem because I examine it as a distinct piece in dialogue with Marlowe's other work within the larger discourses about the Mediterranean. For a queer analysis of Chapman's continuation, see Masten, *Queer Philologies*. For an analysis of cross-cultural and mercantile references in it, see Jacobson, *Barbarous Antiquity*. For a helpful review on critical discussions of Marlowe's poem as complete or not, see Darcy, "Under my hands . . . a double duty."

CHAPTER 2. MAPPING BOYS ON THE HORIZON

1. On Aşık Çelebi's biography and works, see Aynur and Niyazioğlu, *Aşık Çelebi ve Şairler Tezkiresi Üzerine Yazılar*.

2. This line is a translation of an idiomatic term. Water gets dirty when it stops running, yet murky water also flows faster. This refers to the young person's maturation through mistakes: one cannot become mature unless they get dirty or naughty.

3. This is a reference to the winter periods when the river freezes.

4. The river has an erotic mingling with the naked youth yet no more than that; hence, he is chaste. This might be referring to the uncontaminated, clean waters of the river.

5. "*Yarlardan atılup taşlara urur başını / Aşık-ı divane vü Mecnun-ı uryandur Tuna. / Su bulanmayınca turılmaz acep midür eger / Taş u toprak oynar ise dahi oğlandur Tuna / . . . / Kisver-i kafirden iman ehline akup gelür / Kıbleye tutmış yüzini bir müselmandur Tuna / Habs-i kafirden boşanmış gibi zencirin sürür / Şâh-ı Islama gelür bir ehl-i imandur Tuna / . . . / Yüzi üstine sürinerek ider her hidmetün / Bir yumuş oğlanı gibi bendefermandur Tuna / Gerçi tongunlıgla uşşaka sovukluk gösterür / Hublar nerm eylemekde nar-ı suzandur Tuna / Sine-ber-sine olur simin-bedenlerle veli / Sade pehluyile kani' pak-damandur Tuna*." Qtd. in Kılıç, "Tuna Kasidesi'nin Düşündürdükleri," 34–35. All translations from the poem are my own.

6. On representation of space, see Lefebvre (*The Production of Space*), for whom representations of space are tied to the relations of production, knowledge, and signification. For de Certeau, space is a narrated place, a place in stories, movements, and speech-acts:

"Stories thus carry out a labor that constantly transforms places into spaces or spaces into places" (*The Practice of Everyday Life*, 118). My focus on "space" draws from conceptualizations of space in relation to gender, sexuality, and representation. On the relationship between space-gender and sexuality, see Lefebvre; Massey, *for space* and *Space, Place, and Gender*; Barnes and Gregory, *Reading Human Geography*; Bell and Valentine, "Introduction: Orientations"; Duncan, "Introduction: (Re)placings"; Grosz, *Architecture from the Outside*; Higgs, *Queer Sites*; Johnston and Longhurst, *Space, Place, and Sex*; McDowell, *Gender, Identity, Place*; and Colomina and Bloomer, *Sexuality and Space*.

7. On gendered and sexualized spaces, see Hiscock, *The Uses of This World*; Sanders, *The Cultural Geography of Early Modern Drama*; Boulton, *Neighborhood and Society*; Burford and Wotton, *Private Vices—Public Virtues*; Crane, "Illicit Privacy and Outdoor Spaces in Early Modern England"; Flather, *Gender and Space in Early Modern England*; Friedman, "Inside/Out"; Fumerton, *Cultural Aesthetics*; Howard, *Theater of a City*; Turner, *The English Renaissance Stage*; Wall, *Staging Domesticity*; Helgerson, *Adulterous Alliances*; Capp, "Gender and the Culture of the English Alehouse in Late Stuart England"; Gowing, "'The freedom of streets'"; Guy-Bray, *Homoerotic Space*; Mullaney, *The Place of the Stage*; Johnson, "'To what bawdy house doth your Maister belong?'"; Dabhoiwala, "The Pattern of Sexual Immorality in Seventeenth- and Eighteenth-Century London"; Gillies, *Shakespeare and the Geography of Difference*; McJannet, "Genre and Geography"; Stanivukovic, "Cruising the Mediterranean"; and Bly, "Carnal Geographies."

8. Montrose, "The Work of Gender in the Discourse of Discovery." Some other exemplary works that presented a land/woman association in early modern cultural imagination are Kolodny, *The Lay of the Land*; Hulme, "Polytropic Man"; Vickers, "'The blazon of sweet beauty's best'"; Stallybrass, "Patriarchal Territories." On gender, sex, and the conquest of the Americas, see Trexler, *Sex and Conquest*.

9. My use of the concept of the horizon is influenced by Sara Ahmed's explication of the horizon as an imaginary phenomenon that generated and is generated by a directionality (*Queer Phenomenology*) and by Muñoz's argument that "queerness is always in the horizon" that emerges in the aesthetic realm (*Cruising Utopia*, 11). Also helpful for my conceptualization of horizon as an edge blurring what is here and what is not is Bronwen Wilson's reading of the sixteenth-century cartographer Melchior Lorck's mapping of Istanbul by focusing on the horizon and prospect of the map ("The Itinerant Artist and the Islamic Urban Prospect"). I use "horizon" more in terms of an imaginary space, including allegorical and iconographic representations.

10. In the early modern Ottoman language, terrestrial maps were usually termed *resm* (drawing/picture) or *suret* (representation/image/face), signifying the representational, topographical, and artistic aspects of cartography.

11. Andrews and Kalpaklı, *The Age of Beloveds*, 63–73.

12. Qtd. in Andrews and Kalpaklı, *The Age of Beloveds*, 64.

13. "Frank" also appears in early modern European travel accounts with this meaning, although etymologically it goes back to Old English, signifying Germanic people. The early modern usage mainly refers to "a name given by the nations bordering on the Levant to an individual of Western nationality" (*OED*, s.v. "frank," n. and adj., 1 and 2) Also, the term *franj* or *il-franj* is common in medieval Arabic sources, simply meaning white or from Western Christendom.

14. Lewis, "Sexual Occidentation," 707.

15. Andrews and Kalpaklı, *The Age of Beloveds*, 159–60.

16. Mehmed used Avni as his pen name (*mahlas*) in his poems. It was a common practice for an Ottoman poet to use a pen name and to use it as a signature in the last couplet; hence the change in the pronoun addressing the speaker.

17. "*Bir güneş yüzlü melek gördüm ki alem mahıdur. / Ol kara sünbülleri aşıklarınun ahıdur. / Karalar geymiş meh-i taban gibi ol serv-i naz, / Mülk-i efrengün meğer kim hüsn içinde şahıdur. / Ukde-i zünnarına her kimse kim dil bağlamaz, / Ehl-i iman olmaz ol aşıklarınun güm-rahıdur. / Gamzesi öldürdüğine lebleri canlar virür, / Var ise ol ruh-bahşün din-i İsa rahıdur. / Avniya kılma güman kim sana ram ola nigar, / Sen Sitanbul şahısun, ol (da) Kalata şahıdur.*" Doğan, *Fatih Divanı ve Şerhi*, 55. My translation is largely based on Andrews and Kalpaklı's translation (*The Age of Beloveds*, 3); I made some modifications in terms of rhymes, inverted sentence structure, and pronouns. For Mehmed II's *Divan* [Collected poems], with facsimiles in Ottoman Turkish and transcriptions into modern Turkish, see Doğan.

18. Qtd. in Lewis, "Sexual Occidentation," 698.

19. In the mystic Sufi tradition—i.e., the writings of Rumi or Ibn al-Arabi—Jesus's miracle of bringing someone back to life by his breath or his kiss is depicted as love's power of healing. On Jesus's miracles, especially breathing life, see the Qur'an 3:49. For more on Jesus's kiss in the Sufi tradition, see Leirvik, *Images of Jesus Christ in Islam*, 92–94; and Ridgeon, "Christianity as Portrayed by Jalal al-Din Rumi."

20. For early modern Arabic examples of the boy as a medium for reaching divine love, see El-Rouayheb, "The Love of Boys." For Persian examples, see Lewis, "Sexual Occidentation." For comparative readings of Arabic, Hebrew, and European traditions, see Roth, "'Deal Gently with the Young Man.'"

21. Kevser, or Kausar in Arabic, is the fountain of paradise in Islamic tradition.

22. "*Bağlamaz Firdevs'e gönlini Kalata'yı gören / Servi anmaz anda ol serv-i dil-arayı gören / Bir firengi şiveli İsa'yı gördüm anda kim, / Lebleri dirisidür dir idi İsa'yı gören / Akl ü fehmin din ü imanın nice zabt eylesün / Kafir olur hey müselmanlar o tersayı gören. / Kevseri anmaz ol içdüğü mey-i nabi içen / Mescide varmaz o vardugı kilisayı gören / Bir firengi kafir oldugun bilürdü Avniya / Belde zünnarını boynunda çelipayı gören.*" Doğan, *Fatih Divanı ve Şerhi*, 202. The translation to English is my own. In the original, the rhyming repetition is "*gören*" (one who sees), yet taking into consideration the conditional and momentary implication of the word, which is derived from the verb "*gör*" (to see), as well as the repetitive use of "*anda*" (that moment), I used "once" or "but once" 1) to emphasize the sense of "the moment" or the "abrupt" in the act of laying eyes, 2) to convey conditionality (once/if one sees the boy), and 3) to better reflect the rhyme.

23. Lefebvre, *The Production of Space*, 195.

24. Arvas, "The Ottomans in and of Europe."

25. In Islamic tradition, Constantinople was considered a promised city because of a hadith (a saying of the Prophet Muhammed) in which the Prophet anticipated its conquest by Muslims and praised the future commander of the conquest. When the Ottomans finally captured it, Muslim rulers had tried to conquer the city several times from the seventh century to the fifteenth century. For competing discourses on Constantinople, see Fleming, "Constantinople: From Christianity to Islam."

26. "*Rind isen meyli koma cam-ı musaffadan yana / Arif isen götür ayağı Galatadan yana / Mülk-i Rum içre firengistanı görmek isteyen / Seyre geçsün dayima ol şehr-i ra'nadan yana / Şol fireng oğlanların sofi göreydün bir nazar / Göz açup bakmaz idün cennetde havradan yana / Ṣanuram oldı mukarin gökde Pervine hilal / Keştiye binüp güzeller gitse deryadan yana / Din yağmasın ider kafirbeçe mahbublar / Sakınun varman müselmanlar kilisadan yana / Bu felek anun mücella kasrıdur kim afitab / Seyr içün revzen açupdur ana dünyadan yana / Hur u gılman ile pür olmış Revani her taraf / Bakmaz içine giren firdevs-i a'ladan yana.*" Revani, "Gazeller: 7," my translation. For an alternative translation, see Andrews and Kalpaklı, *The Age of Beloveds*, 65–66.

27. El-Rouayheb, "The Love of Boys," 14.

28. Imber, *The Ottoman Empire*, 121.

29. Brookes, "The Ottoman Gentleman of the Sixteenth Century," 220.

30. On semantic analysis of maps, see Harley, "Silences and Secrecy," "Maps, Knowledge, and Power," and "Deconstructing the Map." On maps as objects, documents, imperial agents, and subject makers, see Davies, *Renaissance Ethnography and the Invention of the Human*; Helgerson, "The Land Speaks"; Edney, *Mapping an Empire*; and Akerman, *Cartographies of Travel and Navigation*.

31. Traub, "Mapping the Global Body," 45.

32. The early modern atlases were often titled or called "theaters of the world."

33. San Juan, "The Transformation of the Rio de la Plata."

34. Lazzaro, "River Gods," 94.

35. Rubin, "'Che è di questo culazzino!,'" 437.

36. This is particularly because of Florence's reputation for male homosexuality. In Germany, "*florenzen*" was used to mean "to sodomize" (Rocke, *Forbidden Friendships*, 3).

37. Saslow, *Ganymede in the Renaissance*, 102–119.

38. For more on Ganymede as Aquarius, see Barkan, *Transuming Passion*; Saslow, *Ganymede in the Renaissance*; and Trzaskoma et al., *Anthology of Classical Myth*, 105.

39. Hyginus, *Fabulae*, 224.

40. Phelan, *Unmarked*, 51.

41. Foucault, *The Use of Pleasure*, 200.

CHAPTER 3. (IN)VISIBLE BOYS IN ENGLISH ABDUCTIONS

1. Campana, "Shakespeare's Children," 10. Campana includes boys in the category of children, emphasizing the complexity of terms such as child, boy, and infant in the early modern context (11).

2. Campana, "Traffic in Children," 38. On local boys, see also Campana, "Boy Toys and Liquid Joys"; and Busse, "Profitable Children."

3. Hendricks, "'Obscured by dreams,'" 44, 43. For other postcolonial readings of the play, see Raman, *Framing "India"*; Shahani, "The Spiced Indian Air in Early Modern England"; Buchanan, "'India' and the Golden Age in *A Midsummer Night's Dream*"; Habib, "Bengal as Shakespeare's India and the Stolen Indian Boy."

4. Loomba, "The Great Indian Vanishing Trick," 169.

5. Loomba, "The Great Indian Vanishing Trick," 184.

6. Loomba, "The Great Indian Vanishing Trick," 181.

7. I use the Indian boy as a template for these abducted boys in the early modern English imagination, as "Indian" was often used as an all-encompassing signifier for exotic and unknowable places and cultures, bringing into proximity Asian, African, and American as racially different from the white English boy. India, in Raman's terms, was "the name for both physical and metaphysical limits to the European world" (*Framing "India,"* 15). On various significations of the term "India," see also Harris, *Indiography*, 1–20; and Buchanan, "'India' and the Golden Age in *A Midsummer Night's Dream*," 58–60.

8. On medieval oblation, see Boswell, *The Kindness of Strangers*; and Orme, *Medieval Children*. On child actors and children taken up for theater and choirs, see Bryan, "In the Company of Boys"; and Campana, "Traffic in Children." On theatrical apprenticeship and the physical labor of boy actors, see Belsey, "Shakespeare's Little Boys"; and McCarthy, *Boy Actors in Early Modern England*.

9. Bryan, "In the Company of Boys," 260.

10. Bryan writes, "In May 1609 the governing council of the Virginia Company sent out Instructions for running the Virginia colony to Sir Thomas Gates, the English governor of Virginia, 'You must procure from them (the natives) some convenient number of their children to be brought up in your language, and manners.' Taking native children and "training" them to be English motivated much support, both financial and moral, in England for the Virginia Company" ("In the Company of Boys," 253–54).

11. For more on English existence in the Mediterranean and English piracy activities, see Vitkus, *Piracy, Slavery, and Redemption*; Jowitt, *The Culture of Piracy, 1580–1630*; Fisher, *Barbary Legend*; and Skilliter, *William Harborne and the Trade with Turkey*. On Ottoman captives and other Mediterranean piracy activities, see Dávid and Fodor, *Ransom Slavery along the Ottoman Borders*.

12. On kidnapping and trading of boys in Asian trade by the East India Company, see Habib, "Bengal as Shakespeare's India and the Stolen Indian Boy."

13. Habib, *Black Lives in the English Archives*, 67.

14. For examples of accounts, see Kaufmann, *Black Tudors*. For more on the presence of black people in England, see Amussen, *Caribbean Exchanges*; Fryer, *Staying Power*; Shyllon, *Black People in Britain*; Ungerer, *The Mediterranean Apprenticeship of British Slavery*; Dabydeen, Gilmore, and Jones, *The Oxford Companion to Black British History*; and Onyeka, *Blackamoores*.

15. For a detailed analysis of the event, see Knutson, "A Caliban in St. Milfred Poultry."

16. Habib, *Black Lives in the English Archives*, 142.

17. For more on the assimilation of native boys in the New World, see Bryan, "In the Company of Boys." On boys brought from India, see Habib, *Black Lives in the English Archives*, 239–60; and "Bengal as Shakespeare's India and the Stolen Indian Boy." For Raleigh's transportation of boys, see Habib, *Black Lives in the English Archives*, 252–53; and Vaughan, "Sir Walter Raleigh's Indian Interpreters." On Native Americans brought to England, see Vaughan, "Trinculo's Indian." For a discussion of conversion and slavery, see Lowe, "Introduction" 12–13; and Hall, *Things of Darkness*.

18. On crossings between slavery and domestic service in England, see Chakravarty, *Fictions of Consent*.

19. For decrees, see Habib, *Black Lives in the English Archives*, 112–14. Loomba suggests that these decrees functioned as attempts at the "preservation of the white race"

(*Gender, Race, Renaissance Drama*, 40). See also Bartels, "Too Many Blackamoors"; and Kaufmann, "Caspar van Senden, Sir Thomas Sherley and the 'Blackamoor' Project." Kaufmann suggests that the decrees did not really aim to expel black people but were used as a profitable means by merchants against some debtors.

20. The image of a black boy was on a bookshop sign, called "blacke boye," from 1550 to 1553, according to the churchyard records of St Paul's Cross. See Blayney, *The Bookshops in Paul's Cross Churchyard*, 82. Valerie Wayne's paper "The Black Boy Bookshops in Sixteenth-Century London," submitted for the 2021 Shakespeare Association of America meeting, showed that the sign of black boy was used at least by two booksellers in the vicinity of St Paul's Churchyard, as well as by other shops.

21. Lowe, "Introduction," 2.

22. Qtd. in Matar, "Muslim Conversion to Christianity in the Early Modern Period," 215.

23. Qtd. in Habib, *Black Lives in the English Archives*, 127.

24. *OED*, s.v. "lusty," adj., 1, 3, 4.

25. *OED*, s.v. "lusty," adj., 5.

26. Cooper, *Thesaurus*, s.v. "firmus."

27. Rycaut, *The Present State of the Ottoman Empire*, 25.

28. Earle and Lowe's collection *Black Africans in Renaissance Europe* shows that the black servant appears in the visual culture of almost all European traditions, including Spanish and Portuguese, in the Renaissance. See Kaplan, "Titian's 'Laura Dianti' and the Origins of the Motif of the Black Page in Portraiture" and "Isabella d'Este and Black African Women," for the motif of the black servant in Italian art, and Blakely, *Blacks in the Dutch World*, for the motif in Dutch art. On black bodies in English paintings, see Erickson, "Invisibility Speaks," "Representations of Race in Renaissance Art," and "Representations of Blacks and Blackness in the Renaissance"; and Erickson and Hulse, *Early Modern Visual Culture*. For a collection of Western images of black people, see Bindman and Gates, *The Image of the Black in Western Art* (for early modern images, see vol. 3, parts 1 and 2). On black female bodies, see Hall, *Things of Darkness* and "Object into Object?"

29. Hall argues that these representations "chart the ongoing commodification of black bodies as England becomes more dependent on an involvement with Africa for economic expansion and symbolic definition" (*Things of Darkness*, 227). Similarly, Erickson notes that "the overall tendency in Renaissance portraiture is to present the black attendant primarily not as subject but as object—appurtenance, status symbol, exotic touch" ("Representations of Race in Renaissance Art," 4–5).

30. For biographical analysis of the portrait, see Wendorf, *The Elements of Life*. For an analysis of it in a colonial frame, see Gilma, "Madagascar on My Mind."

31. Hall, *Things of Darkness*, 232.

32. For Rupert's biography, see Morrah, *Prince Rupert of the Rhine*; Spencer, *Prince Rupert*; and Wilkinson, *Prince Rupert the Cavalier*. Both Hall (*Things of Darkness*, 228) and Spencer (*Prince Rupert*, 229) associate the boy in the painting with the captured boy.

33. Morrah, *Prince Rupert of the Rhine*, 264.

34. Morrah, *Prince Rupert of the Rhine*, 287.

35. Morrah, *Prince Rupert of the Rhine*, 288.

36. Morrah, *Prince Rupert of the Rhine*, 288.

37. Wilkinson, *Prince Rupert the Cavalier*, 117–19; Spencer, *Prince Rupert*, 126–28.

38. Qtd. in Morrah, *Prince Rupert of the Rhine*, 54.

39. On enslaved black boys itemized as commodities, see Hall, "I can't love this the way you want me to."

40. For accounts and poems suggesting unnatural, even satanic aspects of their relationship, see Morrah, *Prince Rupert of the Rhine*, 105–106; and Spencer, *Prince Rupert*, 127–28.

41. Aravamudan, *Tropicopolitans*, 34. On symmetries between servants and pets, see Tuan, *Dominance and Affection*.

42. Qtd. in Morrah, *Prince Rupert of the Rhine*, 105.

43. Interestingly, biographers of Rupert are either silent or defensive about his sexuality. Morrah, for example, sounds resentful about homosexuality attributed to Rupert, and states, "Nothing in his career gives the slightest suggestion that he was not a man of perfectly normal passions" (*Prince Rupert of the Rhine*, 400). Whatever these perfectly normal passions were, one must ask about his intimate closeness to his loyal soldier, Honest Will Ledge, who was "Rupert's most faithful servant. . . . As time went on the trust and intimacy between the Prince and Legge grew steadily, as is revealed in their correspondence. Legge wrote to Rupert with uninhibited candour, always with his best interest in heart. Rupert wrote to his beloved Will with an informality which he seldom showed in letters to anybody else" (*Prince Rupert of the Rhine*, 104). So Morrah's own language makes one wonder about Rupert's intimacy with male companions. Although Morrah presses against "abnormal" passions, he can find that male-male intimacy was "normal" and often went unseen unless it caused social disorder in early modern England.

44. Anonymous, *An Exact description of Prince Ruperts Malignant She-Monkey*, A2.

45. Anonymous, *An Exact description of Prince Ruperts Malignant She-Monkey*, A3, A4.

46. Anonymous, *The Humerous Tricks and Conceits of Prince Roberts Malignant She-Monkey*, A4.

47. Coke, *The Third Part of the Institutes of the Laws of England*, 59. For more on bestiality as a part of sodomy, see Bray, *Homosexuality in Renaissance England*, 13–18.

48. Anonymous, *An Exact description of Prince Ruperts Malignant She-Monkey*, A5.

49. Erickson, "Representations of Race in Renaissance Art," 6.

50. Hall, *Things of Darkness*, 228.

51. Lowe, "The Stereotyping of Black Africans in Renaissance Europe," 21, 23–24.

52. Hall, *Things of Darkness*, 298.

53. Erickson, "Invisibility Speaks," 24.

54. Sandys, *A Relation of a Journey*, 10–25, 77–84.

55. Lithgow, *The Totall Discourse of the Rare Adventures, and Painefull Peregrinations*, 75, 71–73.

56. Habib suggests that the "spiced air of tropical high summer Bengali nights" harmonizes with the "cooler English early spring seasons of 'oxlips', 'nodding violets', and 'wild thyme[s]'" ("Bengal as Shakespeare's India and the Stolen Indian Boy," 4).

57. Since the 1940s, critics have identified the boy as an erotic object of desire. Miller writes that Titania is "in love with the changeling" ("Titania and the Changeling," 69); Kott (*Shakespeare Our Contemporary*) suggests that he is a sexual toy for Oberon; and Green identifies sodomy in "Oberon's obsession with the changeling boy" ("Preposterous Pleasures," 376). He is the child object of love for all in Garner ("*A Midsummer Night's Dream*") and "the single "master-mistress" of each one's passion" (Crewe, *Hidden Desires*, 148). See also

Sinfield, "Cultural Materialism and Intertextuality"; Jacobson, "A Note on Shakespeare's *A Midsummer Night's Dream*"; Faber, "Hermia's Dream"; and Garber, *Vested Interests*.

58. On English abductions in India and Titania's "stealing" in this context, see Habib, "Bengal as Shakespeare's India and the Stolen Indian Boy."

59. Hendricks, "'Obscured by dreams,'" 53. On female homoeroticism in the play, see Traub, *The Renaissance of Lesbianism in Early Modern England*, 65–69.

60. Loomba, "The Great Indian Vanishing Trick," 184.

61. Garner, "*A Midsummer Night's Dream*," 129.

62. Hendricks writes, "The displacement of the changeling child and the substitution of the adult changeling foreground the problem of unregulated female sexuality and its effect on the existing concept of race" ("'Obscured by dreams,'" 58). For more on Bottom as an erotic substitution for the Indian boy, see Montrose, *The Purpose of Playing*; Hendricks, "'Obscured by dreams'"; Schwartz, *Tough Love*; Lamb, "Taken by Fairies"; Paster and Howard, *A Midsummer Night's Dream*; Garner, "*A Midsummer Night's Dream*"; and Boehrer, "Economies of Desire in *A Midsummer Night's Dream*." For feminist readings that emphasize female submission in the play as a part of the "natural" sexual and gender economy, see Gohlke, "'I wooed thee with my sword'"; Desmet, "Disfiguring Women with Masculine Tropes"; Garner, "*A Midsummer Night's Dream*"; Traub, "(In)Significance of 'Lesbian' Desire in Early Modern England"; and Callaghan, "What Is an Audience?"

63. Masten, *Queer Philologies*, 74.

64. Hall, "Culinary Spaces, Colonial Spaces," 168–90.

65. *OED*, s.v. "squire," n., 4.

66. *OED*, s.v. "perforce," adv., 1.

67. Garner, "*A Midsummer Night's Dream*," 129–30. See also Paster and Howard, for whom "the play identifies the emotional violence of this radical separation of mother and son with Titania and her ferocious refusal to let her godson go" (*A Midsummer Night's Dream*, 168).

68. Challenging Montrose's reading of Oberon's realm as a masculine fatherly space, Hendricks "view[s] Oberon's quest for the boy less as the embodiment of fatherly love or pride than as the manifestation of a perceived prerogative to claim possession—to have "all . . . tied to" him. The paternal interest that many critics argue lies at the heart of Oberon's desire is not evident in his words" ("'Obscured by dreams,'" 53).

69. *OED*, s.v. "henchman," n., etym. and 1.

70. For an analysis of these images, see Hall, *Things of Darkness*, 235–39.

71. Philips, "Schoolmasters, Seduction, and Slavery," 148. For the black stable boy in an English textbook, see 147–158.

72. Rambuss, "What It Feels Like for a Boy," 245.

73. Sodomy laws were rarely invoked in England despite widespread anti-sodomy theological and legal discourses. As Smith notes, during the Elizabethan and Jacobean periods, there was only one case that was related to sodomitical rape (*Homosexual Desire in Shakespeare's England*, 48). On patronage, service, and royal favorites, see Bray, *Homosexuality in Renaissance England*; and DiGangi, *Sexual Types*. On humanism, pedagogy, and classical writings, see Shannon, *Sovereign Amity*; Stewart, *Close Readers*; and Smith, *Homosexual Desire in Shakespeare's England*.

74. Goldberg, *Sodometries*, 19. Bray (*Homosexuality in Renaissance England*) also notes that sodomy appears in connection with crimes such as treason and witchcraft and remains invisible in the context of such bonds as friendship, patronage, bedfellows, servants and masters, students and teachers, and kings and their minions.

75. Sinfield, *Shakespeare, Authority, Sexuality*, 115.

76. Gowing, *Common Bodies*, 61. Gowing further writes, "Servants had little private space, rarely a room or even a bed of their own, and they had little autonomy over their bodies" (64). See also Cynthia Herrup's work on the household of the second Earl of Castlehaven, showing how Castlehaven sexually dominated members of his household, particularly his boy servants (*A House in Gross Disorder*). Of course, not all servant boys were used sexually; however, they were all potential sexual objects within the social hierarchy. Servants also figured in major same-sex scandals, including Francis Bacon's relationship with his servant (Bray, *Homosexuality in Renaissance England*, 48–53).

77. Smith, *Homosexual Desire in Shakespeare's England*, 195, 118.

78. Sinfield, "Cultural Materialism and Intertextuality."

79. Lowe, "The Stereotyping of Black Africans in Renaissance Europe," 31.

80. Qtd. in Habib, *Black Lives in the English Archives*, 304, my italics.

81. Habib argues that these slaves are black boys (*Black Lives in the English Archives*, 229–30).

82. Qtd. in Bray, *Homosexuality in Renaissance England*, 40. Masten notes the ambiguous language in this account and suggests that the record is not explicit enough to clarify whether the boy William participated in the buggery or he just witnessed the buggery with another person or animal. Nevertheless, it is Drago who is on trial and the English boy who provides testimony. Masten also suggests that Drago's name might be connected to his profession as a traveling *dragoman* (the term used for the Ottoman translators and guides). In this sense, Masten suggests, "*drago* and *dragoman*, as a word and activity, crosses between Here and There" ("Glossing and T*pping," 579).

83. Bray, *Homosexuality in Renaissance England*, 72. Little observes that the "vast majority of black men appearing in early modern tragedy find themselves directly or indirectly implicated in a rape scene, making it all the more likely that an early modern audience would see—would have a history of seeing—black men as natural rapists" (*Shakespeare Jungle Fever*, 5). Often interracial relations between black men and white women were considered aberrant, excessive, and unnatural and hence sodomitical.

84. On the Spanish context, see Berco, *Sexual Hierarchies*; and Savvadis, "Male Prostitution and the Homoerotic Sex-Market in Early Modern England," 51–55.

85. Historical accounts of black women can give us clues about the exploitation of slave boys. Black women were forced into prostitution and/or sexually abused. When they were impregnated, they gave birth to "bastard" children (Habib, *Black Lives in the English Archives*, 76–112). An example on stage is the unnamed, unseen black woman in *The Merchant of Venice* who is pregnant with Lancelot's child (3.5.32). On the sexual exploitation of enslaved black men in in the early American context, see Foster, *Rethinking Rufus*.

86. See, for instance, Anthony Guy Patricia's study of queer filmic productions of the play: "To be sure, conceding that the possibility exists that Oberon's and Titania's interest in the youth may cross the line between the appropriately paternal and the disturbingly criminal forces an entirely discomfiting confrontation with one of the darkest sides of humanity—the

abuse of children perpetrated by adults who are afflicted with a deformity in mind, character, and spirit as devastating as it is repulsive" (*Queering the Shakespeare Film*, 14).

87. Williams, *Our Moonlight Revels*, 275n104.

88. Montrose, *The Purpose of Playing*, 127; Sinfield, "Cultural Materialism and Intertextuality," 74.

89. *OED*, s.v. "changeling," n., 1.

90. *OED*, s.v. "child," n., 9.

91. *OED*, s.v. "child," n., 6.

92. As I discuss in chapter 6, some artists and theater makers also represented the boy not as a child but an adolescent serving a fairy king or queen.

93. On the emergence of domestic heterosexuality in early modern England, see Traub, *The Renaissance of Lesbianism in Early Modern England*.

94. On this potentiality as presented on stage, see chapter 6.

95. DiGangi, "Asses and Wits," 180.

96. Sinfield, *On Sexuality and Power*, 115.

97. Sinfield, "Cultural Materialism and Intertextuality," 75.

98. I discuss creative survivance in the introduction. I revisit the future of the boy and reimaginations and presentations of him by theater makers in chapter 6.

CHAPTER 4. REFASHIONING BOYS

1. Sanders, "The voyage made to Tripolis in Barbarie," 192. Subsequent references appear parenthetically throughout the chapter.

2. Burton, *Traffic and Turning*, 106–126.

3. Malieckal, "Wanton Irreligious Madness," 25–43.

4. Britton, "Muslim Conversion and Circumcision as Theater," 74.

5. Rawlins, *The famous and wonderfull recoverie of a ship of Bristoll*, B1–B1v 4; Purchas, *Hakluytus Posthumus*, 10:425, 9:483.

6. I use the term "cutting pricks" in the sense of its early modern usage as circumcision to evoke that for Christians, circumcision was terrifying and therefore conflated with castration. For more on the use of the term, see Holmberg, *Jews in the Early Modern English Imagination*, 88; and Shapiro, *Shakespeare and the Jews*, 265n14.

7. Araz notes that circumcision was usually done as a coming-of-age event when the boy was six or seven years old, ages that were crucial in the boy's transition to the next phase of boyhood toward adulthood in early modern Ottoman society (*16. Yüzyıldan 19*, 33).

8. Baudier, *The history of the imperiall estate of the grand seigneurs*, 77.

9. Arslan, "Osmanlı," 169–89.

10. Şahin cogently notes the paradigm shift from marriage to circumcision as a symbolic demonstration of royalty's reproductive power. As he remarks, "before the mid-fifteenth century, dynastic marriages (through which the Ottoman dynasty established alliances in Anatolia and the Balkans), not circumcisions, were occasions for public and semi-public celebrations.... [A] prince's circumcision ceremonies became the major occasion for emphasizing the dynasty's biological virility" ("Staging an Empire," 485). For more on these ceremonies, see Peirce, *The Imperial Harem*, 28–30.

11. Şahin, "Staging an Empire," 463–64.

12. For other contemporary depictions of this celebration, see Tursun Beg, *Tarih-i Ebü'l-Feth*, 84–91; and Chalkokondyles, *The Histories*, 259–61.

13. Aşıkpaşazade, *Manakib u Tevarih-u Al-i Osman*, 495. Edirne was the royal site for these events when Istanbul was being reconstructed during the three years after the conquest.

14. Aşıkpaşazade, *Manakib u Tevarih-u Al-i Osman*, 496.

15. Aşıkpaşazade, *Manakib u Tevarih-u Al-i Osman*, 225.

16. Metin And claims that there is no other festivity that is recorded in as much detail as this celebration, either in the Islamic or in the European world (*16. Yüzyılda Istanbul*, 145). Since there are numerous extant manuscripts of the *Surname* in various museums and libraries, I am referring to the manuscript in the Topkapı Palace, which is considered to be the complete copy presented to the sultan. For a facsimile of this copy with selected miniatures, see Atasoy, *1582 Sûrnâme-i Hümayun*. For more on the surname tradition and the 1582 circumcision celebrations, see And, *Osmanlı Şenliklerinde Türk Sanatları, Kırk Gün Kırk Gece* and *A History of Theatre and Popular Entertainment in Turkey*; Stout, "The Sur-ı Humayun of Murad III"; Gökyay, "Bir Saltanat Düğünü"; Terzioğlu, "The Imperial Circumcision Festival of 1582"; and Atasoy, *1582 Sûrnâme-i Hümayun*. On earlier circumcision festivals, see Şahin, "Staging an Empire"; and Yelçe, "Evaluating Three Imperial Festivals."

17. On the influence of Romans on Ottoman celebrations, see And, *Kırk Gün Kırk Gece*, 73; Atasoy, *1582 Sûrnâme-i Hümayun*, 20–22; and Tansuğ, *Şenlikname Düzeni*. On the Ottomans' reclaiming of Byzantium conventions in these celebrations, see Şahin, "Staging an Empire." On the Ottomans as new Romans, see Kafadar, "A Rome of One's Own."

18. Qtd. in Andrews and Kalpaklı, *The Age of Beloveds*, 151.

19. Qtd. in Andrews and Kalpaklı, *The Age of Beloveds*, 154.

20. On the participation of Europeans in these celebrations, see And, *16. Yüzyılda Istanbul*.

21. Baudier, *The history of the imperiall estate of the grand seigneurs*, 78–79.

22. Baudier, *The history of the imperiall estate of the grand seigneurs*, 78.

23. For the list of European accounts and the letter, see And, *Osmanlı Şenliklerinde Türk Sanatları*, 259–60, and *A History of Theatre and Popular Entertainment in Turkey*, 118–30; Stout, "The Sur-ı Humayun of Murad III"; and Terzioğlu, "The Imperial Circumcision Festival of 1582."

24. Goulart, *Admirable and memorable histories containing the wonders of our time*, 39–43. On the English translation of Lebelski, see And, *A History of Theatre and Popular Entertainment in Turkey*, 118–30; Stout, "The Sur-ı Humayun of Murad III," 17-17; and Terzioğlu, "The Imperial Circumcision Festival of 1582," 97n2.

25. Goulart, *Admirable and memorable histories containing the wonders of our time*, 39, Grimeston's italics.

26. Qtd. in Loomba and Burton, *Race in Early Modern England*, 41.

27. On Jews and circumcision in the context of medieval conversions in Europe, see Tartakoff, *Conversion, Circumcision, and Ritual Murder in Medieval Europe*. In early modern England, see Shapiro, *Shakespeare and the Jews*; and Holmberg, *Jews in the Early Modern English Imagination*.

28. Shapiro, *Shakespeare and the Jews*, 115.

29. Geuffroy, *The order of the greate Turckes courte*, Iiiii.

30. Geuffroy, *The order of the greate Turckes courte*, Ib.

31. Women have indeed been excluded from mosques in some places and times, not because of circumcision but because of other excuses such as menstruation or the risk of temptation.

32. Geuffroy, *The order of the greate Turckes courte*, Ib. Geuffroy's text in translation mistakenly uses the Turkish word "*sunet*" for "uncircumcised." (The word "*sünnet*" means circumcision).

33. Geuffroy, *The order of the greate Turckes courte*, Iiii.

34. On the association of sodomy with Italy, see Daileader, "Back Door Sex"; Bredbeck, *Sodomy and Interpretation*; DiGangi, *The Homoerotics of Early Modern Drama*; and Jones, "Italians and Others."

35. Georgieuiz, *The Offspring of the House of Ottomanno*, D1.

36. Following this gendered coding, the text describes quite accurately how the surgery takes place, the feasts following the ceremony, the tradition of using henna in celebrations, and so on.

37. Sandys, *A Relation of a Journey*, 55–57.

38. On medieval perceptions of Islam in Europe, see Akbari, *Idols in the East*; Tolan, *Saracens*; Strickland, *Saracens, Demons, and Jews*; and Cohen, "On Saracen Enjoyment."

39. Kellet, *A Returne from Argier*, 18–19, 2.

40. Kellet, *A Returne from Argier*, 32; *OED*, s.v. "nastie," adj., 4.

41. MacLean and Matar, *Britain and the Islamic World*, 220.

42. James I, *Lepanto*, A4v.

43. Shapiro also remarks, "Shakespeare's contemporaries used circumcision as a metaphor for castration" (*Shakespeare and the Jews*, 114).

44. Bulwer, *Anthropometamorphosis*, 211.

45. Bulwer, *Anthropometamorphosis*, 213.

46. Bulwer, *Anthropometamorphosis*, 214.

47. Bulwer, *Anthropometamorphosis*, 213.

48. Bulwer, *Anthropometamorphosis*, 214.

49. Vitkus, *Turning Turk*, 104.

50. Degenhardt, *Islamic Conversion and Christian Resistance*, 2. Burton remarks, referring to the interrelationship between conversion and desire on the English stage, that "the Turkish plays enact a fantastic recuperation of imperiled English masculinity by situating heterosexual desire at the center of Anglo-Islamic relations" (*Traffic and Turning*, 93).

51. All citations to the play refer to page numbers from Vitkus, *Three Turk Plays from Early Modern England*.

52. Vitkus, *Turning Turk*, 84.

53. Daileader, "Back Door Sex," 304, 305.

54. Burton, *Traffic and Turning*, 202.

55. For more on how environmental understandings of bodies, especially venery in relation to sexualized Muslims, see LaFleur, *The Natural History of Sexuality in Early America*, especially 44–80.

56. Loomba, "'Delicious Traffick,'" 207.

57. Qtd. in Vitkus, *Three Turk Plays from Early Modern England*, 346.

58. Greenblatt et al., *The Norton Shakespeare*, 2190n9.

59. On *Othello* in the Ottoman Mediterranean context, see Vitkus, *Turning Turk*; Burton, *Traffic and Turning*; Britton, *Becoming Christian*; and Degenhardt, *Islamic Conversion and Christian Resistance*.

60. Othello's name is Shakespeare's creation. In its primary source, *Un Capitano Moro* (A Moorish Captain) by Giovanni Battista Giraldi (Cinthio) (1565), he is just called "Moor." Gillies identifies "Othello" as an Ottoman name (*Shakespeare*, 99).

61. Smith, "The Queer Moor." For more on bestiality, blackness, and sodomy in the play, see Little, "'An Essence that's Not Seen.'" On sodomy discourse in the play, see Matz, "Slander, Renaissance Discourses of Sodomy, and 'Othello.'"

62. Boyarin, "Othello's Penis," 258. On Othello's circumcision, see Lupton, "Othello Circumcised"; Vitkus, *Turning Turk*; and Parker, "Preposterous Conversions."

63. *OED*, s.v. "defunct," adj. & n., etym.; s.v. "function," n., etym.

64. *OED*, s.v. "effeminate," adj., 2; s.v. "effeminacy," n., 2.

65. On Othello's failure in heterosexuality, see Neill, "Unproper Beds"; Nelson and Haines, "Othello's Unconsummated Marriage"; Matz, "Slander, Renaissance Discourses of Sodomy, and 'Othello'"; Smith, *Homosexual Desire*, 61–64; Dollimore, *Sexual Dissidence*, 182–200; Adelman, "Iago's Alter Ego"; and Calbi, "Unshap't Bodies."

66. Foucault, *The History of Sexuality*, 75.

67. Sandys, *A Relation of a Journey*, 78.

68. Traub, *The Renaissance of Lesbianism in Early Modern England*, 196.

69. Baudier, *The history of the imperiall estate of the grand seigneurs*, 93–94.

70. Bulwer, *Anthropometamorphosis*, 206.

71. Similar accounts on Barbary corsairs in in the late seventeenth and early eighteenth centuries, LaFleur has persuasively argued, contributed tremendously to the formation of an "environmental theory of early sexuality" (*The Natural History of Sexuality in Early America*, 94). My focus on the circumcised body as a confusing racial and sexual marker shows that such environmental articulations follow earlier templates and accounts of Barbary captivity narratives. See LaFleur, especially 63–102.

72. On European accounts of conversions for sexual reasons as well as the instruction of boys on European vessels in the Mediterranean, see Malcolm, "Forbidden Love in Istanbul."

73. *OED*, s.v. "unhappy," adj., 5.a.

74. On analyses of sadness as related to complex homoerotic affects and nonprocreation, see DiGangi, "Shakespeare after Queer Theory"; Sinfield, "How to Read *The Merchant of Venice* without Being Heterosexist"; and Lenthe, "Antonio's Sad Flesh."

75. *OED*, s.v. "fancy," v., 8, 8a.

76. Gainsford, *The Glory of England*, 199.

77. Gainsford eroticizes this youth who would later become an icon for Christian liberation from the Ottomans: "When a mighty Champion of *Persia* made a challenge to fight with any Turke for the honour of both Empires hand to hand, starknaked, and with single *Semiter* at last this *George Castriot* out of some diuine inspiration, and generous spirit, stepped foorth in the presence of the Emperour, not fully 18 yeere old, and without procrastinating the matter, stripped himselfe before them, and made them as much amazed at the beautifulnes . . . and comelinesse of his person, as greatnesse of courage, and shaking his sharp and glistring curtelax triumphantly ouer his head, approached the *Persian*, who by this time was prepared to the encounter, and in lesse then one quarter of

an houres trauersing the ground, closed with him, wrastled with him, stradled ouer him like a *Colossus*, after hee had layd him on his backe, and strucke off his head: for which hee was presently embraced in his sweat by the great Emperour, inuested with a robe of honour, proclaimed by the sound of a trumpet *Scanderbeg, quasi Alexander Magnus*, and aduanced to the dignity of *Generall* of the army" (*The Glory of England*, 199–200).

78. On European depictions of tortures Christian captives experienced in sexual terms, including sodomitical images of penetrating male bodies, see LaFleur, *The Natural History of Sexuality in Early America*, 63–102.

79. Burton, *Traffic and Turning*, 96–97.

80. Parker, "Preposterous Conversions," 4.

81. For more on Islam and Elizabethan Protestant relations as well as anti-Catholic sentiments and nationalism, see Robinson, *Islam and Early Modern Literature*.

82. Hakluyt, *The Principal Navigations*, 200.

83. Hakluyt, *The Principal Navigations*, 200.

84. Hakluyt, *The Principal Navigations*, 200–201.

CHAPTER 5. REGENDERING BOYS

A part of chapter 5 appeared as "Early Modern Eunuchs and the Transing of Gender and Race," *Journal for Early Modern Cultural Studies* 19, no. 4 (2019): 116–36, https://doi.org/10.1353/jem.2019.0040.

1. Neill, *The Tragedy of Anthony and Cleopatra*, 113.

2. I use "they/them" pronouns to refer to eunuchs to emphasize that their embodiments were historically perceived as gender nonconforming or beyond gender binary.

3. Matthew 19:11–12. Terence's *Eunuchus* is not about a real eunuch; it is about a lascivious young man disguised as a eunuch in order to enter the female space, where he often violates and then marries a woman. Fake eunuchs on Terence's model were the subject of several plays, especially toward the mid-seventeenth century. Examples include Thomas Middleton's *A Game at Chess* (1624), Peter Hausted's *The Rival Friends* (1632), John Ford's *The Fancies, Chaste and Noble* (1638), and William Wycherley's *The Country Wife* (1675).

4. Bosman, "'Best Play with Mardian,'" 124.

5. Such studies on eunuchs on the English stage rarely examine their probable links with Ottoman eunuchs. Elam ("The Fertile Eunuch"), for instance, traces the theatrical eunuch via Terence's *Eunuchus*. Bosman ("'Best Play with Mardian'") traces the influence of classical and Christian traditions in the theatrical figurations of the eunuch and notes that emerging racial ideologies associated eunuchs with black bodies, but he does not recognize black Ottoman eunuchs. Crawford (*Eunuchs and Castrati*) conflates eunuchs with castrated men in her examination of disability and does not consider Ottoman eunuchs in her exploration of theatrical eunuchs; she devotes her last chapter to race and Ottoman eunuchs, where she overemphasizes the power of black eunuchs, which in fact only a few had, to explain the racialized accounts of eunuchs in western texts.

6. Bosman, "'Best Play with Mardian,'" 124.

7. Gender crossings have historically been attributed to elsewhere, usually the "orient." Greco-Romans attributed sexual perversion, extravagance, luxury, decadence, effeminacy, and eunuchs to oriental Persians and Syrians, as is evident in stories of the

mythical Sardanapalus of Assyria, Nanarus of Babylonia, and the cross-dressing Assyrian queen Semiramis. See Isaac, *The Invention of Racism in Classical Antiquity*; and Balsdon, *Romans and Aliens*.

8. Qtd. in Taylor, *Castration*, 171.

9. Junne, *The Black Eunuchs of the Ottoman Empire*, 2–9.

10. The Byzantines invented the role of the castrated male vocalist in religious ceremonies, a practice that made its way to the castrati of early modern Europe. The Mamluks assigned a corps of eunuchs to the sacred duty of protecting the tomb of the Prophet Muhammad in Medina, a practice that the Ottomans also undertook in the early modern period. Eunuchs continued to oversee the Prophet's tomb until the mid-twentieth century. On eunuchs in Mesopotamia, see Asher-Greve, "Mesopotamian Conceptions of the Gendered Body." For Egypt, see Kadish, "Eunuchs in Ancient Egypt." For China, see Anderson, *Hidden Power*; and Chiang, *After Eunuchs*. For the Near East, see Weidemann, *Greek and Roman Slavery*. For the Mamluk Sultanate, see Ayalon, *Eunuchs, Caliphs, and Sultans*; and Marmon, *Eunuchs and Sacred Boundaries in Islamic Society*. For the Byzantine Empire, see Ringrose, *The Perfect Servant*; and Kuefler, *The Manly Eunuch*. For Europe, see Crawford, *Eunuchs and Castrati*; and Taylor, *Castration*. For the Ottoman Empire, see Hathaway, *Beshir Agha* and *The Chief Eunuch of the Ottoman Harem*.

11. Lad, "Panoptic Bodies," 162. For more on Ottoman harems, see Peirce, *The Imperial Harem*, which notes that a harem was the private quarters of a household—the inner circle—not just female space. The harem, with its signification of prohibited and sacred space, was where the sultan's body was. For more on the complex symbolic architectural structure of harems and the apartments of eunuchs, see Lad, "Panoptic Bodies."

12. For a biography of Beshir Agha in the context of Ottoman eunuchs, see Hathaway, *Beshir Agha*.

13. Peirce, *The Imperial Harem*, 11.

14. On mutes and dwarfs in the imperial palace, see Miles, "Signing in the Seraglio."

15. Ringrose (*The Perfect Servant*) analyzes eunuchs who were marked as a third gender that crossed and mediated between male and female worlds. Marmon (*Eunuchs and Sacred Boundaries in Islamic Society*) notes that their gender ambiguity enabled them to protect the Prophet's tomb in Islamicate societies. Taylor (*Castration*) notes their demarcation as a third gender in Latin texts. Most recently, Crawford (*Eunuchs and Castrati*) examined eunuchs with a focus on disability and normativity under the general rubric of castrates.

16. Hathaway, *Beshir Agha*, 13.

17. Penzer, *The Harem*, 149.

18. Noting that references to the ugliness of Africans "obviously smack of racism," Junne also stresses cultural differences in the method of castration: "the White eunuchs were not necessarily completely 'shaved,' while the Africans were" (*The Black Eunuchs of the Ottoman Empire*, 4). Crawford makes the same observation but points out that contemporary writers did not make such a distinction at all (*Eunuchs and Castrati*, 178–80).

19. For more on Galenic influences on gender in the early modern Ottoman world, see Ze'evi, *Producing Desire*, 16–47. On the regimes of the scrotum and the penis, see Taylor, *Castration*.

20. Bach, "Tennis Balls," 5. For more on the difference between premodern and modern conceptualizations of male sex, see Simons, *The Sex of Men in Premodern*

Europe. See also Howard and Rackin, who note that, in contrast to feudal patrilineal inheritance and reproductive prowess, a "performative masculinity" emerged in the early modern period that was shaped by the sexual conquest of women (*Engendering a Nation*, 17).

21. Fisher, *Materializing Gender in Early Modern English Literature and Culture*, 70.
22. Fisher, *Materializing Gender in Early Modern English Literature and Culture*, 70.
23. Bulwer, *Anthropometamorphosis*, 203.
24. Bulwer, *Anthropometamorphosis*, 204.
25. Cocles, *A Brief and most pleasant epiyomyne of the whole art of physiognomie*, sig. d2r.
26. Bulwer, *Anthropometamorphosis*, 243. Withers's account reads: "All eunuchs in the Seraglio may be in number about two hundred, what with old ones, middle aged, and young ones; they are all of them not only gelt, but have their yards also clean cut off, and are chosen of those *Renegado* youths, which are presented from time to time to the Grand Signior" (qtd. in Bon, *The Sultan's Seraglio*, 84).
27. Penzer, *The Harem*, 183.
28. I draw on Geraldine Heng's definition of race as "a structural relationship for the articulation and management of human differences, rather than a substantive content" (*The Invention of Race in the European Middle Ages*, 19). On premodern race, see Loomba and Burton, *Race in Early Modern England*; Loomba, "Identities and Bodies in Early Modern Studies"; Erickson and Hall, "A New Scholarly Song"; and Kaplan, *Figuring Racism in Medieval Christianity*.
29. Hathaway, *Beshir Agha*, 16.
30. Hathaway, *Beshir Agha*, 15.
31. Hathaway, *The Chief Eunuch of the Ottoman Harem*, 35.
32. Hathaway, *The Chief Eunuch of the Ottoman Harem*, 35.
33. Hathaway, *The Chief Eunuch of the Ottoman Harem*, 36.
34. Hathaway, *The Chief Eunuch of the Ottoman Harem*, 37. Likewise, Tezcan's cogent analysis of antiblack Ottoman treatises underlines "phobias" as "amplified in certain socio-political contexts" ("*Dispelling the Darkness* of the *Halberdier's Treatise*," 44). Lad notes the impact of changing racial discourses and market values on the separation of white and black eunuchs, yet still, he writes, it "may not be entirely understandable in terms of modern racial attitudes" ("Panoptic Bodies," 143).
35. Hall, *Things of Darkness*, 6, my italics.
36. See Goldenberg, *The Curse of Ham*; Lewis, *Race and Slavery in the Middle East*; Walz and Cuno, *Race and Slavery in the Middle East*; Gomez, *African Dominion*; and El Hamel, *Black Morocco*.
37. Qtd. in Lewis, *Race and Color in Islam*, 33.
38. Qtd. in Lewis, *Race and Color in Islam*, 34.
39. Qtd. in Lewis, *Race and Color in Islam*, 34.
40. Ibn Khaldun, *Muqaddimah*, 58–64.
41. Ibn Khaldun, *Muqaddimah*, 117.
42. For more on the animalization of slaves and "natural slaves," see Davis, *Inhuman Bondage*, 27–76.
43. El Hamel, *Black Morocco*, 58.
44. El Hamel, *Black Morocco*, 198.

45. As early as the late tenth century, the widespread practice of African eunuchism became a part of the slave market, as is evident in a Persian treatise written in 982CE: "The merchants steal their children and bring them with them. Then they castrate them, import them to Egypt, and sell them. Among themselves there are people who steal each other's children and sell them to the merchants when the latter arrive" (qtd. in Lewis, *Race and Color in Islam*, 35).

46. Erdem, *Slavery in the Ottoman Empire and Its Demise*, 58. On European slaves and differences between ethnicities, see Sobers-Khan, *Slaves without Shackles*.

47. For more on African slavery in the empire, see Toledano, *As If Silent and Absent* and *Slavery and Abolition in the Ottoman Middle East*; Erdem, *Slavery in the Ottoman Empire and Its Demise*; and Powell, "Will that Subaltern Ever Speak?"

48. For antiblack treatises in the context of preexisting templates, see Tezcan, "*Dispelling the Darkness* of the *Halberdier's Treatise*" and "*Dispelling the Darkness*: The Politics of 'Race' in the Early Seventeenth Century Ottoman Empire."

49. Brookes, "The Ottoman Gentleman of the Sixteenth Century," 53–55

50. Brookes, "The Ottoman Gentleman of the Sixteenth Century," 55–56.

51. Brookes, "The Ottoman Gentleman of the Sixteenth Century," 43.

52. Brookes, "The Ottoman Gentleman of the Sixteenth Century," 218.

53. Brookes, "The Ottoman Gentleman of the Sixteenth Century," 218–19.

54. Brookes, "The Ottoman Gentleman of the Sixteenth Century," 151. Nubia is traditionally the region along the Nile from south of the First Cataract to just north of today's Khartoum.

55. Brookes, "The Ottoman Gentleman of the Sixteenth Century," 152.

56. On Mullah Ali's life and work, see Tezcan, "*Dispelling the Darkness*: The Politics of 'Race' in the Early Seventeenth Century Ottoman Empire."

57. Tezcan records the ulema's resistance against Mullah Ali's escalation by noting that almost half of top positions in the ulema hierarchy in the period came from a total of eleven families ("*Dispelling the Darkness*: The Politics of 'Race' in the Early Seventeenth Century Ottoman Empire," 75).

58. Tezcan, "*Dispelling the Darkness*: The Politics of 'Race' in the Early Seventeenth Century Ottoman Empire," 74.

59. All these accounts are quoted in Tezcan, "*Dispelling the Darkness*: The Politics of 'Race' in the Early Seventeenth Century Ottoman Empire," 83.

60. Tezcan, "*Dispelling the Darkness*: The Politics of 'Race' in the Early Seventeenth Century Ottoman Empire," 85.

61. For more on the Latin "genus" and eunuchs as a third sex, see Taylor, *Castration*, 146–54. On how historical transformations of the concept of *cins/genus* informed the debates and enabled the contemporary dominant concepts and practices that shaped them and how *cins* came to mean sex and how this matters, see Najmabadi, who notes that the pre-nineteenth-century definition of *cins* or *jins* as "genus, kind, stock, sort, mode; gender; goods, movables, articles, things; grain, corn; crop, products" began to refer to sexuality in the mid-twentieth-century in Iran ("Genus of Sex or the Sexing of *Jins*," 212). Loomba suggests that like the racial, sexual, and gender connotations of Latin *gens* (kind), race in early modern England, with its connotations of family and lineage, was also related to sex and

that it "sometimes was used in the sense of species, or race, or nation, or national groups" ("Identities and Bodies in Early Modern Studies," 232).

62. Hathaway writes that "Africans of various 'races' (singular, *cins*, which derives from Latin *genus*)—Habeshi, Nubi, Sudani, Takruri—along with the *evlad-i 'Arab*, occupied a spectrum that also included eastern Anatolians, Kurds, and populations from the Caucasus" (*The Chief Eunuch of the Ottoman Harem*, 36).

63. Taylor, *Castration*, 147.

64. "*Un Enuque noir quy est auiourduy cadillesquier* [*kadiasker,* chief judge] *gouverne maintenant tout cet Empire*" (qtd. in Tezcan, "*Dispelling the Darkness*: The Politics of 'Race' in the Early Seventeenth Century Ottoman Empire," 81).

65. Qtd. in Tezcan, "*Dispelling the Darkness*: The Politics of 'Race' in the Early Seventeenth Century Ottoman Empire," 74. Tezcan notes that as the judge of Galata, Mullah Ali implemented a poll tax on foreign Christians residing in Istanbul. Despite many diplomatic and personal appeals, the judge did not relent. He was often criticized by European diplomats, merchants, and writers in Istanbul as a strict judge.

66. Brookes, "The Ottoman Gentleman of the Sixteenth Century," 231.

67. Brookes, "The Ottoman Gentleman of the Sixteenth Century," 44–45.

68. See *Risale-i teberdariyye fi ahval-ı aga-yı daru's-sa'ade* [Halberdier's treatise on the affairs of the chief black eunuch] written in 1741 by Dervis Abdullah, which sets essential genealogies of good and evil that are essentially linked with whites and blacks. This account also targets a black eunuch, the prominent chief black eunuch Beshir Agha. For more on this treatise, see Tezcan, "*Dispelling the Darkness* of the *Halberdier's Treatise.*"

69. Tezcan, "*Dispelling the Darkness* of the *Halberdier's Treatise*," 57.

70. For an extensive analysis of Mullah Ali's treatise, see Tezcan, "*Dispelling the Darkness*: The Politics of 'Race' in the Early Seventeenth Century Ottoman Empire." This genre goes back to early Islamicate writings. Jahiz of Basra, one of the most celebrated prose writers of classical Arabic literature, penned a treatise titled "Superiority of the Blacks against the White" in which he celebrates the beauty of blacks (Lewis, *Race and Color in Islam*, 31). Such accounts, as El Hamel proposes, are "evidence of color consciousness and a literary discourse in defense of blacks against Arab ethnocentricism" (*Black Morocco*, 85).

71. Qur'an 30:22; Tezcan, "*Dispelling the Darkness*: The Politics of 'Race' in the Early Seventeenth Century Ottoman Empire," 90.

72. Qtd. in Tezcan, "*Dispelling the Darkness*: The Politics of 'Race' in the Early Seventeenth Century Ottoman Empire," 93.

73. Taylor, *Castration*, 30.

74. Crawford, *Eunuchs and Castrati*, 124.

75. Late sixteenth-century records include information about two English-born eunuchs in the households of Uluç Ali Pasha and Ciğalazade Yusuf Sinan Pasha. Samson Rowlie, son of a Bristol merchant, was captured and castrated and served in the household of Uluç Ali. Rowlie reported that Ciğalazade's wife had one English eunuch in their household who was murdered because of her jealousy of the relationship between him and her husband (Graf, *The Sultan's Renegades*, 155–57).

76. For Dallam, see MacLean, *The Rise of Oriental Travel*, 3–47.

77. Qtd. in Junne, *The Black Eunuchs of the Ottoman Empire*, 134.

78. Sandys, *A Relation of a Journey*, 71.

79. Taylor, *Castration*, 152–53.

80. Sandys, *A Relation of a Journey*, 71.

81. Qtd. in Loomba and Burton, *Race in Early Modern England*, 204.

82. Baudier, *The history of the imperiall estate of the grand seigneurs*, 60–61.

83. Ringrose calls eunuchs "perfect servants," especially because of their ability to cross boundaries with bodies that did not reproduce (*The Perfect Servant*).

84. Baudier, *The history of the imperiall estate of the grand seigneurs*, 133. Accounts that called attention to the existence of individuals who chose to become eunuchs are not rare. Robert Withers claims that "few, or none of them, are gelt and cut against their will" (Bon, *The Sultan's Seraglio*, 84). Stories of eunuchs who were widely recognized to have consented to their gender transformation included that of the well-known Hungarian convert Gazanfer Agha, who voluntarily underwent a castration operation in order to become the sultan's companion and thereby maintain physical intimacy with him beyond the prohibited gates of the palace. Hathaway's observation that "there are accounts of castration performed within Topkapı Palace" also confirms that some recruited servant boys (*devşirme*) might have been asked to become eunuchs (*Beshir Agha*, 19). Whether they are true or not, such accounts force us to think about the possibility that this may have been a form of voluntary gender transition for at least some individuals. However, there appears to have been a racial dynamic involved in this process, since it was mostly white European boys rather than black Africans who underwent voluntary castration. Black Africans were usually already castrated when they were brought to the Ottoman court. Thus, this issue of will and consent in the making of eunuchs appears to have been racialized.

85. Rycaut, *The Present State of the Ottoman Empire*, 37.

86. Shakespeare also referred to eunuchs in *Cymbeline, Henry VI Part II, A Midsummer Night's Dream, Titus Andronicus*, and *Two Noble Kinsman*.

87. On the eunuch in *Anthony and Cleopatra* and the pairing of eunuchs and blackamoors, see Bosman, "'Best Play with Mardian.'"

88. Loomba, *Anthony and Cleopatra*.

89. *OED*, s.v. "renege," v., 2a.

90. *OED*, s.v. "renegado," n., 2. On *renegados*, see Matar, "The Renegade in English Seventeenth-Century Imagination" and *Islam in Britain, 1558–1685*; and Fuchs, "Faithless Empires." Birchwood traces the imagery of the renegade into the Civil War and argues that the figure of the renegade intensified in this period as Oliver Cromwell was depicted as a Turkish despot and his followers as renegades who betrayed the crown (*Staging Islam in England*, 96–128).

91. *OED*, s.v. "neger," n. and adj., 1a.

92. The stage directions in the folio edition list Mardian in 5.2.

93. The term "gypsy" signifies sorcery or magic and was attributed to Egyptians in the period. See Loomba's introduction to *Anthony and Cleopatra*. For more on the racialization of the "gypsy," see Wagner, "Outlandish People."

94. Some productions where Mardian is racialized are those at the Shakespeare Memorial Theater (1953), the Royal Shakespeare Company (1972, 2006, and 2017), the Globe

(2014), Stratford (2014), and Cape Town (2010). On performance history and the blackness of Cleopatra, see Rutter, *Anthony and Cleopatra*.

95. Blount, *A Voyage into the Levant*, 54. Attribution of gender inversion to Egyptians go back to Herodotus; see Loomba and Burton, *Race in Early Modern England*, 40–41.

96. Hanson, "*Antony and Cleopatra*," 49.

97. Elam, "The Fertile Eunuch," 1.

98. Elam, "The Fertile Eunuch," 6.

99. On Cesario's name and gender ambiguity in the play, see Orgel, *Impersonations*, 53.

100. Masten, *Queer Philologies*, 112.

101. On hermaphrodites, see Gilbert, *Early Modern Hermaphrodites*; Long, *Hermaphrodites in Renaissance Europe*; and DeVun, *The Shape of Sex*. On the parallels between anti-Jewish and anti-Muslim racism in premodern Christianity, see Kaplan, *Figuring Racism in Medieval Christianity*.

102. On the influence of the Ottomans in shaping the castrati, see Scholz, *Eunuchs and Castrati*. On Volpone's household as evocative of Mediterranean trade and consumerism, see Kolb, "'A Turk's mustachio.'" On Epicene's household as a seraglio, see Zeman, "Sultanic Drag in Ben Jonson's Epicene."

103. On Dryden's eunuch in the frame of "deformity," see Chow, "Showing the Eunuch."

104. Other Turk plays where eunuchs figure include Mason's *The Turke*, Daborne's *A Christian Turned Turk*, Glathorne's *The Revenge for Honor*, Carlell's *Osmond the Great Turk*, Davenant's *The Siege of Rhodes*, May's *Cleopatra*, and Massinger's *The Emperor of the East*.

105. Traub, "Mapping the Global Body," 84.

106. See, for instance, the Netherlandish painting of Rembrandt Harmenszoon van Rijn, Pieter Lastman, Leonaert Bramer, Salomon de Bray, Claes Corneliszoon Moayaert, and Salomon Koninck, among others.

107. See, for example, paintings by Jean-Auguste-Dominique Ingres, Jean-Léon Gérôme, Jean-Jules-Antoine Lecomte du Nouÿ, and Rudolf Ernst.

108. For the story of the black eunuch and the dildo, see Bardakçı, *Osmanlı'da Seks*, 197–200.

CHAPTER 6. STAGING BOYS, 1690–1990

1. Williams, *Our Moonlight Revels*, 24.
2. For the importance of the context and politics of each production in casting, be it colorblind or racialized, see Thompson, *Colorblind Shakespeare*.
3. Garber, *Vested Interests*, 92.
4. Menon, "Desire," 330.
5. Gui, "Bottom's Dream."
6. Jacobson, "A Note on Shakespeare's *A Midsummer Night's* Dream," 23.
7. Slights, "The Changeling in *A Dream*."
8. Dunn, "The Indian Boy's Dream."
9. Frosch, "The Missing Child in *A Midsummer Night's Dream*."
10. Faber, "Hermia's Dream," 188.
11. I thank the director Danny Scheie for sharing the recording of the production with me. For an image of the boy, see Hendricks, "'Obscured by dreams,'" 40.

12. Hendricks, "'Obscured by dreams,'" 38.
13. Hendricks, "'Obscured by dreams,'" 60.
14. Sinfield, "Cultural Materialism and Intertextuality," 74.
15. Sinfield, "Cultural Materialism and Intertextuality," 74.
16. Sinfield, "Cultural Materialism and Intertextuality," 75.
17. Unless stated otherwise, all references to promptbooks are from copies held at the Folger Shakespeare Library.
18. In 1662, Thomas Killigrew's staging was based on the complete text with dance sequences. Partial adaptations include *The Comedy of Pyramus and Thisbe* (before 1624), *Merry Conceited Humours of Bottom the Weaver* (in 1646); and Garrick's opera, *The Fairies* (in 1755). For the stage history in the eighteenth century, see Kehler, *A Midsummer Night's Dream*; Williams, *Our Moonlight Revels*; Chaudhuri, *A Midsummer Night's Dream*; and Griffiths, *A Midsummer Night's Dream*. For a history of scholarly approaches to the play, see Kehler, *A Midsummer Night's Dream*, 3–76.
19. Griffiths, *A Midsummer Night's Dream*, 127; Williams, *Our Moonlight Revels*, 25.
20. Reynolds, *A Midsummer Night's Dream*, 18.
21. Reynolds, *A Midsummer Night's Dream*, 18.
22. Williams, *Our Moonlight Revels*, 87.
23. Griffiths, *A Midsummer Night's Dream*, 127.
24. Burton, *Prompt book made by John Moore*, 6, Burton's italics.
25. Burton, *Prompt book made by John Moore*, 9.
26. Keene, *A Midsummer Night's Dream*, vi.
27. For such paintings of mistresses and exotic servants, see chapter 3.
28. Griffiths, *A Midsummer Night's Dream*, 126n120.
29. After Lucia Elizabeth Vestris acted Oberon in 1840s, "Oberon was played by a woman in every major English and American production of the play until 1914" (Williams, *Our Moonlight Revels*, 93).
30. I discuss Bottom as an erotic replacement for the Indian boy in chapter 3.
31. For more on Purcell's influence on Britten's adaptation and the popularity and influence of that adaptation, see Case, "Britten's Dream"; Godsalve, *Britten's "A Midsummer Night's Dream"*; and Küpper, *William Shakespeare's "A Midsummer Night's Dream."*
32. Case, "Britten's Dream," 108.
33. Williams, *Our Moonlight Revels*, 222.
34. Williams, *Our Moonlight Revels*, 222.
35. Williams, *Our Moonlight Revels*, 202.
36. Tommasini, "In Britten's Complex 'Dream,' a Balance of Light and Dark."
37. White, "ENO's Shocking New Paedophile *Midsummer Night's Dream* Is Brilliant."
38. White, "ENO's Shocking New Paedophile *Midsummer Night's Dream* Is Brilliant."
39. Harkins, "Foucault, the Family and the Cold Monster of Neoliberalism," 103. The "sex panics" that emerged in the late 1980s with "spectacularly mediatized" testimonies of adult survivors of incest and a series of rapes and murders of girls, as Amin notes, "have durably installed the pedophile as a figure of fear and loathing and an alibi for the extralegal extension of neoliberal surveillance, control, and regulation" (*Disturbing Attachments*, 24).
40. Fischel, *Sex and Harm in the Age of Consent*, 19.
41. Amin, *Disturbing Attachments*, 35, 26, Amin's italics.

42. Amin, *Disturbing Attachments*, 40–42. For more on the attribution of pederasty to the Orient, see El-Rouayheb, *Before Homosexuality in the Arab-Islamic World*; Al-Kassim, "Epilogue," 300–302; and Boone, "Modernist Re-Orientations" and *The Homoerotics of Orientalism*.

43. For Lim (*Brown Boys and Rice Queens*), sex between "brown boys and rice queens" and the eroticization of Asians and Asia as boyish are deeply interlinked with putative distinctions in maturity, temporal development, and power between Euro-North America and the Asias. Likewise, Pérez (*A Taste for Brown Bodies*) has noted that the civilizational temporality of Western modernity not only casts the figure of the premodern, childlike savage as backward but also produces nonegalitarian erotic encounters between him and the civilized white man.

44. Qtd. in Wood, "Creating the Sensual Child," 164. On the idealization of classical pederasty among nineteenth-century writers and intellectuals, see Cleves, *Unspeakable*.

45. On medieval clerics' formulation of pederasty as "the sin not fit to be named," see Elliott, *The Corrupter of Boys*, especially 230–35.

46. Sinfield, "Cultural Materialism and Intertextuality," 75.

47. On homosexual subcultures in New York City of the early twentieth century, see Chauncey, *Gay New York*.

48. Menon, "Desire," 330. Since Menon does not engage with any productions (as if all embodiments are the same and thus productions are not worth close examination), one can only guess, by references to Hendricks, that she has in mind this SSC production. For a critique of Menon, see DiGangi, who suggests that Menon "develops an antithesis between 'desire' and 'the body' that has significant, and I think troubling, implications for our understanding of the representation of gender, sexuality, and power in early modern dramatic texts" ("Early Modern Bodies that Matter," 33–34).

49. Glassman, "The Bondsman's New Clothes," 282.

CHAPTER 7. THE ORIENTALIZATION OF BOY LOVE

1. Citations to Atayi's story are from Andrews and Kalpaklı's translation (*The Age of Beloveds*, 59–62), which is followed by a profound analysis of the story in the context of homoerotic dynamics in early modern Istanbul (62–84). For an alternative translation and examination of homoeroticism in the story, see Boone, *The Homoerotics of Orientalism*, 10–16. For an edited version of *Heft Han* in modern Turkish, see Karacan, *Heft-han mesnevisi*.

2. Borris, *Same-Sex Desire in the English Renaissance*, 90.

3. Traub, *The Renaissance of Lesbianism in Early Modern England*.

4. On the Kadızadeli movement, see Zilfi, "The Kadızadelis." On the impact of this movement on the expression of homoeroticism, see Andrews and Kalpaklı, *The Age of Beloveds*, 320–24.

5. Jem first resided in Rhodes, which was under the control of the Knights of St. John. After that, he lived in safe custody in France, followed by papal custody in the Vatican. He was finally handed to Charles XII of France upon his entrance to Rome, who demanded that Pope Alexander Borgia give him Jem before his march on Naples, during which Jem suddenly fell ill and died in 1495, most probably as a result of being poisoned

by order of the pope. For the biography of Jem, see Altınay, *Sultan Cem*; and Okur, *Cem Sultan Hayatı ve Şiir Dünyası*.

6. Castiglione, *The Book of the Courtier*, 141.

7. In early modern Ottoman poetry, Jemshid is a literary figure who represents the mythic inventor of wine, evoking Bacchus.

8. Gibb, *A History of Ottoman Poetry*, 2:90–91. I made some alterations to Gibb's translation: I changed "this city with the King's Son of the Franks" to "this city of the French Prince" ("*şehrinde bu sehzade-i Efrenginun*"); "fair the frankish lovelings show" to "fair Frankish beauty" ("*Efrengi mahbub-i melik*"), and Gibb's use of plural in "their bright beauty" to the singular "his bright beauty," since the lines still refer to the French youth; the sun and moon are drunk because of their love for "his" beauty. For the poem in Turkish, see Ersoylu, *Cem Sultan'ın Türkçe Divanı*.

9. Since Jem was in Europe with his courtiers, who included poets, contemporary biographers disagree about which poems really belong to the prince and which to the poets in his circle. This poem is widely accepted as Jem's, although even if it were not, it still reflects the observations of one Ottoman elite in a European city. For an overview of the poem's authorship, see Çınar ("Geleneğe Direnen Bir Şair ve Şiiri"), who considers Jem to be the author of the poem.

10. *The Renegado* was first staged in 1621 and first printed in 1630. All references to the play, cited parenthetically, are from Vitkus, *Three Turk Plays*, 241–339.

11. See Vitkus, *Three Turk Plays*, 40–41.

12. Qtd. in El-Rouayheb, *Before Homosexuality in the Arab-Islamic World*, 62.

13. Qtd. in El-Rouayheb, *Before Homosexuality in the Arab-Islamic World*, 61.

14. Burton, "Terminal Essay," 206–207. See Boone, *The Homoerotics of Orientalism*, especially 50–100. On Burton's geographic zone in relation to the emerging field of sexology, see Kahan, *The Book of Minor Perverts*, 45–65.

15. For changing sexual discourses in the Ottoman Empire, see Sarıtaş, *Cinsel Normalliğin Kuruluşu*; and Ze'evi, *Producing Desire*. On Arabic-speaking regions under the Ottoman Empire, see El-Rouayheb, *Before Homosexuality in the Arab-Islamic World*. On a similar shift in Iranian context, see Najmabadi, *Women with Mustaches and Men without Beards*.

16. Sarıtaş, *Cinsel Normalliğin Kuruluşu*, 102.

17. "*Zen-dostlar çoğalup mahbublar azaldı. Kavm-i Lut sanki yere battı. Istanbul'da öteden beru delikanlılar icum maruf u muted olan aşk u alaka, hali tabiisi üzre kızlara muntahil oldu. . . . Kubera içinde gulamparelikle meşhur Kamil ve Ali Paşalar ile anlara mensub olanlar kalmadı. Halbuki Ali Paşa da ecanibin itirazlarindan ihtiraz ile gulampareliğini ihfaya çalışırdı*" (Ahmed Cevdet Paşa, *Maruzat*, 9). The translation to English is mine.

18. El-Rouayheb, *Before Homosexuality in the Arab-Islamic World*, 112–115; Peirce, "Seniority, Sexuality, and Social Order," 178.

19. See Ze'evi's examination of such historical shifts in medical, religious, legal and theatrical spheres in *Producing Desire*.

20. For more on heterosexualization in the process of modernization, see Sarıtaş, *Cinsel Normalliğin Kuruluşu*; and Kandiyoti, "Some Awkward Questions on Women and Modernity in Turkey," "Patterns of Patriarchy," and "Gendering the Modern."

21. Peirce, "Writing Histories of Sexuality in the Middle East," 1336.
22. Sarıtaş, *Cinsel Normalliğin Kuruluşu*, 27.
23. I follow the deployment of the genealogical method by Halperin, Traub, and Najmabadi, among others.
24. Sedgwick, *Epistemology of the Closet*, 47; Arvas, "From the Pervert Back to the Beloved," 145–63.
25. Lim, *Brown Boys and Rice Queens*, 4. See also Pérez, *A Taste for Brown Bodies*.
26. Hakluyt, *The Principal Navigations*, 200.

Bibliography

Adelman, Janet. "Iago's Alter Ego: Race as Projection in Othello." *Shakespeare Quarterly* 48, no. 2 (1997): 125–44.
Ahmed, Sara. *Queer Phenomenology: Orientation, Objects, Others*. Durham, NC: Duke University Press, 2006.
Ahmed Cevdet Paşa. *Maruzat*. Istanbul: Çağrı, 1980.
Akbari, Suzanne Conklin. *Idols in the East: European Representations of Islam and the Orient, 1100–1450*. Ithaca, NY: Cornell University Press, 2009.
Akerman, James R., ed. *Cartographies of Travel and Navigation*. Chicago: University of Chicago Press, 2006.
Akgündüz, Ahmet. *Osmanlı Kanunnameleri ve Hukuk Tahlilleri*. Vol 2. Istanbul: Fey Vakfı, 1990.
Akhimie, Patricia. *Shakespeare and the Cultivation of Difference: Race and Conduct in the Early Modern World*. New York: Routledge, 2018.
Aksan, Virginia. "Locating the Ottomans among Early Modern Empires." *Journal of Early Modern History* 3, no. 2 (1999): 103–34.
Aldrich, Robert F. *Colonialism and Homosexuality*. New York; London: Routledge, 2003.
Ali, Abdullah Yūsuf, trans. *The Holy Qur'ān: Text, Translation and Commentary*. New York: Tahrike Tarsile Qur'an, 2001.
Al-Kassim, Dina. "Epilogue: Sexual Epistemologies, East in West." In *Islamicate Sexualities: Translations across Temporal Geographies of Desire*, edited by Kathryn Babayan and Afsaneh Najmabadi, 297–339. Cambridge, MA: Harvard University Press, 2008.
Altınay, Ahmet Refik. *Sultan Cem*. Istanbul: İş Bankası Yayınları, 2001.
Amer, Sahar. *Crossing Borders: Love between Women in Medieval French and Arabic Literatures*. Philadelphia: University of Pennsylvania Press, 2008.
Amin, Kadji. *Disturbing Attachments: Genet, Modern Pederasty, and Queer History*. Durham, NC: Duke University Press, 2017.
Amussen, Susan. *Caribbean Exchanges: Slavery and the Transformation of English Society, 1640–1700*. Chapel Hill: University of North Carolina Press, 2007.
And, Metin. *A History of Theatre and Popular Entertainment in Turkey*. Ankara: Forum, 1963.

And, Metin. *Kırk Gün Kırk Gece: Eski Donanma ve Şenliklerinde Türk Sanatları.* Istanbul: Tac, 1959.

And, Metin. *Osmanlı Şenliklerinde Türk Sanatları.* Ankara: Kültür ve Turizm Bakanlığı, 1982.

And, Metin. *16. Yüzyılda Istanbul: Kent, Saray, Günlük Yaşam.* Istanbul: Yapı Kredi Yayınları, 2011.

Anderson, Mary. *Hidden Power: The Palace Eunuchs of Imperial China.* Buffalo: Prometheus, 1990.

Andrea, Bernadette. *The Lives of Girls and Women from the Islamic World in Early Modern British Literature and Culture.* Toronto: University of Toronto Press, 2017.

Andrea, Bernadette. *Women and Islam in Early Modern English Literature.* Cambridge: Cambridge University Press, 2007.

Andrea, Bernadette, and Linda McJannet. *Early Modern England and Islamic Worlds.* New York: Palgrave Macmillan, 2011.

Andrews, Walter G. *Poetry's Voice, Society's Song: Ottoman Lyric Poetry.* Seattle: University of Washington Press, 1985.

Andrews, Walter G. "Suppressed Renaissance: Q: When Is a Renaissance Not a Renaissance? A: When It Is the Ottoman Renaissance!" In *Other Renaissances: A New Approach to World Literature,* edited by Brenda Deen Schildgen, Gang Zhou, and Sander L. Gilman, 17–33, New York: Palgrave Macmillan, 2006.

Andrews, Walter G., and Mehmet Kalpaklı. *The Age of Beloveds: Love and the Beloved in Early Modern Ottoman and European Culture and Society.* Durham, NC: Duke University Press, 2005.

Andrews, Walter G., and Mehmet Kalpaklı. *Sevgililer Çağı: Erken Modern Osmanlı-Avrupa Kültürü ve Toplumunda Aşk ve Sevgili.* Translated by Y. Zeynep Yelçe. Istanbul: Yapı Kredi Yayınları, 2016.

Anonymous. *The Estate of Christians, living under the subjection of the Turke.* London, 1595.

Anonymous. *An Exact description of Prince Ruperts Malignant She-Monkey, a great Delinquent having approved her selfe a better servant then his white Dog called Boy.* London, 1643.

Anonymous. *The Humerous Tricks and Conceits of Prince Roberts Malignant She-Monkey, discovered to the world before her marriage. Also the manner of her marriage to a cavaleer and how within three dayes space, she called him cuckold to his face.* London, 1643.

Aravamudan, Srinivas. *Enlightenment Orientalism: Resisting the Rise of the Novel.* Chicago: University of Chicago Press, 2012.

Aravamudan, Srinivas. *Tropicopolitans: Colonialism and Agency, 1688–1804.* Durham, NC: Duke University Press, 1999.

Araz, Yahya. *16. Yüzyıldan 19. Yüzyıl Başlarına Osmanlı Toplumunda Çocuk Olmak.* Istanbul: Kitap, 2013.

Ariès, Philippe. *Centuries of Childhood: A Social History of Family Life.* New York: Alfred A. Knopf, 1962.

Arifi. *Süleymanname.* Edited by Esin Atıl. London: National Gallery of Art, 1986.

Arondekar, Anjali. "The Voyage Out: Transacting Sex under Globalization." *Feminist Studies* 33, no. 2 (2007): 227–349.

Arslan, Mehmet. "Osmanlı Saray Düğünleri ve Şenlikleri ve Bu Konuda Yazılan Eserler: Sûrnâmeler." In Arslan, *Osmanlı (Edebiyat-Tarih-Kültür) Makaleleri*, 169–89. Istanbul: Kitabevi, 2000.

Artan, Tulay, and Irvin Cemil Schick. "Ottomanizing Pornotopia: Changing Visual Codes in Eighteenth-Century Ottoman Erotic Miniatures." In *Eros and Sexuality in Islamic Art*, edited by F. Leoni and M. Natif, 157–207. London: Ashgate, 2013.

Arvas, Abdulhamit. "From the Pervert Back to the Beloved: Homosexuality and Ottoman Literary History, 1453–1923." In *The Cambridge History of Gay and Lesbian Literature*, edited by E. L. McCallum and Mikko Tuhkanen, 145–63. Cambridge: Cambridge University Press, 2014.

Arvas, Abdulhamit. "The Ottomans in and of Europe." In *England's Asian Renaissance*, edited by Carmen Nocentelli and Su Fang Ng, 31–54. Newark: University of Delaware Press, 2021.

Arvas, Abdulhamit. "Queers In-Between: Globalizing Sexualities, Local Resistances." In *The Postcolonial World*, edited by Jyotsna Singh and David D. Kim, 97–116. New York: Routledge, 2017.

Asher-Greve, Julia M. "Mesopotamian Conceptions of the Gendered Body." In *Gender and the Body in the Ancient Mediterranean*, edited by Maria Wyke, 8–37. Malden, MA: Blackwell, 1998.

Aşık Çelebi. *Meşa'irü'ş-Şu'ara*. Edited by Filiz Kılıç. Istanbul: Istanbul Araştırmaları Enstitüsü, 2010.

Aşıkpaşazade. *Manakib u Tevarih-u Al-i Osman: Osmanlıoğulları'nın Tarihi*. Edited by Kemal Yavuz and Yekta Sarac. Istanbul: K Kitaplığı, 2003.

Atasoy, Nurhan, ed. *1582 Sûrnâme-i Hümayun/An Imperial Celebration*. Istanbul: Koç, 1997.

Atshan, Sa'ed. *Queer Palestine and the Empire of Critique*. Stanford, CA: Stanford University Press, 2020.

Ayalon, David. *Eunuchs, Caliphs, and Sultans: A Study of Power Relationships*. Jerusalem: Magnes, 1999.

Aynur, Hatice, and Aslı Niyazioğlu, eds. *Aşık Çelebi ve Şairler Tezkiresi Üzerine Yazılar*. Istanbul: Koç, 2011.

Babinger, Franz. *Mehmed the Conqueror and His Time*. Princeton, NJ: Princeton University Press, 1978.

Bach, Rebecca Ann. "Tennis Balls: *Henry V* and Testicular Masculinity; or, According to the OED, Shakespeare Doesn't Have Any Balls." *Renaissance Drama*, n.s., 30 (2001): 3–23.

Balsdon, J. P. V. D. *Romans and Aliens*. Chapel Hill: University of North Carolina Press, 1979.

Barbour, Richmond Tyler. *Before Orientalism: London's Theatre of East, 1576–1626*. Cambridge: Cambridge University Press, 2003.

Bardakçı, Murat. *Osmanlı'da Seks*. Istanbul: Inkılap, 2005.

Barkan, Leonard. *Transuming Passion: Ganymede and the Erotics of Humanism*. Stanford, CA: Stanford University Press, 1991.

Barkey, Karen. *Empire of Difference: The Ottomans in Comparative Perspective*. Cambridge: Cambridge University Press, 2008.

Barnfield, Richard. *The Complete Poems*. Edited by George Klawitter. Selinsgrove, PA: Susquehanna University Press, 1990.

Barnes, Trevor J., and Derek Gregory, eds. *Reading Human Geography: The Poetics and Politics of Inquiry*. London: Arnold, 1997.

Bartels, Emily. *Spectacles of Strangeness: Imperialism, Alienation, and Marlowe*. Philadelphia: University of Pennsylvania Press, 1993.

Bartels, Emily. "Too Many Blackamoors: Deportation, Discrimination, and Elizabeth." *Studies in English Literature 1500–1900* 46, no. 2 (2005): 305–22.

Barthelemy, Anthony. *Black Face, Maligned Race: The Representation of Blacks in English Drama from Shakespeare to Southerne*. Baton Rouge: Louisiana State University Press, 1987.

Baudier, Michel. *The history of the imperiall estate of the grand seigneurs, their habitations, liues, titles . . . gouernment and tyranny*. Translated by E. G. [Edward Grimeston]. London, 1635.

Bell, David, and Gill Valentine. "Introduction: Orientations." In *Mapping Desire: Geographies of Sexualities*, edited by David Bell and Gill Valentine, 1–27. New York: Routledge, 1994.

Belsey, Catherine. "Shakespeare's Little Boys: Theatrical Apprenticeship and the Construction of Childhood." In *Rematerializing Shakespeare: Authority and Representation on the Early Modern Stage*, edited by Bryan Reynolds and William N. West, 53–72. New York: Palgrave Macmillan, 2005.

Ben-Amos, Ilana Krausman. *Adolescence and Youth in Early Modern England*. New Haven, CT: Yale University Press, 1994.

Berco, Christian. *Sexual Hierarchies, Public Status: Men, Sodomy, and Society in Spain's Golden Age*. Toronto: University of Toronto Press, 2007.

Bernstein, Robin. *Racial Innocence: Performing American Childhood from Slavery to Civil Rights*. New York: New York University Press, 2011.

Bindman, David, and Henry Louis Gates Jr. *The Image of the Black in Western Art*. 5 vols. Cambridge, MA: Harvard University Press, 2010.

Birchwood, Matthew. *Staging Islam in England: Drama and Culture, 1640–1685*. Cambridge, UK: Boydell and Brewer, 2007.

Birchwood, Matthew, and Matthew Dimmock, eds. *Cultural Encounters between East and West, 1453–1699*. Newcastle-on-Tyne: Cambridge Scholars Press, 2005.

Bisaha, Nancy. *Creating East and West: Renaissance Humanists and the Ottoman Turks*. Philadelphia: University of Pennsylvania Press, 2004.

Blakely, Allison. *Blacks in the Dutch World: The Evolution of Racial Imagery in a Modern Society*. Bloomington: Indiana University Press. 1993.

Blayney, Peter W. M. *The Bookshops in Paul's Cross Churchyard*. London: Bibliographical Society, 1990.

Bloom, Gina. "'Thy Voice Squeaks': Listening for Masculinity on the Early Modern Stage." *Renaissance Drama* 29 (1998): 39–71.

Blount, Henry. *A Voyage into the Levant: A brief Relation of a Journey lately performed from England . . . with particular observations concerning the modern condition of the Turks*. London, 1634.

Blount, Thomas. *Glossographia: or, a Dictionary Interpreting all such Hard Words . . . as are now used in our refined English Tongue*. London, 1656.

Bly, Mary. "Carnal Geographies: Mocking and Mapping the Religious Body." In *Masculinity and the Metropolis of Vice, 1550–1650*, edited by Amanda Bailey and Roze Hentschell, 89–113. New York: Palgrave Macmillan, 2010.

Bly, Mary. *Queer Virgins and Virgin Queans on the Early Modern Stage*. Oxford: Oxford University Press, 2000.

Boehrer, Bruce. "Economies of Desire in *A Midsummer Night's Dream*." *Shakespeare Studies* 32 (2004): 99–117.

Bon, Ottaviano. *The Sultan's Seraglio: An Intimate Portrait of Life at the Ottoman Court*. Edited by Godfrey Goodwin. London: Saqi Books, 1996.

Boone, Joseph. *The Homoerotics of Orientalism*. New York: Columbia University Press, 2014.

Boone, Joseph. "Modernist Re-Orientations: Imagining Homoerotic Desire in the 'Nearly' Middle East." *Modernism/modernity* 17, no. 3 (2010): 561–605.

Borris, Kenneth, ed. *Same-Sex Desire in the English Renaissance: A Sourcebook of Texts, 1470–1650*. New York: Routledge, 2004.

Bosman, Anston. "'Best Play with Mardian': Eunuch and Blackamoor as Imperial Culturegram." *Shakespeare Studies* 34 (2006): 123–57.

Boswell, John. *Christianity, Social Tolerance, and Homosexuality: Gay People in Western Europe from the Beginning of the Christian Era to the Fourteenth Century*. Chicago: University of Chicago Press, 1980.

Boswell, John. *The Kindness of Strangers: The Abandonment of Children in Western Europe from Late Antiquity to the Renaissance*. Chicago: University of Chicago Press, 1998.

Boulton, Jeremy. *Neighborhood and Society: A London Suburb in the Seventeenth Century*. Cambridge: Cambridge University Press, 1987.

Boyarin, Daniel. "Othello's Penis: Or, Islam in the Closet." In *Shakesqueer: A Queer Companion to the Complete Works of Shakespeare*, edited by Madhavi Menon, 254–62. Durham, NC: Duke University Press, 2011.

Braudel, Fernand. *The Mediterranean and the Mediterranean World in the Age of Philip II*. Vol. 2. New York: Harper and Row, 1972.

Bray, Alan. *The Friend*. Chicago: University of Chicago Press, 2003.

Bray, Alan. *Homosexuality in Renaissance England*. London: Gay Men's Press, 1982.

Bredbeck, Gregory W. *Sodomy and Interpretation: Marlowe to Milton*. Ithaca, NY: Cornell University Press, 1991.

Britton, Dennis. *Becoming Christian: Race, Reformation, and Early Modern English Romance*. New York: Fordham University Press, 2014.

Britton, Dennis. "Muslim Conversion and Circumcision as Theater." In *Religion and Drama in Early Modern England: The Performance of Religion on the Renaissance Stage*, edited by Jane H. Degenhardt and Elizabeth Williamson, 71–88. Farnham, Surrey, England: Ashgate, 2011.

Bromley, James. "Cruisy Historicism: Sartorial Extravagance and Public Sexual Culture in Ben Jonson's *Every Man Out of His Humour*." *Journal for Early Modern Cultural Studies* 16, no. 2 (2016): 21–58.

Bromley, James. *Intimacy and Sexuality in the Age of Shakespeare*. Cambridge: Cambridge University Press, 2012.

Brookes, Douglas S. "The Ottoman Gentleman of the Sixteenth Century: Mustafa Ali's Mevaidun-Nefais Fi Kavaidil-Mecalis: 'Tables of Delicacies concerning the Rules of Social Gatherings.'" PhD diss., Harvard University, 1998.

Brotton, Jerry. *The Renaissance Bazaar: From the Silk Road to Michelangelo*. Oxford: Oxford University Press, 2002.

Brotton, Jerry. *Trading Territories: Mapping the Early Modern World*. Ithaca, NY: Cornell University Press, 1997.

Brown, Georgia. *Redefining Elizabethan Literature*. Cambridge: Cambridge University Press, 2009.

Brown, Steve. "The Boyhood of Shakespeare's Heroines: Notes on Gender Ambiguity in the Sixteenth Century." *Studies in English Literature 1500–1900* 30, no. 2 (1990): 243–63.

Brummett, Palmira. *Ottoman Seapower and Levantine Diplomacy in the Age of Discovery*. Albany: State University of New York Press, 1994.

Bryan, Emily Drugge. "In the Company of Boys: The Place of the Boy Actor in Early Modern English Culture." PhD diss., Northwestern University, 2005.

Buchanan, Henry. "'India' and the Golden Age in *A Midsummer Night's Dream*." *Shakespeare Survey* 65 (2012): 58–68.

Bulliet, Richard W. *The Case for Islamo-Christian Civilization*. New York: Columbia University Press, 2004.

Bulwer, John. *Anthropometamorphosis: Man Transform'd: or, the Artificial Changeling*. London: Printed for J. Hardesty, 1650.

Burford, E. J., and Joy Wotton. *Private Vices—Public Virtues*. London: Robert Hale Limited, 1995.

Burton, Jonathan. "Race." In *A Cultural History of Western Empires in the Renaissance*, edited by Ania Loomba, 203–23. London: Bloomsbury, 2019.

Burton, Jonathan. *Traffic and Turning: Islam and English Drama, 1579–1624*. Newark: University of Delaware Press, 2005.

Burton, Jonathan. "Western Encounters with Sex and Bodies in Non-European Cultures, 1550–1750." In *The Routledge History of Sex and the Body*, edited by Sarah Toulalan and Kate Fisher, 495–510. New York: Routledge, 2013.

Burton, Richard. "Terminal Essay." In *The Book of a Thousand Nights and a Night: A Plain and Literal Translation of the Arab Nights Entertainments*, vol. 10, translated by Richard F. Burton, 206–7. London: Burton Club, 1886.

Burton, William E. *Prompt book made by John Moore*. 1854. PROMPT M.N.D. 21. Folger Shakespeare Library, Washington, DC.

Busse, Claire M. "Profitable Children: Children as Commodities in Early Modern England." In *Domestic Arrangements in Early Modern England*, edited by Kari Boyd McBride, 209–43. Pittsburgh, PA: Duquesne University Press, 2002.

Cadden, Joan. *The Meanings of Sex Difference in the Middle Ages: Medicine, Science, and Culture*. Cambridge: Cambridge University Press, 1993.

Çakırlar, Cüneyt, and Serkan Delice. *Cinsellik Muamması: Turkiye'de Queer Kültür ve Muhalefet (The Sexuality Conundrum: Queer Culture and Dissidence in Turkey)*. Istanbul: Metis, 2012.

Calbi, Maurizio. "Unshap't Bodies: Masculinity Travels East." In *Cultural Encounters between East and West, 1453–1699*, edited by Matthew Birchwood and Matthew Dimmock, 132–44. Newcastle-upon-Tyne: Cambridge Scholars Press, 2005.

Callaghan, Dympna. "What Is an Audience?" In *Shakespeare without Women: Representing Gender and Race on the Renaissance Stage*, edited by Dympna Callaghan, 139–65. London: Routledge, 2000.

Campana, Joseph. "Boy Toys and Liquid Joys: Pleasure and Power in the Bower of Bliss." *Modern Philology* 106, no. 3 (2009): 465–96.

Campana, Joseph. "Shakespeare's Children." *Literature Compass* 8, no. 1 (2011): 1–14.

Campana, Joseph. "Traffic in Children: Shipwrecked Shakespeare, Precarious Pericles." In *Childhood, Education, and the Stage in Early Modern England*, edited by Richard Preiss and Deanne Williams, 37–57. Cambridge: Cambridge University Press, 2017.

Capp, Bernard. "Gender and the Culture of the English Alehouse in Late Stuart England." In *The Trouble with Ribs: Women, Men and Gender in Early Modern Europe*, edited by Anu Korhonen and Kate Lowe, 103–27. Helsinki: Collegium, 2007.

Carter, Sarah. *Ovidian Myth and Sexual Deviance in Early Modern English Literature*. New York: Palgrave Macmillan, 2011.

Casale, Giancarlo. *The Ottoman Age of Exploration*. Oxford: Oxford University Press. 2010.

Casale, Giancarlo. "Seeing the Past: Maps and Ottoman Historical Consciousness." In *Writing History at the Ottoman Court: Editing the Past, Fashioning the Future*, edited by H. Erdem Çıpa and Emine Fetvacı, 80–99. Bloomington: Indiana University Press, 2013.

Case, Sue-Ellen. "Britten's Dream." In Philip Brett, *Music and Sexuality in Britten: Selected Essays*, edited by George E. Haggerty, 106–28. Berkeley: University of California Press, 2006.

Castiglione, Baldassare. *The Book of the Courtier*. Translated by L. E. Opdycke. New York: Charles Scribner's Sons, 1903.

Chakrabarty, Dipesh. *Provincializing Europe: Postcolonial Thought and Historical Difference*. Princeton, NJ: Princeton University Press, 2000.

Chakravarty, Urvashi. *Fictions of Consent: Slavery, Servitude, and Free Service in Early Modern England*. Philadelphia: University of Pennsylvania Press, 2022.

Chakravarty, Urvashi. "More than Kin, Less than Kind: Similitude, Strangeness, and Early Modern English Homonationalisms." *Shakespeare Quarterly* 67, no. 1 (2016): 14–29.

Chalkokondyles, Laonikos. *The Histories*. Vol. 2. Translated by Anthony Kaldellis, 259–61. Cambridge, MA: Harvard University Press, 2014,

Chaudhuri, Sukanta, ed. *A Midsummer Night's Dream*. London: Bloomsbury, 2017.

Chauncey, George. *Gay New York: Gender, Urban Culture, and the Making of the Gay Male World, 1890–1940*. New York: Basic Books, 1994.

Chedgzoy, Kate, Susanne Greenhalgh, and Robert Shaughnessy, eds. *Shakespeare and Childhood*. Cambridge: Cambridge University Press, 2007.

Cheney, Patrick. "'The Passionate Shepherd to His Love' and *Hero and Leander*." In *Christopher Marlowe at 450*, edited by Sara Munson Deats and Robert A. Logan, 163–200. New York: Ashgate, 2015.

Cheney, Patrick, and Brian J. Striar. *The Collected Poems of Christopher Marlowe*. Oxford: Oxford University Press, 2006.

Chiang, Howard. *After Eunuchs: Science, Medicine, and the Transformation of Sex in Modern China*. New York: Columbia University Press, 2018.

Chow, Jeremy. "Showing the Eunuch: Disability, Sexuality, and Dryden's *All for Love*." In *Castration, Impotence, and Emasculation in the Long Eighteenth Century*, edited by Anne Greenfield, 105–24. New York: Routledge, 2020.

Çiçek, Kemal, ed. *Pax Ottomana: Studies in Memoriam Prof. Nejat Goyunc*. Ankara: Yeni Turkiye, 2001.

Çınar, Bekir. "Geleneğe Direnen Bir Şair ve Şiiri: Cem Sultan'ın Frengistan Kasidesi." *Turkish Studies International Periodical for Languages, Literature and History of Turkish or Turkic* 2, no. 4 (2007): 274–82.

Çıpa, H. Erdem. "Changing Perceptions about Christian-Born Ottomans: Anti-kul Sentiments in Ottoman Historiography." In *Disliking Others: Loathing, Hostility, and Distrust in Premodern Ottoman Lands*, edited by Hakan Karateke, H. Erdem Çıpa, and Helga Anetshofer, 1–21. Boston: Academic Studies, 2018.

Cirakman, Asli. *From the "Terror of the World" to the "Sick Man of Europe": European Images of Ottoman Empire and Society from the Sixteenth Century to the Nineteenth*. New York: P. Lang, 2002.

Cleves, Rachel Hope. *Unspeakable: A Life beyond Sexual Morality*. Chicago: University of Chicago, 2020.

Clines, Robert John. *A Jewish Jesuit in the Eastern Mediterranean: Early Modern Conversion, Mission, and the Construction of Identity*. Cambridge: Cambridge University Press, 2020.

Cocles, Bartholomeus. *A Brief and most pleasant epiyomyne of the whole art of physiognomie*. London, 1556.

Cohen, Jeffrey Jerome. "On Saracen Enjoyment: Some Fantasies of Race in Late Medieval France and England." *Journal of Medieval and Early Modern Studies* 31, no. 1 (2001): 113–46.

Coke, Edward. *The Third Part of the Institutes of the Laws of England*. London, 1644.

Colley, Linda. *Captives: Britain, Empire, and the World, 1600–1850*. New York: Anchor Books, 2004.

Colomina, Beatriz, and Jennifer Bloomer. *Sexuality and Space*. New York: Princeton Architectural Press, 1992.

Cooper, Thomas. *Thesarus*. London, 1578.

Crane, Thomas. "Illicit Privacy and Outdoor Spaces in Early Modern England." *Journal for Early Modern Cultural Studies* 9, no. 1 (2009): 4–22.

Crawford, Katherine. *Eunuchs and Castrati: Disability and Normativity in Early Modern Europe*. New York: Routledge, 2019.

Crewe, Jonathan. *Hidden Desires*. New York: Methuen, 1986.

Dabhoiwala, Faramerz. "The Pattern of Sexual Immorality in Seventeenth- and Eighteenth-Century London." In *Londinopolis: Essays in the Cultural and Social History of Early Modern London*, edited by Paul Griffiths and Mark S. R. Jenner, 86–106. Manchester: Manchester University Press, 2001.

Dabydeen, David, James Gilmore, and Cecily Jones, eds. *The Oxford Companion to Black British History*. Oxford: Oxford University Press, 2007.

Daileader, Celia R. "Back Door Sex: Renaissance Gynosodomy, Aretino, and the Exotic." *ELH* 69, no. 2 (2002): 303–34.

Darcy, Robert F. "'Under my hands... a double duty': Printing and Pressing Marlowe's *Hero and Leander*." *Journal for Early Modern Cultural Studies* 2, no. 2 (2002): 26–56.

Dávid, Géza, and Pál Fodor, eds. *Ransom Slavery along the Ottoman Borders: Early Fifteenth–Early Eighteenth Centuries*. Leiden: Brill, 2007.

Davies, Surekha. *Renaissance Ethnography and the Invention of the Human: New World, Maps and Monsters*. Cambridge: Cambridge University Press, 2016.

Davis, David Brion. *Inhuman Bondage: The Rise and Fall of Slavery in the New World*. Oxford: Oxford University Press, 2006.

De Certeau, Michel. *The Practice of Everyday Life*. Berkeley: University of California Press, 1984.

Degenhardt, Jane Hwang. *Islamic Conversion and Christian Resistance on the Early Modern Stage*. Edinburgh: Edinburgh University Press, 2010.

Delany, Samuel R. *Times Square Red, Times Square Blue*. New York: New York University Press, 2009.

Delice, Serkan. "The Janissaries and Their Bedfellows: Masculinity and Male Friendship in Eighteenth-Century Ottoman Istanbul." In *Gender and Sexuality in Muslim Cultures*, edited by Gul Ozyegin, 115–36. New York: Ashgate, 2015.

Deng, Stephen. "Global Œconomy: Ben Jonson's *The Staple of News* and The Ethics of Mercantilism." In *Global Traffic: Discourses and Practices of Trade in English Literature and Culture from 1550 to 1700*, edited by Stephen Deng and Barbara Sebek, 245–63. New York: Palgrave Macmillan, 2008.

Desmet, Christy. "Disfiguring Women with Masculine Tropes: A Rhetorical Reading of *A Midsummer Night's Dream*." In *A Midsummer Night's Dream: Critical Essays*, edited by Dorothea Kehler, 299–329. New York: Garland, 1998.

DeVun, Leah. *The Shape of Sex: Nonbinary Gender from Genesis to the Renaissance*. New York: Columbia University Press, 2021.

DiGangi, Mario. "Asses and Wits: The Homoerotics of Mastery in Satiric Comedy." *English Literary Renaissance* 25, no. 2 (1995): 179–208.

DiGangi, Mario. "Early Modern Bodies that Matter." In *The Routledge Companion to Women, Sex, and Gender in the Early British Colonial World*, edited by Eve Keller and Kimberly Anne Coles, 33–45. New York: Routledge, 2018.

DiGangi, Mario. *The Homoerotics of Early Modern Drama*. Cambridge: Cambridge University Press, 1997.

DiGangi, Mario. *Sexual Types: Embodiment, Agency, and Dramatic Character from Shakespeare to Shirley*. Philadelphia: University of Pennsylvania Press, 2011.

DiGangi, Mario. "Shakespeare after Queer Theory." In *The Book in History, the Book as History: New Intersections of the Material Text*, edited by Heidi Brayman Hackel, Jesse M. Lander, and Zachary Lesser, 65–85. New Haven, CT: Yale University Press, 2016.

Dimmock, Matthew. *New Turkes: Dramatizing Islam and the Ottomans in Early Modern England*. Burlington, VT: Ashgate, 2005.

Dimmock, Matthew. "Tudor Turks: Ottomans Speaking English in Early Modern Sultansbriefe." *English Literary Renaissance* 50, no. 3 (2020): 335–58.

Dinshaw, Carolyn. "Got Medieval?" *Journal of the History of Sexuality* 10, no. 2 (2001): 202–12.

Doğan, Muhammed Nur, ed. *Fatih Divanı ve Şerhi (Metin, Nesre Çeviri ve Şerh)*. Istanbul: Erguvan, 2004.

Dollimore, Jonathan. *Sexual Dissidence*. 2nd ed. Oxford: Oxford University Press, 2018.

Dolven, Jeff. *Scenes of Instruction in Renaissance Romance*. Chicago: University of Chicago Press, 2007.

Duncan, Nancy. "Introduction: (Re)placings." In *Bodyspace: Destabilizing Geographies of Gender and Sexuality*, edited by Nancy Duncan, 1–12. London: Routledge, 1996.

Dunn, Allen. "The Indian Boy's Dream Wherein Every Mother's Son Rehearses His Part: Shakespeare's *A Midsummer Night's Dream*." *Shakespeare Studies* 20 (1988): 15–32.

Dursteler, Eric. *Renegade Women: Gender, Identity, and Boundaries in the Early Modern Mediterranean*. Baltimore, MD: Johns Hopkins University Press, 2011.

Earle, T. F., and K. J. P. Lowe, eds. *Black Africans in Renaissance Europe*. Cambridge: Cambridge University Press, 2005.

Edelman, Lee. *No Future: Queer Theory and the Death Drive*. Durham, NC: Duke University Press, 2004.

Edney, Matthey H. *Mapping an Empire: The Geographical Construction of British India, 1765–1843*. Chicago: University of Chicago Press, 1997.

Elam, Keir. "The Fertile Eunuch: Twelfth Night, Early Modern Intercourse, and the Fruits of Castration." *Shakespeare Quarterly* 47, no. 1 (1996): 1–36.

El Hamel, Chouki. *Black Morocco: A History of Slavery, Race, and Islam*. Cambridge: Cambridge University Press, 2013.

Elliott, Dyan. *The Corrupter of Boys: Sodomy, Scandal, and the Medieval Clergy*. Philadelphia: University of Pennsylvania Press, 2020.

Ellis, Jim. *Sexuality and Citizenship: Metamorphosis in Elizabethan Erotic Verse*. Toronto: University of Toronto Press, 2003.

El-Rouayheb, Khaled. *Before Homosexuality in the Arab-Islamic World, 1500–1800*. Chicago: University of Chicago Press, 2005.

El-Rouayheb, Khaled. "The Love of Boys in Arabic Poetry of the Early Ottoman Period 1500–1800." *Middle Eastern Literatures* 8, no. 1 (2005): 1–22.

Emiralioğlu, M. Pınar. *Geographical Knowledge and Imperial Culture in the Early Modern Ottoman Empire*. Burlington, VT: Ashgate, 2014.

Eng, David L. *Racial Castration: Managing Masculinity in Asian America*. Durham, NC: Duke University Press, 2001.

Eng, David L., Judith Halberstam, and José Esteban Muñoz. "What's Queer about Queer Studies Now?" *Social Text* 23, no. 3–4 (2005): 1–17.

Enterline, Lynn. "Elizabethan Minor Epics." In *The Oxford History of Classical Reception in English*, vol. 2, edited by Patrick Cheney and Philip Hardie, 253–71. Oxford: Oxford University Press, 2016.

Enterline, Lynn. *The Rhetoric of the Body from Ovid to Shakespeare*. Cambridge: Cambridge University Press, 2000.

Enterline, Lynn. *Shakespeare's Schoolroom: Rhetoric, Discipline, Emotion*. Philadelphia: University of Pennsylvania Press, 2012.

Erdem, Hakan Y. *Slavery in the Ottoman Empire and Its Demise, 1800–1909*. New York: St. Martin's, 1996.
Erickson, Peter. "Invisibility Speaks: Servants and Portraits in Early Modern Visual Culture." *Journal for Early Modern Cultural Studies* 9, no. 1 (2009): 23–61.
Erickson, Peter. "Representations of Blacks and Blackness in the Renaissance." *Criticism* 35, no. 4 (1993): 499–526.
Erickson, Peter. "Representations of Race in Renaissance Art." *Upstart Crow: A Shakespeare Journal* 18 (1998): 2–9.
Erickson, Peter, and Kim F. Hall. "'A New Scholarly Song': Rereading Early Modern Race." *Shakespeare Quarterly* 67, no. 1 (2016): 1–13.
Erickson, Peter, and Clark Hulse, eds. *Early Modern Visual Culture: Representation, Race, and Empire in Renaissance England*. Philadelphia: University of Pennsylvania Press, 2000.
Ersoylu, I. Halil. *Cem Sultan'ın Türkçe Divanı*. Ankara: Türk Dil Kurumu, 1989.
Ertaş, Mehmet Yaşar. "Evliya Çelebi'nin Seyahatnamesi'nde Gaza." *Tarih İncelemeleri Dergisi* 27 (2012): 79–100.
Eyüboğlu, İsmet Zeki. *Divan Şiirinde Sapık Sevgi*. Istanbul: Okat, 1968.
Faber, M. D. "Hermia's Dream: Royal Road to *A Midsummer Night's Dream*." *Literature and Psychology* 22 (1972): 179–90.
Faroqhi, Suraiya. *The Ottoman Empire and the World around It*. London: I. B. Tauris, 2004.
Feerick, Jean. *Strangers in Blood: Relocating Race in the Renaissance*. Toronto: University of Toronto Press, 2010.
Ferguson, Roderick A. *Aberrations in Black: Toward a Queer of Color Critique*. Minneapolis: University of Minnesota Press, 2003.
Fischel, Joseph J. *Sex and Harm in the Age of Consent*. Minneapolis: University of Minnesota Press, 2016.
Fisher, Godfrey. *Barbary Legend: War, Trade, and Piracy in North Africa, 1415–1830*. Oxford: Clarendon, 1957.
Fisher, Will. *Materializing Gender in Early Modern English Literature and Culture*. Cambridge: Cambridge University Press, 2006.
Fisher, Will. "The Renaissance Beard: Masculinity in Early Modern England." *Renaissance Quarterly* 54, no. 1 (2001): 155–87.
Flather, Amanda. *Gender and Space in Early Modern England*. Rochester: Boydell, 2007.
Fleet, Kate. *European and Islamic Trade in the Early Ottoman State: The Merchants of Genoa and Turkey*. Cambridge: Cambridge University Press, 1999.
Fleischer, Cornell H. *Bureaucrat and Intellectual in the Ottoman Empire: The Historian Mustafa Ali (1541–1600)*. Princeton, NJ: Princeton University Press, 1986.
Fleischer, Cornell H. "The Lawgiver as Messiah: The Making of the Imperial Image in the Reign of Süleymân." In *Soliman le Magnifique et son temps*, edited by Giles Veinstein, 159–77. Paris: La Documentasyon Française, 1992.
Fleming, K. E. "Constantinople: From Christianity to Islam." *The Classical World* 97, no. 1 (2003): 69–78.
Florio, John. *Queen Anna's New World of Words, or Dictionary of the Italian and English Tongues*. London: Melch. Bradwood, 1611.
Foster, Thomas A. *Rethinking Rufus: Sexual Violations of Enslaved Men*. Athens: University of Georgia Press, 2019.

Foucault, Michel. *The History of Sexuality: An Introduction*. London: Vintage, 1979.
Foucault, Michel. "Nietzsche, Genealogy, History." In *Language, Counter-Memory, Practice: Selected Essays and Interviews*, edited by Donald F. Bouchard, 139–64. Ithaca, NY: Cornell University Press, 1980.
Foucault, Michel. *The Use of Pleasure: Volume 2 of The History of Sexuality*. Translated by Robert Hurley. New York: Vintage Books, 1990.
Foxe, John. *Second Volume of the Ecclesiasticall History Containing the Acts and Monuments of Martyrs*. London, 1641.
Friedman, Alice T. "Inside/Out: Women, Domesticity, and the Pleasures of the City." In *Material London, ca. 1600*, edited by Lena Cowen Orlin, 232–50. Philadelphia: University of Pennsylvania Press, 2000.
Frosch, Thomas R. "The Missing Child in *A Midsummer Night's Dream*." *American Imago* 64, no. 4 (2007): 485–511.
Fryer, Peter. *Staying Power: The History of Black People in Britain*. London: Pluto, 1984.
Fuchs, Barbara. "Faithless Empires: Pirates, Renegadoes, and the English Nation." *ELH* 67 (2000): 45–69.
Fumerton, Patricia. *Cultural Aesthetics: Renaissance Literature and the Practice of Social Ornament*. Chicago: University of Chicago Press, 1991.
Gainsford, Thomas. *The Glory of England*. London, 1618.
Games, Alison. *The Web of Empire: English Cosmopolitans in an Age of Expansion, 1560–1660*. Oxford: Oxford University Press, 2009.
Garber, Marjorie. *Vested Interests: Cross-Dressing and Cultural Anxiety*. New York: Routledge, 1992.
Garner, Shirley Nelson. "*A Midsummer Night's Dream*: 'Jack Shall Have Jill/Nought Shall Go Ill.'" In *A Midsummer Night's Dream: Critical Essays*, edited by Dorothea Kehler, 127–43. New York: Garland, 1998.
Georgieuiz, Bartholomeus. *The Offspring of the House of Ottomanno*. London, 1569.
Geuffroy, Antoine. *The order of the greate Turckes courte, of hys menne of warre, and of all hys conquestes, with the summe of Mahumetes doctryne. Translated out of Frenche*. London: Ricardus Grafton excudebat, 1524.
Gibb, Elias J. W. *A History of Ottoman Poetry*. 6 Vols. London: Luzac & Co, 1902–1908.
Gilbert, Ruth. *Early Modern Hermaphrodites: Sex and Other Stories*. New York: Palgrave Macmillan, 2002.
Gillies, John. *Shakespeare and the Geography of Difference*. Cambridge: Cambridge University Press, 1994.
Gilma, Ernest B. "Madagascar on My Mind: The Earl of Arundel and Arts of Colonization." In *Early Modern Visual Culture: Representation, Race, and Empire in Renaissance England*, edited by Peter Erickson and Clark Hulse, 284–314. Philadelphia: University of Pennsylvania Press, 2000.
Glassman, Jonathon. "The Bondsman's New Clothes: The Contradictory Consciousness of Slave Resistance on the Swahili Coast." *The Journal of African History* 32, no. 2 (1991): 277–312.
Godsalve, William H. L. *Britten's "A Midsummer Night's Dream": Making an Opera from Shakespeare's Comedy*. London: Associated University Press, 1995.
Goffe, Thomas. *The Couragious Turke, or, Amurath the First. A Tragedie*. Oxford, 1618.

Goffman, Daniel. *The Ottoman Empire and Early Modern Europe.* Cambridge: Cambridge University Press, 2004.

Gohlke, Madelon. "'I wooed thee with my sword': Shakespeare's Tragic Paradigms." In *Representing Shakespeare: New Psychoanalytic Essays*, edited by Murray M. Schwartz and Coppelia Kahn, 170–87. Baltimore, MD: Johns Hopkins University Press, 1980.

Gökyay, Orhan Şaik. "Bir Saltanat Düğünü." *Topkapı Sarayı Yıllığı* 1 (1986): 21–55.

Goldberg, Jonathan, ed. *Queering the Renaissance.* Durham, NC: Duke University Press, 1994.

Goldberg, Jonathan. *Sodometries: Renaissance Texts, Modern Sexualities.* Stanford, CA: Stanford University Press, 1992.

Goldberg, Jonathan. "Sodomy and Society: The Case of Christopher Marlowe." In *Staging the Renaissance: Reinterpretation of Elizabethan and Jacobean Drama*, edited by David Scott Kastan and Peter Stallybrass, 75–82. New York: Routledge, 1991.

Goldenberg, David M. *The Curse of Ham: Race and Slavery in Early Judaism, Christianity, and Islam.* Princeton, NJ: Princeton University Press, 2003.

Golding, Arthur. *The xv bookes of P. Ouidius Naso, entytuled Metamorphosis, translated oute of Latin into English meeter, by Arthur Golding Gentleman, A worke very pleasaunt and delectable.* London, 1567.

Gomez, Michael. *African Dominion: A New History of Empire in Early and Medieval West Africa.* Princeton, NJ: Princeton University Press, 2018.

Goulart, Simon. *Admirable and memorable histories containing the wonders of our time. Collected into French out of the best authors.* Translated by Edward Grimeston. London, 1607.

Gowing, Laura. *Common Bodies: Women, Touch and Power in Seventeenth-Century England.* New Haven, CT: Yale University Press, 2003.

Gowing, Laura. "'The freedom of streets': Women and Social Space, 1560–1640." In *Londinopolis: Essays in the Cultural and Social History of Early Modern London*, edited by Paul Griffiths and Mark S. R. Jenner, 130–51. Manchester: Manchester University Press, 2001.

Graf, Tobias P. *The Sultan's Renegades: Christian-European Converts to Islam and the Making of the Ottoman Elite, 1575–1610.* Oxford: Oxford University Press, 2017.

Gratien, Chris. "Race, Slavery, and Islamic Law in the Early Modern Atlantic: Ahmad Baba al-Tinbukti's Treatise on Enslavement." *Journal of North African Studies* 18, no. 3 (2013): 454–68.

Green, Douglas E. "Preposterous Pleasures: Queer Theories and *A Midsummer Night's Dream*." In *A Midsummer Night's Dream: Critical Essays*, edited by Dorothea Kehler, 369–97. New York: Garland, 1998.

Greenblatt, Stephen, Walter Cohen, Jean Howard, and Katharine Eisaman Maus, eds. *The Norton Shakespeare.* 2nd ed. New York: Norton, 2008.

Greene, Robert. *Greene's Arcadia; Or Menaphon.* London, 1589.

Greene, Robert. *Selimus, Emperor of the Turks.* In *Three Turk Plays from Early Modern England*, edited by Daniel Vitkus, 55–144. New York: Columbia University Press, 2000.

Grier, Miles P. *Inkface: Othello and White Authority in the Era of Atlantic Slavery.* Charlottesville: University of Virginia Press, 2023.

Griffiths, Paul. *Youth and Authority: Formative Experiences in England 1560–1640.* Oxford: Clarendon, 1996.

Griffiths, Trevor R., ed. *A Midsummer Night's Dream*. Cambridge: Cambridge University Press, 1996.

Grosz, Elizabeth. *Architecture from the Outside: Essays on Virtual and Real Space*. Cambridge, MA: MIT Press, 2001.

Gui, Weston A. "Bottom's Dream." *American Imago* 9, no. 3–4 (1952): 251–305.

Guy-Bray, Stephen. *Homoerotic Space: The Poetics of Loss in Renaissance Literature*. Toronto: University of Toronto Press, 2002.

Haber, Judith. *Desire and Dramatic Form in Early Modern England*. Cambridge: Cambridge University Press, 2009.

Habib, Imtiaz. "Bengal as Shakespeare's India and the Stolen Indian Boy: The Historical Dark Matter of *A Midsummer Night's Dream*." *Early Modern Literary Studies* 20, no. 1 (2018): 1–27.

Habib, Imtiaz. *Black Lives in the English Archives: 1500–1677*. Burlington, VT: Ashgate, 2008.

Haeckel, Ernst. *A Visit to Ceylon*. Translated by Clara Bell. London: Kegan Paul, 1883.

Hakluyt, Richard. *The Principal Navigations, Voyages, and Discoveries of the English Nation*. London, 1589.

Hall, Kim F. "Culinary Spaces, Colonial Spaces: The Gendering of Sugar in the Seventeenth Century." In *Feminist Readings of Early Modern Culture: Emerging Subjects*, edited by Valerie Traub, Lindsay Kaplan, and Dympna Callaghan, 168–90. Cambridge: Cambridge University Press, 1996.

Hall, Kim F. "I can't love this the way you want me to: Archival Blackness." *postmedieval: a journal of medieval cultural studies* 11, no. 2–3 (2020): 171–79.

Hall, Kim F. "Object into Object? Some Thoughts on the Presence of Black Women in Early Modern Culture." In *Early Modern Visual Culture: Representation, Race, and Empire in Renaissance England*, edited by Peter Erickson and Clark Hulse, 346–79. Philadelphia: University of Pennsylvania Press, 2000.

Hall, Kim F. *Things of Darkness*. Ithaca, NY: Cornell University Press, 1995.

Halperin, David. *How to Do the History of Homosexuality*. Chicago: University of Chicago Press, 2002.

Hanson, Ellis. "*Antony and Cleopatra*: Aught an Eunuch Has." In *Shakesqueer: A Queer Companion to the Complete Works of Shakespeare*, edited by Madhavi Menon, 48–54. Durham, NC: Duke University Press, 2001.

Harkins, Gillian. "Foucault, the Family and the Cold Monster of Neoliberalism." In *Foucault, the Family and Politics*, edited by Leon Rocha and Robbie Duschinsky, 82–120. London: Palgrave Macmillan, 2012.

Harley, J. B. "Deconstructing the Map." *Cartographica* 26, no. 2 (1989): 1–20.

Harley, J. B. "Maps, Knowledge, and Power." In *The Iconography of Landscape: Essays on the Symbolic Representation, Design, and Use of Past Environments*, edited by Denis Cosgrove and Stephen Daniels, 277–312. Cambridge: Cambridge University Press, 1988.

Harley, J. B. "Silences and Secrecy: The Hidden Agenda of Cartography in Early Modern Europe." *Imago Mundi* 40, no. 1 (1988): 57–76.

Harper, James. "Turks as Trojans, Trojans as Turks: Visual Imagery of the Trojan War and the Politics of Cultural Identity in Fifteenth-Century Europe." In *Translating Cultures: Postcolonial Approaches to the Middle Ages*, edited by Ananya Jahanara Kabir and Deanne Williams, 151–79. Cambridge: Cambridge University Press, 2005.

Harris, Jonathan Gil, ed. *Indography: Writing the "Indian" in Early Modern England.* New York: Palgrave Macmillan, 2012.
Hathaway, Jane. *Beshir Agha: Chief Eunuch of the Ottoman Imperial Harem.* London: Oneworld, 2005.
Hathaway, Jane. *The Chief Eunuch of the Ottoman Harem: From African Slave to Power-Broker.* Cambridge: Cambridge University Press, 2018.
Helgerson, Richard. *Adulterous Alliances: Home, State, and History in Early Modern European Drama and Painting.* Chicago: University of Chicago Press, 2000.
Helgerson, Richard. "The Land Speaks: Cartography, Chorography, and Subversion in Renaissance England." *Representations* 16 (1986): 50–86.
Hendricks, Margo. "'Obscured by dreams': Race, Empire, and Shakespeare's *A Midsummer Night's Dream*." *Shakespeare Quarterly* 47, no. 1 (1996): 37–60.
Hendricks, Margo, and Patricia Parker, eds. *Women, Race, and Writing in Early Modern England.* New York: Routledge, 1994.
Heng, Geraldine. *The Invention of Race in the European Middle Ages.* Cambridge: Cambridge University Press, 2018.
Herbert, Thomas. *Travels in Persia, 1627–1629.* Edited by Sir William Foster. New York: Routledge, 2005.
Herrup, Cynthia. *A House in Gross Disorder: Sex, Law, and the 2nd Earl of Castlehaven.* Oxford: Oxford University Press, 1999.
Hershenzon, Daniel. *The Captive Sea: Slavery, Communication, and Commerce in Early Modern Spain and the Mediterranean.* Philadelphia: University of Pennsylvania Press, 2018.
Heywood, Thomas. *The Fair Maid of the West, Parts I and II.* Edited by Robert K. Turner Jr. Lincoln: University of Nebraska Press, 1967.
Higginbotham, Jennifer. *The Girlhood of Shakespeare's Sisters: Gender, Transgression, Adolescence.* Edinburgh: Edinburgh University Press, 2013.
Higgs, David. *Queer Sites: Gay Urban Histories since 1600.* London: Routledge, 1999.
Higonnet, Anne. *Pictures of Innocence: The History and Crisis of Ideal Childhood.* London: Thames and Hudson, 1998.
Hiscock, Andrew. *The Uses of This World: Thinking Space in Shakespeare, Marlowe, Cary, and Jonson.* Cardiff: University of Wales Press, 2004.
Holland, Sharon Patricia. *The Erotic Life of Racism.* Durham, NC: Duke University Press, 2012.
Holmberg, Eva J. *Jews in the Early Modern English Imagination.* Burlington, VT: Ashgate, 2012.
Homer. *The Iliad.* Translated by Samuel Butler. London: Longmans, 1898.
Howard, Jean. *The Stage and Social Struggle in Early Modern England.* New York: Routledge, 1994.
Howard, Jean. *Theater of a City: The Places of London Comedy, 1598–1642.* Philadelphia: University of Pennsylvania Press, 2007.
Howard, Jean, and Phyllis Rackin. *Engendering a Nation: A Feminist Account of Shakespeare's English Histories.* New York: Routledge, 1997.
Hulme, Peter. "Polytropic Man: Tropes of Sexuality and Mobility in Early Colonial Discourse." In *Europe and Its Others: Proceedings of the Essex Conference on the Sociology*

of Literature, July 1984, vol. 2, edited by Francis Barker, P. Hulme, M. Iverson, and D. Loxley, 1–15. Colchester: University of Essex, 1985.

Hulse, Clark. *Metamorphic Verse: The Elizabethan Minor Epic*. Princeton, NJ: Princeton University Press, 1981.

Hutchings, Mark. *Turks, Repertories, and the Early Modern English Stage*. New York: Palgrave Macmillan, 2017.

Hyginus. *Fabulae*. Translated by Mary Grant. Lawrence: University of Kansas Publications, 1960.

Ibn Khaldun. *An Introduction to History: The Muqaddimah*. Translated by Franz Rosenthal. New York: Routledge, 1967.

Ibn Manzur. *Lisān al-'Arab*. Vol. 6. Beirut: Dar Iḥya al-Turath al-Arabi, 1883.

Imber, Colin. *The Ottoman Empire, 1300–1650*. 2nd ed. New York: Palgrave Macmillan, 2009.

Inalcik, Halil. "Military and Fiscal Transformation in the Ottoman Empire (1600–1700)." *Archivum Ottomanicum* 6 (1980): 283–339.

Inderpal, Grewal, and Caren Kaplan. "Global Identities: Theorizing Transnational Studies of Sexuality." *GLQ: A Journal of Lesbian and Gay Studies* 7, no. 4 (2001): 663–79.

Ingram, Anders. *Writing the Ottomans: Turkish History in Early Modern England*. New York: Palgrave Macmillan, 2015.

Isaac, Benjamin H. *The Invention of Racism in Classical Antiquity*. Princeton, NJ: Princeton University Press, 2004.

Jackson, Louise. *Child Sexual Abuse in Victorian England*. New York: Routledge, 2000.

Jacobson, Gerald F. "A Note on Shakespeare's *A Midsummer Night's Dream*." *American Imago* 19 (1962): 21–26.

Jacobson, Miriam. *Barbarous Antiquity: Reorienting the Past in the Poetry of Early Modern England*. Philadelphia: University of Pennsylvania Press, 2014.

James I. *His Maiesties Lepanto, or heroicall song being part of his poetical exercises at vacant hours*. London, 1603.

Jardine, Lisa. *Reading Shakespeare Historically*. London: Routledge, 1996.

Jardine, Lisa, and Jerry Brotton. *Global Interests: Renaissance Art between East and West*. Ithaca, NY: Cornell University Press, 2000.

Johnson, Mark Albert. "'To what bawdy house doth your Maister belong?': Barbers, Bawds, and Vice in Early Modern London Barbershop." In *Masculinity and the Metropolis of Vice, 1550–1650*, edited by Amanda Bailey and Roze Hentschell, 115–35. New York: Palgrave Macmillan, 2010.

Johnston, Lynda, and Robyn Longhurst. *Space, Place, and Sex: Geographies of Sexualities*. Lanham, MD: Rowman & Littlefield, 2010.

Jones, Ann Rosalind. "Italians and Others: Venice and the Irish in *Coryat's Crudities* and *The White Devil*." *Renaissance Drama* 17 (1987): 101–19.

Jones, Eldred. *Othello's Countrymen: The African in English Renaissance Drama*. Oxford: Oxford University Press, 1965.

Jonson, Ben. *Volpone, or the Fox*. New Haven. CT: Yale University Press, 1962.

Jowitt, Clare. *The Culture of Piracy, 1580–1630: English Literature and Seaborne Crime*. Farnham, Surrey, England: Ashgate, 2010.

Junne, George. *The Black Eunuchs of the Ottoman Empire: Networks of Power in the Court of the Sultan*. New York: I. B. Taurus, 2016.

Kadish, Gerald E. "Eunuchs in Ancient Egypt." In *Studies in Honor of J. A. Wilson*, edited by G. E. Kadish, 55–62. Chicago: University of Chicago Press, 1969.

Kafadar, Cemal. *Between Two Worlds: The Construction of the Ottoman State*. Berkeley: University of California Press, 1995.

Kafadar, Cemal. "On the Purity and Corruption of the Janissaries." *Turkish Studies Association Bulletin* 15, no. 2 (1991): 275–76.

Kafadar, Cemal. "The Ottomans and Europe." In *Handbook of European History, 1400–1600*, vol. 1, *Structures and Assertions*, edited by Thomas A. Brady Jr., Heiko A. Oberman, and James D. Tracy, 589–635. Leiden: Brill, 1994.

Kafadar, Cemal. "A Rome of One's Own: Reflections on Cultural Geography and Identity in the Lands of Rum." *Muqarnas* 24 (2007): 7–25.

Kahan, Benjamin. *The Book of Minor Perverts: Sexology, Etiology, and the Emergences of Sexuality*. Chicago: University of Chicago Press, 2019.

Kandiyoti, Deniz. "Gendering the Modern: On Missing Dimensions in the Study of Turkish Modernity." In *Rethinking Modernity and National Identity in Turkey*, edited by Sibel Bozdogan and Resat Kasaba, 133–56. Seattle: University of Washington Press, 1997.

Kandiyoti, Deniz. "Patterns of Patriarchy: Notes for an Analysis of Male Dominance in Turkish Society." In *Women in Modern Turkish Society: A Reader*, edited by Sirin Tekeli, 306–18. London: Zed, 1991.

Kandiyoti, Deniz. "Some Awkward Questions on Women and Modernity in Turkey." In *Remaking Women: Feminism and Modernity in the Middle East*, edited by Lila Abu-Lughod, 270–87. Princeton, NJ: Princeton University Press, 1998.

Kaplan, Lindsay M. *Figuring Racism in Medieval Christianity*. Oxford: Oxford University Press, 2019.

Kaplan, Paul H. D. "Isabella d'Este and Black African Women." In *Black Africans in Renaissance Europe*, edited by T. F. Earle and K. J. P. Lowe, 125–54. Cambridge: Cambridge University Press, 2005.

Kaplan, Paul H. D. "Titian's 'Laura Dianti' and the Origins of the Motif of the Black Page in Portraiture." *Antichità Viva* 21, no. 1 (1982): 11–18.

Karacan, Turgut. *Heft-han mesnevisi*. Ankara: Sevinç, 1974.

Karateke, Hakan, H. Erdem Çıpa, and Helga Anetshofer, eds. *Disliking Others: Loathing, Hostility, and Distrust in Premodern Ottoman Lands*. Boston: Academic Studies Press, 2018.

Karras, Ruth Mazo. *From Boys to Men: Formations of Masculinity in Late Medieval Europe*. Philadelphia: University of Pennsylvania Press, 2003.

Kathman, David. "How Old Were Shakespeare's Boy Actors?" *Shakespeare Survey* 58 (2005): 220–46.

Kaufmann, Miranda. *Black Tudors: The Untold Story*. London: Oneworld, 2017.

Kaufmann, Miranda. "Caspar van Senden, Sir Thomas Sherley and the 'Blackamoor' Project." *Historical Research* 81, no. 212 (May 2008): 366–71.

Keach, William. *Elizabethan Erotic Narratives: Irony and Pathos in the Ovidian Poetry of Shakespeare, Marlowe, and Their Contemporaries*. New Brunswick, NJ: Rutgers University Press, 1977.

Keene, Laura. *Shakspeare's Play of* A Midsummer Night's Dream. *Arranged for Representation at Laura Keene's Theatre*. New York: O. A. Roorbach, Jr., 1859.
Kehler, Dorothea, ed. *A Midsummer Night's Dream: Critical Essays*. London: Garland, 1998.
Kellet, Edward. *A Returne from Argier: A sermon Preached at Minhead in the County of Somerset the 16 March, 1627, at the re-admission of a relapsed Christian into our Church*. London, 1628.
Kılıç, Filiz. "Tuna Kasidesi'nin Düşündürdükleri." *Türk Kültürü Dergisi* 441 (2000): 32–48.
Kincaid, James R. *Child-Loving: The Erotic Child and Victorian Culture*. New York: Routledge, 1992.
Kinoshita, Sharon. "Locating the Medieval Mediterranean." In *Locating the Middle Ages: The Spaces and Places of Medieval Culture*, edited by Julian Weiss and Sarah Salih, 39–52. London: Center for Late Antique and Medieval Studies, 2012.
Kinoshita, Sharon. "Medieval Mediterranean Literature." *PMLA* 124, no. 2 (2009): 600–8.
Kinoshita, Sharon. "Romance in/and Medieval Mediterranean." In *Thinking Medieval Romance*, edited by Katherine C. Little and Nicola McDonald, 187–202. Oxford: Oxford University Press, 2018.
Knolles, Richard. *The Generall Historie of the Turkes*. London, 1603.
Knowles, Katie. *Shakespeare's Boys: A Cultural History*. New York: Palgrave Macmillan, 2014.
Knutson, Roslyn. "A Caliban in St. Milfred Poultry." In *Shakespeare and Cultural Traditions*, edited by Tetsuo Kishi, Roger Pringle, and Stanley Wells, 110–26. Newark: University of Delaware Press, 1991.
Kolb, Justin. "'A Turk's mustachio': Anglo-Islamic Traffic and Exotic London in Ben Jonson's *Every Man Out of His Humour* and *Entertainment at Britain's Burse*." In *Early Modern England and Islamic Worlds*, edited by Linda McJannet and Bernadette Andrea, 197–214. New York: Palgrave Macmillan, 2011.
Kolodny, Annette. *The Lay of the Land*. Chapel Hill: University of North Carolina Press, 1975.
Kott, Jan. *Shakespeare Our Contemporary*. New York: Norton, 1974.
Krstić, Tijana. *Contested Conversions to Islam: Narratives of Religious Change in the Early Modern Ottoman Empire*. Stanford, CA: Stanford University Press, 2011.
Kuefler, Matthew. *The Manly Eunuch: Masculinity, Gender Ambiguity, and Christian Ideology in Late Antiquity*. Chicago: University of Chicago Press, 2001.
Kunt, Metin. "Kulların Kulları." *Boğaziçi Üniversitesi Dergisi* 3 (1975): 27–42.
Kunt, Metin. "State and Sultan up to the Age of Suleyman: Frontier Principality to World Empire." In *Suleyman the Magnificient and His Age: The Ottoman Empire in the Early Modern World*, edited by Metin Kunt and Christine Woodhead, 3–29. London: Longman, 1995.
Kunt, Metin. *The Sultan's Servants: The Transformation of Ottoman Provincial Government, 1559–1650*. New York: Columbia University Press, 1983.
Küpper, Ulrike. *William Shakespeare's "A Midsummer Night's Dream" in the History of Music Theater*. London: Peter Lang, 2010.
Kursar, Vjeran. "Ambigious Subjects and Uneasy Neighbors: Bosnian Franciscans' Attitudes toward the Ottoman State, 'Turks,' and Vlachs." In *Disliking Others: Loathing, Hostility, and Distrust in Premodern Ottoman Lands*, edited by Hakan Karateke, H. Erdem Çıpa, and Helga Anetshofer, 148–86. Boston: Academic Studies Press, 2018.

Kuru, Selim. "Naming the Beloved in Ottoman Turkish Gazel: The Case of Ishak Celebi (d. 1537/8)." In *Ghazal as World Literature II: From a Literary Genre to a Great Tradition: The Ottoman Gazel in Context*, edited by Angelika Neuwirth, Michael Hess, Judith Pfeiffer, and Börte Sagaster, 163–73. Beirut: Beiruter Texte und Studien, 2005.

Kuru, Selim. "Scholar and Author in the Sixteenth-Century Ottoman Empire: Deli Birader and His Work *Dâfi'ü 'l-gumûm râfi'ü 'l-humûm*." PhD diss., Harvard University, 2000.

Lad, Jateen. "Panoptic Bodies: Black Eunuchs as Guardians of the Topkapi Harem." In *Harem Histories: Envisioning Places and Living Spaces*, edited by Marilyn Booth, 136–76. Durham, NC: Duke University Press, 2010.

LaFleur, Greta. *The Natural History of Sexuality in Early America*. Baltimore, MD: Johns Hopkins University Press, 2018.

Lamb, Edel. *Performing Childhood in the Early Modern Theatre: The Children's Playing Companies (1599–1613)*. New York: Palgrave Macmillan, 2009.

Lamb, Mary Ellen. "Taken by Fairies: Fairy Practices and the Production of Popular Culture in *A Midsummer Night's Dream*." *Shakespeare Quarterly* 51, no. 3 (2000): 277–312.

Laqueur, Thomas. *Making Sex: Body and Gender from Greeks to Freud*. Cambridge, MA: Harvard University Press, 1992.

Lazzaro, Claudia. "River Gods: Personifying Nature in Sixteenth-Century Italy." *Renaissance Studies* 25, no. 1 (2011): 70–94.

Lefebvre, Henri. *The Production of Space*. Malden, MA: Blackwell. 1991.

Leirvik, Oddbjørn. *Images of Jesus Christ in Islam*. New York: Continuum, 2010.

Lenthe, Victor. "Antonio's Sad Flesh." *Shakespeare* 19, no. 4 (2023): 569–85.

Levend, Agah Sirri. *Türk Edebiyatında Şehrengizler ve Şehrengizlerde İstanbul*. Istanbul: Fetih Cemiyeti, 1958.

Levine, Laura. *Men in Women's Clothing: Anti-Theatricality and Effeminization, 1579–1642*. Cambridge: Cambridge University Press, 1994.

Lewis, Bernard. *Race and Color in Islam*. New York: Harper & Row, 1971.

Lewis, Bernard. *Race and Slavery in the Middle East: An Historical Enquiry*. Oxford: Oxford University Press, 1990.

Lewis, Franklin. "Sexual Occidentation: The Politics of Conversion, Christian-Love and Boy-Love in 'Attar." *Iranian Studies* 42, no. 5 (2009): 693–723.

Lim, Eng-Beng. *Brown Boys and Rice Queens: Spellbinding Performance in the Asias*. New York: New York University Press, 2014.

Lithgow, William. *The Totall Discourse of the Rare Adventures, and Painefull Peregrinations of long Nineteene Yeares Travayles from Scotland to the most famous Kingdomes in Europe, Asia and Affrica*. London, 1632.

Little, Arthur L. "'An Essence that's Not Seen': The Primal Scene of Racism in *Othello*." *Shakespeare Quarterly* 44, no. 3 (1993): 304–24.

Little, Arthur L. *Shakespeare Jungle Fever: National-Imperial Re-Visions of Race, Rape, and Sacrifice*. Stanford, CA: Stanford University Press, 2000.

Long, Kathleen P. *Hermaphrodites in Renaissance Europe*. Aldershot: Ashgate, 2006.

Loomba, Ania, ed. *Anthony and Cleopatra*. New York: Norton, 2011.

Loomba, Ania. "'Delicious Traffick': Alterity and Exchange on Early Modern Stages." In *Shakespeare and Race*, edited by Catherine M. S. Alexander and Stanley Wells, 203–24. Cambridge: Cambridge University Press, 2000.

Loomba, Ania. *Gender, Race, Renaissance Drama*. Manchester: Manchester University Press, 1989.

Loomba, Ania. "The Great Indian Vanishing Trick: Colonialism, Property, and the Family in *A Midsummer Night's Dream*." In *A Feminist Companion to Shakespeare*, edited by Dympna Callaghan, 163–87. Malden, MA: Blackwell, 2001.

Loomba, Ania. "Identities and Bodies in Early Modern Studies." In *The Oxford Handbook of Shakespeare and Embodiment: Gender, Sexuality, and Race*, edited by Valerie Traub, 225–50. Oxford: Oxford University Press, 2016.

Loomba, Ania. "Introduction." In *A Cultural History of Western Empires in the Renaissance*, edited by Ania Loomba, 1–26. London: Bloomsbury, 2018.

Loomba, Ania. "Race and the Possibilities of Comparative Critique." *New Literary History* 40 (2009): 501–22.

Loomba, Ania. *Shakespeare, Race, Colonialism*. Oxford: Oxford University Press, 2002.

Loomba, Ania, and Jonathan Burton, eds. *Race in Early Modern England: A Documentary Companion*. New York: Palgrave Macmillan, 2007.

Loomba, Ania, and Melissa Sanchez, eds. *Rethinking Feminism in Early Modern Studies: Gender, Race and Sexuality*. New York: Routledge, 2016.

Low, Jennifer A. *Manhood and the Duel: Masculinity in Early Modern Drama and Culture*. New York: Palgrave Macmillan, 2003.

Lowe, Kate. "Introduction." In *Black Africans in Renaissance Europe*, edited by T. F. Earle and K. J. P. Lowe, 1–16. Cambridge: Cambridge University Press, 2005.

Lowe, Kate. "The Stereotyping of Black Africans in Renaissance Europe." In *Black Africans in Renaissance Europe*, edited by T. F. Earle and K. J. P. Lowe, 17–47. Cambridge: Cambridge University Press, 2005.

Lowe, Lisa. *The Intimacies of Four Continents*. Durham, NC: Duke University Press, 2016.

Lupton, Julia Reinhard. "Othello Circumcised: Shakespeare and the Pauline Discourse of Nations." *Representations* 57 (1997): 73–89.

Lyne, Raphael. "Ovid in English Translation." In *The Cambridge Companion to Ovid*, edited by Philip Hardie, 249–63. Cambridge: Cambridge University Press, 2002.

MacDonald, Joyce G. "Marlowe's Ganymede." In *Enacting Gender on the English Renaissance Stage*, edited by Viviana Comensoli and Anne Russell, 97–113. Urbana: University of Illinois Press, 1999.

MacDonald, Joyce G. *Women and Race in Early Modern Texts*. Cambridge: Cambridge University Press, 2002.

MacLean, Gerald. *Looking East: English Writing and the Ottoman Empire before 1800*. New York: Palgrave Macmillan, 2007.

MacLean, Gerald. *The Rise of Oriental Travel: English Visitors to the Ottoman Empire, 1580–1720*. New York: Palgrave Macmillan, 2004.

MacLean, Gerald, and Nabil Matar. *Britain and the Islamic World, 1558–1713*. Oxford: Oxford University Press, 2011.

MacMaster, Thomas J. "The Origin of the Origins: Trojans, Turks and the Birth of the Myth of Trojan Origins in the Medieval World." *Atlantide* 2 (2014): 1–12.

Malcolm, Noel. "Forbidden Love in Istanbul: Patterns of Male-Male Sexual Relations in the Early-Modern Mediterranean World." *Past & Present* 257, no. 1 (2022): 55–88.

Malcolm, Noel. "Positive Views of Islam and Ottoman Rule in the Sixteenth Century: The Case of Jean Bodin." In *The Renaissance and the Ottoman World*, edited by Anna Contadini and Clarie Norton, 197–217. Burlington, VT: Ashgate, 2013.

Malieckal, Bindu. "Slavery, Sex, and the Seraglio: 'Turkish' Women in Early Modern Texts." In *The Mysterious and the Foreign in Early Modern England*, edited by Helen Ostovich, Mary V. Silcox, and Graham Roebuck, 58–73. Newark: University of Delaware Press, 2008.

Malieckal, Bindu. "'Wanton Irreligious Madness': Conversion and Castration in Massinger's *The Renegado*." *Essays in Arts and Science* 31 (2002): 25–43.

Manalansan, Martin. *Global Divas: Filipino Gay Men in the Diaspora*. Durham, NC: Duke University Press, 2003.

Marlowe, Christopher. *Dido, Queen of Carthage: The Complete Plays*. Edited by Mark Thornton Burnett. London: Everyman, 1999.

Marlowe, Christopher. *Doctor Faustus*. In *Doctor Faustus and Other Plays*, edited by David Bevington and Eric Rasmussen. Oxford: Oxford University Press, 2008.

Marlowe, Christopher. *Edward II*. In *Doctor Faustus and Other Plays*, edited by David Bevington and Eric Rasmussen. Oxford: Oxford University Press, 2008.

Marlowe, Christopher. *Hero and Leander*. In *The Collected Poems of Christopher Marlowe*, edited by Patrick Cheney and Brian J. Striar. Oxford: Oxford University Press, 2006.

Marlowe, Christopher. *The Jew of Malta*. Edited by David Bevington and Eric Rasmussen. Oxford: Oxford University Press, 2008.

Marlowe, Christopher. *Tamburlaine, Part I*. Edited by David Bevington and Eric Rasmussen. Oxford: Oxford University Press, 2008.

Marmon, Shaun E. *Eunuchs and Sacred Boundaries in Islamic Society*. Oxford: Oxford University Press, 1995.

Marston, John. *The Metamorphosis of Pigmalion's Image and Certaine Satyres*. London, 1598.

Mason, John. *The Turke: A Worthie Tragedie*. London, 1607.

Massad, Joseph A. *Desiring Arabs*. Chicago: University of Chicago Press, 2007.

Massey, Doreen B. *for space*. London: Sage, 2005.

Massey, Doreen B. *Space, Place, and Gender*. Minneapolis: University of Minnesota Press, 1994.

Massinger, Philip. *The Renegado*. In *Three Turk Plays from Early Modern England*, edited by Daniel Vitkus, 241–339. New York: Columbia University Press, 2000.

Masten, Jeffrey. "Ben Jonson's Head." *Shakespeare Studies* 28 (2000): 160–68.

Masten, Jeffrey. "Glossing and T*pping: Editing Sexuality, Race, and Gender in *Othello*." In *The Oxford Handbook of Shakespeare and Embodiment*, edited by Valerie Traub, 569–92. Oxford: Oxford University Press, 2016.

Masten, Jeffrey. *Queer Philologies: Sex, Language, and Affect in Shakespeare's Time*. Philadelphia: University of Pennsylvania Press, 2016.

Masten, Jeffrey. *Textual Intercourse: Collaboration, Authorship, and Sexualities in Renaissance Drama*. New York: Cambridge University Press, 1997.

Matar, Nabil. *Islam in Britain, 1558–1685*. Cambridge: Cambridge University Press, 1998.

Matar, Nabil. "Muslim Conversion to Christianity in the Early Modern Period: Arabic Texts European Contexts." In *Mediterranean Identities in Premodern Era: Entrepôts,*

Islands, Empires, edited by John Watkins and Kathryn L. Reyerson, 211–30. Burlington, VT: Ashgate, 2014.

Matar, Nabil. "The Renegade in English Seventeenth-Century Imagination." *Studies in English Literature, 1500–1900* 33, no. 3 (1993): 489–505.

Matar, Nabil. *Turks, Moors, and Englishmen in the Age of Discovery*. New York: Columbia University Press, 1999.

Matar, Nabil. "Wives, Captives, Husbands, and Turks: The First Women Petitioners in Caroline England." *Explorations in Renaissance Culture* 23 (1997): 111–28.

Matz, Robert. "Slander, Renaissance Discourses of Sodomy, and *Othello*." *English Literary History* 66, no. 2 (1999): 261–76.

McCarthy, Harry R. *Boy Actors in Early Modern England: Skill and Stagecraft in the Theatre*. Cambridge: Cambridge University Press, 2022.

McClintock, Anne. *Imperial Leather: Race, Gender, and Sexuality in the Colonial Contest*. New York: Routledge, 1995.

McDowell, Linda. *Gender, Identity, Place: Understanding Feminist Geographies*. Oxford: Blackwell, 1999.

McJannet, Linda. "Genre and Geography: The Eastern Mediterranean in *Pericles* and *The Comedy of Errors*." In *Playing the Globe: Genre and Geography in English Renaissance Drama*, edited by J. Gillies and V. Vaughan, 86–106. Madison, NJ: Fairleigh Dickinson University Press, 1998.

McJannet, Linda. *The Sultan Speaks: Dialogue in English Plays and Histories about the Ottoman Turks*. New York: Palgrave Macmillan, 2006.

Menage, V. L. "Some Notes on Devşirme." *Bulletin of the School of Oriental African Studies* 29, no. 1 (1966): 64–78.

Menon, Madhavi. "Desire." In *Early Modern Theatricality*, edited by Henry S. Turner, 327–45. Oxford: Oxford University Press, 2013.

Middleton, Thomas, and Thomas Dekker. *The Roaring Girl*. London: Benn, 1976.

Mignolo, Walter. *The Darker Side of the Renaissance: Literacy, Territoriality, and Colonization*. Ann Arbor: University of Michigan Press, 2003.

Miles, M. "Signing in the Seraglio: Mutes, Dwarfs and Jestures at the Ottoman Court 1500–1700." *Disability & Society* 15, no. 1 (2000): 115–34.

Miller, Donald C. "Titania and the Changeling." *English Studies* 22 (1940): 66–70.

Miller, Naomi J., and Naomi Yavneh, eds. *Gender and Early Modern Constructions of Childhood*. Burlington, VT: Ashgate, 2011.

Mills, Robert. *Seeing Sodomy in the Middle Ages*. Chicago: University of Chicago Press, 2015.

Montrose, Louis. *The Purpose of Playing: Shakespeare and the Cultural Politics of Elizabethan Theatre*. Chicago: University of Chicago Press, 1996.

Montrose, Louis. "The Work of Gender in the Discourse of Discovery." *Representations* 33 (1991): 1–41.

Morrah, Patrick. *Prince Rupert of the Rhine*. London: Constable, 1976.

Mullaney, Steven. *The Place of the Stage: License, Play, and Power in Renaissance England*. Chicago: University of Chicago Press, 1988.

Muñoz, José Esteban. *Cruising Utopia: The Then and There of Queer Futurity*. New York: New York University Press, 2009.

Muñoz, José Esteban. *Disidentifications: Queers of Color and the Performance of Politics*. Minneapolis: University of Minnesota Press, 1999.

Munro, Lucy. "Coriolanus and the Little Eyases: The Boyhood of Shakespeare's Hero." In *Shakespeare and Childhood*, edited by Kate Chedgzoy, Susanne Greenhalgh, and Robert Shaughnessy, 80–95. Cambridge: Cambridge University Press, 2007.

Musser, Amber Jamilla. *Sensational Flesh: Race, Power, and Masochism*. New York: New York University Press, 2014.

Najmabadi, Afsaneh. "Genus of Sex or the Sexing of *Jins*." *International Journal of Middle East Studies* 45, no. 2 (2013): 211–31.

Najmabadi, Afsaneh. *Women with Mustaches and Men without Beards: Gender and Sexual Anxieties of Iranian Modernity*. Berkeley: University of California Press, 2005.

Nash, Jennifer C. *The Black Body in Ecstasy: Reading Race, Reading Pornography*. Durham, NC: Duke University Press, 2014.

Ndiaye, Noémie. *Scripts of Blackness: Early Modern Performance Culture and the Making of Race*. Philadelphia: University of Pennsylvania Press, 2022.

Necipoğlu, Gülru. *Architecture, Ceremonial, and Power: The Topkapi Palace in the Fifteenth and Sixteenth Centuries*. Cambridge, MA: MIT Press, 1992.

Neill, Michael. *The Tragedy of Anthony and Cleopatra*. Oxford: Oxford University Press, 1994.

Neill, Michael. "Unproper Beds: Race, Adultery, and the Hideous in *Othello*." *Shakespeare Quarterly* 40, no. 4 (Winter 1989): 383–412.

Nelson, T. G. A., and Charles Haines. "Othello's Unconsummated Marriage." *Essays in Criticism* 33, no. 1 (1983): 1–18.

Newman, Karen. "Directing Traffic: Subjects, Objects, and the Politics of Exchange." *differences* 2, no. 2 (1990): 41–54.

Nicholson, Catherine. *Uncommon Tongues: Eloquence and Eccentricity in the English Renaissance*. Philadelphia: University of Pennsylvania Press, 2014.

Nixon, Anthony. *The Three English Brothers: Sir Thomas Sherley His Trauels, vvith his three yeares imprisonment in Turkie*. London, 1607.

Nocentelli, Carmen. *Empires of Love: Europe, Asia, and the Making of Early Modern Identity*. Philadelphia: University of Pennsylvania Press, 2013.

Norris, John. *A Collection of Miscellanies: Consisting of Poems, Essays, Discourses, and Letters*. 6th ed. London, 1717.

Okur, Münevver. *Cem Sultan Hayatı ve Şiir Dünyası*. Ankara: Kültür Bakanlığı Yayınları, 1992.

Onyeka, Nubia. *Blackamoores: Africans in Tudor England: Their Presence, Status, and Origins*. London: Narrative Eye, 2013.

Orgel, Stephen. *Impersonations: The Performance of Gender in Shakespeare's England*. Cambridge: Cambridge University Press, 1996.

Orgel, Stephen. "Tobacco and Boys: How Queer Was Marlowe?" *GLQ: A Journal of Lesbian and Gay Studies* 6, no. 4 (2000): 555–76.

Orme. Nicholas. *Medieval Children*. New Haven, CT: Yale University Press, 2001.

Ortaylı, İlber. *Osmanlı Barışı*. Istanbul: Timaş, 2007.

Ortega, Stephen. "'Pleading for Help': Gender Relations and Cross-Cultural Logic in the Early Modern Mediterranean." *Gender and History* 20, no. 2 (2008): 332–48.

Ortiz, Fernando. *Cuban Counterpoint: Tobacco and Sugar*. New York: Alfred A. Knopf, 1947; repr., Durham, NC: Duke University Press, 1995.

Öztekin, Dilek. "Şehrengizler ve Bursa: Edebiyat ve Eşcinsel Eğilim." *Kuram* 14 (1997): 37–41.

Parker, Patricia. "Preposterous Conversions: Turning Turk, and Its 'Pauline' Rerighting." *Journal for Early Modern Cultural Studies* 2, no. 1 (2002): 1–34.

Paster, Gail Kern. *The Body Embarrassed: Drama and the Discipline of Shame in Early Modern England*. Ithaca, NY: Cornell University Press, 1993.

Paster, Gail Kern, and Skiles Howard, eds. *A Midsummer Night's Dream: Texts and Contexts*. Boston: Bedford, 1999.

Patricia, Anthony Guy. *Queering the Shakespeare Film: Gender Trouble, Gay Spectatorship and Male Homoeroticism*. London: Bloomsbury, 2017.

Patterson, Orlando. *Slavery and Social Death: A Comparative Study*. Cambridge, MA: Harvard University Press, 1982.

Peirce, Leslie. "Abduction with (Dis)honor: Sovereigns, Brigands, and Heroes in the Ottoman World." *Journal of Early Modern History* 15 (2011): 311–26.

Peirce, Leslie. *The Imperial Harem: Women and Sovereignty in the Ottoman Empire*. New York: Oxford University Press, 1993.

Peirce, Leslie. "Seniority, Sexuality, and Social Order: The Vocabulary of Gender in Early Modern Ottoman Society." In *Women in the Ottoman Empire: Middle Eastern Women in the Early Modernity*, edited by Madeline Zilfi, 169–96. Leiden: Brill, 1997.

Peirce, Leslie. "Writing Histories of Sexuality in the Middle East." *American Historical Review* 114, no. 5 (2009): 1325–39.

Penzer, N. M. *The Harem: Inside the Grand Seraglio of the Turkish Sultans*. New York: Dover, 2005.

Pérez, Hiram. *A Taste for Brown Bodies: Gay Modernity and Cosmopolitan Desire*. New York: New York University Press, 2015.

Phelan, Peggy. *Unmarked: The Politics of Performance*. New York: Routledge, 1993.

Philips, Susan E. "Schoolmasters, Seduction, and Slavery: Polyglot Dictionaries in Pre-Modern England." In *Medievalia et Humanistica 34*, edited by Paul Maurice Clogan, et. al., 129–58. Lanham, MD: Rowman & Littlefield, 2009.

Pittenger, Elizabeth. "'To Serve the Queere': Nicholas Udall, Master of Revels." In *Queering the Renaissance*, edited by Jonathan Goldberg, 162–89. Durham, NC: Duke University Press, 1994.

Plato. *Laws. The Collected Dialogues of Plato*. Edited by Edith Hamilton and Huntington Cairns. Translated by A. E. Taylor. New York: Pantheon, 1961.

Povinelli, Elizabeth A. *The Empire of Love: Toward a Theory of Intimacy, Genealogy, and Carnality*. Durham, NC: Duke University Press, 2006.

Povinelli, Elizabeth A., and George Chauncey. "Thinking Sexuality Transnationally: An Introduction." *GLQ: A Journal of Lesbian and Gay Studies* 5, no. 4 (1999): 439–50.

Powell, Eve M. Troutt. "Will that Subaltern Ever Speak? Finding African Slaves in the Historiography of the Middle East." In *Middle East Historiographies Narrating the Twentieth Century*, edited by Israel Gershoni, Ami Singer, and Y. Hakan Erdem, 242–61. Seattle: University of Washington Press, 2006.

Purchas, Samuel. *Hakluytus Posthumus; or, Purchas His Pilgrimes: Contayning a History of the World in Sea Voyages and Lande Travells by Englishmen and Others*. 20 vols. New York: James MacLehose and Sons; MacMillan, 1905.

Rackin, Phyllis, and Michael Shapiro. "Boy Heroines." *PMLA* 102, no. 5 (1987): 836–38.

Raman, Shankar. *Framing "India": The Colonial Imaginary in Early Modern Culture*. Stanford, CA: Stanford University Press, 2002.

Rambuss, Richard. "Christ's Ganymede." *Yale Journal of Law and the Humanities* 7 (1995): 77–96.

Rambuss, Richard. *Closet Devotions*. Durham, NC: Duke University Press, 1998.

Rambuss, Richard. "What It Feels Like for a Boy: Shakespeare's *Venus* and *Adonis*." In *A Companion to Shakespeare's Works*, vol. 4, *The Poems, Comedies, and Late Plays*, edited by Richard Dutton and Jean E. Howard, 240–58. Malden, MA: Blackwell, 2003.

Rawlins, John. *The famous and wonderfull recoverie of a ship of Bristoll, called the Exchange, from the Turkish pirates of Argier [. . .] from Turkish slauerie*. London, 1622.

Revani. "Gazeller: 7." In *Revani Divanı*, edited by Mehmet Çavuşoğlu. Ottoman Text Archive Project, University of Washington, Seattle. http://courses.washington.edu/otap/archive/data/arch_txt/texts/a_rgaza.html.

Reynolds, Frederic. *A Midsummer Night's Dream . . . as it is performed at the Theater Royal, Covent Garden*. London, 1816.

Ridgeon, Lloyd. "Christianity as Portrayed by Jalal al-Din Rumi." In *Islamic Interpretations of Christianity*, edited by Lloyd Ridgeon, 99–126. New York: Routledge, 2011.

Ringrose, Kathryn M. *The Perfect Servant: Eunuchs and the Social Construction of Gender in Byzantium*. Chicago: University of Chicago Press, 2003.

Robinson, Benedict. "Harry and Amurath." *Shakespeare Quarterly* 60, no. 4 (2009): 399–424.

Robinson, Benedict. *Islam and Early Modern Literature: The Politics of Romance from Spenser to Milton*. New York: Palgrave Macmillan, 2007.

Rocke, Michael. *Forbidden Friendships: Homosexuality and Male Culture in Renaissance Florence*. Oxford: Oxford University Press, 1976.

Rodriguez, Juana Maria. *Queer Latinidad: Identity Practices, Discursive Spaces*. New York: New York University Press, 2003.

Roth, Norman. "'Deal Gently with the Young Man': Love of Boys in Medieval Hebrew Poetry of Spain." *Speculum* 57, no. 1 (1982): 20–51.

Rubin, Gayle. "The Traffic in Women: Notes on the 'Political Economy of Sex.'" In *Toward an Anthropology of Women*, edited by Rayna Reiter, 157–209. New York: Monthly Review Press, 1975.

Rubin, Patricia. "'Che è di questo culazzino!': Michelangelo and the Motif of the Male Buttocks in Italian Renaissance Art." *Oxford Art Journal* 32, no. 3 (2009): 427–46.

Rutter, Carol Chillington, ed. *Antony and Cleopatra*. Manchester: Manchester University Press, 2020.

Rutter, Carol Chillington. *Shakespeare and Child's Play: Performing Lost Boys on Stage and Screen*. New York: Routledge, 2007.

Rycaut, Paul. *The Present State of the Ottoman Empire*. 1668; repr., New York: Arno Press, 1971.

Şahin, Kaya. *Empire and Power in the Reign of Süleyman: Narrating the Sixteenth-Century Ottoman World*. Cambridge: Cambridge University Press, 2013.

Şahin, Kaya. "Staging an Empire: An Ottoman Circumcision Ceremony as Cultural Performance." *American Historical Review* 123, no. 2 (2018): 463–92.

Said, Edward W. *Culture and Imperialism*. New York: Vintage, 1994.

Said, Edward W. *Orientalism*. New York: Pantheon, 1978.

San Juan, Rose Marie. "The Transformation of the Rio de la Plata and Bernini's *Fountain of the Four Rivers* in Rome." *Representations* 118, no. 1 (2012): 72–102.

Sanders, Julie. *The Cultural Geography of Early Modern Drama, 1620–1650*. Cambridge: Cambridge University Press, 2011.

Sanders, Thomas. "The voyage made to Tripolis in Barbarie, in the yeere 1584, with a ship called the *Jesus*, wherein the adventures and distresses of some Englishmen are truely reported, and other necessary circumstances observed." In Richard Hakluyt, *The Principal Navigations, Voyages, and Discoveries of the English Nation*, 192–200. London, 1589.

Sandys, George. *A Relation of a Journey Begun An. Dom. 1610*. London, 1615.

Sarıtaş, Ezgi. *Cinsel Normalliğin Kuruluşu: Osmanlı'dan Cumhuriyet'e Heteronormatiflik ve İstikrarsızlıkları*. Istanbul: Metis, 2000.

Saslow, James. *Ganymede in the Renaissance: Homosexuality in Art and Society*. New Haven, CT: Yale University Press, 1986.

Sasser, Marvin Tyler. "Shakespeare and Boyhood: Early Modern Representations and Contemporary Appropriations." PhD diss., University of Mississippi, 2015.

Savvadis, Dimitris. "Male Prostitution and the Homoerotic Sex-Market in Early Modern England." PhD diss., University of Sussex, 2011.

Schick, Irvin Cemil. "Representation of Gender and Sexuality in Ottoman and Turkish Erotic Literature." *Turkish Studies Association Journal* 28, no. 1–2 (2007): 81–103.

Schleck, Julia. *Telling True Tales of Islamic Lands: Forms of Mediation in Early English Travel Writing, 1575–1630*. Selinsgrove, PA: Susquehanna University Press, 2011.

Scholz, Piotr O. *Eunuchs and Castrati: A Cultural History*. Princeton, NJ: Markus Wiener, 2001.

Schwartz, Kathryn. *Tough Love: Amazon Encounters in the English Renaissance*. Durham, NC: Duke University Press, 2000.

Scott, Christopher P. "Queer Rapture: Translating Ganymede from Ovid to Marlowe." MA thesis, Wesleyan University, 2011.

Sedgwick, Eve Kosofsky. *Between Men: English Literature and Male Homosocial Desire*. New York: Columbia University Press, 1985.

Sedgwick, Eve Kosofsky. *Epistemology of the Closet*. Berkeley: University of California Press, 2008.

Şeker, Mehmet, ed. *Gelibolulu Mustafa Ali ve Meva'idu'n-nefais fi-kava'idil'l-mecalis*. Ankara: Türk Tarih Kurumu, 1997.

Şentürk, Atilla. "Osmanlı Şiirinde Aşka Dair." *Doğu Batı* 7, no. 26 (2004): 55–68.

Shahani, Gitanjali. "The Spiced Indian Air in Early Modern England." *Shakespeare Studies* 42 (2014): 122–40.

Shakespeare, William. *All's Well That Ends Well*. In *The Norton Shakespeare*, 2nd ed., edited by Stephen Greenblatt, Walter Cohen, Jean Howard, and Katharine Eisaman Maus, 2193–2262. New York: Norton, 2008.

Shakespeare, William. *Anthony and Cleopatra*. In *The Norton Shakespeare*, 2nd ed., edited by Stephen Greenblatt, Walter Cohen, Jean Howard, and Katharine Eisaman Maus, 2633–2722. New York: Norton, 2008.
Shakespeare, William. *As You Like It*. In *The Norton Shakespeare*, 2nd ed., edited by Stephen Greenblatt, Walter Cohen, Jean Howard, and Katharine Eisaman Maus, 1615–82. New York: Norton, 2008.
Shakespeare, William. *Coriolanus*. In *The Norton Shakespeare*, 2nd ed., edited by Stephen Greenblatt, Walter Cohen, Jean Howard, and Katharine Eisaman Maus, 2793–2880. New York: Norton, 2008.
Shakespeare, William, *Love Labor's Lost*. In *The Norton Shakespeare*, 2nd ed., edited by Stephen Greenblatt, Walter Cohen, Jean Howard, and Katharine Eisaman Maus, 767–836. New York: Norton, 2008.
Shakespeare, William. *The Merchant of Venice*. In *The Norton Shakespeare*, 2nd ed., edited by Stephen Greenblatt, Walter Cohen, Jean Howard, and Katharine Eisaman Maus, 1111–76. New York: Norton, 2008.
Shakespeare, William. *A Midsummer Night's Dream*. In *The Norton Shakespeare*, 2nd ed., edited by Stephen Greenblatt, Walter Cohen, Jean Howard, and Katharine Eisaman Maus, 839–96. New York: Norton, 2008.
Shakespeare, William. *Othello*. In *The Norton Shakespeare*, 2nd ed., edited by Stephen Greenblatt, Walter Cohen, Jean Howard, and Katharine Eisaman Maus, 2109–92. New York: Norton, 2008.
Shakespeare, William. *Romeo and Juliet*. In *The Norton Shakespeare*, 2nd ed., edited by Stephen Greenblatt, Walter Cohen, Jean Howard, and Katharine Eisaman Maus, 897–972. New York: Norton, 2008.
Shakespeare, William. "Sonnets." In *The Norton Shakespeare*, 2nd ed., edited by Stephen Greenblatt, Walter Cohen, Jean Howard, and Katharine Eisaman Maus, 1937–2010. New York: Norton, 2008.
Shakespeare, William. *Twelfth Night*. In *The Norton Shakespeare*, 2nd ed., edited by Stephen Greenblatt, Walter Cohen, Jean Howard, and Katharine Eisaman Maus, 1785–1846. New York: Norton, 2008.
Shakespeare, William. *Two Gentlemen of Verona*. In *The Norton Shakespeare*, 2nd ed., edited by Stephen Greenblatt, Walter Cohen, Jean Howard, and Katharine Eisaman Maus, 103–58. New York: Norton, 2008.
Shakespeare, William. *Venus and Adonis*. In *The Norton Shakespeare*, 2nd ed., edited by Stephen Greenblatt, Walter Cohen, Jean Howard, and Katharine Eisaman Maus, 629–62. New York: Norton, 2008.
Shakespeare, William. *The Winter's Tale*. In *The Norton Shakespeare*, 2nd ed., edited by Stephen Greenblatt, Walter Cohen, Jean Howard, and Katharine Eisaman Maus, 2881–2962. New York: Norton, 2008.
Shannon, Laurie. *Sovereign Amity: Figures of Friendship in Shakespearean Contexts*. Chicago: University of Chicago Press, 2002.
Shapiro, James. *Shakespeare and the Jews*. New York: Columbia University Press, 1996.
Shapiro, Michael. *Children of the Revels: The Boy Companies of Shakespeare's Time and Their Plays*. New York: Columbia University Press, 1977.
Shyllon, Folarin. *Black People in Britain 1555–1833*. Oxford: Oxford University Press, 1977.

Sılay, Kemal. *Nedim and the Poetics of the Ottoman Court: Medieval Inheritance and the Need for Change*. Bloomington: Indiana University Press, 1994.

Simons, Patricia. *The Sex of Men in Premodern Europe: A Cultural History*. Cambridge: Cambridge University Press, 2011.

Sinfield, Alan. "Cultural Materialism and Intertextuality: The Limits of Queer Reading in *A Midsummer Night's Dream* and *The Two Noble Kinsmen*." *Shakespeare Survey* 56 (2003): 67–78.

Sinfield, Alan. "How to Read *The Merchant of Venice* without Being Heterosexist." In *Alternative Shakespeares*, vol. 2, edited by Terrence Hawkes, 123–40. London: Routledge, 2005.

Sinfield, Alan. *On Sexuality and Power*. New York: Columbia University Press, 2004.

Sinfield, Alan. *Shakespeare, Authority, Sexuality: Unfinished Business in Cultural Materialism*. London: Routledge, 2006.

Singh, Jyotsna G. *Colonial Narratives/Cultural Dialogues: "Discovery" of India in the Language of Colonialism*. New York: Routledge, 1996.

Singh, Jyotsna G., ed. *A Companion to The Global Renaissance: English Literature and Culture in the Era of Expansion*. Malden, MA: Wiley-Blackwell, 2009.

Skilliter, Susan A. *William Harborne and the Trade with Turkey, 1578–1582: A Documentary Study of the First Anglo-Ottoman Relations*. Oxford: Oxford University Press, 1977.

Slade, Adolphus. *Records of Travels in Turkey, Greece, etc. . . . in the Years 1829. 1830, and 1831*. London, 1833.

Slights, William E. "The Changeling in *A Dream*." *Studies in English Literature 1500–1900* 28, no. 2 (1988): 259–72.

Smith, Bruce. *Homosexual Desire in Shakespeare's England: A Cultural Poetics*. Chicago: University of Chicago Press, 1991.

Smith, Ian. "The Queer Moor: Bodies, Borders, and Barbary Inns." In *A Companion to The Global Renaissance: English Literature and Culture in the Era of Expansion*, edited by Jyotsna G. Singh, 190–204. Malden, MA: Wiley-Blackwell, 2009.

Snorton, C. Riley. *Black on Both Sides: A Racial History of Trans Identity*. Minneapolis: University of Minnesota Press, 2017.

Sobers-Khan, Nur. *Slaves without Shackles: Forced Labour and Manumission in the Galata Court Registers, 1560–1572*. Berlin: Klaus Schwarz Verlag, 2014.

Somerville, Siobhan B. *Queering the Color Line: Race and the Invention of Homosexuality in American Culture*. Durham, NC: Duke University Press, 2000.

Spencer, Charles. *Prince Rupert: The Last Cavalier*. London: Weidenfeld and Nicolson, 2007.

Spencer, Terence. "Turks and Trojans in the Renaissance." *Modern Language Review* 47, no. 3 (1952): 330–33.

Spenser, Edmund. *The Faerie Queene*. London: Penguin, 1987.

Spurlin, William. *Imperialism within the Margins: Queer Representations and the Politics of Culture in Southern Africa*. New York: Palgrave Macmillan, 2006.

Spurlin, William. "Shifting Geopolitical Borders/Shifting Sexual Borders: Textual and Cultural Renegotiations of National Identity and Sexual Dissidence in Postcolonial Africa." *Studies in Ethnicity and Nationalism* 13, no. 1 (2013): 69–79.

Stallybrass, Peter. "Patriarchal Territories: The Body Enclosed." In *Rewriting the Renaissance: The Discourse of Sexual Difference in Early Modern Europe*, edited by Margaret W. Ferguson, Maureen Quilligan, and Nancy J. Vickers, 123–43. Chicago: University of Chicago Press, 1984.

Stallybrass, Peter. "Transvestism and the 'Body Beneath': Speculating on the Boy Actor." In *Erotic Politics: Desire on the Renaissance Stage*, edited by Susan Zimmerman, 64–83. New York: Routledge, 1992.

Stanivukovic, Goran V. "Cruising the Mediterranean: Narratives of Sexuality and Geographies of the Eastern Mediterranean in Early Modern English Prose Romances." In *Remapping the Mediterranean World in Early Modern English Writings*, edited by Goran V. Stanivukovic, 59–74. New York: Palgrave Macmillan, 2007.

Stanivukovic, Goran. *Knights in Arms: Prose Romance, Masculinity, and Eastern Mediterranean Trade in Early Modern England, 1565–1655*. Toronto: University of Toronto Press, 2018.

Steedman, Carolyn. *Strange Dislocations: Childhood and the Idea of Human Interiority, 1780–1930*. New York: Routledge, 1992.

Stetkevych, Suzanne P. "Intoxication and Immortality: Wine and Associated Imagery in Al-Maʿarri's Garden." In *Homoeroticism in Classical Arabic Literature*, edited by J. W. Wright and Everett K. Rowson, 210–32. New York: Columbia University Press, 1997.

Stewart, Alan. *Close Readers: Humanism and Sodomy in Early Modern England*. Princeton, NJ: Princeton University Press, 1997.

Stewart-Robinson, James. "A Neglected Ottoman Poem: The Sehrengiz." In *Studies in Near Eastern Culture and History: In Memory of Ernest T. Abdel-Massih*, edited by James Bellamy, 201–11. Ann Arbor: University of Michigan Press, 1990.

Stockton, Kathryn Bond. *The Queer Child, or Growing Sideways in the Twentieth Century*. Durham, NC: Duke University Press, 2009.

Stoler, Ann Laura. *Race and the Education of Desire: Foucault's "History of Sexuality" and the Colonial Order of Things*. Durham, NC: Duke University Press, 1995.

Stout, Robert E. "The Sur-ı Humayun of Murad III: A Study of Ottoman Pageantry and Entertainment." PhD diss., Ohio State University, 1966.

Strickland, Debra Higgs. *Saracens, Demons, and Jews: Making Monsters in Medieval Art*. Princeton, NJ: Princeton University Press, 2003.

Subrahmanyam, Sanjay. "Connected Histories: Notes towards a Reconfiguration of Early Modern Eurasia." In *Beyond Binary Histories: Re-imagining Eurasia to c.1830*, edited by Victor Lieberman, 289–316. Ann Arbor: University of Michigan Press, 1999.

Subrahmanyam, Sanjay. *Explorations in Connected History: Mughals and Franks*. Oxford: Oxford University Press, 2005.

Subrahmanyam, Sanjay. "On World Historians in the Sixteenth Century." *Representations* 91, no. 1 (2005): 26–57.

Subrahmanyam, Sanjay. "A Tale of Three Empires: Mughals, Ottomans, and Habsburgs in A Comparative Context." *Common Knowledge* 12, no. 1 (2006): 66–92.

Tansuğ, Sezer. *Şenlikname Düzeni*. Istanbul: Yapı Kredi Yayınları, 1993.

Tartakoff, Paola. *Conversion, Circumcision, and Ritual Murder in Medieval Europe*. Philadelphia: University of Pennsylvania Press, 2020.

Taylor, Gary. *Castration: An Abbreviated History of Western Manhood*. New York: Routledge, 2000.

Terzioğlu, Derin. "The Imperial Circumcision Festival of 1582: An Interpretation." *Muqarnas: An Annual on Islamic Art and Architecture* 12 (1995): 84–100.

Tezcan, Baki. "*Dispelling the Darkness* of the *Halberdier's Treatise*: A Comparative Look at Black Africans in Ottoman Letters in the Early Modern Period." In *Disliking Others: Loathing, Hostility, and Distrust in Premodern Ottoman Lands*, edited by Hakan Karateke, H. Erdem Çıpa, and Helga Anetshofer, 43–74. Boston: Academic Studies, 2018.

Tezcan, Baki. "*Dispelling the Darkness*: The Politics of 'Race' in the Early Seventeenth Century Ottoman Empire in the Light of the Life and Work of Mulla Ali." In *Identity and Identity Formation in the Ottoman World: A Volume of Essays in Honor of Norman Itzkowitz*, edited by Baki Tezcan and Karl K. Barbir, 73–96. Madison: University of Wisconsin Press, 2007.

Tezcan, Baki. *The Second Ottoman Empire: Political and Social Transformation in the Early Modern World*. Cambridge: Cambridge University Press, 2010.

Thompson, Ayanna, ed. *Colorblind Shakespeare: New Perspectives on Race and Performance*. Routledge, 2006.

Tokson, Elliot H. *The Popular Image of the Black Man in English Drama, 1550–1688*. Boston: G. K. Hall, 1982.

Tolan, John V. *Saracens: Islam in the Medieval European Imagination*. New York: Columbia University Press, 2002.

Toledano, Ehud R. *As if Silent and Absent: Bonds of Enslavement in the Islamic Middle East*. New Haven, CT: Yale University Press, 2007.

Toledano, Ehud R. "The Concept of Slavery in Ottoman and Other Muslim Societies." In *Slave Elites in the Middle East and Africa: A Comparative Study*, edited by Miura Toru and John E. Philips, 159–76. London: Kegan Paul, 2000.

Toledano, Ehud R. *Slavery and Abolition in the Ottoman Middle East*. Seattle: University of Washington Press, 1998.

Tommasini, Anthony. "In Britten's Complex 'Dream,' a Balance of Light and Dark." *New York Times*, November 24, 1996.

Traub, Valerie. "(In)Significance of 'Lesbian' Desire in Early Modern England." In *Erotic Politics: Desire on the Renaissance Stage*, edited by Susan Zimmerman, 150–69. New York: Routledge, 1991.

Traub, Valerie. "Mapping the Global Body." In *Early Modern Visual Culture: Representation, Race, and Empire in Renaissance England*, edited by Peter Erickson and Clarke Hulse, 44–97. Philadelphia: University of Pennsylvania Press, 2000.

Traub, Valerie, ed. *The Oxford Handbook of Shakespeare and Embodiment: Gender, Sexuality, and Race*. Oxford: Oxford University Press, 2018.

Traub, Valerie. "The Past Is a Foreign Country? The Times and Spaces of Islamicate Sexuality Studies." In *Islamicate Sexualities: Translations across Temporal Geographies of Desire*, edited by Kathryn Babayan and Afsaneh Najmabadi, 1–40. Cambridge, MA: Harvard University Press, 2008.

Traub, Valerie. *The Renaissance of Lesbianism in Early Modern England*. Cambridge: Cambridge University Press, 2002.

Traub, Valerie. "Sexuality." In *A Cultural History of Western Empires in the Renaissance*, edited by Ania Loomba, 147–80. London: Bloomsbury, 2019.

Trexler, Richard C. *Sex and Conquest: Gendered Violence, Political Order, and the European Conquest of the Americas*. Ithaca, NY: Cornell University Press, 1995.

Trzaskoma, Stephen, R. Scott Smith, Stephen Brunet, and Thomas G. Palaima, eds. *Anthology of Classical Myth: Primary Sources in Translation*. Indianapolis: Hackett Publishing, 2004.

Tuan, Yi-Fu. *Dominance and Affection: The Making of Pets*. New Haven, CT: Yale University Press, 1984.

Tuğcu, Emine. "Şehrengizler ve Ayine-i Huban-I Bursa: Bursa Şehrengizlerinde Guzeller." PhD diss., Bilkent University, 2007.

Türkiye Diyanet Vakfı İslâm Ansiklopedisi. Istanbul: Türkiye Diyanet Vakfi, 1988.

Turner, Henry S. *The English Renaissance Stage: Geometry, Poetics, and the Practical Spatial Arts 1580–1630*. Oxford: Oxford University Press, 2006.

Tursun Beg. *Tarih-i Ebü'l-Feth*. Edited by A. Mertol Tulum. Istanbul: Baha, 1977.

Ungerer, Gustav. *The Mediterranean Apprenticeship of British Slavery*. Madrid: Verbum, 2008.

Uzunçarşılı, Ismail H. *Osmanlı Devleti Teşkilatında Kapıkulu Ocakları*. Ankara: Türk Tarih Kurumu, 1943.

Vakalopoulos. Apostolos E. *The Greek Nation, 1453–1669: The Cultural and Economic Background of Modern Greek Society*. New Brunswick, NJ: Rutgers University Press, 1976.

Vaughan, Alden T. "Sir Walter Raleigh's Indian Interpreters, 1585–1618." *William and Mary Quarterly* 59, no. 2 (2002): 341–76.

Vaughan, Alden T. "Trinculo's Indian: American Natives in Shakespeare's England." In *The Tempest and Its Travels*, edited by Peter Hulme and William Sherman, 49–59. Philadelphia: University of Pennsylvania Press, 2000.

Vickers, Nancy. "'The blazon of sweet beauty's best': Shakespeare's *Lucrece*." In *Shakespeare and the Question of Theory*, edited by Patricia Parker and Geoffrey Hartman, 95–115. New York: Methuen, 1985.

Virgil. *Virgil's Aeneid*. 1697. Translated by John Dryden. New York: P. F. Collier and Son, 1909.

Vitkus, Daniel, ed. *Piracy, Slavery, and Redemption: Barbary Captivity Narratives from Early Modern England*. New York: Columbia University Press, 2001.

Vitkus, Daniel, ed. *Three Turk Plays from Early Modern England*. New York: Columbia University Press, 2000.

Vitkus, Daniel. *Turning Turk: English Theatre and the Multicultural Mediterranean, 1570–1630*. Basingstoke: Palgrave Macmillan, 2003.

Wagner, Sydnee. "Outlandish People: Gypsies, Race, and Fantasies of National Identity in Early Modern England." PhD diss., CUNY, 2020.

Wall, Wendy. *Staging Domesticity: Household Work and English Identity in Early Modern Drama*. Cambridge: Cambridge University Press, 2002.

Wallace, Andrew. *Virgil's Schoolboys: The Poetics of Pedagogy in Renaissance England*. Oxford: Oxford University Press, 2010.

Walz, Terence, and Kenneth M. Cuno, eds. *Race and Slavery in the Middle East: Histories of Trans-Saharan Africans in Nineteenth-Century Egypt, Sudan, and the Ottoman Mediterranean*. New York: American University in Cairo Press, 2010.

Warner, Michael. "New English Sodomy." *American Literature* 64, no. 1 (1992): 19–47.
Weaver, William P. *Untutored Lines: The Making of the English Epyllion*. Edinburgh: Edinburgh University Press, 2012.
Weidemann, Thomas, ed. *Greek and Roman Slavery*. Baltimore, MD: Johns Hopkins University Press, 1982.
Weissbourd, Emily. *Bad Blood: Staging Race between Early Modern England and Spain*. Philadelphia: University of Pennsylvania Press, 2023.
Wendorf, Richard. *The Elements of Life: Biography and Portrait in Stuart and Georgian England*. Oxford: Clarendon Press, 1990.
White, Michael. "ENO's Shocking New Paedophile *Midsummer Night's Dream* Is Brilliant, and I Hated It." *The Telegraph*, May 20, 2011.
Wilkinson, Clennell. *Prince Rupert the Cavalier*. London: J. B. Lippincott, 1935.
Williams, Gary Jay. *Our Moonlight Revels: A Midsummer Night's Dream in the Theatre*. Iowa City: University of Iowa Press, 1997
Wilson, Bronwen. "The Itinerant Artist and the Islamic Urban Prospect: Guillaume-Joseph Grélot's Self-Portraits in Ambrosio Bembo's *Travel Journal*." *Artibus et Historiae* 38, no. 76 (2017): 157–80.
Wintle, Michael. *The Image of Europe: Visualizing Europe in Cartography and Iconography throughout the Ages*. Cambridge: Cambridge University Press, 2009.
Wood, Noami. "Creating the Sensual Child: Paterian Aesthetics, Pederasty, and Oscar Wilde's Fairy Tales." *Marvels & Tales* 16, no. 2 (2002): 156–70.
Yelçe, Zeynep. "Evaluating Three Imperial Festivals: 1524, 1530 and 1539." In *Celebration, Entertainment and Theater in the Ottoman World*, edited by Suraiya Faroqi and Arzu Öztürkmen, 71–109. London: Seagull, 2014.
Yermolenko, Galina I. "Tartar-Turkish Captivity and Conversion in Early Modern Ukrainian Songs." In *Mediterranean Identities in Premodern Era: Entrepots Islands Empires*, edited by John Watkins and Kathryn L. Reyerson, 191–209. Burlington, VT: Ashgate, 2014.
Yılmaz, Gülay. "Becoming a *Devşirme*: The Training of Conscripted Children in the Ottoman Empire." In *Children in Slavery through the Ages*, edited by Gwyn Campbell, Suzanne Meiers, and Joseph C. Miller, 119–34. Athens: Ohio University Press, 2009.
Yılmaz, Gülay. "The Devshirme System and the Levied Children of Bursa in 1603–4 A.D." *Belleten* 78, no. 286 (2015): 901–31.
Ze'evi, Dror. *Producing Desire: Changing Sexual Discourse in the Ottoman Middle East, 1500–1900*. Berkeley: University of California Press, 2006.
Zeikowitz, Richard E. *Homoeroticism and Chivalry: Discourses of Male Same-Sex Desire in the Fourteenth Century*. New York: Palgrave Macmillan, 2003.
Zeman, Corinne. "Sultanic Drag in Ben Jonson's Epicene." *Shakespeare Studies* 47 (2019): 134–40.
Zilfi, Madeline C. "The Kadızadelis: Discordant Revivalism in Seventeenth-Century Istanbul." *Journal of Near Eastern Studies* 45, no. 4 (1996): 251–69.
Zilfi, Madeline C. *Women and Slavery in the Late Ottoman Empire: The Design of Difference*. Cambridge: Cambridge University Press, 2010.

Index

Abdulaziz, Karaçelebizade, 181
Abyssinians, 66, 179, 180
administrators, 47, 65, 144, 176, 229
adolescents, 8, 18, 37, 107, 135, 213–14, 219, 226, 261n92
adults, 7–8, 11–12, 18, 26, 36, 41, 50, 67, 74, 77–78, 99–100, 106, 108, 123, 134, 140, 143, 146, 149, 159, 173, 180, 183, 200, 202, 211, 213–17, 220, 231, 245n143, 259n62, 261n86, 272n39; transition to, 2, 64, 146, 150, 211, 234n7, 249n60, 261n7
aestheticization, 4, 107, 222; representational, 3, 8, 10–11, 23, 34, 36, 74, 96, 107, 111, 228, 253n9
Africa, 17, 21, 23, 28, 33, 40, 110–11, 117, 161, 178, 193, 194, 222, 246n14, 257n29; African, 94, 118, 169–70, 175–76, 189, 195, 200, 225, 238n71, 256n7, 257n28, 268nn45–47, 269n62, 270n84; African American, 41, 200, 213, 234n10; Africans in England, 112–13, 118, 123, 133; attacks against Africans, 66, 177–85, 188, 243n122, 266n18
agency, 4, 37, 63, 217–19, 245n141. *See also* resistance; subjectivity
Ahmed, Sara, 253n9
Ahmed Cevdet Paşa, 228–29
Ahmed Pasha, 55, 58–59, 64, 248n47
Alexander the Great, 24, 26, 91
Ali, Mullah, 180–85, 269n65. *See also* hyacinths
Al-Jahiz of Basra, 177, 269n70

Allston, Washington, 207
All's Well That Ends Well (Shakespeare), 189
Al-Masudi, 178
ambassadors, 21, 69, 83, 118, 147, 164, 172, 183, 229
Amer, Sahar, 9, 25
Americas, 17, 20, 24, 110, 112, 253n8, 260n85; personifications of, 96, 106–7. *See also* New World
Amin, Kadji, 6–7, 18, 215
Anatolia, 24, 30, 65–67, 261n10, 269n62
anatomy, 171, 187
And, Metin, 262n16
Andrea, Bernadette, 36, 239n79
Andrews, Walter, 22–23, 248n45; and Mehmet Kalpaklı, 9, 26–27, 64, 84, 87, 94, 233n3, 239nn83–85, 241n102, 241–42n104, 242nn105–6, 246n22, 248nn42–43, 248nn49–52, 249n57, 249nn59–60, 253nn11–12, 254n15, 254n17, 255n26, 273n1, 273n4
androgynous, 2, 4, 193, 230
animals, 65, 97, 118–19, 127–28, 130, 132, 145, 158, 178, 258n40, 260n82, 267n42. *See also* bestiality; dehumanization; grooms; henchmen
Anne of Denmark, 130
Anthony and Cleopatra (Shakespeare), 169–71, 186–95, 200, 234n9
apprentices, 2, 3, 50, 111, 132, 223, 256n8. *See also* mastery; service

Arab: as black, 176, 178–84, 269n62; as ethnicity, 9, 25, 65, 67, 146, 177, 227, 269n70; Islamicate, 7, 25, 33, 177, 185, 215; language and literature, 11, 23–24, 52, 54–55, 86–87, 185, 215, 241n101, 247n35, 248n42, 250n69, 254nn20–21, 269n70, 274n15. *See also* black; Islam

Aravamudan, Srinivas, 118, 258n41

archive, queering of, 4–5

Arifi, 52, 54–55, 63–64. See also *Süleymanname*

Aristotle, 26, 241n101

army, 48–49, 52, 63–64, 149, 247n35, 248n55, 265n77. *See also* military

Arondekar, Anjali, 46, 237n65, 246n3

Asia, 23, 92, 99, 103, 106, 110–12, 126, 160, 193, 231; abductions in, 111–12, 126, 256n12; Asian, 94, 103, 159, 181, 212–13, 217, 256n7, 256n12, 273n43; embodied as boy, 231, 273n43; personifications of, 99, 103

Aşık Çelebi, 228, 248n57, 250n70, 252n1; "Ode to Danube," 39, 81–84, 92, 94–95, 102, 108

As You Like It (Shakespeare), 13, 137, 217, 245n141

Atayi, Nev'izade: *Heft Han*, 221–23, 273n1

Athens, 37, 40, 109–11, 125, 127, 129, 136, 206. *See also* Greece

atlases, 99, 108. *See also* cartography

Attar, Farid al-Din, 88

Avicenna (Ibn Sina), 26, 226, 241n101

Avni. *See* Mehmed II

Bacchus, 100, 274n7

Bach, Rebecca Ann, 175, 266n20

Bacon, Francis, 260n76

Balkans, 17, 51, 172, 174, 176, 261n10

Barbary, 21, 47–48, 141, 157, 160, 165–66, 200, 261n1, 264n71. *See also* Africa; black; Moor

Bardakçı, Murat, 241n103, 271n108

Barnfield, Richard, 13, 137, 236n49

bathhouses, 2, 19, 26–27, 84, 227–28, 241n103, 249n57

Baudier, Michel, 16, 72, 144, 147–48, 159–60, 187, 251n87

Bayezid I, 144, 223

beards, 100, 103, 175, 230; boys without, 27, 65–68, 95, 143, 173, 193, 228, 249n57; as signs of adulthood, 64–65, 95, 173, 234n7, 249n60. *See also* hair

beauty: blackness as, 185, 243n122, 269n70; changing norms of, 3–4, 234n13; whiteness as, 34, 66, 68, 75–76, 179, 184, 188, 224; of boys, 2, 12–13, 17, 27, 36–37, 39–40, 50–51, 55, 58, 63, 65, 67–74, 88–89, 91, 95, 107, 113, 167, 206, 220, 224–26, 228, 236n49, 242n105, 249n62. *See also* Joseph

Beshir Agha, 172, 176, 266n12, 269n68

bestiality, 119, 125, 153, 157–58, 184, 258n47, 264n61. *See also* animals; buggery; sodomy

Betterton, Thomas, 203

Bible, 26; allusions to, 99, 170, 185

biography, 26, 33, 67, 82, 117–18, 228, 241n103, 243n119, 244n128, 250n70, 252n1, 257n32, 258n43, 266n12, 274n5, 274n9

black: antiblack racism, 41, 171, 177–85, 243n122, 267n34, 268n48, 269n68; black boys, 7, 33, 40–41, 112–13, 128, 130–33, 169–70, 189, 194, 257n20, 258n39, 260n81; blackamoor, 113, 118, 170, 186; black women, 175, 200, 260n85; exotic servants in portraiture, 114–20, 124, 257n28; negro, 113–14, 133–35, 161, 174, 178, 181, 183, 189, 193. *See also* Africa; Arab; eunuch; exoticized; foreign; Hamitic curse; Moor; race; skin

Blaeu, Willem, 99–105, 108

blazon, 75–76, 251n98

Blount, Henry, 72, 190

Blount, Thomas, 13, 72

Bodin, Jean, 23

body. *See* beards; black; clothing; embodiment; gender; hair; humoral theory; penis; skin

Boone, Joseph, 8–10, 215, 241n103, 273n1, 273n42

borders, 8, 38, 46, 65, 81, 87, 94–95, 103–4, 147, 232, 253n13; fluidity of, 39, 79, 83, 106, 108; linguistic and cultural, 4, 9, 11, 20, 24, 239n79, 241n103

Bosman, Anston, 170, 265n5, 270n87

Bostanzade Yahya, 181

boy: abuse of, 6–7, 16, 13, 37, 49, 72, 134, 143, 214, 219, 237n63, 245n144, 260n85, 261n86; actors, 3, 134–35, 226, 233n3, 245n141, 256n8; the age of, 2, 7–8, 27, 35–36, 49–50, 54, 65, 71, 113–14, 134–36, 143, 149–50, 170,

207, 213–14, 216–17, 219, 234n8, 247n28, 261n7, 261n92; definitions and categories of, 2–3, 65, 134–35, 192, 213, 233n1; as iconic, 11–12, 17–18, 27, 39, 54, 67, 72, 77, 87, 105, 126, 133, 226, 264; innocence of, 4, 36–37, 245n139, 245n143; in liminal spaces, 39, 83–84, 86–93, 94–96, 100–108; as a literary trope, 13, 19, 36, 38, 40, 45, 55, 62, 79, 80, 83–89, 222, 241n102, 245n2; in portraiture, 114–24; racial cataloguing of, 63–68; as seducer, 11, 13, 16, 19, 37, 76, 86, 245n141; selection of, 34, 51–52, 63, 113–14, 247n29; transition from, 2, 64, 146, 150, 211, 234n7, 249n60, 261n7. *See also* cupbearers; devşirme; Ganymede; grooms; henchmen; janissaries; pages; squires

Boyarin, Daniel, 158

Bray, Alan, 19, 133, 223, 238n71, 250n69, 258n47, 259n73, 260n74, 260n76

Britten, Benjamin, 212–15, 272n31

Britton, Dennis, 142, 242n107, 264n59

Bromley, James, 79, 251n91

Brook, Peter, 217

brothels, 2, 227

Bryan, Emily, 111, 237n61, 245n141, 256nn8–10, 256n17

buggery, 14, 19, 119, 133, 223, 260n82. *See also* bestiality; sodomy

Bulwer, John, 152–53, 158, 160, 175

Burges, Richard, 162–65

Burton, Jonathan, 29, 142, 155, 163, 238n71, 238n75, 239nn77–78, 242nn107–8, 246nn15–16, 246n21, 263n50, 263n54, 264n59, 267n28, 271n95

Burton, Richard, 227, 274n14

Burton, Robert, 187

Burton, William E., 206

Byzantine, 11, 24, 50, 92, 95, 146, 171, 266n10

Caesar (character), 91, 190, 234n9

Caesar (title), 23, 91–92, 240n87

Campana, Joseph, 110, 234n11, 255nn1–2, 256n8

cannibalism, 184

capitalism, 223

captains, 155–56, 161, 192, 264n60

captives and captivity, 3–4, 8–9, 17, 40, 48–50, 65, 73, 95, 103, 138, 142, 157, 160–67, 234n11, 239n77, 246n14, 264n71. *See also* slaves and slavery

cartography: developments in, 23, 239n85, 240n88; representations, 24, 37–39, 83–84, 87, 95–97, 99–106, 253nn9–10. *See also* rivers

Casale, Giancarlo, 24, 239n85

Case, Sue-Ellen, 213, 272n31

Castiglione, Baldassare, 25, 224

Castlehaven, Earl of, 238n71, 260n76

castration, 40, 71, 178, 187, 189, 192; circumcision as, 143, 152, 154–59, 160, 169–70, 261n6, 263n43; conversion as, 142, 153–57; methods of, 174–76, 266n18; voluntary, 270n84. *See also* circumcision; deformity; eunuch; gender

catamite, 2, 13, 36, 64, 66, 72, 226, 230, 236n48, 251n85. *See also* Ganymede

Cavendish, William, 130

Cecil, Robert, 112

Certeau, Michel de, 252n6

changeling, 110–11, 126–29, 134–35, 201, 204, 214, 216, 258n57, 259n62. *See also* Indian boy; substitutions

Chapman, George, 80, 252n107

Charles I, 117, 119, 130

Charles II, 117

Chauncey, George, 217, 237n65, 273n47

child, 2, 6, 16, 71, 110, 112–13, 118, 126–29, 134–37, 149–50, 157, 173, 177, 186–87, 193, 200–201, 206, 211, 213–16, 233n1, 245n139, 245n144, 255n1, 256n8, 256n10, 258n57, 261n86, 261n92, 274n85. *See also* boy

Christianity: conversion to, 86, 89, 152, 156; Euro-Christian, 17, 22, 39, 63, 68, 83, 86, 88, 106, 147, 171, 222–23, 227; versus Islam, 8, 22, 82–83, 88, 94, 103, 106, 165, 222, 263n38, 265n81. *See also* conversion; Frank

chronicle, 21, 23, 25, 38, 40–41, 49, 51, 55, 144, 146, 147, 151, 157, 171, 240n87, 240n99

churches, 83–84, 90–93, 149, 151, 222, 241n99

cins (jins/genus), 181–83, 268n61, 269n62

circumcision, 40–41, 71, 141; as castration, 142–43, 154–59, 160, 169–70, 189, 261n6, 263n43; in Ottoman Empire, 143–48; as racialized conversion, 149–53, 163–67

class, 2, 6, 8, 27, 35, 48, 51, 62, 65, 137, 144, 145, 156, 181–82, 185, 202, 217, 219, 220, 223, 234n7, 235n26, 242n107

INDEX 311

Claudianus, Claudian, 182
Cleves, Rachel Hope, 6, 235n23, 237n63, 245n140, 245n143, 273n44
climatic theory, 33, 177–78, 184–85, 237n66, 242n107
clothing: codpieces, 175, 192; cross-dressing, 13, 134, 146, 192, 206, 217, 226, 266n7; of servant boys, 52, 54–55, 69, 115–16, 123–24, 206, 212; as a sign of religious difference, 4, 30, 86, 88, 90–91, 152–53, 155; turban, 102, 116, 151, 154, 156–57, 193, 201, 207, 211–12, 216–17, 219. *See also* beards; embodiment; hair
Cocles, Bartholomeus, 175
coffeehouses, 25, 227–28, 249n57
Coke, Edward, 19, 119
Colman, George, 205
colonialism, 7, 9–10, 17, 24, 28, 30, 32, 39, 42, 83, 106, 110–11, 115, 124, 127, 138, 200, 203, 205, 223, 228–29, 231, 242n107. *See also* postcolonialism
companions, 11–12, 16, 67–68, 71, 107, 180, 236n49, 270n84; in bed, 74, 118, 128, 189, 194, 202, 260n74, 260n76; reproductive unions, 34, 83, 111, 132, 170, 173–74, 230, 267n20. *See also* eroticism; friend
conquest, 30, 77, 84, 87, 92–93, 95, 108, 144, 163, 170, 177, 179, 205, 237n60, 243n115, 253n8, 254n25, 262n13, 267n20
consent, 8, 31, 36, 136, 165, 187, 245n140, 270n84
Constantinople, 19, 37, 69, 71, 84, 87, 91–92, 144, 147–48, 164, 166, 187, 237n60, 254n25. *See also* Istanbul
contacts: cross-cultural, 2, 10, 19–20, 29, 39, 50, 83, 142, 238n73; erotic, 176, 183, 249n57. *See also* exchanges
continents, 23–25, 96–97, 103
contrapuntal reading, 1, 4, 9–11, 29, 38, 41, 54, 223, 230
convention, 6, 34, 38, 55, 79, 80, 83, 87, 96, 106, 146, 161, 170, 200, 203, 213, 216–17, 228–29, 241n102, 251n98, 262n17
conversion: as perversion, 5–6, 49, 86, 142–43, 149, 153–60, 163, 189, 246n16; homoerotics of, 83, 89–94, 162. *See also* circumcision; renegados
Copland, Patrick, 112

Coriolanus (Shakespeare), 189
Coryat, Thomas, 49, 143
courtiers, 25, 55, 62, 82, 84, 224, 250n69, 250n78
Crawford, Katherine, 265n5, 266n10, 266n15, 266n18
cross-dressing. *See* clothing
crossings, 1, 5–6, 8, 19, 20–21, 25, 38, 46, 50, 83, 106, 193, 203, 220, 226, 239n77, 265n7. *See also* contacts; conversion; exchanges; gender; Mediterranean
cruising, 79, 83; as method, 5–6, 234n14
cupbearers, 8, 12–13, 17, 27, 45, 54–55, 59, 68, 73, 76–77, 80, 86, 93, 100, 105, 133, 136, 207, 222, 224, 231. *See also* boy; Ganymede; service
Cupid, 13, 71, 99, 135, 146, 170, 191, 245n141
Cymbeline (Shakespeare), 270n86

Daborne, Robert: *A Christian Turned Turk*, 40, 153–56, 225, 271n104
Daileader, Celia R., 155, 263n34
Dallam, Thomas, 186, 269n76
Daly, Augustin, 206
Danube. *See* rivers
decadence, 49, 265n7
decrees, 84, 113, 256n19, 257n19
Dederj, 112
deformity, 70, 183, 187, 191, 193, 195, 261n86, 271n103. *See also* castration
Degenhardt, Jane, 153, 238n71, 239n77, 264n59
dehumanization, 118–19, 134, 158, 180, 200, 205, 234n10. *See also* animals; black; slaves and slavery
De Jode, Gerard, 97
Dekker, Thomas, 236n49
Deli Birader Gazali, 250n69
dervishes, 60, 67, 144
devşirme, 2, 31, 162, 172; celebration of, 54–64, 222; emergence and process of, 50–52, 243n118, 247n27; English accounts of, 49, 68–73, 160; as a racial practice, 29–32, 185. *See also* boy; janissaries
Dido, Queen of Carthage (Marlowe), 73, 79, 236n49
Dieterle, William, 211
DiGangi, Mario, 136, 223, 233n3, 236n49, 238n71, 246n22, 249n68, 250n69, 259n73, 263n34, 264n74, 273n48

Dinshaw, Carolyn, 6
diplomats and diplomacy, 10, 48–49, 83, 112, 147, 166, 171, 229, 238n73, 239n85, 269n65
domestic, 3, 26, 33, 40, 50, 52, 72, 94, 107, 112, 118, 132, 172, 180, 223, 235n28, 256n18
domination, 10, 24, 34, 40, 84, 89, 92, 94, 96, 104, 108, 123, 132, 146, 163, 167, 205, 243n115
Drago, Domingo Cassedon, 133, 260n82
dragomans, 260n82
Dryden, John, 271n103; *All for Love*, 194
dwarf, 173, 183, 193, 266n14

East India Company, 17, 112, 126, 220, 256n12
east versus west, 22–23, 28–31, 38, 40, 79, 91–94, 102–6, 166, 184, 215, 227–32, 240n87, 273n43
economy, 5, 8, 17–18, 23, 35, 38, 40, 46–47, 110, 114, 126, 128, 142, 159, 160, 162, 165–66, 193, 222–23, 235n28, 257n29, 259n62
Edirne, 144, 181, 262n13
Edward II (Marlowe), 73, 79, 236n49
effeminacy, 107, 119, 158–59, 183, 190, 212, 230, 265n7. *See also* emasculation; femininity; masculinity
Egypt, 67, 157, 171, 187, 189, 191, 221, 266n10, 268n45; Egyptian, 75, 148, 152, 158, 169–70, 190, 226–27, 270n93, 271n95
Elam, Keir, 192, 265n5
El Hamel, Chouki, 32–33, 178, 244n126, 267n36, 269n70
elites, 23–24, 30, 34, 36, 39, 41, 47–48, 50–52, 65, 68, 84, 87, 172, 176, 179, 181, 185, 249n57, 274n9
Elizabeth I, 21, 113, 120, 148, 165–66, 186, 223, 232, 239n77
Elizabeth of Bohemia, 117
El-Rouayheb, Khaled, 93, 227, 242n105, 248n42, 249n60, 250n69, 254n20, 273n42, 274n15
emasculation, 143, 153, 156, 183, 189, 234n10. *See also* effeminacy; femininity; masculinity
embodiment, 24, 39, 82–83, 87, 89–90, 92, 106, 108, 123, 142, 174, 182, 191, 195, 200–201, 216–17, 244n131, 259n68, 265n2, 273n48; on maps, 96–105
employment. *See* mastery; patronage; service
encounters. *See* contacts; exchanges; Mediterranean

enderun, 52, 172
English National Opera, 213–14
Enlightenment, 28, 175
enslavement. *See* slaves and slavery
Enterline, Lynn, 75, 233n3, 246n6
epyllion, 36, 38, 47–48, 80, 222
Erickson, Peter, 35, 120, 124, 244n125, 257nn28–29, 267n28
eroticism, 4, 16, 20, 79, 127, 136, 201, 215, 232, 236n49; age-differentiated, 6–8, 18, 100–106, 214–16, 219–20, 231–32, 245n143; literary, 3, 13, 16, 20, 27, 38, 46, 50, 73, 222–23, 235n34. *See also* companions; friend; pederasty
Ethiopian, 66, 170, 178, 180, 184
ethnography, 10, 20, 40, 48, 65, 96, 143, 157, 159
eunuch: abductions from Africa, 169; attacks against black eunuchs, 179–85; as a distinct racialized gender, 33, 41, 171–78, 191–94; on English stage, 169–71, 189–95; in travelogues, 26, 186–88. *See also* Africa; black; castration; gender
Eurasia, 103
Eurocentricism, 9, 21–22, 26, 194
Evliya Çelebi, 228, 249n57
exchanges, 10, 18, 77, 87, 118, 124–26, 134, 137, 166, 234n11; cross-cultural and transnational, 2–4, 9, 11, 16–22, 25–26, 28–29, 38–39, 46, 48, 50, 83, 84, 106, 108, 110, 126–27, 136, 142, 171, 185–86, 199–200, 223, 225–26, 231–32, 235n28, 237n65, 238n71, 238n75, 239n77, 239n85, 245n141
exoticized, 1, 3, 19, 40, 86–87, 109, 115–16, 118, 123, 127, 130, 189, 193, 201, 203, 222, 226. *See also* black; exoticized; foreign; race
expansion, 33–34, 41, 63, 68, 92, 94, 96, 106, 114, 177–78, 200, 238n73, 257n29
Eyüboğlu, Ismet Zeki, 230, 241n102

faith, 66, 82, 88–90, 92–93, 142, 153, 156, 189, 250n70
femininity, 66, 99, 107, 127, 129, 135, 166, 174, 185, 190, 206, 227, 229. *See also* effeminacy; emasculation; masculinity
feminism, 35, 202, 242n107, 259n62
festivals, 25, 99, 104, 143–44, 148, 150, 167, 213; accounts of, 38, 41, 145–48, 262n16
fetish, 127, 138

INDEX 313

Fevri, 250n70
Fielding, William, 115–16, 123
Fischel, Joseph J., 215, 235n24
Fisher, Will, 175, 233n3, 234n7, 249n60
Fleischer, Cornell, 67, 239n85
Florence, 255n36
Ford, John, 265n3
foreign, 19, 21, 35, 39, 47, 83, 94, 112, 116, 133, 147, 166, 194, 195, 202, 228, 229, 238n71. *See also* black; exoticized; race
Fortunatus, 112
Foucault, Michel, 28, 107, 159, 227, 242n110, 250n75
Frank, 27, 66, 86–93, 224, 253n13
French, Samuel, 206
friend, 7, 11, 50, 68–69, 128, 132, 150, 166, 180, 221–23, 228, 230, 243n119, 249n69, 250n69, 260n74. *See also* companions; eroticism
futurity, 95, 107, 108, 112, 116, 125, 170, 201, 220

Gainsford, Thomas, 72, 162, 264n77
Galata, 27, 39, 71, 83–86, 107–8; poems on, 87–96. *See also* Frank
Galen, 26, 241n101, 266n19. *See also* humoral theory
Ganymede: catamite as a corrupt form of, 72, 236n48, 251n85; as a common noun, 2, 13, 26; ganimet as, 17, 39, 52–54, 62, 68, 72, 80, 164, 247n35; Ganymede-effect, 18–19, 46, 83, 104, 138, 231; Indian boy as, 133–36, 207; origins and explications of the myth, 11–12, 235n39; as seen from behind, 105; servants as, 26–27, 72, 126, 237n58; various historical figurations of, 3, 13–17, 217, 222, 224–26, 236n40, 236n44, 236n49, 236n52, 245n141. *See also* boy; cupbearers
Garber, Marjorie, 201, 233n3, 237n62, 259n57
gardens, 55, 64, 80, 84, 87, 104, 203, 221, 248n45, 249n57. *See also* paradise
Garner, Shirley Nelson, 127, 129, 258n57
Garrick, David, 204–5, 272n18
gender: changes in, 6, 169–72; circumcision as a mark of, 142–51, 157–59; fluidity of, 2–3, 76, 82, 84, 100, 111, 133, 167, 192, 206, 233n1; gendered personifications, 95–104; gendering spaces, 83, 87–94, 172–75; in spectrum, 2, 7–8, 135; racialized, 176–85, 187–95. *See also* adults; beards; black; boy; cloth-

ing; embodiment; eunuch; hair; humoral theory
genealogy, 28, 31, 32, 176, 195, 200, 203, 230, 242n110. *See also* history
genre, 25–27, 36, 38, 47, 80, 114, 222, 241n103, 250n70, 269n70
geopolitics, 1, 16, 20, 38, 45–46, 82, 96, 155, 170
Georgieuiz, Bartholomeus, 150–51
Geuffroy, Antoine, 149–50, 155, 186, 263n32
ghazal, 26, 36, 38, 58, 80, 86, 222
Gibb, E. J. W., 21–22, 227, 241n103, 274n8
Giraldi, Giovanni Battista (Cinthio), 264n60
Glassman, Jonathon, 218
global Renaissance, 11, 20, 28
globe, 15, 120, 153
Globe Theater, 200, 271n94
Goffe, Thomas, 16
Goldberg, Jonathan, 50, 132, 223, 233n3, 238nn71–72, 242n107, 244n131, 251n90, 260n74
Golding, Arthur, 13, 236n42
Goulart, Simon, 148
Gowing, Laura, 132, 253n7, 260n76
Gramaye, J. M., 49, 164
grand signior, 175, 193, 267n26
grand vizier, 33, 52, 172, 237n58, 243n119, 247n31
Greco-Roman, 3, 12, 47, 72, 75, 111, 170, 226, 265n7. *See also* Roman; Troy
Greece, 1, 125; Greek, 3, 11, 25, 45, 47, 51, 54, 72, 76, 107, 125, 146, 237n60, 240n87, 249n60, 249n69. *See also* Athens; Greco-Roman; Troy
Greene, Robert: *Menaphon*, 12, 126; *Selimus, Emperor of Turks*, 194
Grimeston, Edward, 148, 251n87
grooms, 2, 112, 118, 130, 133. *See also* animals; henchmen; mastery; pages; service; squires
guilds, 145–46
gypsy, 169, 189, 193

Habib, Imtiaz, 112–13, 255n3, 256n17, 256n19, 258n56, 259n58, 260n81, 260n85
Habsburgs, 23, 39, 95, 102–3
Haeckel, Ernst, 237n58
hair, 2, 4, 63–65, 146–47, 177–78, 187, 212, 234n7, 248n54, 249n60. *See also* beards; clothing

Hajji Ahmed, 23, 30
Hakluyt, Richard, 26, 166, 240n98; *The Principal Navigations*, 21, 141, 165
Halil, Çandarlı, 51
Hall, Kim F., 35, 116, 128, 234n11, 242n107, 244n125, 256n17, 257nn28–29, 257n32, 267n28, 272n39
Halperin, David, 7, 242n110, 275n23
hamam. *See* bathhouses
Hamitic curse, 33, 177–78, 184–85. *See also* black; race
Hamlet (Shakespeare), 134
Hanson, Ellis, 191
Harborne, William, 21
harem, 9, 33, 162, 172–77, 180, 183, 186–87, 193, 195, 234n11, 266n11
Harkins, Gillian, 215
Hathaway, Jane, 176–77, 266n10, 266n12, 269n62, 270n84
Hausted, Peter, 265n2
Hayali, 59, 60, 62, 64, 67, 248n51
Hellespont, 5, 38, 45–48, 73–82, 109, 125, 129, 246n10
henchmen, 112, 116, 130, 132, 134–35, 138. *See also* boy; grooms; mastery; pages; service; squires
Hendricks, Margo, 110, 127, 201–3, 216, 240n98, 242n107, 259n62, 259n68, 271n11, 273n48
Heng, Geraldine, 32, 243n125, 267n28
Henry VI Part II (Shakespeare), 270n86
Henry VIII, 96, 223
Herbert, Thomas, 16
heresy, 19, 90–91, 93, 95, 132, 165–66, 195, 238n71
hermaphrodite, 12, 193, 230, 271n101
Hero and Leander (Marlowe), 37–39, 45–50; continuation of, 80, 252n107; Hellespont in, 46–73, 251n93; Leander as Ganymede in the Mediterranean, 73–80
Herodotus, 148, 171, 271n95
heterosexuality, 9, 107, 153, 156, 159, 228, 238n71, 250n75, 263n50, 264n65; domestic heterosexuality, 96, 136, 205, 223, 261n93; heteronormativity and heterosexualization, 3, 45, 136, 162, 216, 223, 228, 230, 274n20
Heywood, Thomas, 194

hierarchy, 2, 4, 6–7, 9, 16, 18–19, 22, 28, 30–41, 46, 60, 62–63, 66–68, 89, 100, 110, 112, 124–25, 132–36, 138, 144, 150, 167, 172, 175–76, 179, 181–82, 184, 188, 216–17, 219, 220, 222–23, 229, 231–32, 245n141, 260n76, 268n57. *See also* mastery; service
history: historical and literary, 5, 11, 16, 19, 34–37, 50, 80, 110, 124, 203, 216, 219–20, 222, 230–31; historiography, 3, 5–6, 18, 26, 34; transhistorical, 8, 28, 32, 41–42, 195, 199, 223. *See also* genealogy
Hoffman, Michael, 212
homosexuality, 227–31. *See also* cruising; eroticism; pederasty; perversion; sodomy
Hondius, Jodocus, 103
Hoppner, John, 206
horizon, 1, 83–84, 93–95, 97, 102, 106, 108, 120, 253n9
households, 1, 2, 17, 31, 37, 51, 54, 75, 112, 123, 132–33, 161, 172, 193, 223, 235n28, 247n29, 260n76, 266n11, 269n75, 271n102
Howard, Frank, 206
Howard, Jean, 233n3, 253n7, 259n62, 259n67, 267n20
humanism: humanist accounts of Turks, 23, 25, 240n87; pedagogy and training in, 16, 38, 47, 132, 246n6, 259n73
humoral theory, 76, 175–78, 183, 233n2. *See also* embodiment; Galen; gender
Hungary, 65, 94–95; Hungarian, 25, 51, 66, 72, 103, 270n84
hyacinths, 87–88, 146–47; as epithet (*Sünbül*), 181–82
Hyginus, 105

Ibn al-Arabi, 254n19
Ibn al-Faqih, 177
Ibn Khaldun, 178
Ibn Qutayba, 177
Ibn Sina. *See* Avicenna
Ibrahim Pasha, 243n119
identity, 5, 7–8, 25, 35, 52, 89, 123, 144, 149, 152, 156, 170, 192, 195, 201, 215, 219, 227, 230, 238n73, 240n87
ideology, 9–10, 19, 22, 29–32, 35, 40, 42, 107, 110, 175, 177, 180, 187, 195, 201–3, 265n5
imperialism, 4, 7, 28–30, 110, 215, 231. *See also* colonialism; Orientalism

INDEX 315

Imtiyazi, 145. See also *Surname-i Humayun*
India, 17, 40, 75, 110–11, 115, 123, 127, 201, 205–6, 222, 256n17, 259n58. *See also* Indian boy
Indian boy, 27, 37, 40–42, 109, 199, 256n7; the age of, 134, 216–17; critical approaches to, 110–11, 200–202; differing abductions of, 110–11; as Ganymede, 129–31, 134–36, 207; Indian boys in England, 112–13; as object of love, 125–28, 131–33, 137–38, 259n62; staging history of, 200–206, 213–20; in visual arts, 114–24, 206–12. See also *Midsummer Night's Dream, A* (Shakespeare)
infidels, 19, 31, 82, 92, 108, 147, 150, 163, 164, 221
interactions. *See* contacts; exchanges
intersections, 6, 9–10, 27, 29, 34–35, 40, 42, 110, 142, 158, 195, 202–3, 220, 230, 232, 242n107, 244n131
Islam: associated with Judaism, 155; versus Christianity, 8, 22, 82–83, 88, 94, 103, 106, 165, 222, 263n38, 265n81; as deviation from Christianity, 151; Islamicate, 10, 25, 29–31, 33, 55, 86, 91, 93, 143, 147, 178, 185, 231, 249n62, 266n15, 269n70; and racialized slavery, 83–84, 29–34, 177–87. *See also* Arab; conversion; east versus west
Istanbul, 1, 4, 17, 23, 26, 33, 39, 52, 60, 67, 69, 83–94, 108, 144, 178, 181, 186, 221–22, 228, 237n60, 253n9, 262n13, 269n65, 273n1. *See also* Constantinople
Italy, 22, 24, 104, 215, 224, 263n34; Italian, 9, 23, 25, 50, 92, 114, 148, 150, 155, 225, 236n48, 238n71, 257n28. *See also* Florence; Venice

Jacobson, Miriam, 47, 75–76, 251n93, 252n107
James VI and I, 117; "Lepanto," 152
janissaries, 27, 227; eroticization of, 59–72, 249n57, 250n78; in European accounts, 26, 47–48, 73; origins of, 17, 51; recruitment of, 51–59, 247n29. *See also* boy; devşirme
Jem (Cem/Djem), 223–24, 273n5, 274n9
Jesus, 86–91, 96, 102, 141, 160–62, 165, 235n39, 236n40, 254n19
Jewett, Henry, 206
Jew of Malta, The (Marlowe), 75, 155
Jews, 25, 89, 122, 151; and circumcision, 149, 150, 153, 157, 262n27; as linked with Muslims, 155–56, 193, 271n101; in the Ottoman Empire, 30, 84, 88, 92, 146
Johnson, Robert, 17
Jonson, Ben, 52; *Epicene*, 193, 271n102; *Volpone*, 41, 75, 193
Joseph, 65, 67, 269n62
Jove, 11–13, 45, 54, 73–74, 77, 80, 126, 235n39, 236n49, 237n58. *See also* Ganymede
judges, 60, 81, 180; black Ottoman, 180–85, 269nn64–65. *See also* Ali, Mullah

Kadızadeli, 223, 273n4
Kafadar, Cemal, 239n85, 240n87, 240n92, 247n29, 262n17
Kathman, David, 135, 233n3
Kean, Charles, 206
Keene, Laura, 206
Kellet, Edward, 151–52
Kemble, John Philip, 219
Killigrew, Thomas, 272n18
kingdoms, 74, 77, 137, 145, 170, 213, 224
kings, 12, 16–17, 45, 55, 73, 102, 109, 125–27, 136–37, 141, 147, 161–64, 184, 197, 204, 206, 212, 214, 216, 224, 260n74, 261n92
Knolles Richard, 72; *The Generall Historie of the Turkes*, 21, 171, 225
Koçi Bey, 248n56

Lad, Jateen, 172, 266n11, 267n34
Lane, Edward, 227
Latifi, 100
laws, 84, 113; Islamic laws, 31–32, 51, 180; janissary laws, 51–52, 247n29; people of law, 181–82, 185, 268n57; sodomy laws, 223, 259n73; taxation, 30–31, 112, 269n65. *See also* judges
Lazzaro, Claudia, 104
Lebelski, George, 148, 262n24
Le Brun, Charles, 96
Lefebvre, Henri, 90, 252n6, 253n6
Leo Africanus, 157
lesbianism, 23, 25, 128, 205, 230, 259n59; as located in Ottoman lands, 19–20, 238n71
letters, 73, 163–64, 258n43, 262n23; between the Ottomans and the English, 21, 165–66, 239n77, 240n99
Levant Company, 35, 48, 125
Le Vigne de Pera, 148

Lewenklaw, Johannes, 148
Lewis, Bernard, 244n126, 254n20, 267n36, 268n45, 269n70
Lewis, Franklin, 86, 254n20
Lim, Eng-Beng, 215, 231, 273n43
Lithgow, William, 19, 125
Little, Arthur, 242n107, 244n131, 260n83, 264n61
London, 1, 4, 165, 241; blacks in, 40, 112–13
Loomba, Ania, 23, 43, 110, 127, 156, 189, 242n107, 244n131, 256n19, 267n28, 268n61, 270n93, 271n95
Lorck, Melchior, 253n9
Love Labor's Lost (Shakespeare), 189
Lowe, Kate, 113, 123, 133, 256n17
Lubenau, Reinhold, 148
lust, 9, 19, 49, 64, 67, 69, 74, 77, 86, 113–14, 119, 135, 152–53, 158, 169, 184, 189, 213, 229, 249n57. *See also* eroticism; perversion; sodomy

Machiavelli, Niccolò, 25
MacLean, Gerald, 152, 239n75, 239n77, 269n76
Mahmud II, 227
Malieckal, Bindu, 142, 234n11
Mamluks, 50, 171, 179, 266n10
man. *See* adults; beards; gender; hair; humoral theory; masculinity; mastery
Manakıb u Tevarih-i Âl-i Osman (Aşıkpaşazade), 52, 144, 237n59, 246n24, 247nn33–34, 247n36, 262nn13–15
Mandeville's travels, 193
map. *See* cartography
mappa mundi, 193
Marlowe, Christopher, 13, 48–49, 81, 110, 125, 136–37, 245n141, 251n90. *See also individual works*
marriage, 2, 8, 26, 111, 135–36, 144, 200, 228, 234n7, 261n10
Marston, John, 16
Mary I, 223
masculinity, 39, 92, 87, 96, 99–100, 107–8, 116, 123, 128, 138, 142–43, 149, 153, 159, 163, 174–76, 181, 189, 191–92, 227, 230, 249n60, 250n69, 259n68, 263n50, 267n20. *See also* effeminacy; emasculation; femininity
Mason, John: *The Turke*, 16, 48, 271n104
masque, 16, 145

Massinger, Philip: *The Emperor of the East*, 271n104; *The Renegado*, 16, 194, 224–26
Masten, Jeffrey, 5, 37, 73, 77–78, 128, 192, 233n3, 236n52, 251n91, 260n82
mastery, 2, 3, 77, 83, 115, 117, 120, 129, 132, 138, 141, 218; the homoerotics of, 118, 132–38, 215, 221–22, 260n74; in households, 2; masterless boys, 3; masters and servants, 2, 16–17, 31, 39, 42, 54, 62, 67–74, 100, 111, 116, 118–24, 164, 187, 202, 216. *See also* hierarchy; patronage; service
Matar, Nabil, 152, 234n11, 238n71, 239n75, 239n77, 242n108, 246n21, 270n90
Mediterranean: England's engagements in, 10, 17, 19, 21, 48–49, 75, 108, 125, 138, 141–42, 186; plots set in, 12, 40–41, 73, 109–11, 126, 141, 169, 191–94, 199–200, 225; racialized slavery in, 33, 177–84; as a sexualized site, 50, 79, 112, 136, 137, 157, 160–67. *See also* captives and captivity; contacts; crossings; exchanges; pirates and piracy; slaves and slavery
Mehmed Agha, 179–81
Mehmed II, 37, 39, 55, 72, 84, 87–93, 108, 137, 144, 223, 224, 240n87, 243n117, 254nn16–17
Menon, Madhavi, 201, 217, 273n48
Merchant of Venice, The (Shakespeare), 137, 200, 260n85
metamorphosis, 47, 246n6. *See also* Ovid
metaphor, 27, 34, 55, 64, 68, 81, 87, 88, 91, 93–94, 106–7, 127, 201, 241n102, 263n43
Metropolitan of Thessaloniki, 49
Metropolitan Opera, 213
Michelangelo, 13, 216, 226, 236n44
Middle Ages (medieval), 5, 9, 12, 22, 25, 88, 96, 111, 152, 171, 178–79, 186, 198, 235n39, 237n66, 241n103, 245n144, 250n69, 253n13, 256n8, 262n27, 263n38, 273n45
Middleton, Thomas: *A Game at Chess*, 265n3; *The Roaring Girl* (Middleton and Dekker), 236n46
Midsummer Night's Dream, A (Shakespeare), 27, 37, 40–42, 109–12, 115, 119, 192, 251n99, 270n86; as a dream of sexual liberation, 213–20; female eroticism, 125–28; as a Mediterranean play, 40, 124–25; pederastic homoeroticism in, 128–38; performance history of, 199–201, 203–6, 211–15; in visual arts, 206–10. *See also* Indian boy

Mignolo, Walter, 28
military, 21, 33, 39, 51–52, 92, 102, 116, 124, 158, 159, 162, 172, 235n28, 239n85, 247n29. *See also* army
miniature, 27, 38, 52, 54, 68–69, 145, 147, 173, 262n16
minions, 2, 16, 36, 72, 100, 132, 260n74
misogyny, 12, 183, 249n69
Montrose, Louis, 83, 134, 259n62, 259n68
Moor, 21, 112–14, 135, 156–57, 183, 187, 189, 193–94, 238n71, 264n60. *See also* black; *Othello* (Shakespeare); race
Morocco, 33, 178, 200
Morrah, Patrick, 117, 257n32, 258n40, 258n43
Moryson, Fynes, 71
Mosaval, Johaar, 213
mosques, 71, 90–91, 146, 149, 151, 263n31
movement, 82, 87, 93, 173–74, 195, 205, 212, 218, 243n122, 252n6, 273n4
Muhammad, 71, 152–55, 160, 162–63, 227, 254n25
Muñoz, José Esteban, 5–6, 237n65, 244n134, 253n9
Murad I, 144
Murad II, 51
Murad III, 71, 144, 165, 174, 180, 186
Murad IV, 250n78
Musaeus, 45
Mustafa Ali of Gallipoli: *Description of Cairo*, 176; *Kavaʾiduʾl-mecalis*, 39, 63–68, 72, 91, 95, 179–83, 185, 228, 248n53, 248n57, 249n69; *Künh ül-ahbar*, 66, 184
Mustafa Çelebi, 144
mutability, 48, 142, 156, 167, 184
mutes, 173, 183, 192–93, 266n14
Mytens, Daniel, 117, 120, 130

Nagy, Jakab Harsány, 25
Najmabadi, Afsaneh, 234n13, 249n59, 268n61, 274n15, 275n23
Narcissus, 76, 187, 225–26
Nash, Jennifer C., 35
Nasuh, Matrakçı, 84–87
nation, 4, 20, 25–26, 50, 65, 71, 86, 95–96, 141, 152–53, 158, 178, 182, 190, 226, 238n71, 244n125, 253n13, 269n61; national literature paradigm, 4, 9–11, 24, 38; nation state, 20, 24, 194, 229, 230

Necipoğlu, Gülru, 55
Neill, Michael, 170, 264n65
New World, 20, 24; abductions in, 17, 40, 111–13, 222, 256n17; sodomy in, 238n71. *See also* Americas
Noble, Adrian, 212
Nocentelli, Carmen, 34, 238n71, 242n107
Norris, John, 70

objectification, 35, 76, 78, 84, 92, 104, 106–8, 111, 124, 134, 137, 200
Orientalism, 8–10, 16, 21, 28–30, 170, 186, 195, 201, 203, 215, 219, 227, 229–31, 237n58, 242n109, 242n111, 250n75. *See also* imperialism; Said, Edward
Ortiz, Fernando, 9–10
Othello (Shakespeare), 40, 114, 152, 156–59, 180, 200, 264nn59–62, 264n65
Ovid, 12–13, 16, 38, 236n42, 245n141, 246n6

pages, 2, 6, 52, 58, 66, 67, 70–71, 112, 126, 130, 132, 135, 151, 160, 192–94, 230, 248n47, 257n28. *See also* boy; grooms; henchmen; mastery; service; squires
palaces, 31, 52, 55, 63–64, 68, 69–71, 74, 84, 92–93, 162, 172, 174–75, 181, 183–84, 187, 266n14, 267n26, 270n84, 271n102
Palerne, Jean, 148
palimpsest, 19, 28, 125
pamphlets, 118–19, 152
paradise, 55, 84, 87, 89–92, 153, 248n44, 254n21; boys in, 63, 68, 93–94. *See also* gardens
Parmigianino, 105
Passionate Shepherd to His Love, The (Marlowe), 78, 251n91
patriarchy, 3, 7, 33, 106–7, 132, 138, 202, 219
patronage, 23, 50, 67, 92, 114–15, 119, 132, 193, 180, 182, 202, 223, 259n73, 260n74. *See also* mastery; service
Pax Ottomanica, 30, 243n115
Peacham, Henry, 14
pearls, 47, 66–67, 74–76, 123–25, 251n93, 251n99
pederasty: attribution to the Orient, 16, 42, 72, 111, 119, 215–16, 227–31, 273n42; as conventional and literary mode, 37, 74–80, 132–38, 212–14, 217, 235n39, 252n105, 273n44; as historically ordinary, 6–8, 11–12,

18, 37, 219, 235nn22–23, 236n50, 237n63, 245n144; versus pedophilia, 6–7, 200, 213–16, 235n24, 272n39. *See also* boy; eroticism; homosexuality; sodomy
pedophilia. *See* pederasty
Peirce, Leslie, 172, 233n3, 234nn6–7, 234n11, 239n85, 249n60, 261n10, 266n10
penis, 142, 158, 166, 174–75, 178, 186, 191–92, 266n19. *See also* castration; circumcision; eunuch; testicles
Penzer, N. M., 174
Pérez, Hiram, 215, 273n43, 275n25
performance, 17, 25, 111, 125, 143–48, 150, 157–58, 170, 201, 203, 205–6, 216, 219, 271n94
performative, 19, 37, 79, 82, 199, 238n73, 267n20
Persian, 11, 16, 23–25, 54–55, 66, 72, 86–88, 92, 146, 153, 171, 241n102, 247n37, 248n42, 249n62, 254n20, 264n77, 265n7, 268n45
personifications, 78; of lands, 96–104, 107, 110. *See also* continents
perversion, 5, 42, 69, 71, 214, 227, 229–30, 241n102, 250n75, 265n7; conversion as, 5–6, 49, 86, 142–43, 149, 153–60, 163, 189, 246n16. *See also* lust; sodomy
Petowe, Henry, 252n107
pets. *See* animals
Phelan, Peggy, 106–7
philology, 9, 77, 128
physiognomy, 26, 33, 63, 67, 152, 175
Pickenoy, Nicolaes Eliaszoon, 120
Pindar, Paul, 183
pirates and piracy, 12, 46, 49, 74, 112, 123, 153, 155–56, 164, 246n11, 251n93, 256n11. *See also* Mediterranean
Plato, 12, 26, 216, 250n69
platonic love, 4, 12, 68–70, 72–73, 93
Plutarch, 190
poetics, 47, 50, 88, 96, 109
population, 30, 31, 33–35, 51, 55, 63, 66–67, 71, 83, 86, 90, 111, 124, 171, 175, 178, 184–85, 218, 240n92, 269n62
portraiture, 114–20, 123–24, 130, 138, 239n77, 257n28, 257n29
postcolonialism, 7, 42, 127, 202, 232, 237n65, 255n3. *See also* colonialism; imperialism; Orientalism
Pountney, David, 213

promotions, 7, 34, 71, 171–72, 179, 183, 185, 228, 231
pronouns, 89, 91, 227, 241n102, 254nn16–17, 265n2
prototypes, 3, 46, 68, 105
Purcell, Henry, 212, 272n31; *The Fairy-Queen*, 203, 206, 212–13
Purchas, Samuel, 21, 175
Puritans, 118–19, 149, 223

Qur'an, 26, 55, 67, 146, 184, 248n42, 248n44, 249n62, 254n19

race: circumcision as a racial mark, 148–58; in Islamic and Ottoman context, 27–33, 176–85; premodern critical race studies, 242n107; and queer, 4, 6–8, 34–37; racialized catalogue of boys, 63–68; racialized gender, 176–85, 187–95. *See also* animals; black; cins (jins/genus); dehumanization; exoticized; foreign; Hamitic curse; hierarchy; slaves and slavery; whiteness
Rackham, Arthur, 207
Raleigh, Walter, 112, 256n17
Rambuss, Richard, 132, 236n40
Rawlins, John, 49, 142
Reinhardt, Max, 211
renegados, 16, 47–48, 149, 163–64, 189, 194, 224–25, 238n71, 267n26, 270n90. *See also* conversion; Islam
resistance, 31, 36–37, 77, 95, 107, 142, 163, 202, 213; silence as, 217–18. *See also* agency; subjectivity
Revani, 92–93
Reynolds, Frederic, 205–6
rites of passage, 47, 143
rivers, 5, 55, 78, 252n4; abductions around, 94–96; Danube, 39, 65, 81–84, 107–8; mapping of, 96, 100–106; Rhine, 99–100; river gods, 99–100, 103–4; Thames, 3, 148. *See also* cartography
Roaring Girl, The (Middleton and Dekker), 236n49
Roe, Thomas, 21
Roman, 23–24, 26, 30, 32, 65–67, 91–92, 95, 103, 146, 170, 176, 182, 186, 189–90, 192, 240n87, 240n92, 262n17. *See also* Greco-Roman; Troy

romance, 12, 36, 38, 69, 126, 222, 235n34, 238n71
Romeo and Juliet (Shakespeare), 78
Romney, George, 206
roses, 55, 64, 93, 146, 187, 248n41
Rotz, Jean, 96
Roundheads, 118
Rowe, Nicholas, 204
Rowlie, Samson, 269n75
Royal African Company, 117
Royal Opera House, 213
Royal Shakespeare Company, 212, 217, 270n94
Rubens, Peter Paul, 13
Rubin, Gayle, 234n11
Rubin, Patricia, 104
Rum. *See* Roman
Rumelia. *See* Roman
Rupert, Prince, 117–24, 128, 257n32, 258n43
Rycaut, Paul, 21, 24, 69–71, 77, 114, 183, 188, 250n72, 250n75

Safiye Sultan, 21, 239n77
Şahin, Kaya, 144, 239n85, 261n10, 262nn16–17
Said, Edward, 9–10, 28–29. *See also* Orientalism
Sanders, Thomas, 40, 141–43, 157, 160–66
Sanderson, John, 49, 143
Sandys, George: *A Relation of a Journey*, 19, 21, 48, 71, 125, 150–52, 159, 186, 225
Saracens, 112, 152, 158
Sarıtaş, Ezgi, 227, 229, 274n15, 274n20
Saslow, James, 104–5, 235n35, 236n41, 236n46, 236n48, 251n85, 255n38
Scheie, Danny, 201, 216–17, 219, 271n11
Schick, Irvin Cemil, 240n85, 241n103
scholars, 144, 180–81, 226, 250n69
schools, 2, 17, 47, 50, 52, 70, 132, 214, 233n3
Sedgwick, Eve Kosofsky, 230, 234n11
şehrengiz, 26, 59, 228, 241n103, 242n105. *See also* biography; boy
Selim II, 55, 180
seraglio. *See* palaces
servants. *See* boy; cupbearers; Ganymede; grooms; henchmen; mastery; pages; service; squires
service, 2, 8, 50–51, 63, 67–68, 71–72, 82, 105, 132, 135–36, 172, 187, 191–92, 194, 216, 222–23, 249n57, 256n18, 259n73. *See also* mastery; patronage
Shakespeare, William, 13, 40–41, 110–11, 134–35, 188, 199–201, 203, 213–14, 216. *See also individual works*
Shakespeare Memorial Theater, 270n94
Shakespeare Santa Cruz (SSC), 42, 201, 202, 216, 218, 219, 273n48
Shapiro, James, 149, 261n6, 262n27, 263n43
ships, 1, 5, 12, 84, 113, 117, 126–28, 135, 137, 141, 160–61, 165, 221, 240n98. *See also* Mediterranean
Sinfield, Alan, 18, 132–33, 134, 136, 202–3, 216, 235n22, 235n26, 250n69, 259n57, 264n74
Singh, Jyotsna, 20, 242n107
skin, 148, 152, 186; the color of, 33–34, 66–67, 75, 82, 123, 176–78, 181–82, 184, 207. *See also* black; embodiment
Slade, Adolphus, 237n58
slaves and slavery: in captivity narratives, 141–43, 160–67; in England, 113–19; in the Mediterranean, 28–34, 40, 51–72, 177–79, 194, 121–22. *See also* captives and captivity
Smith, Bruce, 76, 132, 223, 233n3, 234n8, 235n34, 236n49, 236n53, 245n2, 251n91, 252n105, 259n73, 264n65
Smith, Ian, 5, 35, 158, 242n107
Smith, James, 162–64
sodomy: attributed to Italians, 104, 263n34; attributed to Turks and Muslims, 9, 19–20, 49–50, 71–72, 133–34, 226, 229, 237n66, 238n71; as bestiality, 119, 157–59, 258n47, 264n61; laws and trials, 2, 222–23, 234n8, 259n73. *See also* bestiality; buggery; laws; pederasty; perversion
soldiers, 49, 52, 58, 65, 76–77, 84, 164, 172, 258n43. *See also* army; military
Sonnets (Shakespeare), 27, 134, 137, 200, 216
Spenser, Edmund, 75
squires, 127–30, 134, 205. *See also* grooms; henchmen; mastery; pages; service
Stanivukovic, Goran, 68, 234n14, 235n34, 238n71, 253n7
Stanley, Edward, 133
status. *See* class, gender, hierarchy; mastery; race; service
Stepney, William, 132
Stratford, 271n94; Shakespeare Festival in, 213

subjectivity, 36–37, 47, 124, 201, 217. *See also* agency; resistance
submission, 67, 76–77, 82, 84, 89, 95, 99, 107–8, 116, 120, 124, 178, 249n60, 259n62
Subrahmanyam, Sanjay, 20, 238n74
substitutions, 106, 119, 127–28, 134, 211, 227, 259n62. *See also* changeling
Sufi, 70, 89, 92–93, 144, 221, 228, 248n42, 254n19
sugar, 9, 128, 146–47, 249n57. *See also* sweetness
Suleyman I, 24, 54, 67, 89, 174
Suleymaniye, 146, 181
Süleymanname (Arifi), 52, 54
Surname-i Humayun, 41, 145, 147, 262n16
survival. *See* survivance
survivance, 36, 137, 261n98. *See also* agency; resistance; subjectivity
sweetness, 58, 74, 109, 126–29, 134–36, 146–47, 179, 224. *See also* sugar
swords, 102, 104, 106, 153–54, 189

Tahta'wi, Rifai'ah, 227
Tamburlaine (Marlowe), 48–49, 149, 202, 246n15
Taming of the Shrew, The (Shakespeare), 75
taverns, 2, 25, 63, 64, 84, 221, 228, 248n57
Taylor, Gary, 175, 186, 266n10, 266n15, 266n19, 268n61
Tempest, The (Shakespeare), 125, 200
Terence, 170, 192, 265n3, 265n5
testicles, 171. *See also* body; castration; eunuch; masculinity; penis
Tezcan, Baki, 181–82, 239n85, 243n122, 244n128, 267n34, 268n48, 268nn56–57, 269n65, 269n70
tezkire. *See* biography
Titian, 114, 119
Titus Andronicus (Shakespeare), 270n86
Tommasini, Anthony, 214
touch, 6, 73, 79, 108, 119–20, 136, 174, 218, 227, 257n29
trade, 112–13, 118, 120, 123, 125–27, 138, 141–42, 145, 150, 161, 165–66, 170, 177, 186, 256n12, 271n102. *See also* Mediterranean
transgression. *See* gender; perversion; sodomy
translation, 11, 13, 23, 55, 148, 151, 182, 187, 225, 227, 236n42, 241nn101–2, 241n104, 251n87, 263n32

Traub, Valerie, 35, 36, 96, 159, 195, 223, 237n65, 238n71, 242n107, 244n131, 259n59, 259n62, 261n93, 275n23
travel writing, 16–17, 25–26, 37–38, 40–41, 48–49, 110, 138, 143, 149, 151, 157, 171, 174, 186, 190, 222, 229, 238n71, 246n10, 249n57, 250n72
Tree, Herbert Beerbohm, 206
Troy, 54; Trojan, 11, 13; Turks as Trojans, 23, 240n87. *See also* Greco-Roman; Greece; Roman
turban. *See* clothing
Turkey Company, 21, 48, 125, 220
Twelfth Night (Shakespeare), 41, 137, 186, 191–93, 217
Two Gentlemen of Verona, The (Shakespeare), 5
Two Noble Kinsman (Shakespeare), 270n86

Uluç Ali Pasha, 269n75

Van der Helst, Bartholomeus, 120
Van Diepenbeck, Abraham, 130
Van Dyck, Anthony, 114, 115, 120
Van Somer, Paul, 130
Vasfi, 60
Venice, 147, 155, 157–59, 164–65; Venetian, 16, 146, 150, 156, 166, 193, 224–25. *See also* Florence; Italy
Venus and Adonis (Shakespeare), 132
Vickers, Nancy, 76, 253n8
Virginia Company, 111–12, 256n10
virility, 99, 107, 159, 175, 261n10
Vitkus, Daniel, 5, 153, 238n71, 238n75, 239n77, 242n108, 246n11, 246nn15–16, 256n11, 264n59, 264n62
vizier, 33, 51, 52, 172, 237n58, 243n119, 247n31
Von Haunolth, Nicholas, 148
voyeurism, 67, 68, 94, 96, 100, 104, 108, 115, 162, 218

Ward, John, 153–56
Warner, Michael, 134, 238n71
Weaver, William P., 47
westernization, 223, 227–28, 230. *See also* east versus west

White, Michael, 214
whiteness, 4, 21, 33–34, 65–68, 114–20, 171–79, 181–85, 190, 224. *See also* beauty; black; exoticized; race
Wilde, Oscar, 215–16
Williams, Gary Jay, 134, 200, 203, 205, 213
Williams, Raymond, 10
Wilson, Bronwen, 253n9
wine. *See* cupbearers
Winter's Tale, The (Shakespeare), 135
Withers, Robert, 175, 267n26, 270n84
Wladus, Dracula, 72
woman. *See* embodiment; femininity; gender; hierarchy; humoral theory; race; slaves and slavery
Wycherley, William, 265n3

Yahya (poet), 59–60, 64, 250n70
Yılmaz, Gülay, 64, 247nn27–29
youth. *See* boy
Yusuf Sinan Pasha, Ciğalazade, 269n75

Ze'evi, Dror, 227, 233n3, 241n101, 242n105, 248n42, 249n60, 266n19, 274n15, 274n19
Zeman, Corinne, 193, 271n102

www.ingramcontent.com/pod-product-compliance
Lightning Source LLC
Chambersburg PA
CBHW031448250426
43671CB00041B/316